Coming
to
Terms

WILLIAM

DOUBLEDAY

SAFIRE

Coming to Terms

New York   London   Toronto   Sydney   Auckland

PUBLISHED BY DOUBLEDAY

a division of Bantam Doubleday Dell Publishing Group, Inc.

666 Fifth Avenue, New York, New York 10103

DOUBLEDAY and the portrayal of an anchor
with a dolphin are trademarks of Doubleday,
a division of Bantam Doubleday Dell
Publishing Group, Inc.

Book design by Chris Welch

Library of Congress Cataloging-in-Publication Data
Safire, William
Coming to terms / William Safire. — 1st ed.
p. cm.
Essays originally appeared in *The New York Times*, 1986–1988.
1. English language—Usage. 2. English language—Style.
I. Title.
PE1421.S216 1991
428'.00973—dc20   90-23376
CIP
ISBN 0-385-41300-9

For Sir Basil and Lady Feldman

ACKNOWLEDGMENTS

Language users have been "coming to terms" for more than two centuries. According to the Oxford English Dictionary, the infinitive phrase *to come to terms* first had a meaning of "to reach a settlement, to agree upon conditions," when the British biographer Roger North wrote prior to 1734: "The creditors . . . rather than to contest accounts, came to terms, and agreed to take shares." By the early twentieth century, a second sense of "to reconcile oneself" had also come to this term.

Lexicographers who have assisted me in coming to terms include Robert Barnhart of Barnhart Books, Robert Burchfield of the O.E.D., Frederic Cassidy and Joan Hall of the *Dictionary of American Regional English,* Sol Steinmetz of Random House, Victoria Neufeldt of Webster's New World, Frederick Mish of Merriam-Webster, and Anne Soukhanov of the American Heritage Dictionary. Jacques Barzun has provided guidance in usage, James McCawley in linguistics, though both of these academic giants must get exasperated at my triumphant judgmentalism (they have come to terms with the difficulty of educating me). Helping me to track quotations have been Justin Kaplan of Bartlett's, the quotation anthologist Len Safir, and Jeanne Smith at the Library of Congress. The lexicographer Stuart Berg Flexner, who died in 1990, deserves special note.

Those who assist me at the New York Times bureau in Washington, D.C., include my assistant, Ann Elise Rubin; my research associate, Jeffrey McQuain; our chief librarian, Barclay Walsh; our other librarians, Monica Borkowski and Marjorie Goldsborough; and our communications manager, Earl Smith. At Doubleday, I'm grateful to Herman Gollob, Joel Fishman, Wendy Goldman, and Chaucy Bennetts.

Of course, I am especially grateful to the legion of Lexicographic Irregulars, flanked by the tireless troops of the Squad Squad and the heavy hitters of the Gotcha! Gang, for their assistance—even when cloaked in gleeful one-upmanship.

The Gotcha! Gang
Strikes Again

Certitude is the wrong attitude.

A name I answer to is U. Ofallpeople. That is the salutation on corrections from the Gotcha! Gang, members of which believe that self-proclaimed language mavens, above all others in the writing dodge, have an obligation to be 100 percent accurate.

A few years back, I alluded to a subtle kinship of grammatical terms with "like the Colonel's Lady and Rosie O'Grady"—recalling, as Kipling fans know, "sisters under the skin."

A Gotcha! Gangster, Jerrold Weinberg of Norfolk, Va., promptly set me straight: The character who is sister under the skin to the Colonel's Lady is *Judy* O'Grady, not *Rosie*, whom Mr. Weinberg cautiously identified as "the subject and title of the 1890s song attributed to Maude Nugent." (Maude Nugent did write both the words and music of the song "Sweet Rosie O'Grady," copyrighted in 1896.)

Corrections of fact and grammar are received here with equanimity bordering on grim glee. This particular correction from one of my equi-poisoned pen pals, however, got to me. I have been inaccurately pairing the Colonel's Lady with the wrong O'Grady woman all my life—hundreds of times in conversation, dozens of times in print. Many listeners or readers must have said to themselves, "He's got the poem mixed up with the song, but it's not for me to tell him what sort of jerk that makes him in my eyes."

The realization of that long-perpetuated embarrassment caused a *klong*, a word coined by Frank Mankiewicz to describe "a sudden rush of crud to the heart." The repeated damage was done: it is now too late to thread my way back through life to fix that mistake.

A copy editor in my youth saved me from another one of those always-belated klongs. Beach Conger, the *New York Herald Tribune* editor who read my copy in the late 1940s, changed *gilding the lily* to *painting the lily*. When I asked why, he pointed to the line in Shakespeare's *King John:* "To gild refined gold, to paint the lily."

"Everybody says *gilding the lily*—that's the expression," I argued, holding that any copy-desk requirement that the idiomatic phrase be used strictly as originated was arrant pedantry. (The dour Mr. Conger destroyed my village by countering that *arrant pedantry* was a cliché. I almost replied that that was arrant nonsense, but I didn't want either to use another cliché or lose my job.)

Forty years from painted roses to sweet Rosies, and I have never again used the phrase *gilding the lily*. That misquoted metaphor, now so ingrained in the language as to be a nonsolecism, was consciously avoided a hundred times in my life. But what worries me now—and what should worry you, if you don't want to be afflicted with similar klongs in life—is this: how many other citations that are not quite right are we carrying around in our heads?

Once more into the breach, my friends. I've said that, too, a hundred times, usually with a satisfied sigh of world-weariness. But when it came to using that quotation from Shakespeare's *Henry V* in a piece making predictions for the coming year, I had to stop and think: how do you spell that opening into which Henry was urging his troops—*breech* or *breach*? A breech is a rump, so called because the anatomy's posterior, with its split between buttocks, appeared to the literal-minded to be broken. Accordingly, the *breech of a gun* is the back end, the part behind the barrel; a *breech delivery* is with the baby's backside first, and a cub reporter occasionally gets *too big for his breeches*, or trousers.

Why, you wonder, did the Geneva Bible of 1560 become known to book collectors as the Breeches Bible? Because of its depiction of Adam and Eve in Genesis 3:7: "They sewed figge leaves together, and made themselves breeches." Although the earlier Wyclif Bible used the same word with the variant spelling *brechis*, it was the Geneva Bible that gained the nickname; the later King James version substituted *aprons* for *breeches*. Modern dictionaries usually include *breeches* as well as the variant *britches*.

A *breach*, spelled with an *a*, is a break that causes a fissure, gap or opening—whether between wings of an army, between nations breaking relations, or between a leaping whale and the water it springs out of. (Ahab blanched when Moby Dick *breached.*)

Breach, in the sense of "break," is perhaps most familiar in the phrase *breach* of promise. Now usually reserved for reneging on an agreement to marry, this phrase originally applied to any broken promise.

I concluded that the military word I had in mind was spelled "into the *breach,*" my friends. But wait—did Shakespeare get it right? He suffered at times from a lack of a copy editor, and members of the Gotcha! Gang have not been loath to beard the Bard himself. In this passage, fortunately, the First Folio (no longer the last word on what Shakespeare wrote, but 'tis enough, 'twill serve) has the word spelled properly: *breach.*

However *(klong!),* I now see the line reads not *"my* friends," but *"dear* friends," and worse—*(klong klong!)*—the correct version goes, "Once more *unto* the breach, dear friends."

Who would have figured that Will Shakespeare, in need of a syllable to balance a line, would have rejected the simple *into* and turned to a poetic variant of *to* now archaic and written *unto?*

Some arrant pedants would make a big point of the way smoothing usage has worn down Shakespeare's original phrase to "into the breach, my friends," but they would be painting the lily, as they like to say. The rest of the G.G. (shock troops of the Nitpickers' League), professing a reluctance to quibble but getting our secret thrill out of quibbling, realize that by correcting each other, we help avoid language klongs.

"Better to know when you're young," writes Colonel Judith O'Grady of Bombay, an honorary member of the Gotcha! Gang, "about a quotation you have askew, and to correct it, than to go through life with the mental equivalent of a piece of spinach on your tooth."

Eschew certitude. Embrace the existential attitude of cheery correctability. As Mark Twain once said, "It ain't what we don't know that hurts us. It's what we do know that ain't so." (I think that's what he said. It was Mark Twain, wasn't it?)*

---

* No; the Oxford Dictionary of Quotations attributes it to Josh Billings, in the words: "The trouble with people is not what they don't know but that they know so much that ain't so." Walter Mondale, in a debate with Ronald Reagan, credited it to Will Rogers. Ain't so.

Coming
to
Terms

Advise and Repent

During his record-setting thirty-five hours of testimony at the Senate confirmation hearings, Judge Robert H. Bork was criticized for "rigidity" and "inflexibility" on his views that had not changed, and criticized for what Senator Patrick J. Leahy called "this metamorphosis" on views that had changed. Bork supporters used "consistency," "predictability" and "coherence" to characterize unchanged views, and "growth" and "not set in concrete" to explain shifts in position over the decades. The judge himself tried to point out that his role changed—from precedent-challenging professor to Solicitor General to precedent-following judge—which had an effect on what he had to say.

The assertion of views different from those held when he wrote as a professor in 1971 led to Senator Leahy's charge of *metamorphosis.* That is a word that came into English in Sir Thomas More's 1533 writing about witchcraft (thereby lending ammunition to those who defended Judge Bork as a victim of a "witch hunt"). It is from the Greek for "transformation," and gained a meaning in biology as "a profound change in form during the life of an organism." In its figurative meaning today, the word denotes more than mere alteration or modification of views, which is why it was rejected by Bork supporters.

An attack phrase used by opponents of the nominee, especially Senator Leahy, was *confirmation conversion.* This was an alliterative play on *deathbed conversion,* a variant of *deathbed repentance,* slyly suggesting that the imminence of punishment led to a change of heart. The new phrase—unfound in the computer files before these hearings—is likely to be used often in the future to impugn a nominee's motives in adopting any views of the confirming senators. It ain't on a level with *innocuous desuetude,* but it shows that the coinage of slashing phrases is not a lost art.

Airheads

The retronym watch—that backward-looking battalion of Lexicographic Irregulars that keeps track of new names for old things—has come up with one that ranks with *acoustic guitar* and *day baseball.*

An incensed Howard Baker ("mildly peeved" would be a more accurate description of the easygoing man when he was White House chief of staff, but that day he was doing his best to appear incensed, a word rooted in the Latin for "to set on fire," and a parenthesis this long makes a sentence sag in the middle) issued a statement when three television networks—ABC, CBS and NBC—turned down the opportunity of broadcasting President Reagan's speech to the nation about aid to the Nicaraguan contras.

He denounced as "an attempt to substitute their judgment for that of the President" this "decision by the three over-the-air networks. . . ."

Just as electric guitars made it necessary to call regular guitars *acoustic guitars,* cable networks have now created the retronym *over-the-air networks.* By choosing this locution, Mr. Baker subtly underscored both the importance and the difference of Cable News Network, which had agreed to show the President's speech.

Big change: the *networks* no longer refer to the three we have grown accustomed to; now that grouping must be called the *over-the-air networks.* Decades hence, when we all carry satellite-receiving dishes in our teeth, we will look back fondly on the days of over-the-air networks as we watch round-the-clock baseball.

And So On

How do we dribble off assertively? This department has long taken careful note of the changes in derogatory summations of what other people say; in olden times, *and so forth and so on* was in vogue (in Germany, *und so weiter*), followed by *et cetera, et cetera, et cetera.* A generation ago, *yakety-yakety-yak* had its day, and in the 1970s *stuff-stuff-stuff* came and went. To some, *whatever* was the preferred way to indicate three dots at the end of a sentence (the "spoken ellipsis"), and perhaps the longest-lasting dribble-off was *blah-blah-blah.*

"There is a new, widespread verbal shortcut making the rounds these days," writes Professor Dennis Baron, director of freshman rhetoric at the University of Illinois at Urbana-Champaign, "one so recent that so far as I know it hasn't appeared in print before and consequently has no official spelling. . . . It is imitative, like its equally slangy, more negative and possibly obsolescent equivalent *blah-blah-blah.*"

I will represent the new dribble-off, which Professor Baron calls a "summative," in this way: *duh-DAH-duh-DAH-duh-DAH-duh-DAH.*

Perhaps you have heard it; so have I, and attention should be paid. The example the professor cites is "The President said on television that the stock-market crash was just a mild correction and not to panic about it and, you know, the dollar is strong and duh-DAH-duh-DAH-duh-DAH-duh-DAH."

Among folks who work in computer science, artificial intelligence and cognitive science, the term *mumble* has become a mildly self-deprecatory way to terminate a thought that has gotten beyond the control of its thinker. This happens not infrequently at the cutting edge of the information sciences. The user can safely exit to "mumble" when he is at risk of *flaming*—another Silicon Valley locution that means "getting intellectually outrageous or otherwise losing it."
        Arnold S. Wasserman
        Blue Bell, Pennsylvania

Still heard among high literates who use Latinisms is *ad infinitum.* To be truly derogatory, *ad nauseam* is tagged on.

The duh-DAH's remind me of Foster's refrain in "De Camptown Races" which is "Oh, doo-dah day!" Which brings to mind ta-TUM ta-TUM ta-TUM, sometimes used as dummy lyrics by composers. Both suggest a singsong quality of speech.

This is reaching, but calling blah-blah-blah a "dribble-off" strikes me as clever, as the similar "blather" or "blither" derives from the Old Norse *bladha* for bladder. To blather, of course, is to talk nonsense, which is neatly akin to blabber, which is to indulge in idle chatter (but one who blabs is indiscreet). Blub-blub-blub has a nice ring—I think I've seen it in cartoons about drowning—and to describe a run-on-artist as being blubbery (fatty speechifying) I think is apt.

Street slang includes "running at the mouth" for both chatterers and those who let secrets slip. I could go on, but . . .

> *Sylvia S. Gellman*
> *New York, New York*

I have heard a verbal shortcut similar to that described by Professor Baron. It has been circulating this area for several years. As in the professor's example, it is used to terminate a statement which is running on without saying very much. It sounds something like this: YAH-duh YAH-duh YAH-duh.

> *Bruce Giordano*
> *Union, New Jersey*

I'm appalled that in compiling examples of what you call the "spoken ellipsis" you omitted to mention one that I first heard at Yale ten years ago and which seems to be quite popular still: yah-de-yah-de-yah. Always five syllables, and always said as cavalierly as possible.

> *Jack Stone*
> *Cambridge, Massachusetts*

I hope you haven't missed the ways they dribble off in New York's Outer Boroughs:
1) . . . and what not.
2) . . . and like that.

> *Dan Cooper*
> *New York, New York*

Is it possible that the "new, widespread verbal short cut" stated by Professor Dennis Baron is a variation on the spoken words for the International Morse Code symbol for period? The period •_•_•_ is spoken dit-DAH-dit-DAH-dit-DAH. This represents the spoken ellipsis.

> *Charles T. Soltesz*
> *Wilton, Connecticut*

Arrogance of Power

The power craze began when they started calling the baseball slugger a *power hitter*. Then, in 1956, the sociologist C. Wright Mills labeled the movers and shakers of society the *power elite*; in the 1960s, the journalist-historian Theodore H. White coined *power broker*. Campus slanguists soon picked up on the use of *power* as an attributive noun (lending its meaning to an adjacent noun) with *power tool*, meaning "one who studies fiercely," and *power boot*, "unusually forceful regurgitation." *Vogue* magazine referred to the hairdressing of celebrities as *power cuts*.

The modifier is now being applied to meals. In October of 1980, the *Washington Post Magazine* writer Rudy Maxa wrote of the *power lunch* being served at four distinguished D.C. eateries: Mel Krupin's, the Palm, Joe & Mo's and Gary's. These were the places where "the elite meet ta eat," in the phrase of radio's "Duffy's Tavern," which antedated Professor Mills's coinage. Vito Zappala, who runs Gary's, recalls the phrase being used first in connection with the original Duke Zeibert's restaurant—"the *power lunch* was where the *power people* ate."

Within one month, the *power* combining form was applied to an earlier meal: in a story by Florence Fabricant of *The New York Times*, the literary agent Morton Janklow coined *power breakfast*, about the low-key hard sell early in the morning at the Regency Hotel in New York. The power breakfast was political, not literary: "The literary types wander into their offices after ten," said Mr. Janklow.

Brenda Fine and Jane E. Lasky, in their new and remarkably useful *Women's Travel Guide* (I read everything), have a special section for *power breakfasts* in their Washington listings of "best bets for early-morning power grabbing," and remind us that the new term has its origin in *working breakfast*.

The meaning of the attributive noun changed as the phrase took hold: from the original "lunch of the powerful people," *power lunch* and *power breakfast* came to mean "the type of meal eaten by the powerful"—that is, cholesterol-free and nonfattening to the point of lacking in nourishment altogether. Bacon and eggs was a dish for the impotent; the power-breakfasters preferred a small dish of out-of-season berries, dry bran, weak tea and a two-cents-plain imported from a bankrupt Yugoslavian spa. Even simple meals, however, can distract too much from getting work done, so the power meals are being replaced. A *Newsweek* business article offered the latest course: "Goodbye power lunch, hello power tea."

Another recent compound noun in this line is *power dressing*, which in a woman is a severe suit, in a man is an intimidating Italian sport jacket, and in a power lunch, presumably, is a vinaigrette with lots of garlic.

As author of *The Dictionary of American Food & Drink*, I've been tracking neologisms in the food and foodie world for some time. The first reference to "power lunch" was in an article in *Esquire* entitled "America's Most Powerful Lunch," by Lee Eisenberg (now editor of self-same magazine) in the October 1979 issue (see, you don't read everything). Eisenberg says he coined the term.

"Power breakfast" was coined at the Regency Hotel in New York, as you said, but the term belongs to Robert Tisch, president of the Loews Corporation, which owns the hotel.

In November 1984 author Ron Rosenbaum wrote an article for *Manhattan, inc.* on Roy Cohn's dining habit of bringing his own tuna fish (canned) to restaurants like Le Cirque. Rosenbaum entitled his article, "Roy Cohn: All Power, No Lunch."

John F. Mariani
Tuckahoe, New York

The headline "Arrogance of Power" led me to think you were going to talk about "power trips." A "power trip," of course, has nothing to do with travel or necessarily even leaving one's office. The expression "he's on a power trip" refers to some hyper-ambitious executive (or other individual) who is arrogantly seeking to take control. I guess it's rather like an old-fashioned "power play," which, you might also have cited, is an early antecedent of "power" as an attributive noun. The substitution of the word "trip" instead of "play" incorporates the more trendy drug culture language to be "on a trip."

Richard H. Jenrette
Chairman of the Board
Donaldson, Lufkin & Jenrette
New York, New York

In the early 1980s, Egon von Furstenberg wrote a book entitled *The Power Look* in which he told non-princes and non-heirs how to dress.

And, of course, in New York a yellow silk tie has been called a "power tie," I believe because Donald Trump wears them.

Ed Lucaire
New York, New York

An associate recently suggested that the ultimate *power lunch* is a knuckle sandwich.

Richard Newton
Santa Rosa, California

Bankuage

"This time Citibank has gone too far." Nancy Sharkey, an assignment editor on the metropolitan desk of the *Times* (I miss the old "city desk"), can put up with Citicorp, Citibank, Citicard and even the slogan "the Citi never sleeps," but objects to what the bank calls its "Mentor/Mentee Profile."

The -corp, -bank, or whatever it is has a fine public-relations project going that encourages employees to help students. It usually refers to *mentors and fellows*, which is unobjectionable, but in its press releases often changes that to *mentors and mentees*.

"I think it's time to break the bank's coinage," writes my colleague on what I am tempted to call the "citi-desk." "What next? Does an *illuminator* enlighten *illuminatees?* Are vaudevillians introduced by an *interlocutor* to be called *interlocutees?*"

The use of -*ee* as the automatic complement to -*or* should be resisted. (So should the passive construction: don't use -*ee* every time you need a word to complement a word ending in -*or.*) If the word exists—lessee—use it; if it does not readily come to mind, don't lazily coin a new one ("The people crawling through the field of sensors are sensees . . .").

Look for the word that exists. The person who goes to a *mentor* (from the name of the adviser to Odysseus in the Greek myth) can be called a *protégé*. The French Academy gets huffy about adopting English words, but we are free to adopt French words; especially when an English word for *acolyte* does not readily come to mind, the foreign word is not pretentious. (If the protégé is a woman, the mentor will advise spelling it protégée.) If you want a less voguish word for a sage adviser, try *nestor*, from the counselor to the Greeks at Troy; steer clear of "nestee," and use *student* or *disciple* or *follower*. Like a *tutor* with a *tutee*, an *instructor* with an *instructee* doesn't know how to teach.

While I have the folks from Citibank on the line, let me pat them on the head for the use of a word in advertising long used by people and long eschewed by bankers. The colloquial is the verb *bounce*, as in "Gee, they bounced my check." For years, genteel bankers referred to the tendency of customers to write checks without having money in the bank as *overdrafting*; comes now the Citi-adman with a pitch for "bounce-free checking." That's saying it plain. Next year, some enterprising banker will take the next step: "customized, designer-color, real rubber checks!"

In an effort to reach out to a targeted portion of our entering freshman class to help them adjust to the requirements of college life through added support, we introduced the Faculty Mentor Program.

I was not in on the planning of this program (which I think is a wonderful idea) or the choosing of its name, but I am a mentor (a difficult image to apply to myself as a teacher of Classical literature). At our early meetings my mentor colleagues and I struggled with what to call the group of five students each of us was assigned, and struggle we did. 'Students' was not even considered because that was too confusing: our classes are filled with 'students.' 'Mentoree' was knocked about for a while, but somehow, with a good deal of uneasiness, the majority settled on 'mentee,' and memoranda we now receive refer to the Mentor/Mentee Program.

Until someone can come up with an appropriate alternative, we will be uncomfortable co-conspirators with Citicorp in our Mentor/ Mentee relationships.

Arlene R. Fromchuck
Associate Professor of Classics
Brooklyn College
Brooklyn, New York

Besides, the Wench Is Dead

The writer of a language column recently used the slang word *roundheeled* as an intensifier for "descriptivist." The editor (all this took place long ago on another planet) held that *roundheeled* was unsuitable for a family newspaper, because the noun *roundheel* is defined in Webster's New World Dictionary as "a woman who yields readily to sexual intercourse," and that such a term was therefore sexist.

The word, in widespread use but not defined in Merriam-Webster's Ninth New Collegiate Dictionary, appears in Thorndike-Barnhart's two-volume World Book Dictionary, with the first definition of *roundheel* being "a person who is easily swayed or unable to resist a particular appeal." The second definition offered by that superb dictionary is the earlier and more specific sense of the term, "a promiscuous woman."

In the language columnist's view, the dictionaries err in using the singular form for the noun: nobody ever says, "That person is a roundheel," if only for the simple reason that people have two feet, and an easy mark would be called a *roundheels.*

More to the point, the adjective *roundheeled* has outstripped the noun in frequency of use, and in so doing has adopted the extended-metaphor sense as defined in Thorndike-Barnhart: "easily swayed," or readily susceptible to persuasion.

The writer, unfairly charged with unwitting sexism, is both institutionally loyal and personally collegial; that is why he accepted with good grace the editor's judgment. He does, however, argue that the adjective *roundheeled* is more expressive and colorful than the bland synonym "permissive," and is needed in the language because the metaphor from which it springs—*pushover*—has no adjective form.

A *pushover* is, as defined in Webster's New World, "1. anything very easy to accomplish; 2. a person, group, etc., easily persuaded, defeated, seduced, etc."

Someone easy to push over (or seduce) has round heels; hence that extension of the original metaphor. As in the case of *pushover,* popular use has weakened the original, sexual meaning of *roundheeled,* and now it is most often applied to the general "easy to persuade; complaisant." Through frequent use, *roundheeled* has dropped its hyphen, unlike other parasynthetic combinations such as *round-eyed* and *round-shouldered.*

The dictionaries will come around, you'll see. Then the editors will. Readers have just seen *roundheeled* used, with no sexist intent or reception, in the language column. Next, it will appear in the run of the paper, and finally in learned and formal discourse.

I can wait.

I recall Al Capp's movie-star character of maybe thirty years ago, Roland Roundheels. He superficially resembled Clark Gable and had a wig, false teeth, a tight corset, and elevator shoes. Flashing his toothy smile, he confessed to one and all, "I'm just a pullover."

John C. Thomas
Wilmington, Delaware

You instruct us that the noun "roundheel" could never, despite what dictionaries say, refer to an individual, ". . . if only for the simple reason that people have two heels, and an easy mark would be called a *roundheels.*"

Presumably, by that same rule, you propose to call a singular native of North Carolina "a Tarheels," or a passionate lover of literature "a bluestockings." A blacklegs, a gumshoes—the history of usage turns fluid beneath our feet. Absurd as it is to imply retaining the services of only one side of a human being. You would probably wish us to speak of a farm laborer as "a hired hands."

My point is that the proper study of language does not consist of adducing simplistic "rules" from insufficient example, then trying to force usage into their unreal but constrictive mold. That was the way of "science" when it was still ruled over by theology, leading to the construction of ever-more-bizarre models of how the universe *ought* to be. Idiom is altogether a more various, more flexible, more maddeningly and delightfully elusive subject of study than seems to be dreamt of in your philosophy.

Edwin Ahearn
Brooklyn, New York

Beware the W-Word

The *Washington Post* was bewailing the reluctance of candidates to mention the dread word *taxes*. "They've been Mondaled," the editorialist wrote, making a verb out of the name of the last candidate to suggest that a rise in taxes was inevitable, "you say the T-*word* and you die."

"These days," wrote a *New York Times* editorialist the same week, "the mere mention of the *U-word*—unemployment—sends shivers through the ranks of Moscow's economic reformers."

Earlier, when a reporter "went all the way"—asked Gary Hart if he had ever committed adultery—the press corps began referring to that question as the *A-question.* The same construction applied when a Harvard colleague ratted on Judge Douglas H. Ginsburg, forcing the Supreme Court nominee to admit having smoked marijuana in the early 1970s; ABC's Sam Donaldson promptly dubbed that "the *M-question.* "

To what do we owe this outbreak of initialese?

Children learn to speak before they learn to spell. Secure in that knowledge, parents from time immemorial have spelled out what they did not want their small children to understand. Dogs, too; I have two large dogs, bred to roam the outdoor peaks, that go crazy when they hear the word *out.* That sound causes them to bark furiously, paw the windows, tear the leashes off the wall peg and assume threatening positions on the best rug. Therefore, in my house you can hear, "I think it's time to take the dogs O-U-T." That fooled them for a while, but now I have the only Bernese mountain dogs that can spell.

Among parents, a modern worry is the use of obscene epithets by kids who hear the words all the time at the movies and may not understand how those words shock adults (or may understand all too well).

"The Rating Code office told me a mandatory R went to any film using one of seventeen words," explained Roy E. Disney, producer of the film *Pacific High,* to the Associated Press in 1980. "The picture has four of what my mother calls 'that F-word.' I asked about *All the President's Men.* That was different, they said—'it was a picture that all Americans should have seen.' I couldn't understand that."

Mr. Disney appealed the rating decision and lost; however, his may have been the first citation in print of the baby-talk euphemism that is at the etymological root of what is now used so widely as an ironic commentary.

Irony is what is in the fire here. The trick of alluding to a word by its first initial may be quickly overcome ("What the hell do you mean by the 'H-word,' Papa?"), but the ineffective parental practice has been given a new dimension: now the *-word* construction is used to express mock horror at a plain word too blunt for the pusillanimous to allow to pass their lips. I joined the voguish parade of those using spurious unmentionables recently, explaining in this space that the *D-word* had become the chosen euphemism in Washington for the now-naughty *détente.*

This vogue will probably peter out in a few years, after we go through the alphabet and begin to get confused about what a given letter is supposed to signify. Already the *Washington Post* has done in print what cannot be done easily in speech, ostentatiously leaving blanks in a pseudo-dirty word: "The only way even to begin to do these things is to raise *t___s.* "

Perhaps you have forgotten the 1878 use of an initial to stand for a swearword.

As Captain Corcoran (in *H. M. S. Pinafore*) in his opening song says, "I am the captain of the *Pinafore*. . . . I never use the big, big D___." "What, never?" ask his crew. "Well, hardly ever," sings he. "Hardly ever swears a big, big D___," they conclude.

I am sure there are numerous other examples of such in literature, but this one comes to mind.

> *Louise F. Rossmassler*
> *Flourtown, Pennsylvania*

Our dog can spell C-O-O-K-I-E.

> *Joan Chesler*
> *Ann Arbor, Michigan*

Biden v. Bimbo et al.

Senator Joseph R. Biden, Jr., of Delaware, in an interview with the *Wilmington News-Journal*, accused the Reagan Justice Department of choosing for judgeships candidates of "lower and lower standards," and added that the Administration could no longer expect to "run these bimbos through anymore."

The Administration took heavy umbrage. "It is astonishing," responded Terry Eastland, press agent for the Department of Justice, "that the man likely to be chairman of the Senate Judiciary Committee should use a word like *bimbo* to describe candidates for the bench. . . . Is *bimbo* really a suitable characterization for any prospective or sitting judge?"

Dan Buck, a Democratic Congressional aide whose stationery announces that it is "printed on paper made with recycled fibers," passes on these clippings with this observation: "The word is a gift from Italian, where it means child, infant, or kid. In English, *bimbo* has become a generalized term of disparagement, bringing to mind, perhaps, *nitwit* or *Manion*." This last was a recycled-fiber slam at a federal judge whose nomination was a matter of recent controversy. Mr. Buck also suggests, in greater seriousness, that *airhead* is a current synonym for *bimbo*.

In the United States, an Italian baby is a *bambino*, not a *bimbo*; Robert L. Chapman in the New Dictionary of American Slang records that *Bimbo* was often the name of the monkey holding out the hat for organ grinders.

The word came into American slang at the turn of this century to mean "a menacing man," and was used by writers Dashiell Hammett and Raymond Chandler in the 1930s to mean "a bank robber." P. G. Wodehouse, the British humorist, wrote in 1947 of *"Bimbos* who went about the place making passes at innocent girls after discarding their wives." However, a second sense developed in America of "a prostitute," and the word lent itself to alliteration with the adjectives *blond* and *blowzy.* In this generation, *bimbo* has come to mean "a woman of easy morals," usually calling up the image of one glitzily attractive, bosomy and leggy, and devoid of cunning: *airhead* and *dumbo* are the frequent derogations of these armpieces, who are sometimes not as lamebrained as they try to appear.

Because of that female connotation, this cannot be the word that Senator Biden had in mind. I think a related word, *bozo,* was what he was reaching for: *bozo* is often used as the name of a clown, and is applied to any person (usually, but not particularly, male) of large size and sappy expression. *Bozo* is of uncertain origin, but speculations include a Spanish dialectal word from *vosotros* (the plural "you"), a rhyming compound formed from *bo* (a variant spelling of *beau*) and the Spanish *bozo,* a word for the facial hair of youths. It is more emphatically derogative than *fella* or *guy,* as in "As for this *bozo* next to me . . ."

An irritated and critical senator might easily, and without risk of effective riposte, object to an Administration "running these *bozos* through anymore." It is synonymous with "these clowns," and is a locution that politicians are reluctant to thunder against: "I am not a *bimbo"* would be acceptable from a sitting judge, but a political leader would flirt with pomposity by insisting, "I am not a *bozo."*

> I have often heard and just as often used *bimbo* as a synonym for "airhead" or "dumbo." Donald Dale Jackson also used it in the same sense in an issue of *The Smithsonian* (January 1987). In his article on alligators ("Old Bigtooth Returns," p. 43), he says, ". . . with a brain no larger than a poker chip, an alligator is no mental marvel, but it's not a total bimbo either."
>
> *Connor P. Hartnett*
> *Jersey City, New Jersey*

> I have often used "bimbos" interchangeably with "bozos"; perhaps it's a usage that has filtered through freelance writers and U.S. senators, but has not yet reached word usage mavens and political pundits.
>
> Furthermore, the female version of the word is "bimbettes." A bimbette is an airhead, a this-elevator-doesn't-stop-at-every-floor girl, but definitely not a floozy.
>
> *Dan Woog*
> *Most definitely not a bimbo*
> *Westport, Connecticut*

During the 1920s, a very popular film star named Bimbo was quite a sensation.

By 1924 Max and Dave Fleischer (pioneer animators of Betty Boop and Popeye the Sailorman fame) and their hired head animator Dick Huemer introduced a doggish character to the American theater-going public named Bimbo. In some of the early "Song Car-Tunes," Bimbo would invite the viewers to follow the bouncing ball and sing along. (Dave Fleischer invented the bouncing ball concept.) In "My Old Kentucky Home," according to author Leslie Cabarga in *The Fleischer Story* (Nostalgia Press, New York, 1976), Bimbo walks into a room, plays a trombone and clumsily mouths the words, "Now let's all follow the bouncing ball and sing along." Bimbo later became the playful if mischievous companion of the lauded Koko the Clown, one of the earliest animated stars.

Michael Ward
Cambridge, Massachusetts

You write: "In the United States, an Italian baby is a *bambino*, not a *bimbo* . . ." In Italy, however, both indeed mean baby or child. As does *pupo*. My husband's pet names for me were *bimba* and *pupa*, and I'm sure he wasn't thinking about monkeys, menacing men, or prostitutes. But all areas and even cities in Italy have their own separate dialects, which have little or nothing to do with proper Florentine Italian and are completely unintelligible to people from other parts of the country. It is, therefore, entirely possible that *bimbo*, a perfectly good Italian word to be found even in my simple dictionary, means other things in other parts of Italy—in Sicily, for example, the land of origin of so many Italo-Americans.

Naturally, were I Mr. Manion, I'd much rather be described as a *bimbo* than a *bozo*.

Phyllis Borea
New York, New York

Compare *bembo*, in Francisco J. Santamaría's "Diccionario de Mejicanismos" (1959). He said it is of African origin and refers to a thick lip. (Maybe that's why the organ grinder monkeys were called "bimbos.") By extension, a *bembo* refers to a dunce, dolt, fool, idiot, simpleton, etc. Also to someone who is coarse, unpolished, ill-bred, clownish, clumsy, etc. (Similar uses in Cuba and Puerto Rico.)

See these entries in Santamaría: *bemba*, *bembo*, *bembón*. Also see *bimba*, a drunken woman.

Gaines Kincaid
Fort Stockton, Texas

Bravo Zulu!

"Chain that young man to a computer," said John Tower, "and feed him baloney sandwiches." Thus did the chairman of the Reagan-appointed board to investigate Iran-contra arms dealings assign the task of writing "Appendix B" to Nicholas Rostow, a staff member borrowed from the State Department who had academic training in diplomatic history.

The result was the most stunning reverse appendectomy in government report-writing in years. (A reverse appendectomy puts an inflamed appendix *in*.) Mr. Rostow's riveting narrative, piecing together the sometimes contradictory evidence in a dramatic fashion, was not the portion of the report printed in most newspapers, but is the guts of the paperback book —*The Tower Commission Report*—that became an overnight best seller.

Lexicographers and linguists found that section to be of special interest because its selections from interoffice computer memos revealed, in raw form, the arcane lingo of the military bureaucrats on the National Security Council staff. We have at last available for scholarly analysis the down-home patois of our home-grown patsies.

"*Bravo Zulu* on Jenco's release," wrote former national security adviser Robert C. McFarlane to Vice Admiral John M. Poindexter, after an arms shipment obtained the release of an American held hostage in Lebanon. Colonel McFarlane used that same expression, *Bravo Zulu*, at the end of a message to Lieutenant Colonel Oliver L. North, a fellow Naval Academy ring-knocker. Some reporters immediately suspected South African involvement in the dealings.

In Navy signal code, *Bravo* stands for B and *Zulu* for Z. Merriam-Webster dates the use of these terms from the North Atlantic Treaty Organization phonetic alphabet back to circa 1962 and 1952, respectively. When the two signals are put together as *B-Z*, or spoken or written out as *Bravo Zulu*, the message means "job well done."

Why? Why do the letters *B-Z* not mean "I'm busy, *Titanic*, try another ship"? Nobody I reached at the Naval Academy or the Naval Institute at Annapolis had the answer, though commendably nobody there refused to answer on constitutional grounds. Somewhat defensively, one old-salt librarian suggested the letters *B-Z* were used by signal communicators to mean "well done" for the same reason CB operators use *10-4* for "great" or "so long"—that is, for no reason at all.

Five unusual verb phrases also studded the appendix: *stand down, promise paper, went through the overhead, be teed up* and *stay off the skyline*. This has caused terrible headaches at the KGB decoding station in Dzerzhinsky Square. In the spirit of international amity, these explanations:

"I was advised to do nothing and basically to *stand down,*" testified Howard Teicher, then the National Security Council's Middle Eastern specialist. That same expression, using the past participle of *stand,* was repeated to me in this connection by Secretary of State George P. Shultz: "They told me the whole thing was '*stood down.*' "

The earliest use of *stand down* dates back to 1681, as a clause in a trial transcript directing a witness to leave the box after giving evidence: "You say well, stand down." In the nineteenth century, the infinitive phrase *to stand down* gained a nautical sense of "to sail with the wind or tide." In the 1890s, it became a sports term meaning "to withdraw from a race or game." In World War I, it became the opposite of the order *stand to,* an ellipsis for "stand to one's arms," or come on duty.

"*Stand down* is the order countermanding *stand to,*" wrote Edward Samuel Farrow in his 1918 Dictionary of Military Terms. This sense of coming off military duty was transferred to "closing down an operation" by military men working in the diplomatic area during the past decade.

"If pressed for action you can credibly *promise paper* within the next few days," wrote the late Donald R. Fortier, deputy to Colonel McFarlane. This is the first appearance anywhere of this locution. Closest is the 1976 comment in *The Economist* of London that "the Tory government, facing defeat, had to promise a white paper on the subject to quell the mutineers." In the sense used in the NSC memo, *paper* is a memorandum or other documentation to back up a position; the infinitive phrase *to promise paper,* I assume from the context, means "to promise a report in writing" to a senior who is worried about all these words flying around on the phone.

When informed of the Central Intelligence Agency's involvement in an early shipment of arms to Iran, then-Deputy Director John N. McMahon wrote a self-protecting memo for his file saying that he "*went through the overhead* pointing out that there was no way we could become involved . . . without a finding."

Overhead, in this context, seems to be an intensified term for *roof;* the overhead has long meant "sky, firmament," and someone who goes through it is far angrier than the fiddler who stops after penetrating the roof. This sense may be influenced by computerese, which defines a *high-overhead function* as "one that places heavy demands on a computer," using *overhead* in an extended sense of "cost of doing business." (Observe the double meaning in "Larry Tisch has gone through the overhead.")

Now to *be teed up.* Was President Reagan informed by his aides of the risk inherent in a secret operation that, if it leaked, would be interpreted as a swap of arms for hostages? "The President was told," Donald T. Regan, then the White House chief of staff, told the Tower Commission, "but by no means was it really teed up for him of what the downside risk would be here as far as American public opinion was concerned."

The infinitive phrase *to tee up* is from golf, more recently from football: "to place a ball on a tee, a device for setting it in place above the ground, to be hit or kicked." In the passive voice used by Mr. Regan, the phrase means "be spelled out, as if to a child or someone unfamiliar with the language; be explained so that understanding is easy."

This is not to be confused with *to tee off*, which in golf means "to begin," and by extension, "to hit the ball or problem a long way on the first shot." However, the passive *to be teed off* does not mean "to have begun," but "to be very angry." If you are asked to use both phrases in a single sentence, try: "When President Reagan discovered the risk had not been properly *teed up*, he was *teed off.*"

The nervous investor reading Donald Regan's teed-up sentence will be attracted by the former Merrill Lynch chairman's use of *downside risk*. This is a phrase probably first used in *The Wall Street Journal* on Sept. 10, 1953, according to Sol Steinmetz of Barnhart Books. The paper warned, "There is a downside risk in common stocks at this juncture. . . ." *Downside*, first spotted in 1946, is based on the flip side of *upside*, which appeared in the fourteenth century's *upside down*.

One of the great grabbers of the Prof system (an IBM acronym for Professional Office System, turned into a verb as in "Prof it to me") is the McFarlanism *to stay off the skyline*. In a memo from Oliver North to John Poindexter, the marine colonel reported to the admiral that the Israeli contact, Amiram Nir, was being told not to make his presence known: "Nir has been told to *stay off the skyline* on this issue."

Use a computer to catch a computer: a fast check of Nexis, the computerized library of the past decade's media output, reveals only one other use of this phrase by anyone in the reported world. Bud McFarlane told Richard Halloran, a reporter for *The New York Times*, in September of 1985 that the recently released Reverend Benjamin F. Weir had been asked not to make major public appearances lest the other hostage-takers in Lebanon intensify their competition. "That had been discussed with Mr. Weir, Mr. McFarlane said," wrote Halloran, "and he had agreed to '*stay off the skyline*' until the chances for the release of the others could be clarified."

More drama permeates this phrase than the synonymous "remain out of sight" or "lie low" or even "keep a low profile." *Stay off the skyline* is not merely alliterative, but evokes a poetic image of publicity breaking over the spires of a great city. "Instead of the literal skyline, the outline of tall objects against the sky," suggests Sol Steinmetz, "it's possible that this expression refers to a 'skyline chart,' showing relative sizes on a graph."

In a coming article, more mining of this mother lode: CIA *annuitant*, *disgruntlement*, *buy onto*, *wiring diagram*, *pallet*, *grosso modo*.* Until then, *stay off the skyline*. (*Bravo Zulu*, Bud!)

You left hanging the question of the derivation of the meaning "to be very angry" for *teed off*, when *teed up* and *teed off* were defined in

---

* See "The Gruntled Employee," pages 122–25.

the obvious golf context. This created the impression that *teed off* also had its origin in golf. However, it is more likely that the *tee* in this case is not a golf tee, but is a *t'*, a corruption of *p'*, otherwise *pee*, and meaning *piss*.

No doubt you know all this, but avoided the subject because the origin was in *pissed off*, widely used in World War II. Another variant that was sometimes used to avoid the tabooed version was *ticked off*, which also avoided the *peed off* taboo, yet sounded a bit like the basic *pissed off*.

> *Murray Berdick*
> *Branford, Connecticut*

In defining "overhead," you can lower your sights from the firmament. It's simply more Navy jargon; "overhead" substitutes for "ceiling," just as "bulkhead" equals "wall," and "deck" equals "floor."

Read McMahon, presumably another old salt, as saying he was so incensed at CIA involvement that he "went through the ceiling . . ."

> *Eugene Carlson*
> *Washington, D.C.*

Bill:

You wrote, "CB operators use *10-4* for 'great' or 'so long'—that is, for no reason at all."

Breaker, good buddy; they may use 10-4 mindlessly, but it does have a legit meaning that depending on context may work for "great" or "so long." It is one of a series of coded messages used generally in (I think only land-based) radio communications. These messages go from 10-1 to at least 10-20. 10-4 means "acknowledge," the same way "roger" did in air communications during the war. 10-19, for another example, means "return to base."

You need me over on that there magga-zeen write-up, ol' buddy. I go double nickels, keep Smokey off your tail.

> *Best,*
> *Steve [Pickering]*
> *The New York Times*
> *New York, New York*

"10-4" is generally used by CB'ers to indicate agreement with a statement just communicated by another "operator." For example, Charlie says something like, "Man, this traffic is terrible today!" and Joe replies, "10-4, good buddy." If Joe wants to show enthusiastic agreement with the statement, he can say, "That's a *big* 10-4!" The original meaning of "10-4" (and still used by police departments) is "message received" or "OK."

However, 10-4 isn't used to say "so long," as you wrote. For good-byes, the CB'er reverts to a corruption of the old railroad (and now ham radio) signal—"73." "73" is generally stated as "73's" or just plain "threes." Since "73" was originally intended as an abbreviation for "best regards," this pluralization literally means "best regardses."

Edward D. Hesse
North Merrick, New York

Re "stand down," you are right in translating it as "coming off military duty" but you failed to mention the origin commonly as-signed it.

In the construction of medieval castles (which, of course, were mili-tary forts more than dwelling places for nobility), there were quite wide slits cut in the stone of the upper walls (I guess you'd call them the "ramparts") for the archers to shoot through when besieged by the enemy. Below the line of slits ran the stone walkway by which the archers reached the slits. But the stone walkway was too far below the slits to enable the archers to aim. So a wooden step was installed between the walkway and the slit.

When it came time to shoot their arrows or whatever they were using, the defenders would step up from the stone walkway to the wooden step and shoot through the slit. When the wave of attackers was decimated, the commander of the defending force would order: "Stand down!" The archers then would step off the wooden perch onto the stone walkway. They wouldn't be free to leave their post; they'd just be "at ease" for a while, standing down from their slit, ready to stand up to it at any time.

It's sort of a break during a cease-fire. A very rough translation today would be "cease fire, suspend the attack for a while."

Richard Patrick Wilson
Mobile, Alabama

Teed Off Over Teed Up

"By no means was it really teed up for him. . . ." That phrase, *teed up*, was used by then-White House chief of staff Donald T. Regan in testimony before the Tower Commission. I defined it here to mean "spelled out, as if to a child or someone unfamiliar with the language . . . explained so that understanding is easy."

Not his meaning at all, Mr. Regan corrects me. Although he has suffered in silence the savagings of the media, and has saved for his memoirs any ripostes to backstabbing from the East Wing, he has taken pen in hand to

set straight for future historians and committee chairmen a couple of matters linguistic. The man has his priorities straight.

"Since I play golf as often as possible," he writes about *teed up*, "but
never as much as I want, I was using it in a true golf sense. To *tee up* the
ball means for someone to put a tee (peg) into the ground and place a ball
on it. All the golfer then has to do is hit the ball (assuming he has the
capability)."

Mr. Regan interrupts himself to reminisce: "In the old days, a caddy
actually used to tee up a ball for his player. I must add, though, today one
usually has to tee up one's own ball, due to the lack of caddies." (Presumably those absent caddies now have better, higher-paying jobs because a
rising economic tide in the Reagan years has lifted all the golf carts.)

"I was trying to tell the commission," he continues, "that the issue had
not been really defined well enough to be ready for the President. Later, we
did discuss in more detail the downside risk of revelation of swapping arms
for hostages."

Let the record show that *tee up*, which to some linguistic duffers means
"spell out patiently," means to others more adept with a niblick "define
for decision." (To *tee off*, in golf, is "to begin play"; in slang, it has become
a euphemism for a mild vulgarism meaning "to upset or irritate.")

Donald Regan was not the only former serviceman to take issue with
some of the terms discussed in that philological analysis of the Tower
report. A broadside from Old Salts has been followed by an invasion of
my mailbox by irate grunts, or infantrymen. Subject: etymology, inaccurate or incomplete, of terminology, military. (That's how to write in ser-
vice-ese; always follow the noun with a comma and the modifier. The War
Department bought a billion extra commas during World War II, and the
Defense Department is determined to use them up. Hence signs like "Garbage, inedible.")

"Add this to the pile of letters you are receiving about *overhead,*" writes
Garland Hicks of Mount Kisco, N.Y., referring to my definition of this
term as "roof"; I had assumed *to go through the overhead* was a simple
variant of *to go through the roof.* "In the Navy, the stairs are the *ladder*; the
floor is the *deck*; the wall is the *bulkhead*; and the ceiling is the *overhead.*"

I didn't get a *Bravo Zulu* for that; in fact, my explanation of this phrase
as radio phonetic code for "job well done" was shallow. The Naval Institute in Annapolis, to which I had turned for guidance in this, came sailing
back with this added thought from Captain Jim Barber, its executive director: "B-Z is one of the two-letter designators for specific flag hoist/flashing
light signals."

Aha! It comes from semaphore and the use of flags to indicate letters; a
phonetic practice was picked up by the radio operators from the wavers of
signal flags. The letter B can be signaled by a solid red flag, which by itself
stands for "Take care, ammunition is being taken aboard." The hoist of B

over Z meant "job well done"; now the question is why that particular combination was chosen to have that meaning.

Nobody has yet come forward with a reason. Generations ago, B over Z was expressed as *Baker Zebra*; when North Atlantic Treaty Organization codes changed *Baker* to *Bravo*, the meaning of "job well done" was reinforced and passed into the everyday speech of military bureaucrats.

The question arises: What is the opposite of *Bravo Zulu?* "The Delta flag," says Captain Barber, not quite addressing the issue, "is what you'd want to show to indicate trouble." In the International Code, the letter U is used for "You are standing into danger" and the delta (D) means "Keep clear of me. I am maneuvering with difficulty."

However, whenever you ask anybody in Annapolis or at the Pentagon for the code that is the precise opposite of *Bravo Zulu,* you get a lot of double-talk about secret codes. Is there no signal for "Boyoboy, did you botch that!"? Must the signal for criticism be classified as secret? Are reactions limited to ayes-only?

Here's the real story, which you will not find in any reference book or secret NATO code, and which has been passed to me from a non-Annapolis source strictly for nonattribution: the phrase used in blistering criticism is *Delta Sierra.* The closest I can come to giving its meaning in this space is "dumb stunt," which will do for a euphemism. (Do not confuse it with *Sierra Hotel,* an aviator's term defined by modern Bowdlers as "specially hot," used to hail pilots who have just shot down an enemy.)

Next time a cowboy in the basement comes up with a plan to swap arms for hostages, or to divert profits from such a deal to finance insurgencies elsewhere, we can expect the message from the alert brass: *"Delta Sierra* re your recent Prof message, and a copy of this objection is being sent directly to the appropriate oversight committees."

What sent infantrymen through the overhead, or disgruntlement through the grunts, was the metaphoric origin of *stay off the skyline,* meaning "try to avoid publicity" or "keep out of sight."

"The phrase has nothing to do with a city skyline or a skyline chart," writes Allan W. Cameron of Washington. "It has to do with making oneself a target or drawing fire." He recalled the Bill Mauldin cartoon of a young officer standing erect on the top of a ridge; a doughface on the ground asks him, "Sir, do ya hafta draw fire while yer inspirin' us?"

United States Army Field Regulations, page 33 of the 1914 edition, has this citation sent in by John G. McGarrahan of New York City: "Troops on outpost keep concealed as much as is possible . . . especially do they avoid appearing on the sky line." In the Korean conflict, the phrase was better known as *ridgeline.*

Don Regan tees that up best of all: "When one goes through combat-patrol work," he writes, "one quickly learns that the best target is the person who 'stands on the skyline. . . .' Indians knew it, Indian scouts knew it, soldiers, sailors and all marines know it.

"I might add, a chief of staff is supposed to know it," concludes Mr. Regan, with what strikes me as a note of rue, "but sometimes there is no way a chief of staff can *stay off the skyline.*"

You brought back memories of my days as a quartermaster aboard a pitching destroyer while I ran signal flags up the flag hoists on the signal bridge.

The opposite of Bravo Zulu is the use of the Negat flag, N, above the signal. I copied and enclose the pertinent page from the 1943 *Bluejacket's Manual.* The meaning would be "Not Well Done."

I saw this signal used before the war when during practice torpedo runs our captain forgot that we were hoisting a torpedo aboard and called for full speed ahead. The torpedo became fouled in the screws. The commodore flew a "Not Well Done" signal from his flag hoist addressed to our ship "D361." The whole fleet read the signal to the great discomfiture of the captain.

That's one way the Navy punishes mistakes.

Walter A. Becker
Pullman, Washington

The ceiling of a *cabin* (room) in a naval ship, British, Canadian or American, is called, strictly speaking, the *deckhead. Overhead* refers to the space between the *deckhead* proper and the false ceiling which provides sound and heat insulation for the captain's cabin, though not for those occupied by the crew. There is a reference to the term in the play *Mr. Roberts,* when Ensign Pulver plans to revenge himself on the captain by putting "marbles in his overhead," which would roll around with the motion of the ship and keep that unfortunate officer awake at night.

Mr. Hicks might have added another term to his below-decks list, the cheerful word *companionway,* meaning a corridor in a large ship, or the steps leading down from the deck to the cabin in a smaller boat. A short glossary of sailing terms can be found in *The Annapolis Book of Seamanship* by John Rousmanière, published by Simon and Schuster.

I must also let you know that a flag hoist does not in fact refer to semaphore flags waved by sailors, but to signal flags of various designs hoisted into the rigging of a ship to inform other ships or shore installations of situations in which the hoisting ship, or another ship for that matter, may find itself.

Gary Plaxton
Île-des-Soeurs, Québec

Fore

Watch out for golf metaphors and spellings. In a piece about *tee up* (to prepare for play and, by extension, to ready for decision), I used the words *niblick* and *caddy*.

"Your use of *niblick* in connection with *tee up* is, to be kind, infelicitous," writes Alistair Cooke from his library chair in some television studio. "The long-gone *niblick* is now known as a 9-iron. The only time you tee up for a niblick shot is when you are about to play a very short par 3 hole. 'Adept with a driver' would have been right, since everybody tees up the ball to drive off the tee on a par 4 or par 5."

Then my friend Alistair, who was trained in linguistics, whales the dickens out of the ball I teed up for him: "A *caddy* is a box you put tea in. A *caddie*, from the French *cadet*, used to tee up the ball on a tiny mound of sand he made from the sand box which used to stand by the tee markers. When wooden pegs came in, the player was deemed capable of pressing them in the ground himself."

Former White House chief of staff Donald T. Regan had written to me that caddies teed up the ball for players, much as aides now provide Presidents the bases for decision-making. Mr. Cooke notes: "I never saw a caddie put a tee (peg) in for anybody. Don Regan must belong to a club whose members must average between ninety and one hundred years of age."

These flying divots are not in my game. I play the Victrola.

As a Victrola player, you may not realize that under the rules of golf the use of a wooden tee is permissible only on the tee—the space reserved for the first shot on the hole. Perhaps what Don Regan was referring to was the use of a tee for the second or third shot—in the rough or on remote parts of the fairway. One of the traditional duties of a caddie at many clubs—particularly for, but not limited to those whose members are between ninety and one hundred—is to "improve the lie" of his employer's ball wherever it may be found.

Alistair is right when he observes that caddies do not put the tee (peg) in the ground on the tee. But that handful of sand, the accidental kick, the judicious weeding of neighboring foliage when the player's ball is not on the fairway, is the very essence of caddyship (?), following the ancient golf principle that the lower the employer's score, the higher the tip.

J. M. Hartley
St. Davids, Pennsylvania

I had heard "caddie" was of Scottish origin from a word used in falconry. This would make sense, as I believe the Scotch are more famous for their contributions to the game of golf than are the French. I refer to an article in the December 1920 *National Geographic* magazine by Louis Agassiz Fuertes entitled "Falconry, the Sport of Kings." The sport of falconry was probably at its peak in medieval Europe and Mr. Fuertes states as follows: "A peculiar set of traditions and an equally picturesque language have become inseparably attached to the art of falconry; and it is only fair to the Scotch, who, in their conservatism, have been responsible for the colorful language of golf, to give them the credit for preserving the romantic terminology of falconry." Under an illustration of a "cadge" (a particular kind of perch used for falcons), Mr. Fuertes also stated, "The carrier of the cadge was usually a country boy—a tenant of the owner of the hawks. From 'cadger' came 'codger,' a countryman, and doubtless cad and caddie, both typical Scottish derivatives only slightly different in their present-day applications."

I know I've seen other similar references in books on falconry, but I think I'll bow to Mr. Fuertes whom many consider the most outstanding naturalist and illustrator ever, for the credits.

Eugene E. Kelley
Pleasantville, New York

The Dough Also Rises

In describing a World War II cartoon by Bill Mauldin, I referred to one of the G.I.'s as a *doughface*.

"You seem to have mixed both your metaphors and your wars," writes Brigadier General Richard J. Toner, Commandant of the Air Force Institute of Technology in Ohio. "The *grunt* of Vietnam was the *dogface* of Korea and World War II, whose father was, in turn, the *doughboy* of World War I."

Where did I get *doughface* from? "A *doughface*," writes Charles S. Treat of Chicago, "was a Northern politician who sympathized with Southern views on slavery. Many *doughfaces* no doubt became known as *copperheads* during the Civil War."

Doughface was defined in 1860 by John Russell Bartlett in his Dictionary of Americanisms as "a contemptuous nickname, applied to the Northern favorers and abettors of Negro slavery." However, the coinage, perhaps derived from the English derogation of a pliant politician with a "nose of wax," was credited to John Randolph of Roanoke, Va., in a speech in 1820 castigating abolitionists.

The old word for a pliant politician with an easily changeable image might be useful today, stripped of its racial connotations; under no circumstances should it be confused with the proud moniker of enlisted men, *dogfaces.*

"Doughboy" goes back much farther than World War I slang for soldier. It was applied first to British soldiers in the Peninsular War after the dough cakes they cooked in the ashes of their camp fires. Two World War II slang terms for soldiers in addition to "dogface" were "snuffy" and "yardbird," both from the Barney Google comic strip which had its protagonist, Snuffy Smith, frequently occupying the camp prison yard, thus "yardbird."

"Grunt" applied to a person has another meaning going back to at least just before World War I. A grunt was the man on a telephone or telegraph line inspection crew. While a lineman was up the pole inspecting the condition of wire and insulators, the grunt with pick and shovel was digging down around the base of the pole to inspect for rot and termites; sort of a "low man on the totem pole."

Brooke Nihart
Colonel, USMC (Ret)
McLean, Virginia

The discussion of doughface, dogface, etc. prompts me to write of what the usage was to U.S. Marines of the '40s and '50s, at least.

We always referred to members of the U.S. Army as "doggies" and also were known to mutter "bow-wow" when passing an Army unit during the Korean War.

They had terms of derision for us, too, but that is not the issue.

Come to think of it, we even yelled "arf-arf," from time to time.

Paul H. Finch
The New York Times Syndication
Sales Corporation
Los Angeles, California

I was interested in your reference to John Randolph "of Roanoke, Va."

I think the reference implied (and many readers must have inferred) that John Randolph had a connection with this city. As many readers whose knowledge exceeds mine must have told you by now, that is not the case.

John Randolph, to differentiate himself from a relative of the same name, used the name of his home at Roanoke Plantation in Virginia. Roanoke Plantation was in Charlotte County, an area of Southside Virginia that is generally south of Farmville. Randolph's plantation lay along the Staunton River, which is an extension of the Roanoke River.

This city also took the name of the Roanoke River, but it is located in the southwestern part of the state. It's a relatively young community, incorporated as the Town of Big Lick in 1874. The residents incorporated again as the Town of Roanoke in 1882 and, two years later, Roanoke became a city. The name itself is interesting. Roanoke is one variant of the spelling of an Indian word for the marine shells that served as their medium of exchange. I believe its first use was for the Lost Colony at Roanoke Island off North Carolina.

You can, however, claim the reference was correct in one sense. I have been told that Roanoke Plantation once had a post office, but I can find no written reference for this.

Magdalen A. Poff
Roanoke, Virginia

Isn't the "from" in the sentence "Where did I get doughface from?" excessive?

Louise T. Holmes
South Hadley, Massachusetts

Brother, Can You Spare a Question?

"Why are today's women so unhappy in their relationships with men?" writes Cary McMullen to the editor of *The New York Times.* "The experts you cite mostly beg the question by saying that women should not feel this way. . . ."

Does that really *beg the question?* What does that phrase mean? If you practice panhandling on interrogatories, how much should you ask for?

Professor James Van Cleve of Brown University's philosophy department caught me out on this. I wrote that the habit of schedulers in the railroad business of skipping the meridiem (they go from 11:59 A.M. to 12:01 P.M. in a split second) ". . . begs the question of what to designate the mass transit of the meridiem." That was a mistake: "On the contrary," writes the professor, "since the railroads assume nothing one way or the other on this question, they do not beg it."

Philosophers at Brown know that Aristotelian logic frowns on *petitio principii,* translated as "begging (or seeking) the question (or the beginning)"—the fallacy of assuming what you are supposed to be proving. "I have noticed a trend among journalists," says Van Cleve on solecism, "to use this phrase as though it meant *invites the question, leaves unanswered the question, cries out for an answer to the question* or some such."

Common usage is wearing down *beg the question*, but common usage is not good usage when it loses a useful distinction.

Aristotle explained the idea of *petitio principii*, as it became known in Latin, as "trying to show through itself something that is not knowable through itself." That is one of those definitions that does not get across meaning, which may be why Aristotle never wrote a dictionary. A better one is "a phony argument in which the proof is in the premise." Such a "proof" proves nothing, because it rests on an assumption that has not been proven.

We need examples. When in trouble, exemplify.

Consider the two kinds of question-begging, circular and linear. In circular reasoning, think of a revolving door: you come out where you went in. "Smoking is bad for you because doctors say so, and doctors say so because smoking is bad for you." That's dizzying; to avoid begging the question, you would have to change the last part to "and doctors say so because scientific studies show this, that and the other thing." Philip Howard, my counterpart in London, put it this way: "To state that parallel lines will never meet because they are parallel is to assume as a fact what one is professing to prove."

Now take straight-line question-begging: "What you're reading can't be true, because they never print the truth in the newspapers." The conclusion (what you're reading cannot be true) is based on an unproven, if increasingly popular, premise (that they never print the truth in the newspapers). Even if you were a world-class media-basher, you would have to grant that the premise is in doubt—what you are reading right now, for example, may very well be the truth, although I'm not pushing—and therefore you are resting your argument atop a house of cards. That goes for any argument resting on faith: "What you read in the Bible is true, because the Bible is the word of God." You may believe that; it may be true, but it is *begging the question*.

In this peculiar phrase, the verb *beg*, perhaps rooted in the lay mendicant order of Beghards, is not used to mean "asking for a handout." Nor is it a gentle or formalistic entreaty, as in "I beg to differ" or "Beg pardon, Aristotle, would you care to join me in an Academic game of elenchus?" In the specific use of question-begging, the verb *beg* has the sense of "call up" or "call for"; when you call for the question, you pretend to give an answer, but you merely repeat the question.

Girded for grammatical battle with all this information, we can now address Ms. McMullen's plaint about why today's women are so unhappy in their relationships with men: "The experts you cite mostly beg the question by saying that women should not feel this way. . . ."

No. If we said, "Women are so unhappy in their relationships with men because men are inherently cads," that would be begging the question, setting forth an unproven statement as proof; so would the circular "Today's women are so unhappy in their relationships with men because relationships with men make today's women unhappy." (If we have learned nothing else today, we have learned two ways to beg the hell out of a question.) But when experts answer, "Women should not feel this way," they are evading, ducking or obfuscating the question—not begging it.

Indeed, such experts are *skirting the issue.* But wait: as more female executives rise in corporate America, is the verb *skirt* sexist? Thomas R. Horton, CEO of the American Management Association, wrote me recently about his organization's style decision against the use of periods and apostrophes in the plural of chief executive officer. "Your article successfully skirts this issue," he observed, adding parenthetically, "Yes, there *are* successful female as well as male CEOs."

Most etymologists would vote against taking *skirting* as sexist. *Skirt* and *shirt* probably come from the same root, with *skirt* coming to mean the edge of a man's or woman's shirt or robe. As a verb, *to skirt* started in 1602 to mean "to form the edge or skirt of; to border." Two centuries later, it gained the figurative sense of slipping around the periphery, avoiding the main, as Samuel Taylor Coleridge boasted of being able "to skirt, without crossing, the sandy deserts of utter unbelief." Now we have *skirting* as the verbal substantive. (You like that? Means a noun made from a verb, usually with *-ing* suffixing.) *Skirting* is the act of evading, treating superficially or touching only the edge.

Skirting the issue is no more sexist than *losing your shirt,* something that both men and women on Wall Street do every day.

> The example you give is: Women are unhappy in their relationships with men. To support this someone gives as reason: "because men are inherently cads." This does *not*, however, beg the question. It does not covertly assume that women are unhappy in their relationship with men. It might conceivably be that men are cads but women might still be able to be happy with them. The truth of one does not logically entail the truth of the other. In fact, *if* it were true that men *are* inherently cads, this would be a perfectly good reason to give to someone who wants to know why the claim is made that women are unhappy in their relationships with men.
>
> An example of begging the question would be: women are unhappy in their relationships with men because men just do not sustain happy relationships with women.
>
> *Ernan McMullin*
> *Professor of Philosophy*
> *University of Notre Dame*
> *Notre Dame, Indiana*

> You speak of "skipping the meridiem." I strongly advise you to skip "meridiem" altogether. You are obviously drawing on the phrases *ante meridiem* and *post meridiem,* but it's not right to go around talking

about *meridiem* by itself, without the prepositions, since it is in the accusative case.

In English, we don't talk about a Latin noun in any case but the nominative, which in this case is *meridies,* pronounced, in the English system, muh-RID-ee-eez.

Or, instead of talking about the meridies, which doesn't really make a lot of sense, since *meridies* means "midday" in Latin, you could simply use our English word "meridian."

H. A. Kelly
Department of English
University of California, Los Angeles
Los Angeles, California

Your column prompts me to ask your reaction vis-à-vis the notion of "spare" as in "Can you spare (any) change?" or "Can you spare a dime or a quarter (or whatever amount)?"

I always found this way of asking for help charming and sensitive. There is an apparent will not to cause any problem.

It has no equivalent, to my knowledge, in any other language. And it is almost impossible to translate.

Elie Feuerwerker
Cambridge, Massachusetts

By the Beautiful Sea

"Yes," said President Reagan affirmatively, in defense of his stewardship of foreign policy, "it is in our interest to stand with those who would take arms against the sea of darkness."

That was a play on a Shakespearean phrase that is often misunderstood. Hamlet, contemplating self-destruction in his "To be, or not to be" soliloquy, asks, "Whether 'tis nobler in the mind to suffer/ The slings and arrows of outrageous fortune,/ Or to take arms against a sea of troubles,/ And by opposing end them?"

A *sea of troubles* was, in Shakespeare's day, a way of characterizing this weary life: it did not mean a whole bunch of difficulties as much as it stood for life itself. Just as an optimist in the 1930s would think of life as a *bowl of cherries,* a pessimist in Elizabethan times would call it a *sea of troubles.*

What happens when you "take arms against" life? That means you attack it suicidally. Instead of meaning "to confront one's difficulties energetically," as most people assume, *to take arms against a sea of troubles* meant "to kill yourself." In the same play, Hamlet uses a pun with a similar image in complaining that God prohibits suicide: "Or that the Everlasting had not fix'd/ His canon 'gainst self-slaughter!" *Canon* means "sacred writings" and sounds like *cannon,* the gun, a confusion Shakespeare shows he intended by using a military phrase in the wordplay *fix'd His canon.*

Today, the *sea of troubles* has lost its figurative meaning of "life," and is taken to mean only the oceanful of heavy problems; in a similar way, a *bowl of cherries* is a dish of fruit with pits. Perhaps that is because George Washington in 1789, writing to John Jay, explained, "Having assisted in bringing the ship into port . . . it is not my business to embark upon a sea of troubles." Three years later, the incipient first President added to Henry Knox that he was about "to quit a peaceful abode for an ocean of difficulty."

Mr. Reagan's *take arms against the sea of darkness* gets the quotation wrong and mixes the metaphor: if he wants to dispel a sea of darkness, he should set sail against it or illuminate it with the flares of pitiless publicity.

Dear Bill:

You challenge the President's paraphrase of Hamlet's "Or to take arms against a sea of troubles,/ And by opposing end them.", asserting that Hamlet is here contemplating suicide, not action, as a solution to his dilemma.

Your reading is a possible interpretation of sweet Will's intent, but I submit it's not one often chosen by actors doing the part. This soliloquy is one of only two points in the play (you cite the other) where Hamlet considers suicide as an option—*in the next six lines in the speech.* In performance there's a shift of gears before them. If Shakespeare had meant to include the preceding line in that beat, he'd surely have rendered it, "Or to take arms against myself, and so escape my sea of troubles." Alternatively, "Or to take flight from my vast sea of troubles/ And in oblivion, end them." Shakespeare is never obscure. If he meant it, he would've said it.

Hamlet is a Catholic prince, heir to the throne of Denmark. He can't commit suicide and he knows it. The subtext of the opening "To be, or not to be . . ." is, "To do, or not to do . . ." Throughout the play, while he is passively exploring much of the human condition, Hamlet is actively concerned with finding the way and the will to avenge his father's murder. Look at the "O, what a rogue and peasant slave am I" soliloquy.

Never mind . . . there's room for us to differ on this. Interpretation is subjective and not very important, compared to your vital responsibility in defining and defending the threatened bulwarks of the *language.*

As ever,
Chuck [Charlton Heston]
Beverly Hills, California

" 'Yes,' said President Reagan affirmatively" seems to me redundant. He could hardly say it negatively. It's in a class with " 'Yes,' he agreed" or " 'No,' he refused."

"Said" is a perfectly good word, and can be used over and over without an adverb. In fact, the fewer adverbs the better, in my book.

Mildred Maynard
South Norwalk, Connecticut

Calling Dr. Spin

"It was an event," wrote Paul Taylor in the *Washington Post* about the Michigan Republican primary election, first of the 1988 campaign, ". . . that attracted a phalanx of high-priced political operatives, 'spin doctors,' exit pollsters and reporters who all set out to tease meaning from an election designed to yield none."

The word that first attracted me to that line was *phalanx*, meaning "a close-packed mass of people," from the military formation of infantry assembled with shields overlapping to protect the entire unit, as in the old Nixon phalanstery. To me, a *phalanx*—which is Greek for "log" and can also refer to each finger bone of a hand—carried the connotation of protection, but I suppose it is accurate to think of a politician surrounded by a less-than-protective phalanx.

Spin doctor is a locution we must keep our eyes on. It is based on the slang meaning of the verb *to spin*, which in the 1950s meant "to deceive," perhaps influenced by "to spin a yarn." More recently, as a noun, *spin* has come to mean "twist" or "interpretation"; when a pitcher *puts a spin on* a baseball, he causes it to curve, and when we *put our own spin on* a story, we angle it to suit our predilections or interests.

The phrase *spin doctor* was coined on the analogy of *play doctor*, one who fixes up a limping second act, and gains from the larcenous connotation of the verb *doctor*, to fix a product the way a crooked bookkeeper "cooks" books.

Its earliest citation in the Nexis computer files is from an editorial in *The New York Times* on October 21, 1984, about the Reagan-Mondale televised debates. "Tonight at about 9:30," wrote the editorialist, "seconds after the Reagan-Mondale debate ends, a bazaar will suddenly materialize in the press room. . . . A dozen men in good suits and women in silk dresses will circulate smoothly among the reporters, spouting confident opinions. They won't be just press agents trying to impart a favorable spin to a routine release. They'll be the Spin Doctors, senior advisers to the candidates. . . ."

The *Times* never lets on who writes what editorial, but yell "Spin Doctor!" down the 10th-floor hallway and the one to snap his head around with an explanation was Jack Rosenthal, deputy editor of the editorial page. He recalled the working-over given the press at the Kansas City Municipal Auditorium that night and at the preceding Vice-Presidential debate, and wrote: "Who blundered? Who scored points in rebuttal? . . . Laymen have a right to expect the media to play a mediating role. In a country with a state network or a Government line, such mediation would be dangerous. Not here; even with the Spin Doctors at work, the printed page and the TV screen offer a range of judgments. . . ."

Four days later, Elisabeth Bumiller of the *Washington Post* picked up the phrase, defining *spin doctors*—no longer capitalized—as "the advisers who talk to reporters and try to put their own spin, or analysis, on the story." The term was thus sealed into the new political vocabulary, and will be trotted out by pundits in the coming campaign to prove that their opinions cannot be influenced.

A predecessor term from German and Yiddish is *Kopf-verdreher,* literally "head turner," metaphorically "mind twister"; when I explained to my future father-in-law a generation back that I was in the public-relations field, in which people's attitudes were modified at the introduction of persuasive arguments, he smacked his head and nodded ruefully, "a *Kopf-verdreher.*"

May I add to your observation of the Yiddish origins of *spin?* The *spinning* top enjoyed by children during the Purim celebration is called a *dreidl.* A *finnagler* who twists the facts is a *dreier,* which is short for a *drei-köp,* a head twister. *Tzedreit* denotes confused, twisted, *spun.* Thus a *tzedreiter* is a queer, a nut, his head spun round. There is also the expression: *er dreit a Kup,* which signifies "don't listen to him, he twists, he *spins* the facts."

Hasye Cooperman
New York, New York

Carry a Big One

Writing about New York Mayor Ed Koch, the columnist A. M. Rosenthal defined a Yiddishism that is gaining wider use: "He is so enamored of *shticks*—Latin for making a comedy turn out of almost anything—that his life seems to be a succession of vaudeville performances. . . . *Shticks* and all, he will be remembered. . . ."

In *The Joys of Yiddish*, Leo Rosten found several meanings for *shtick*, which he spells *shtik:* "piece" or "part," as in "Give him a *shtik* cake"; "devious or cheating behavior," as in "How did you ever fall for a *shtik* like that?" and, the most common, "a studied, contrived or characteristic piece of 'business' employed by an actor or actress," exemplified by "Watch him use the same *shtik.*"

Remember Paul Henreid lighting two cigarettes and then passing one to Bette Davis in the 1942 film *Now, Voyager?* I don't know how many holes I burned in pants trying that bit of business, which became his *shtick.* The term has gone beyond show business, however, and has joined the general slanguage in the sense of "one's particular thing."

My primary job is political punditry, but my *shtick*—the special interest that helps me break out of the pundit pack of happy haranguers—is language. A small bit of business, maybe a quick column on synonymy, is a *shtickl.* Rhymes with *pickle.*

A. M. Rosenthal's "shticks" may be Latin, but it is assuredly not Yiddish. In Yiddish, there are no "shticks," but only "shtick," which is both singular and plural.

Jacob Cohen
New York, New York

The plural of shtick is not *chas v'chalila* (an idiom meaning something like God forbid), I repeat, is not shticks. It is shticklech. Just like the plural of crepe is kreplech.

Arnold Feldman
Philadelphia, Pennsylvania

There is also a cognate link to the German word "Stück," which essentially has the same meaning as the Yiddish term: piece, bit, part, even (theater) play, among other meanings.

Lothar Zeidler
New Brunswick, New Jersey

Character Issue

On "Saturday Night Live," the comedian Al Franken asked Bruce E. Babbitt, at that time a Democratic presidential candidate, "Governor, what about the character issue?"

Babbitt: "What about it?"

Franken: "I'm referring to your long history of going into supermarket express lanes with more than 10 items."

Babbitt: "Who told you that—the Dukakis campaign?"

This skit was not exactly a thigh-slapper, but it did have a political barb: the campaign of Governor Michael S. Dukakis was the source of an "attack video," showing that Senator Joseph R. Biden, Jr., had stolen the words—indeed, the entire family background—of a British labor leader, which led to the demise of the Biden candidacy on the rocks of the *character issue.*

In the campaign of 1900, William Jennings Bryan called imperialism the *burning issue* of the campaign, giving more zip to the customary labels of *leading issue* and *paramount issue.* These are the formal, intellectually approved subjects for debate, a cut above the plebeian *bread-and-butter issue* and in contrast to the *gut issue,* which often deals with race or class resentments not to be mentioned in high-toned debate.

Gut issue, probably long bruited about in politics on both sides of the Atlantic, may have been first recorded in *The Economist* of London as recently as 1964: "For Harold Wilson it was a carefully planned campaign . . . the neo-Kennedyism combined with a concentration on gut issues." A generation before, the word *gut*—from the Old English for "bowel"— was a part of college slang as *gut course,* meaning "easily passed course." That referred to the belly's softness; in general slang, *gutsy* means "courageous" and *gut,* used as an adjective, in politics means "visceral," appealing to emotion rather than reason.

A *switcher issue* is known to pollsters as a subject of conflict, such as abortion or gun control, that would cause a voter usually aligned with one party to switch to the opposition on that matter alone. The *social issue,* coined in 1970 by the psephologists Ben J. Wattenberg and Richard M. Scammon, denoted the concern with drug use, alienation, unrest and changing morality that seemed to be replacing the economic, or bread-and-butter, controversies.

Whence *character issue?* (Whence *whence?* That useful adverb means "from what source, place or cause"—*from whence* is considered redundant —and is usually followed by *comes,* but a lot of us are treating that follow-up word as understood. When looking for a neat and punchy opening word to a question about sources, don't say "hence" to *whence*. OK, *hence* has two meanings: 1) "away, over there," as in "Get thee hence," and 2) "therefore," as in "He flouted convention, and hence the convention hooted at him," which brings us back to the *character issue*. Rhetoricians will recognize this as an example of a "boomerang tangent," a lurch off course that unexpectedly returns to the point.)

The problem or shortcoming we call the *character issue* is as old as campaigning, from the iciness of the Romans' Coriolanus to the acknowledgment by Grover Cleveland of paternity of an illegitimate child ("Ma, Ma, where's Pa?" was the slogan used to embarrass him), but the phrase seems to have sprung up in our time.

In October 1979, *Newsweek* attributed the phrase to an unnamed politician in a piece speculating on a bid by Senator Edward M. Kennedy to wrest the Democratic nomination away from President Jimmy Carter: "If Kennedy is the nominee, the 'character' issue will be 'fair game for the Republicans in the fall,' a Democratic strategist agrees." Five months later, the Associated Press observed: "In addition, campaign aides said, Kennedy was not hurt as badly in Massachusetts as in other states by the so-called 'character' issue. For weeks, polls have shown and aides have conceded that Kennedy has been hurt by voter questions about Chappaquiddick and concerns about his marriage."

In the 1984 campaign, a columnist writing about Senator Gary Hart struck first. Mary McGrory wrote that Vice President Walter Mondale was "not, however, ready for Hart and his unexpected, lethal challenge on the character issue. Hart, whose campaign is vaguely 'new' and 'futuristic,' suggests that Mondale is old at heart." Senator John H. Glenn, Jr., then raised what he called the character issue by stressing personal accomplishments rather than position papers. But it was left to Walter Mondale, with his "Where's the beef?" campaign, to imply that Senator Hart was a hollow, or plastic, man; A.P. defined *character issue* as "a synonym for questions about Hart's age and his decision to shorten his name from Hartpence."

The next man to be brought down by the C.I. was Joseph Biden in 1987. (Democrats use this issue on each other; Republicans have not yet learned its efficacy.) When plagiarism charges began to fly, Phil Roeder, an Iowa Democratic spokesman, was quoted by A.P. as sighing, "There's the potential this could raise some of the character issues." When Jane Ann Gephardt was asked about the tribulations of one of her husband Richard's rivals, she replied, "The character issue is important. It is a necessary part of the campaign, as painful as the process may be."

After the furor forced Mr. Biden to abandon his candidacy, a minor flap was caused by the revelation that the Dukakis camp had provided the media with the information that did him in—standard political procedure in the past, but now considered by some antipartisan types as some sort of indelicacy. "This admittedly was a dumb thing for a staff person to do," said the same Iowa Democrat, but "this is not an issue that strikes to the character issue like the Hart incident and the Biden incident both did."

This historical study of the phrase shows how it began in an indirect slam at moral turpitude, swung over to a general uneasiness about uprightness or straight what-you-see-is-what-you-get, then swung back to a suspicion of hanky-panky, coming to rest today in a state of confusion. To some, it means "he's a swinger"; to others, it means "you just can't trust him."

What is *character*, anyway, that makes it an issue that can cripple candidates? This is one of the most powerful and mysterious words in the language; no satisfying synonym exists for it.

Etymologically, it is a fourteenth-century English word from the Greek *kharakter*, which means "engraving tool" and, by extension, the mark made by that tool; the word *character*, for example, contains nine characters, or letters. By further extension, the word came to mean the mark a person makes, the features and qualities that distinguish that person from others.

But character has another sense, beyond "distinguishing trait." It is the mark of an individual with a brave outlook and noble heart; the person with character has the judgment to know what is right and the courage to do what is good. The *character issue* takes aim at the degree to which a candidate falls short of that state, as candidates and most human beings do.

"Politics ruins the character," said Otto von Bismarck in 1881, but Woodrow Wilson less cynically defined it in 1914 as a quality that cannot be deliberately created: "If you will think about what you ought to do for other people, your character will take care of itself. Character is a byproduct. . . ."

William James, the philosopher, explained it to his wife in a letter in 1878: "I have often thought that the best way to define a man's character would be to seek out the particular mental or moral attitude in which, when it came upon him, he felt himself most deeply and intensely active and alive. At such moments there is a voice inside which speaks and says: 'This is the real me!'"

The matter is really very simple. The American people are looking for a leader whose opinions and policies are not designed by pollsters, whose words are not the synthetic or stolen goods of speechwriters and whose conduct with friends and family need not be concealed or excused.

There is a real danger of letting scholarship and sophistication destroy honest and sensible standards. If you continue in this vein, we will no longer be able to find words to distinguish between right and wrong or between good and evil. We will be wonderfully witty dinner guests but rather pathetic citizens of a democracy.

Daniel S. Katz
New York, New York

No satisfying synonym exists for "character"? How about "integrity"?

Carl Bowman
New York, New York

Class Cleavage

"*Stroh's is spoken here.*"
  "*Where you're going is Michelob.*"
"*Pabst is the place.*"

"Is there a name for this sleight of hand with parts of speech?" asks Robert Spillman of the University of Rochester. "While waiting for an answer, I am busy trying to 'live today's Chevy.' "

This is the sort of language spoken in *Marlboro country*. Some grammarians use *functional shift*, a 1942 term, to identify the process by which a word gains a second or third grammatical function. (What's the *process by which* stuff? Belay that; make it read *way*.) Others use the term *class cleavage* to describe how we use words in two ways, splitting their function so they fall into two categories.

Modern advertising is entranced with two techniques: attributive nominating and class cleavage. They don't teach that in advertising copywriting courses, but that's what they do when the client wants a new pitch.

In the country of Marlboro, where the spaces are wide open and the main occupations are inhaling and tattooing, the proper noun *Marlboro* is used both as a name and as a description of the country, which is more a state of mind than a state of the Union. So if it's also used to modify a noun, Marlboro is also being used as an adjective, right? Wrong; in this case, the noun modifier is called an *attributive noun*, which must always be paired tightly with the noun it modifies. (You can say "in cough-racked Marlboro country," but not "in Marlboro cough-racked country.")

What time is it in Marlboro country, or even in the "here" where Stroh's is spoken? Why, it's "Miller time"—another proper noun used also as an attributive noun modifying *time*. Any noun can be used that way: I took out my *travel guide* to see if I could put the man doing my *car repair* under *house arrest*; in that example, *travel, car* and *house* are all nouns that attribute their meaning to the nouns they modify. Same with that "Salem spirit."

Advertising copywriters have turned into attributive-noun freaks because the construction enables them to put the name of the product in a new linguistic function. (*Noun freak* uses the word *noun* as an attributive noun modifying *freak*, probably for the first time in the history of the English language. We really push the envelope in this space.)

But the Madison Avenue types don't stop with attributive nouns: "Tastefully Tareyton" uses the product name as an adjective. Why must it be an adjective? Because it's modified by the adverb *tastefully*; if Tareyton were being used as a proper noun only, the ad would have to read "Tasteful Tareyton."

Now we're into *class cleavage* in a big way, bursting into an area of grammar undreamed of by mere attributive nouns.

Technocrats like class cleavage because it adds a touch of creativity or brings speech closer to the machinery: when a light on a board flashes "go," the message should be "All systems are go" or, as some of us would more likely put it, "The little gizmo on the board that says 'go' is blinking. Maybe we should get out of here." The technocrat prefers "All systems go," with the "go" changing its function from a verb to an adjective—specifically a predicate adjective, which means it follows a linking verb (the understood "are") and describes the subject ("systems") of the sentence. (Look, the *are* has to be understood: the meaning is "all systems are go"; we do not say "all systems *go*" in the sense that every system sooner or later breaks down, like "all people die.")

I have a special wastebasket for letters complaining about the way nouns are being used as verbs. "I want a shoe-leather reporter to shoe-leather this story for me, even if he wears out his shoe-leather," snaps the crusading editor, using *shoe-leather* first as an attributive noun, then as a voguish verb and finally as the original noun. "This door is *alarmed*," a silly warning, uses *alarm*, originally a noun, as a past participle, an example of class cleavage.

"Verbs develop from nouns more than the other way around," observes Enid Pearsons of Random House dictionaries. "The nouns *fish*, *bridge*, *butter*, *cart*, *cradle*, etc., all made it into verbs. But verbs get their own back from time to time: in the *know*, in a *daze*, in the long *run*, taking a *look*." And of course, all systems *go*.

Therefore, I am growing more tolerant of functional shift; in more ways than one, cleavage can be exciting. The slang verb *rip off* becomes the noun *rip-off*, and is used as an attributive noun in *rip-off artist*.

But copywriters should be warned: beware of too much of a good thing. "Is it live or is it *Memorex*?" makes the proper noun seem to be an adjective balancing *live*, creating class cleavage. "Raise your hand if you're *Sure*," says Procter & Gamble's deodorant, its name taken from an adjective, the called-for action subtly exposing an area of the body most in need of deodorant. "Don't send a wimpy bag to do a *Hefty* job," says the Mobil Chemical Company, Hefty bag's manufacturer, using *Hefty* both as a proper noun and as an adjective balancing *wimpy.*

Perhaps the time is near for originality in advertising. Some of us kind of like the idea of a wimpy bag, perhaps as a container for hamburgers, and I'm raising my hand not because I am confident of the condition of my armpit, but to leave the room.

Attributive nouns relate to those they precede in a great variety of ways. Consider the differences between "an iron box," "an iron worker," and "an iron will." Sometimes the linkage is so tenuous or roundabout that only convention makes the combination intelligible. This was borne in on me when I first went to Scotland and discovered that there were two kinds of butchers: pork butchers and family butchers!

To describe all these nouns as "attributive" is to strain the meaning of "attribution" to breaking point. Would they not be better called "associative nouns"?

Pierre Cachia
New York, New York

About the grammatical shifts invented by ad agencies: It is my understanding that trademarks are legally defined as adjectives, and that it is only the popular misuse of them that makes them seem to be nouns. Thus *coffee* is a noun and Sanka® is an adjective.

When a trade name finally becomes part of the language as a true noun, it loses its protected status as a trademark or trade name. This happened to the Bayer Co. in the United States when our court (which one I'm not sure) decided that Aspirin® had become a generic name for salicylic acid (or whatever) and declared "aspirin" in the public domain. The word retains its protected status in many parts of the world, however.

Thus the Robert Young commercials of a few years ago declaiming the virtues of "Sanka brand coffee." General Foods was apparently fearful that the word "Sanka" was losing its status as an adjective modifying *coffee,* and that instead it was becoming a noun with a meaning synonymous with "decaffeinated coffee." They must have done much proselytizing in the restaurant trade; now when one asks for a cup of Sanka, the waitress says, "We have brewed decaf, sir."

Edward M. Roberts
Glen Head, New York

To the extent that the tight pairing of attributive nouns becomes the equivalent of compounding, it seems to me that one could indeed say "in Marlboro cough-racked country." It would be an instance of tmesis.

Russell Eliot Reif
New York, New York

Cockamamie

When Vice Admiral John M. Poindexter used the word *disinforma-tion* in a memo, urging an official policy of duplicity that led to the duping of some reporters, "Credibility Gap" yawned again; the wrath of the press descended, and some of his compatriots wondered if the time had not come for the admiral to leave his National Security Council desk for the bracing refreshment of sea duty.

"The affair will not be wholly disastrous," wrote columnist James J. Kilpatrick, in denouncing such perfidy, "if the President's men will daily ask themselves a probing question: If this particular secret memo is leaked —and it probably will be leaked—how will it look in the papers?" The pundit, who chooses his words with more care than most, concluded, "If the admiral had asked that question about his cockamanie memorandum last August, the memo never would have seen the light of day."

Cockamanie? Should that be *cockamamie?*

The word means "crack-brained, cuckoo, muddled, ridiculous," the kind of action taken by one who does not have all his cups in his cupboard or both oars in the water. It is probably derived from *decalcomania*, the process used by kids a couple of generations ago to transfer pictures from paper to their skin or windows. We'd rub the paper with spit and stick it on our foreheads to roars of laughter, especially as it was often put on askew. We called those decals, as they are now called, "cockamanies."

Decalcomania is rooted in the French *décalquer*, "to trace off or copy from," and the combining form *-mania*, "madness" or "fad." The Latin *calcare*, "to tread, or rub on," is derived from the ultimate root, *calx*, "heel"; often, bastard English has elegant forebears.

In the 1940s, the slang word was spelled *cockamanie*, true to its mania. But then some linguistic shift took place; in the 1958 movie *Teacher's Pet*, Clark Gable used the more widespread *cockamamie* (which Leo Rosten spells *cockamamy*).

In some sections of the United States, the old usage exists, and I am not one to challenge my brother Kilpatrick on his preference in dialects. How-ever, the *n* spelling should be considered a variant; the more common usage and "standard" spelling is now *cockamamie,* accompanied by a circular motion of the finger near the ear, which is what many think is a fair characterization of the admiral's memo.

Contra-Temps

We cannot distance ourselves from solecism. Under the relentless pressure of penetrating interrogation, or sweating in the hallways outside Senate hearing rooms, public figures sometimes crack; to those of us in the language dodge, this manifests itself in the form of mixed metaphors, poorly chosen modifiers or unconscious allusions.

"It will be a cold day in Washington," said Senator David (Call Me Dave) Durenberger, Republican of Minnesota, "before any more money goes into Nicaragua." The expression is usually *a cold day in hell,* a metaphor of unlikelihood; in Washington, there are some fairly cold days and heavy snowfalls. On the other hand, if the senator meant to suggest that Washington, or political life, was hellish, then he is not in error, but merely in the wrong line of work.

Donald Regan, asked if the sending of arms to Iran was the crux of the problem, was quoted in *The Wall Street Journal* answering: "Yes, and the way they were delivered, and the whole seven yards." There goes his credibility with me; it is *the whole nine yards,* from the cubic content of a fully loaded cement truck.

Robert C. McFarlane, the former national security adviser who denies going to Teheran on an Irish passport carrying a cake shaped like a key and a signed copy of the Bible, testified that President Reagan's concern for the hostages "was a very leading underpinning of this whole initiative." *Underpinning* is a good choice of a word here—"a supporting structure"—but *leading* strikes the wrong note as a modifier. *Basic* or *fundamental,* maybe; *concrete* or *solid;* but *leading* is at the front of, and not underneath. The McFarlane patois is often slightly askew; in life, geostrategy and *Weltanschauungs,* not every try is an *initiative.*

Even though he had distanced himself from the Iranian dealings, George Shultz used the phrase, shocking to some, in testimony to a House committee on negotiations with the Soviet Union, in this manner: "Clearly, the negotiations were coming toward the short strokes, and the Soviets were beginning to adjust their position. . . ." Howard J. Lewis of Bethesda, Md., is among the horrified readers who writes: "Is *short strokes* one of those figures of speech with explicitly sexual origins that have inserted themselves into polite conversation?"

Yes. In Francis Grose's 1785 Classical Dictionary of the Vulgar Tongue, the word *stroke* is used as the noun object of the infinitive in the archaic expression *to take a stroke*, which he defined as "to take a bout with a woman," which the Oxford English Dictionary supplement explains is "an act of copulation."

Not every sense of *stroke* (from *strike*) is sexual, of course: the Standard English word covers a single movement in basket-making, similar to a sewing stitch; a strike of the hand or blow delivered by a golf club, and the blow to the gong that is the striking of a clock ("stroke of midnight"). In Eric Berne's 1964 *Games People Play*, the social psychiatrist wrote: "*stroking* may be employed colloquially to denote any act implying recognition of another's presence"; in transactional analysis, an exchange of strokes constitutes a transaction, the unit of social intercourse.

This friendly-gesture sense of *stroke* surfaced in a motto of toleration: the *Houston Chronicle's Texas Magazine* reported in 1973 that the popular saying in a drug-abuse program was "different strokes for different folks," the beginning of which became the basis for the title of the television series, "Diff'rent Strokes."

Another innocent use of *stroke* is the movement of a hand with a brush: in oil painting, the *short strokes* are meant for close detail, contrasted with the *broad brush* sort of painting done by artists and strategists concerned with the big picture.

The slang meaning of *short strokes*, unaccountably, is not defined in the latest slang dictionaries. Nor is its obvious climactic etymon, away from which I avert my eyes in shyness. The phrase is in frequent use and has come to mean "details" or "finishing touches."

George Shultz has a natural linguistic innocence; several years ago, he blinked in wonderment at the snickering that followed his assertion, of "use it or lose it," the etymology of which was duly recorded in this space. (I'm constantly picking up after the Secretary.) The origin of that rhyming advice is not in academia or the construction industry, nor is *toward the short strokes*. But overt usage purifies, and common usage cleanses; the frequent occurrence of *short strokes* in everyday colloquial speech, in print and on the air, has all but obliterated the origin and made the phrase acceptable in polite company. As Dean Acheson never said about Alger Hiss, I will not distance myself from George Shultz.

The motto of another era used to be "different strokes." I'll bet a lot of Americans recognize the motto "short strokes" to be as innocent as golf. I hate golf but I used to cover it, and "short strokes" used to mean those made with shorter clubs to cover shorter distances as one got closer to the hole.

Now then, about "short hair . . ."

Jack [Rosenthal]
The New York Times
New York, New York

As swimmers race in a pool, they must shorten their strokes as they near the edge of the pool. They do this to avoid slamming into the hard concrete. If they are to continue, they also need to be able to quickly touch the edge and press off in a flip turn. So, in this case using short strokes could mean coming toward the finish and such a definition may fit in with the rest of Shultz's sentence.

Jodie Slothower
Boston, Massachusetts

Rowing involves strokes. In competitive rowing a cadence, or stroke repetition rate, is established. This tries to balance maximum output against that endurance needed to complete the race. Just before the finish, however, the rowers greatly increase the cadence and reduce the length of the strokes—concentrating on the middle portion of a normal stroke (that portion of maximum efficiency from a geometric perspective). The resulting strokes are faster and shorter, and are always used as the final tactic just before the finish. Could these be the "short strokes" our Secretary of State mentioned concerning the Soviets?

J. C. Uithol
Captain, U.S. Coast Guard
Governors Island, New York

When a carpenter is cutting a board with a handsaw, he takes long strokes using the full length of the blade for most of that cut.

However, when he is nearly finished—within the last few inches of the cut—he usually changes to short, easy strokes in order to avoid tearing the wood when it separates. Hence, when he is "coming toward the short strokes," he is nearing the end of the job and a bit more delicacy is required.

Carpentry probably is not as old as sex, but it has been around long enough to be the more likely source of that expression.

H. C. Bennett
Syracuse, New York

I'm by any standards a non-prudish person, but I, too, am a little upset at phrases like "short strokes" (which seems to me much more graphic than "use it or lose it") being used publicly by public officials. I think the reason I'm upset is that the use of these phrases creates a sort of men's club or locker-room feeling that makes me feel that the speaker—almost always a man—is speaking exclusively to other men. Probably a woman would not use such phrases publicly and, if she did, would be criticized for it. So . . . I think you should object to this in appropriate language use instead of excusing it.

April Mahnkopf
Plattsburgh, New York

Down heah in the South we have not yet come to the climactic point in your column (that *short strokes* has been cleansed by usage and now is acceptable in polite conversation).

Perhaps that's because we have a similar term which means the same thing but is unburdened by sexual baggage: *short rows.* A member of a work group nearing the end of a long and wearying task might say to his or her fellows, "Hang on, don't give up now, we're getting to the short rows."

Origin? Plots of farm land in the early days often were not laid out in precise rectangles. Near the corners, which were not perfect right angles, there often would be two or three rows of cotton, corn, tobacco, etc., which ran for only a few yards as opposed to the full rows, which were planted from one side of the plot to the other opposite. Tradition had it that the pickers would do these short rows last, as a reward, as they finished their day in the fields. So "getting to the short rows" became synonymous with nearing the end of a task.

Robert J. Haiman
The Poynter Institute
for Media Studies
St. Petersburg, Florida

When you describe the "cubic content of a fully loaded cement truck" as "nine yards," please keep in mind that cubic measures are not measured in yards, since yards is not a measure of volume; at least they shouldn't be in proper English.

Carlos A. Altgelt
Dearborn, Michigan

Put-ti, Put-ti

When he needed criticism least, White House Chief of Staff Don Regan was zapped here for saying "the whole seven yards" when the phrase he had in mind was "the whole *nine* yards." Almost parenthetically, I added that the expression did not come from football or dressmaking but, rather, was derived from the contents of a fully loaded cement truck.

A large load of heavy material was deposited on my head from many readers who lie in wait for writers to misuse the word *cement.* "Just as there are no cement sidewalks," writes Edward B. Finkel, a consulting engineer from Elizabeth, N.J., "there are no cement trucks."

"Cement is an adhesive," instructs Ernest N. Rodbro of Tampa, Fla., a student of semantics, "[and is] mixed with water and an aggregate of sand and stone to make concrete. I am sure your intent was *concrete* instead of *cement* since the cubic content of a fully loaded concrete truck is nine yards."

"Cement is but one constituent of concrete," hammered home Herbert S. Saffir (no kin) of Coral Gables, Fla. "The trucks you made reference to carry concrete and are called 'ready-mix concrete trucks' or 'transit mix trucks.'"

I think it is fine for engineers to call cement "concrete," just as I think mathematicians have every right to get red in the face at the layman's misuse of *parameters.* And I will tut-tut at the inaccuracy of the old-time gangsters who took their victims for a ride and subjected them to what they miscalled "cement shoes" before tossing them in the river.

However, the truck that rolls through the city streets and makes grinding sounds is a *cement truck* to most people. Never mind that it delivers concrete, nine yards to a full load. In this, I remain faithful to Norma Loquendi: the toy she promises her kid for his birthday is a small *cement truck.* On this, my opinion is fixed in concrete.

> These trucks are not misnamed, in that they deliver concrete and not cement. They are in fact named for the device that they carry, namely a cement mixer. As you may guess, the cement mixer . . . mixes . . . the . . . cement . . . with aggregate and water to form concrete.
>
> *John W. Haim*
> *Jamaica Estates, New York*

Regarding the word *parameter,* please do not forget that *both* mathematicians *and* statisticians get red in the face at its misuse. To the statistician, a *parameter* is a *numerical measurement describing some characteristic of a population* (*population* meaning scores, measurements, etc., as well as people).

For example, suppose that 80 percent (one word, please) of *all* the people who read *The New York Times Magazine* read Safire's column. The proportion 0.80 would therefore be the value of the parameter, which is fixed (like your opinion is in concrete) as *all* readers of the Magazine (capitalize, please) were surveyed.

However, because it is neither possible nor financially feasible to locate and survey *all* the readers, a *sample* of them are interviewed, and from this sample we determine a *statistic,* which is used as an estimator of the parameter.

Thus, unless (the opposite of "if") we interview *all* the readers, we *never can say with 100 percent confidence* (or "100 percent certainty"— redundant?) that 80 percent of them read Safire's column, even if (opposite of "unless") in fact 80 percent of them do.

Although politics and statistics (each takes a singular verb, right?) are not mutually exclusive, the latter is still a better bet.

David Bernklau
Brooklyn, New York

Couch Potatoes and Lounge Lizards

There I was, lying on my back, bubble gum wadded in my cheek, a copy of *Sheena, Queen of the Jungle* held before my deliciously shocked eyes, ready to yell the favorite comic-book sound, "Aieeeee!" as the muscular maiden pounced on some unsuspecting leopard, when my mother appeared at the doorway like a Neil Simon heroine to pronounce the awful imprecation: *"Lounge lizard!"*

This meant I was being told to go out and get some fresh air, or get a job, or do something otherwise active and edifying. I did not realize it at the time, but *lounge lizard* was a phrase coined around 1912 to refer not to the merely lazy but to the stingily lascivious: the person being derogated was a young cheapskate who tried to pet in a girl's parlor without first taking her out and springing for a soda and a movie.

Synonymous phrases were *parlor snake* and *chairwarmer,* but the alliteration and *z* sound in *lounge lizard* won out, especially with the later, second meaning of one who hangs out in cocktail lounges. Laziness, without the overlay of stinginess, appeared in such words as *dillydallier, lotus-eater, goldbrick* and, one of my favorite Americanisms, *lollygagger.* In time, the mental picture of a reptile lying on a rock in the sun superseded the meaning of the penny-pinching lecher.

One phrase that never made it to wide use in the earlier part of the century to denote the slothful young male was *couch beetle;* however, the use of *couch* as an attributive noun (a noun modifying another noun) resurfaced in the 1980s and is now sweeping the dens and rec rooms of America: *couch potato.*

"The Doo Dah Parade" was described in a December 30, 1980, dispatch from Pasadena, Calif., in the American Banker as featuring such groups as "the All-City Waitress Band and the World-Famous Couch Potatoes." No group would have named itself the world-famous anything if the phrase was not current, but no earlier written citation has been spotted.

Within a few months, William E. Geist was writing in *The New York Times* about the interweaving of baseball, football, hockey and basketball to form "an almost impenetrable shield of sportscasting" and gave definition to the phrase: "Those who try to penetrate that shield say that the viewers, sometimes known as *couch potatoes*, have long since changed from human beings to receiving components of the broadcasting system."

A leader of the California-based group calling itself by this name, Robert Armstrong, was quoted by the Associated Press in 1982 as seeking to "assuage the guilt of fellow [TV] addicts" by glorifying prolonged viewing. He suggested this etymology: "Potatoes are tubers. They have many eyes. It came to us in a cosmic revelation." Soon an *Official Couch Potato Handbook* was issued by Jack Mingo, including M*A*S*H Potatoes (those addicted to sophisticated situation comedies) and Spec-Taters ("your basic drink-beer-and-watch-football-till-you-pass-out types"). A ladies' auxiliary was reported formed by 1985, the Couch Tomatoes, and by 1986 the term could be said to have become generic for a stupefied boob-tube watcher:

"Yeah, there are other things to do in the world," said high school student James Pol to a *New York Times* reporter, "but it's easier to pop a videotape into the VCR and just become a *couch potato.*" What will become of square-eyed lads like him? Like the readers of *Sheena, Queen of the Jungle* a couple of generations ago, they are in danger of becoming the drones, carpet knights and lounge lizards of the twenty-first century.

> Our firm represents Robert Armstrong, who, as you noted in your column in *The New York Times Magazine*, with some colleagues coined the term *couch potato* for use in a series of *couch potato* works and projects, including comics, publications, fan clubs, and clothing products. Through Mr. Armstrong's use of *couch potato*, and his licensing of the use of that mark to others, he has acquired valuable trademark and service mark rights in it. *Couch potato* is a registered trademark and not a generic term.
>
> *Roberta L. Cairney*
> *Cooper, White & Cooper*
> *San Francisco, California*

Dear Ms. Cairney:

Your letter to William Safire has been referred to this office for reply.

I am afraid that your letter overlooks the fundamental distinction between statements of fact and statements of opinion. Mr. Safire's view concerning the wide acceptance of the term "Couch Potato" is clearly an expression of editorial opinion, and, as the Supreme Court has instructed, there is no such thing as a false opinion. Although you may disagree with this opinion, there is simply no basis for requesting a correction.

David A. Thurm
The New York Times Company
Legal Department
New York, New York

There's disappointment here in Binghamton that you didn't consider the possible derivation of *couch potato* from *boob tuber.*

Faithful reader
[Name withheld]
Binghamton, New York

Dam That Tinker

When General Secretary Mikhail Gorbachev brushed off charges of human-rights violations in the Soviet Union with the question, "What about the *wetbacks?*", Americans cringed—not at the crude attempt of moral equivalency, but at the use of a term now regarded as a slur. A *wetback*—from the condition of a Mexican swimming across the Rio Grande to enter the United States—later become known as an *illegal alien*, and when that became onerous, the name was changed to *undocumented person*, now applied to persons of any nationality who enter the country without a visa. But nobody told the Soviet propagandists.

That brings to mind the subject of ostentatiously kind words, and the subtle change that is taking place in the avoidance through language of harsh reality.

The age-old art of euphemism is being violated. (*Raped* is the word I had in mind, but *violated* seems so much gentler.) In olden times, *limb* was substituted for *leg* to avoid offense, which seems silly, but euphemism had its fair uses: *love child* made life less harsh for *bastards,* and *handicapped* was used when *crippled* stung. Now *-impaired* is the combining form to describe handicaps, which denotes less of a handicap than *disabled.* (An Atlanta business association uses *differently abled,* but that strikes me as a too-kind locution that pretends no handicap exists.) When euphemism lessens pain and does not deny truth, use it.

But when euphemism conceals reality from people who ought to be able to take their vocabulary plain, it should be exposed. *Local prostitutes* is a phrase that is clear and direct, but is never used by the United States Government. In the welcoming packet issued to our Embassy employees in Budapest, there is this phrase: "It must be assumed that *available casual indigenous female companions* work for or cooperate with the Hungarian Government security establishment."

And when names are changed for commercial purposes, let the buyer beware: the Department of Agriculture last year soothed beefing meat producers by replacing the word *good* in its categories of fat content. *Prime* has the highest percentage of fat, or marbling, followed by *choice*, and now by *select*, which used to be *good*. Butchers disliked *good*; they feel that *select* is more appetizing. In that regard, let us recoil in unison from *tube steaks*, the misleading new name for frankfurters. (Is *wurst* closer to bad than good?)

And what about those broadcasters who refer to commercial spots as *announcements*? That's a sneaky way to hide a word from our sponsor. Almost as bad as family counselors describing a simple spanking as an *intensive adversive intervention*.

Big guys who use namby-pamby terms look especially ridiculous. Complaining that his team was being torn apart in the recent football players' strike by a false issue of free agency, Pat Bowlen, owner of the Denver Broncos, said, "That doesn't mean a tinker's darn to three-quarters of the players."

Should he have euphemized *tinker's dam?* Great controversy exists about the small word in this phrase, and whether it should be spelled with an *n* at the end.

Some say a *dam* is a tiny pellet of bread used by a tinker, or mender of pots, to keep patching solder from running through the holes in pans being mended. When the patch was completed, the *dam* would be thrown away, and became known as something without value. Other etymologists hold that tinkers were a blasphemous lot, given to heavy cursing; hence *damn*, from the Latin *damnare*, "to condemn or doom." Whichever of the theories you embrace, never substitute *darn* for *dam* or *damn*.

National Lampoon magazine has issued a list of current euphemisms, including *the homeless* for those unfortunates the hard-hearted used to call *bums* or *derelicts*; *acid-washed* for what wearers of jeans used to call *faded*, and *private person* for the fellow who used to be a *grouchy recluse*.

One of the most callous euphemisms of modern times was recorded by Alexander Solzhenitsyn in his *Gulag Archipelago*. In 1918, a Soviet admiral was sentenced to be shot; however, the death penalty had just been officially abolished, posing a problem for the state prosecutor. He rose to the occasion: "What are you worrying about? Executions have been abolished. But he is not being executed; he is being shot."

The use of the term "differently abled" refines the language. Quite often people with a handicap in one area compensate by trying to excel in other areas.

I too abhor the use of euphemism that obscures the truth, but in this case what may seem to be a euphemism is quite often more accurate than the "plain vocabulary" it replaces.

Nate Butler
Baltimore, Maryland

You imply that "handicapped," "disabled" and "impaired" may be used interchangeably. They are, in fact, distinct classifications pertaining to physical dysfunction. According to the World Health Organization's international classification of 1980:

> *Impairment* refers to the clinical manifestations of disease or trauma.
> *Disability* is the difficulty in performing daily activities as a direct result of the impairment.
> *Handicap* reflects the socioeconomic or environmental consequences of the disability.

For example, in a patient who has had a stroke, the hemiparesis is the impairment, the gait difficulty or trouble with dressing is the disability, and the loss of employment because of the person's inability to function at their job is the handicap.

Barbara S. Giesser, M.D.
Assistant Professor
Department of Neurology
Albert Einstein College
of Medicine
The Bronx, New York

In the jargon of family counselors, a spanking may be called "an intensive *aversive* intervention," but not an *adversive* one. The consequences may indeed prove to be adversive (i.e., unfavorable) but the intent of a punishment is to attenuate if not eliminate maladaptive behavior. Even Webster's Ninth New Collegiate Dictionary refers to "behavior modification by aversive stimulation."

Arnold A. Lazarus
Distinguished Professor of Psychology
The State University of New Jersey
Piscataway, New Jersey

"Tube steaks" is not very new. I have known it, and occasionally used it, since my brief career as student and dropout at Reed College, Portland, Ore., in 1954–55.

The term, beyond the visually obvious, is derived from "down the tube" and "cube steak." "Down the tube" (always singular) implies a drain either within the body or within the plumbing; it means "worthless, gone beyond recall."

"Cube steak," you may recall, is some kind of beef scrap, stamped by enough machine teeth to make it chewable, beyond the budget of two students living on $100 a month ($20 for rent).

Mary W. Roe
Peterborough, New Hampshire

I have for some time now been confused about the meaning and proper use of the term *moral equivalent.*

My profession deals with equivalences of many types. There are algebraic equivalences, geometric congruence, isomorphisms and statistical equivalence. In each of these cases, and in any others that I can think of, there is a common procedure. Rules are set up upon which the likeness (equivalence) of two objects is judged. These rules are agreed upon before the comparison is made, and all subsequent comparisons of the same type are made under the same rules, thus leading to transitive properties of equivalence (i.e. if A is equivalent to B and B is equivalent to C then A is equivalent to C). In some cases (statistical) the equivalence is not determined exactly, but the probability that two objects are the same can be determined. In each case, however, the rules for comparison are defined globally. Moral equivalence is a much different situation for two major reasons. First, morals are held individually, so the rules for comparison are defined locally not globally. In other words, this implies that the equivalence only holds for the speaker or anyone else who shares his moral code. Yet in most circumstances one cannot know the speaker's morals well enough to understand what the basis for comparison is and the term loses all meaning. Also, the transitive property will not be satisfied by any use of the term that I have ever come across. The term is most often used to simplify or generalize something, so use of the transitive property could lead to some ludicrous conclusions. For example, if the fight against inflation is the *moral equivalent* of war and the effort to keep kids drug-free is also referred to as the *moral equivalent* of war, then is the fight against inflation the *moral equivalent* of anti-drug programs? Simply put, my problem is this: A *moral equivalence* does not seem to satisfy the properties of an equivalence, so what meaning does the term have?

William J. Cummings
Department of Physics
Stanford University
Stanford, California

Your mention of the quite proper and unblasphemous origins of the term a "tinker's dam" brings to mind a phrase that is probably getting considerable use of late, but not in polite circles: "cold as a witch's tit." I am sure you know its origins had nothing to do with the milking apparatus of the possessed.

Theodore Lane Bracken
Washington, D.C.

Different Strikes

Linguistic sleuthing into the origin of *surgical strike* has led us into the Kennedy administration, the era of such phrases as *hawks* and *doves, managed news, Irish Mafia, New Frontier, I am a Berliner, Alliance for Progress* and *ask not.*

When last this strike force met, we pinpointed a 1981 Murrey Marder recollection of an early 1960s usage by Stewart Alsop on the subject of the Chinese atomic facility at Lop Nor, which the Russians were thinking about taking out. Concurrently, Martin Nolan of the *Boston Globe*—criticizing the Reagan administration's use of the phrase to describe the attack on Libya—was digging up a more specific citation: Ted Sorensen, in *Kennedy*, a history of the Kennedy White House, wrote in 1964 (and published in 1965), "The idea of American planes suddenly and swiftly eliminating the missile complex [in Cuba] with conventional bombs in a matter of minutes—a so-called 'surgical' strike—had appeal to almost everyone first considering the matter."

If it was in Sorensen, it could also be in Schlesinger, right? Right! On page 252 of *A Thousand Days,* same dates, we see a quotation from an April 5, 1961, memo from Arthur M. Schlesinger, Jr., to President John F. Kennedy: "If we could achieve this [the overthrow of Castro] by a swift, surgical stroke, I would be for it."

Says the historian today: "I don't know when *stroke* evolved into *strike,* but the escalation seems natural enough." Etymologically, it is quite natural: the Middle English *striken* and Old English *strican* meant "to stroke," rather than "to wipe out with a minimum of civilian casualties," a concept not then in use.

Lest anyone think he was what is now termed an unregenerate bomb-'em-back-to-the-Stone-Age hawk, Professor Schlesinger adds, "The memorandum went on to say that I doubted that Castro's regime could be removed surgically and that I was therefore opposed to the Bay of Pigs."

If this were a political column, I would argue that a little air cover that day might have turned the trick, but my friend Arthur, in a kind of surgical estoppel, pre-emptively attacks that: "You might have added to your definition of *surgical* as a military modifier that the impression conveyed of precision, quickness, cleanness and incisiveness is entirely spurious. War, as the late W. T. Sherman pointed out, is not surgical."

(What General Sherman, whose memory is not revered in Georgia, said to the Michigan Military Academy graduation class in 1879, was, "War is barbarism. . . . It is only those who have neither fired a shot nor heard the shrieks and groans of the wounded who cry aloud for blood, more vengeance, more desolation. War is hell.")

Was Professor Schlesinger the coiner of *surgical strike/stroke?* (That is a legitimate use of the virgule.) If you have an earlier written citation, put it on the gurney and wheel it into the operations room. Clue: Hugh Rawson, author of *A Dictionary of Euphemisms & Other Doubletalk,* an excellent 1981 work on the artful dodge, suggests that the Kennedy White House staff "picked up *surgical strike, pre-emptive strike, escalate, option, scenario,* and other war-gaming words from the Pentagon, or from debates by academics over John Foster Dulles's policy of massive retaliation, and that all date in their military senses to the late 1950s."

All right, you guys, go get 'em. (They shouldn't let a pop lexicographer up in a crate like that.)

The Dirtiest Word

Some words sound so harsh that we shrink from using them even when they fit. Such a word is *traitor.*

"The word *spy* is in the news a lot these days," writes Sheldon Vanauken of Lynchburg, Va., "but that word has a certain disreputable dignity and daring about it; there is no connotation of something shameful. When a naval officer, or any American, sells out his country, why are we so hesitant to call him what he is—a *traitor?* Why is there no talk of *treason?*"

When a person is convicted of the crime of espionage, especially when money has changed hands, the criminal can safely be described—with no risk of libel—as having "sold out his country." He is a *traitor,* in the most common sense of the word, rooted in the Latin *tradere:* "to hand over, betray."

Although everybody who has committed *treason* is a *traitor,* not every *traitor* has committed *treason.* The meaning of the word *treason* is spelled out clearly in the United States Constitution, Article III, Section III: "Treason against the United States shall consist only in levying war against them, or in adhering to their enemies, giving them aid and comfort." In those days, *them* meant the United States; we now say *it.* The phrase "levying war against them," it seems to me, means acting against the United States in wartime.

You can betray a friend or be a traitor to a cause, but you can commit treason only against a state and, under United States law, only during wartime. A Soviet citizen who spies on us is a *spy*, but no *traitor*; an American citizen who spies on us is both a *spy* and a *traitor*. But he has not committed *treason*.

Disinformation Prep School

The White House Family Theater is the room in which the Usual Suspects—a motley assortment of pundits, itinerant authors and editorialists—are assembled on the eve of major occasions to hear The Word from The Man.

In a recent session, the President did not feel the need to dissociate himself from charges of using "disinformation." That word was adopted in 1955 from the Russian *dezinformatsiya*, taken from the name of a division of the KGB devoted to black propaganda. (*Propaganda* is "deceitful persuasion"; *black propaganda* goes beyond that to employ outright lying and concealment of sources.)

The word borrowed back from the Russians was used in a secret memo by Vice Admiral John M. Poindexter, the President's national security adviser, as part of a recommendation (never meant to be exposed to public view) of a course of public deception intended to increase the nervous strain on Libya's Colonel Muammar el-Qaddafi.

Disinformation means "the intentional dissemination of lies to the media," and differs from *misinformation* in its intent. Because intentional lying has usually been considered a no-no in the United States, at least in peacetime, some of those in the White House and State Department wished to put some distance between themselves and the word the national security adviser chose.

In verb prefixes, *mis-* usually means "badly, wrongly"; *dis-* means "the opposite of," reversing the meaning of the word that follows. To *misplace* means to put in the wrong place, to *displace* means to substitute for; to *misbelieve* means to be sure that the truth ain't so, and to *disbelieve* is not to believe a word of it.

Misinformation was probably formed from the verb *misinform*, but the noun *disinformation* took the coinage the other way, back-forming the verb. It seemed only natural for the writer Mort Kondracke to ask, "Did the White House disinform the press?"

President Reagan seemed to grasp the meaning of the new verb, evidence of its immediate acceptance into the language; by refusing to answer the question directly, and by ducking two follow-ups, he lent credence to the opinion that he was prepared to adopt a policy of *disinformation* when he felt it was necessary. One of the pundits, accustomed to the tendency of public officials to merely *mislead,* felt this instance went beyond that to become an example of *disleadership.*

Not all Government officials adopted such a cavalier attitude toward official lying; Bernard Kalb, the State Department's top spokesman, resigned on a point of honor rather than associate himself with the word or the practice.

I have long been worried about Vice Admiral Poindexter because of a minor matter that hints at troubles underneath. He has been identified in the persnickety press as head of the National Security Council's "Crisis Preplanning Group," and any bureaucrat who thinks the verb *plan* requires the prefix *pre-* bears watching. (*Preplan* has a fifty-year history of being redundant, but is still worth fighting.)

Worse, the name of the group (it's a committee, but *group* sounds more serious)—*crisis preplanning*—suggests that its task is to "preplan" crises. Aren't we supposed to avoid crises? Even if corrected to "Crisis Planning Group," the name sounds provocative, better suited to a KGB "Active Measures Committee." A spokesman for the National Security Council staff refused to confirm or deny the name of the committee, saying only that such information is classified; however, when I asked whether the NSC had dropped the hyphen in spelling the word "preplanning," reluctant permission was given me to "go with that."

I suspect the misnamed Crisis Preplanning Group's function is to be ready with plans in the event that crises arise, at which point another committee, properly called the Crisis Management Group, chaired by the Vice President, is set to spring into inaction. If my supposition is correct, Vice Admiral Poindexter's group should call itself the Crisis Contingency Committee (nice alliteration there), the Crisis Aversion Group or the Panic Button Removers.

Please remember that the names of these groups are classified, and I hope the sensitive reader will treat my suggested names with the same confidentiality, lest the language dodge require "damage control." The NSC spends a lot of time on nomenclature, and is especially watchful of acronyms. During the Nixon administration, for example, presidential orders were transmitted in National Security Study Memorandums, called NSSM's, pronounced NIS-sims. When the Carter men took over, these papers were renamed, for a single afternoon, Presidential Study Memorandums, until somebody started using the acronym; the situation was tense in the Situation Room until somebody got the authority to change the nomenclature.

Ah, memories; but back to the present. At the same gathering in the Family Theater, the President—who spoke on the record, which meant he could be identified—was followed by a "Senior Administration Official" who can be quoted but not personally identified, according to the rules of background. That struck me as OK because the Administration is getting more senior every day and this official's name is frequently confused with the President's.

Senior Administration Official—I like to think of him as "the SAO"—quoted General Secretary Gorbachev as characterizing the mini-summit in Iceland as "a preliminary meeting—in his words, 'a preparatory meeting' —however you wish to pronounce it. I'll leave that to Mr. Safire."

I wish the SAO wouldn't reveal my background presence that way; I'd just as soon readers not know that my brain is subject to the latherings and rinsings of disinformation. At any rate, he pronounced *preparatory* two ways: PREP-ri-tree, and pre-PAR-a-tor-ee, leaving it for me to choose and thereby avoiding derision in case he got it wrong.

The word is correctly pronounced pre-PAR-a-tor-ee, with the accent on the second syllable. Accenting the first syllable may be due to the influence of *preparation,* which is accented on the first and third syllables, or of *prep school,* a shortening of *preparatory school.* If I had made a mistake and said the answer was PREP-ri-tree, I would have been guilty of passing along *misinformation;* if I had wanted to sabotage the SAO, by deliberately giving him the wrong pronunciation to use incorrectly at the summit, that would have been an example of the triumph of *disinformation.*

You're wrong on "disinformation." It predates the Soviet Union. The German General Staff in fact had a Disinformation Staff during the First World War. It coordinated the fake radio traffic, diplomatic chatter and double-agent plants that Germany used to mislead the allies.

The problem goes beyond dating disinformation. Up until 1980, disinformation was a term of art used by intelligence services to describe the trick used to mislead an adversary's intelligence service. It was a game played between them. With the messages transmitted through private channels, such as agents, not the mass media. For example, a published CIA report, "Soviet Covert Action," differentiates "disinformation" from "propaganda" on the basis that the former is directed to decision-makers and therefore "almost never receives public attention." The KGB defines "disinformation" very similarly. According to a KGB training manual (published by the CIA):

"Strategic disinformation assists in the execution of state tasks and is aimed at misleading the enemy concerning the basic questions of the state policy, the military-economic status and the scientific-technical status of the Soviet Union; the policy of certain imperialistic states with respect to each other and other countries; and the specific counterintelligence tasks of the organs of state security."

In other words, it aims at duping U.S. government leaders and confusing the CIA. It reserves propaganda for the media. This is not just a matter of semantics. The former targets the CIA, and must be remedied by some sort of counterintelligence vetting (i.e., the role of Angleton). The latter targets the media, and requires journalists to be cautious on sources.

Why the CIA decided under Turner to redefine the concept of disinformation therefore is of some concern. The KGB is no doubt still directing its disinformation against the CIA. Turner, by claiming it is a press problem a la Spike, rather than an intelligence problem a la Nosenko, distracts from the CIA's vulnerability.

Apparently, Casey also liked the misdefinition.

Edward Jay Epstein
New York, New York

Your column uses "disinformation" and "black propaganda" interchangeably. I am not sure that they are synonyms. At least the enclosed from the 1976 Church Committee report describes "black propaganda" in a way that differs from what the Administration did in the case of Qaddafi.

"One particular kind of possible 'fallout' has aroused official concern. That is fallout upon the U.S. Government of the CIA's 'black propaganda'—propaganda that appears to originate from an unfriendly source. Because the source of black propaganda is so fully concealed, the CIA recognizes that it risks seriously misleading U.S. policymakers. An Agency regulation specifies that the Directorate of Operations should notify appropriate elements of the DDI and the Intelligence Community if the results of a black operation might influence the thinking of senior U.S. officials or affect U.S. intelligence estimates. Regular coordination between the CIA and the State Department's INR [Bureau of Intelligence and Research] has been instituted to prevent the self-deception of 'senior U.S. officials' through black propaganda. It should be noted that this procedure applies only to black propaganda and only to 'senior U.S. officials.' No mechanism exists to protect the U.S. public and the Congress from fallout from black propaganda or any other propaganda."

Gilbert Cranberg
George H. Gallup Professor
School of Journalism and Mass Communication
The University of Iowa
Iowa City, Iowa

Don't Make Me Blush

Blush—a word associated with maidenly modesty—is coming into vogue, long after women learned to redden with anger at being called modest maidens.

Remember *rouge?* Forget it; gone with the *cold cream.* In 1965, an Ultima II cosmetics ad rhapsodized about a "blushing creme. . . . You can do no wrong with this 'transparesscent' blusher." The copywriter was so transfixed with the blending of *transparent* with *phosphorescent* that he or she missed the first major appearance in print of *blusher* as a noun meaning "a cosmetic used to give a reddish color to the skin, or to accent the cheekbones, or to give 'depth' or contour to other areas of the face."

Blusher, akin to the Old High German for "burning brightly," is like *rouge,* the French word for "red," but it can be in powder form, to be applied with a brush, or quivering in a gel, or lying there in a crème (a French word sometimes pronounced like the English *cream,* but spelled that way here to get around laws demanding that *cream* denote a dairy product).

Blush as a noun is most often used in noncosmetic English as part of the phrase "at first blush," meaning "at first glance." In another sense—the reddening of the skin caused by a flush of blood brought there by embarrassment—we have the meaning preferred by poets. John Keats saw blushes in gradations: "There's a blush for won't, and a blush for shan't and a blush for having done it."

Now there's a blush for brushing on, or dabbing or smearing on. The word has been married to *pink* since at least 1888. In 1955, according to Barnhart Book citations, *The New York Times* began describing bridal gowns as being worn over "blush pink taffeta," and *The Times* of London in 1963 used it as a compound adjective in describing "blush-pink carnations." *The Sunday Times* of London, five years later, was observing that painters tended to choose "blush pink and unsubtle green." Soon the pink was dropped, and *blush* came to stand for pink by itself.

That's when the furriers and vintners moved in on the word.

Full many a flower may be born to blush unseen, as the elegist says, but a fur coat is for looking at and going "wow!" Sidney Sharfstein, of Seventh Avenue's Sharfstein & Feigin, defines a *blush fur* as "a white mink or fox that has been bleached or dyed to a pinkish shade like the glow of a young girl's blush."

Not every furrier agrees with that poetic assessment of the color. "*Blush* is 'tawny' or 'taupe' or 'camelly' at the base," says a refrigerated denizen of

Fred's Fur Vault in New York, "and the hair on the top is cream white. It's a 'high' shade, meaning very fashionable at the moment." Is it dyed, or does some embarrassed animal walk around with blush-colored fur? "We prefer 'color-altered,' " coolly replies the voice from the vault. (I have a short friend who refers to herself as "height-impaired.")

"A California boomlet for *blush wines*" was reported by United Press International in December 1984 and described by the business writer Gail Collins as "white wines made from red varietal grapes." Frank J. Prial, resident wine critic for *The New York Times,* derogated them a few months later as "so-called *blush wines,* which are an attempt to make something akin to white wines out of surplus red grapes. The blush wines, which are usually slightly sweet, bear names such as 'white zinfandel' and 'cabernet blanc.' " California produces plenty of red grapes and drinkers of white wine, leading to the blush boom.

None of the wine dictionaries or neologism sources I've consulted has *blush wine,* so let's take a swig and spit out a definition: "a wine slightly paler and drier than a *rosé.* " As enophiles know, wine juice from red or white (that is, light green) grapes is relatively colorless; the color of the wine comes from the red skins. (*Enophile,* "wine lover," is *oenophile* with the first *o* squeezed out.)

Ray Spencer, who stomps around the Glenora Wine Cellars in Dundee, N.Y., says: "Letting the pulp add color to the juice is called 'leeching.' For *blush wine,* you may allow leeching to occur for less than an hour, while for a ruby red, the leeching process might take several hours or days." He thinks of blush wines as "yuppie rosés." Either rosé will become known as the darker part of a broad blush-wine spectrum or the blush wines will be seen as a pale vanguard in the war of the rosés. We'll sip and see.

I cannot leave the blushful Hippocrene without dealing with the general rise and fast change of *pink.* In American slang, *in the pink* has long meant "in the best condition," playing on the ruddy glow of health; in the 1930s, this word was taken for political use as in *pinko,* meaning "fellow traveler" or Communist sympathizer, sometimes redundantly as in *commie pinko.*

In the 1970s, the feminine association of the color took over, probably rooted in fashion's "Think Pink" and "Shocking Pink"; the adjectival compound *pink-collar* came into use to describe occupations dominated by women, coined on the analogy of *white-collar* (1920) and *blue-collar* (1946).

"*Pink* is now an adjective used to describe a neighborhood, restaurant or shop where yuppies proliferate," says Marissa Piesman, coauthor of *The Yuppie Handbook.* She assumes the usage comes from "the color of the postmodern buildings yuppies inhabit and the Jacuzzis they install in them." That's speculation (permissible in real estate), but I wonder why *gentrification* is associated with the color pink. Ms. Piesman says the new usage can either laud or disparage: either "Here's the neighborhood to buy in—it will be very pink in two years" or "I've got to move out of this place before it gets too pink."

Curious. You might expect to see women in blush furs sitting next to men sipping blush wine in pink neighborhoods.

I am certain many of your local readers have already pointed out your misuse of *leech*, a somewhat repulsive annelid worm, when referring to the *leaching* of color from the skins and pulp of the grape to obtain red wine.

"Leeching" wine may indeed be another way to get red wine, but I don't believe many of your enophiles would approve.

Jon DeBoer
Denver, Colorado

Permit me to call attention to your atypical lack of precision in referring to *blush wine* as being "slightly . . . drier than a *rosé*." Is the rosé you had in mind a mateus (a bit on the sweet side) or a tavel (approximately as dry as any wine I can think of, regardless of color)? This is akin to saying that it is slightly drier than a *red* wine, without specifying whether you have in mind cabernet sauvignon or Mogen David!

Carl Bowman
New York, New York

As you have undoubtedly been notified by now, "blush wine" is a trademark of the Mill Creek Vineyards in Healdsburg, Calif., and not a generic yuppie term for a rosé.

According to part-owner of Mill Creek Vineyards Bill Kreck, "We produced a white Cabernet in 1976, and in an interview with [wine writer] Jerry Mead, he commented on the wine's deep pink color, saying, 'You sure picked up one hell of a blush.' And so we called the wine a Cabernet Blush and started trademark proceedings in 1977," registered in 1981 but applied retroactively to 1977.

Since then other wineries have had to pay a fee to Mill Creek Vineyards for the use of the term "blush wine" on their labels.

John Mariani
author of The Dictionary of American Food & Drink
Tuckahoe, New York

The production operations in making blush wines are far from standardized. Thus, I find no quarrel with your definition of these wines ("slightly paler and drier than a rosé"). As was pointed out in your article, it is very difficult to make a really white wine out of red grapes, and the best of all possible worlds for this salvage operation may be to call them "blush wines." One winery went further in making a virtue of necessity and gave their results the brand name "Opal." Nevertheless, some winemakers who are giving extra care to production of these blanc de noirs (you might have used that phrase) are employing the same methodology used in the production of the most famous of all blancs de noirs, Champagne; that is, to press the grape clusters directly and to avoid the (de-)stemming and crushing operations. Thus, it is hoped that your definition will become more and more inaccurate.

R. E. Kunkee
Professor of "Wheenology"
University of California, Davis
Davis, California

Several years ago, the readers of certain well-known "men's magazines" watched with interest (I imagine) the increasing sexual explicitness of the photographs being published. With almost every issue, it seemed, the editors were becoming bolder and the photographs raunchier. The climax, so to speak, came when *Playboy,* following its competition, also let its centerfolds and other photos "go pink."
Need *I* be more explicit?

Walter J. Klein, Jr.
New York, New York

Don't Touch That Dial

A new language is being pounded into our ears. It is called *dialect*—not the regional speech understood by speakers of the same general language, but the arcane argot of the radio dial.

"Turn off that noise," I used to say to my kids, "and play some nice music." That sentence no longer communicates; in the past, it used to draw raucous laughter, but now the words have been drained of all meaning and evoke looks as blank as tape.

To be understood (if still hooted at) today, I would have to say, "Turn off that *album-oriented rock* and play some *adult contemporary.*"

But that is not what I mean. *Adult,* as a noun, still means "grown-up," but as an adjective, it has come to mean "sexy," verging on "pornographic"; like its synonym, *mature,* as in "mature audience," it means "over fifteen and a half and old enough to flash a learner's permit."

Contemporary has also gone off the linguistic charts. Time was, the word's second syllable clung to the Latin *tempus,* "time," and meant "in the same time, or of the same style as in one time"; one's *contemporaries* are the fellas who used to gather for a hot game of curb ball and now, paunchy and grouchy, twist the dial looking for soothing sounds. *Contemporary* started getting confused with *modern* a few decades ago, and now its meaning wanders like an errant signal from a 250-watt station. *Tempus* fidgets.

"*Adult contemporary* is the category that used to be called *light rock* or *soft rock*," says David Jackson, one of the new breed of nonbroadcast disk jockeys, who spins records for parties, weddings, bar mitzvahs and other social gatherings in Gaithersburg and Rockville, Md. "You can hear it on some *classic rock* stations, but it's not necessarily *oldie*, certainly not *golden oldie*."

Being really middle-aged means not recognizing the songs a younger generation calls *golden oldies.* To avert a mid-dial crisis, I am providing a rundown of my understanding of the new categories of popular music.

Album-oriented rock, or *AOR*, is a catchall term for what used to be *hard rock, heavy metal* and *white rock*, much of which went by the names of *acid rock* in the hippie era of the '60s and then *punk rock.* "It's a mix of older and newer sounds," says Mark Coleman of *Rolling Stone* magazine. "Pop performers like Madonna get little play on AOR, which also stays away from black music for the most part." It includes some *classic rock*, from the Hellenic era of the '70s, favorite of the yuppies, but is mostly *hard-core rock* that is not so hard-core, or obscene, as to get it banished from the airwaves.

For the difference between *AOR* and *adult contemporary*, I turn to Stephen Holden, who writes about popular music for *The New York Times.* "These are demographic terms that refer to a station's targeted audience," he explains. "AOR is the progressive rock format left over on FM from the 1970s, aimed very specifically at white teenage males, with groups like the Rolling Stones and Led Zeppelin. *Adult contemporary*, on the other hand, is aimed at the eighteen-to-thirty-four audience, both male and female, and is *soft rock* compared to the *heavy metal* of AOR."

Contemporary hits radio is a term that has replaced *top forty*, largely because it also covers stations that may play only the top twenty. The term *top forty* never did refer, as the literal-minded might have thought, to music preferred by people over forty years of age. It means the list of the forty most popular numbers compiled by *Billboard* magazine, and the people who listen are akin to the readers who limit themselves to the best-seller lists. Sometimes a highly popular tune is part of an album; for the rest of the album—the unpopular numbers on the flip side—switch to the AOR station.

Urban is the new word for *inner-city*, which replaced *soul*, which means *black*. (There is no *suburban rock*; that is what separates low-growing flowers in a rock garden.) *Blue-eyed soul* comes from whites who sound black; *red-headed soul* is from England.

Rap music, such as that played at a Run-D.M.C. concert in Long Beach, Calif. (which was broken up by gangs who did not like the positive, moral message in the group's lyrics), was described by the Associated Press as "a driving beat and rhyming lyrics delivered in a rhythmic, singsong vocal style." *Rapping* has for several decades meant "talking"; *rap music*, usually performed by black artists, is spoken to a heavy beat. ("Run-D.M.C."? From Run, the nickname of Joseph Simmons, and a play on the name of Darryl McDaniels, members of the group. Astonish your friends with "Would you please tune down that rap music of Joseph and Darryl?")

Other radio stations offer *classical music* (you know, "Tonight We Love," "Full Moon and Empty Arms," the theme from *Elvira Madigan*). *Country music* is in a crisis of stagnancy, as Nashville seems to be blending with *light rock* or giving way to *rockabilly*. What country needs right now is more songs like "My Best Friend Just Ran Off With My Wife, And I Miss Him." *Progressive jazz* and the Detroit-born *Motown* are getting harder to find amid the light rock and adult contemporary merging on the top forty.

You can also get *easy listening*, which until recently meant the music of the '60s played in the '80s in the style of the '40s, as if Jefferson Airplane were flying with Mantovani as pilot. That is the sort of thing you hear in upscale elevators and the best periodontists' offices; it is what many of us meant by "nice music," because it did not demand to be listened to. However, *easy listening* is getting harder; the music that used to go under that moniker is now called *nostalgia*, sometimes called "the music of your life," and studded with commercials for Cadillacs and denture cleaners: the "pop" in that "pop music" is filled with codger power. The phrase *easy listening* has now shifted over to *light rock*, which is softer than *soft rock*. I await the gutsy station that advertises *hard listening*.

The one category in my local paper's listing that could not easily be defined by musical types was MOR. I called WWDC-AM in Washington, and the program director, Bill Scanlan, said, "That's the abbreviation for *middle of the road*. We play the great pop singers and the big-bands era as well as the new material from George Shearing, Mel Torme and the Linda Ronstadt songs she did with Nelson Riddle."

That's middle of the popular road? What, then, is right wing—William Rehnquist and the Supremes? You play your *adult contemporary* while I wait around for Russ Columbo, Al Jolson, Connee Boswell and *Senile Reactionary*.

AOR is not aimed at teenage males of any race. Few AOR stations have significant amounts of teenage listeners. Generally, CHR (Contemporary Hit Radio, a.k.a. Top Forty) and Black/Urban (dance music) stations are dominant with teens.

AOR radio, rather than Adult Contemporary, is aimed at the eighteen-to-thirty-four audience. AOR targets primarily eighteen-to-thirty-four men, while the Adult Contemporary format generally finds its greatest strength among twenty-five-to-forty-four-year-olds, leaning toward women.

AOR plays relatively little heavy metal music compared to two to three years ago. This is because AOR has shifted its focus to the demographic that Madison Avenue finds desirable—listeners over the age of twenty-five. These young adults have far less of a taste for heavy metal's *Sturm und Drang* than younger, ostensibly less sophisticated "earthdogs" that AOR now shuns.

AOR appeals to an older audience than CHR or Black/Urban because it draws from rock 'n' roll's entire thirty-year history, with a concentration on the post-Beatles (1964–present) era. On the other hand, CHR and Black/Urban stations skew younger, generally, because they are more contemporary and play fewer oldies.

The term "AOR" is a registered trademark of R&R. The paper is credited with coining the term "CHR," as well.

> *Steve Feinstein*
> *AOR Editor*
> *Radio & Records*
> *Los Angeles, California*

Dry My Bier

Back in the Nixon era, I remember going to a Redskins football game with Henry A. Kissinger, then national security adviser. We sat in Edward Bennett Williams's box with Earl Warren, who had retired as Chief Justice, all rooting cheerfully until an egregious interference decision was made by a referee that called back a home-team touchdown.

"Bad call!" bawled Williams, one of the owners of the team.

"Poor judgment," agreed Justice Warren.

But Henry was on his feet, fists clenched, yelling at the top of his lungs the words that best expressed all our frustration: "On vot theory?"

Those words came back to me while I was studying the advertisement for a malt beverage that calls itself "Amstel Light Bier." The copy in the ad talks reverently about "this imported beer," spelling the word in English, but then signs off with the German spelling, *Bier.*

On vot theory? Ed O'Halloran, a spokesman for Van Munching & Company, the importer, explains: "We use the Dutch spelling to emphasize that Amstel Light is imported. Also, we wanted to differentiate it from our other imported beer, Heineken." (Heineken spells it *beer.*)

A *bier* in English, however, is a coffin. Some former Miss Rheingolds in New York (Jinx Falkenburg, Emily Banks, where are you?) will remember the joke about a vampire in a watertight coffin singing, as a driving rain flooded the cemetery, "My bier is Rheingold, the dry bier."

I don't want to knock the froth off a good campaign, but it seems to me that to be consistent, Amstel should be selling either *light beer* or *Leichtbier.*

(Some Americans think that *lager* means "light," in contrast to *dunkel*, "dark"; in fact, *lager* means "stored, aged," in contrast to *draft*, or "drawn from a cask.")

Van Munching is following a Madison Avenue trend toward deliberate misspelling, or use of foreign spelling, in order to lend cachet or establish a trademark. Elizabeth Arden did this with Millenium, a moisturizing pore-tightener (I think that's what it does) that has caused a generation of schoolchildren to flunk out when the spelling bee gets to *millennium*, which we all know has two *n*'s (at least until December 31, 2000, when all bets are off).

In the same way, Clairol has a hair coloring (I almost said *dye*, but in the beauty biz, the motto is "Never say *dye!*") that the company calls "Ultress Gel Colourant." The copy claims that "Even Europe never made shades more beautiful" than this *colourant*, which means, I think, that the American *colourant* is supposed to be better than the British *colorant*. That inverts the use of the *u*, and I would rinse out somebody's mouth at Clairol, loved I not honour more.

While I have this file out, let me welcome Christiaan Barnard, with two *a*'s in Christiaan, who has transplanted himself into the world of modern media merchandising. He is pushing a line of products named Glycel, which includes a cellular facial scrub, a cellular toner and a cellular treatment activator. (In Moscow, they must be thinking of a communist cellular creme. *Cellular* is a big new word in cosmetics as well as telephones, part of what the hucksters call "the hard-cellular.") Dr. Barnard says that skin care is "most important in improving the quality of life. This has led my colleagues and I to identify a substance much more abundant in younger skin than in older skin."

In this space, I do not knock the misuse of English by non-native speakers, because my foreignese is nonexistent. However, some copywriter should have caught "my colleagues and I." That phrase is correct as the subject of a sentence ("My colleagues and I are smearing our cellular selves with colourant" would be fine) but is incorrect as an object. In "This has led my colleagues and I," the verb phrase "has led" is transitive, which means it takes a direct object: "This has led my colleagues and me." *I* is in the *subjective* case, the first-person singular pronoun being used as a subject; *me* is the *objective* pronoun.

Between you and me, I'll stick to my good old-fashioned antiaging scruffing toner activator lotion, cellular-free. And you know what I find terrific as a body-building conditioning rinse for what remains of my hair after a shampoo? Stale *Bier!*

One of my obligations, as Officer of the Royal Order of Orange-Nassau, is to defend the language and culture of the Netherlands, particularly against those who confuse it with German.

Allow me therefore to point out:

1. *Bier* is the German spelling, but, more relevant to Amstel, is also the Dutch spelling.

(A digression: Amstel is the name of a river, which gave its name to Amsterdam, originally Amstel-dam, or the dam on the Amstel.)

2. It would never, in any event, be *Leichtbier. Leicht* is German; the Dutch version is *licht. (Licht* also exists in German, but only as a noun, referring to illumination, not to weight or color. The German word for light in color is *hell*—try *hell-bier* in an ad. The Dutch word for light in color is *blond;* very light in color is *helblond.)*

Anyway, you are right about *dunkel* meaning *dark* in German. In Dutch, it would be *donker.*

You will say that Dutch looks like a dialect of German. You could say it, but we wouldn't like it. We say that Dutch and German have common roots somewhere in antiquity.

Dutch has some Spanish *(bodega* is a bar) and French words *(Maréchaussée* is the name of the national police) thanks to Spanish and Napoleonic occupation. And in many ways it is close to English. For example God in Dutch is spelled *God* (although not pronounced our way, for the G is guttural and the *d* sounds almost like a *t* (thus *khot).*

While I trail off into irrelevancy, let me add that the Dutch guttural cannot be pronounced by Germans, which is why, at the time of the German invasion of Holland in 1940, German fifth columnists could be spotted by asking them to pronounce *Scheveningen,* the *Sch* being guttural in Dutch and pronounced by the Germans as *Sh.* A veritable *shibbolet!*

Daniel Schorr
National Public Radio
Washington, D.C.

Your column certainly caught my attention, as no doubt it did many others'. But mine was that of someone conversant in both the English and Netherlands language. It is in that capacity that I write these remarks.

Nederlands, as the language is called by those who speak it in The Kingdom of The Netherlands, once was related to Low German. Dutch, as the language is called in English, had its origins in the West Germanic dialects of the Scheldt-Rhine-Maas delta, dialects unaffected by the High German sound shift. The early political and cultural independence of the Low Countries from Roman times, not to mention interstate separatism and competition among the German States, produced an identifiable Netherlands language sometime in the fifteenth century. The thirteenth century animal epic, "Van den Vos Reynaerde" (Reynard the Fox), for instance, was composed in medieval Dutch, then called "Dietsch."

Thus your confusion of modern German and modern Nederlands is somewhat painful to those who can distinguish, as well as speak both.

I, too, have been struck by the growth of popularity of Amstel Light Bier in this country. Before proceeding to the specific errors in your column, allow me to inform Americans that this word, Amstel, refers to the river on whose mouth Amsterdam was built more than eight hundred years ago. A dam was built on the Amstel; Amstellerdam, Amstelerodam, and other forms of the city name were current before the present form, Amsterdam. That river is pronounced "AHM-stuhl", with accent on the first syllable. I hear in this country Am-STELL, which, I suppose, is an attempt to "Europeanize" the word.

Robert D. Haslach
Assistant to the Counselor
for Press and Cultural Affairs
Royal Netherlands Embassy
Washington, D.C.

"Amstel should be selling . . . *Leichtbier.*" I am afraid that you are in error. The word *leicht* does mean light, but the lightness pertains to weight. Amstel is a *helles Bier.* The word *hell* means light and pertains to color.

Donald L. Cronin
Rolla, Missouri

I don't want to knock the froth off a good campaign, but in your recent comments on Amstel Beer/Bier, you state ". . . *lager* means 'stored, aged,' in contrast to *draft,* or 'drawn from a cask.'" While your definitions are correct, there is no contrast between "lager" and "draft." Whether served from the bottle, can or cask, all bottom-fermented beers are aged weeks or months before leaving the brewery and are thus considered lagers.

John S. Stebbins
Etna, New Hampshire

When I was in grammar school, we educands would perpetrate such sentences as: "Me an' my brudda went ta da stoah." The teacher would correct us: "My brother and I went to the stoah." (Victories against New Yorkese are never more than partial.)

Apparently enough American schoolteachers drummed that correct usage into their charges' heads to cause endemic hypercorrection. Today a significant portion of us speakers of American English, when using a compound construction involving one or more pronouns, construe the pronoun(s) in the nominative case regardless of all other considerations. Hence, beside such sensible constructions as, "My sister and I spoke to him," and, "She and I spoke to him," we hear, "He spoke to my sister and I," and, "He spoke to she and I." And I know more people who say "between you and I" than I know who say "between you and me."

To my knowledge, this particular manifestation of hypercorrection is peculiar to Americans and people who have learned their English from Americans. Dr. Barnard's knowledge of foreignese would therefore not be a factor in his incorrect use of "my colleagues and I." For that he can thank the American colleagues it rubbed off from or the copywriter you postulate, who may well have not only let it pass but interpolated it.

John V. Costa
New York, New York

Your explanation of "me" being in the objective case because it is the object of the transitive verb phrase "has led" is erroneous and, therefore, misleading.

Syntactically, here's how it goes: In the sentence "This has led my colleagues and I to identify a substance much more abundant in younger skin than in older skin," the nominative *I* should be the objective *me*, NOT because it is the object of *has led* but because it is part of the *compound subject* "my colleagues and me," a construction that follows the Indo-European syntax rule that "the subject of an infinitive (to identify) is always in the accusative (objective) case. The group of words beginning with "my colleagues and—" and ending with "skin" constitutes an infinitive clause ("my colleagues and me" is the subject and the verbal "to identify" is the predicate) used as the object of the verb phrase "has led."

Julius B. Kritzer
Adjunct, Department of Communication
Florida Atlantic University
Boca Raton, Florida

The Earth Makes Its Move

"The mountain was really a molehill," said Prime Minister Yitzhak Shamir of Israel, in disparagement of the tepid results of investigations into high-level culpability for his Government's spying in the United States, adding the metaphoric crusher: "and the earth did not move."

This was saying "no big deal" in a ringing way. The alliterative mountain-molehill comparison has been tracked by James Rogers in his 1985 *Dictionary of Clichés* to Nicholas Udall's 1548 book in which the author translates Erasmus: "The Sophistes of Grece coulde through their copiousness make an Elephant of a flye, and a mountaine of a mollehill." (Udall took "an Elephant of a flye" from the second-century Greek writer Lucian, but coined or at least popularized "mountaine of a mollehill" himself. The *Oxford English Dictionary* credits John Foxe with the first mention of mountains and molehills in 1570; I am pleased to call attention today to Nick Udall's turn of the phrase 22 years earlier, which has since been overly used by millions who never saw a mole, much less a molehill. Am I making too much of this?)

The more interesting cliché selected by Shamir was his negative use of "the earth moved." It is possible that he took this from God's response to David's cry of distress in II Samuel 22:8: "Then the earth shook and trembled; the foundations of heaven moved and shook, because he was wroth." More likely, however, it was an unthinking reference to a modern sexual metaphor.

One of Carole King's hit songs in 1971 was titled "I Feel the Earth Move." In 1980, an actress in the play *Passione* was quoted in *The New York Times* describing Frank Langella's direction of her first stage kiss: ". . . he took my face in his hands to show me how to do it—and the earth moved." *The Economist* of London led a 1983 article with "The British television establishment huddled together this week at its annual festival in Edinburgh to ask itself: 'Has the earth moved?' " The writer added a nice note of phrasal etymology: "Borrowing Hemingway's metaphor for female orgasm was bravado."

Right author, although I don't know why *The Economist* limits the orgasm to females. In *For Whom the Bell Tolls*, Hemingway's American hero, Robert Jordan, is fighting on the side of a guerrilla band of Spanish Loyalists against the Fascists; he makes love to Maria, a young woman mistreated by the guerrillas, in a pulsing paragraph that describes the sex act in an exciting but tasteful manner:

"Then there was the smell of heather crushed and the roughness of the bent stalks under her head and the sun bright on her closed eyes . . . and for her everything was red, orange, gold-red from the sun on the closed eyes. . . . For him it was a dark passage which led to nowhere, then to nowhere, then again to nowhere, once again to nowhere, always and forever to nowhere, heavy on the elbows in the earth to nowhere . . . now beyond all bearing up, up, up and into nowhere, suddenly, scaldingly, holdingly all nowhere gone and time absolutely still and they were both there, time having stopped and he felt the earth move out and away from under them."

After a little while, he asks, "But did thee feel the earth move?" and she says yes, "And then the earth moved. The earth never moved before?" He assures her it truly never before had for him. Fourteen pages later, under pressure from one of the guerrilla leaders to tell what happened, Maria looks away and says only, "The earth moved."

It may be easy to snicker now, but "the earth moved" wasn't a cliché when Ernest Hemingway coined it in 1940, even though Udall's "mountaine of a mollehill" may already have been a cliché in 1548.

Besides, if you read that Hemingway passage with the young Ingrid Bergman in mind, her hair cut short as punishment for collaboration, but looking great, you may remember how the earth moved for you when you read the passage or went to the movie, and how truly it all felt then, and how it was so pretty to think we could have a damned good time together, Jake, although I still feel improper about the time we put Grace under pressure and the great bird flew out the window.

Be careful, earth-movers, how you wipe those tectonic plates. Papa's phrase must not be demeaned in its negative form by politicians to mean only "no big deal," nor should writers aware of its orgasmic origin limit its meaning to the satisfaction of one sex. Never send to know for whom the earth moves; if you're lucky, it moves for thee.

I always thought "making mountains out of molehills" was a Maidenform bra slogan.

Seriously, though, the phrase undoubtedly developed from the Aesopic fable *The Mountain in Labor* (A mountain was in labor, and gave birth to a mouse), appearing in Phaedrus's collection of fables about 25 B.C., though Erasmus cites an earlier Greek proverb.

At the end of the movie version of *The Mouse That Roared,* the bomb with which a small European kingdom has threatened the United States and Russia rumbles and threatens to explode . . . and a small mouse comes out.

> *Mac E. Barrick*
> *Shippensburg University*
> *Shippensburg, Pennsylvania*

Do we get a PAW (Poetic Allusion Watch) bonus for your allusion: "Never send to know for whom the earth moves . . ."? It is John Donne's Devotions Number Seventeen: "Never send to know for whom the bell tolls," etc. Which, of course, is where Hemingway got the title.

I'm never quite sure whether or not you are testing us to be sure we are awake.

> *Peter K. Oppenheim*
> *San Francisco, California*

Effective Immediately

The leaders of the free world huddled in Venice and came up with a statement about freedom of navigation in the Persian Gulf that urged "the adoption of just and effective measures by the U.N. Security Council."

But some persnickety reporters wondered why the statement sounded so wishy-washy. Why hadn't a more specific word like *enforceable* been used?

"A discussion came up," President Reagan responded when asked about this, "between a choice of the words *enforceable* and *effective*. And it was decided—a case in semantics here—it was decided that *effective* meant the other, and we didn't need the other word, so it was agreed that we would use *effective* measures."

One meaning of *effective* is "capable of producing the desired effect"—hence, one use of the adjective is to describe something that works. But can the word be used to mean what Mr. Reagan called "the other"—*enforceable*—so much so that the use of the two would be redundant, a case for the Squad Squad?

No. *Effective* is a broad, stretchable word that can be applied as a modifier to people as well as things and events. *Enforceable*, however, cannot be applied to people; you may think Mr. Reagan is an *effective* President, but nobody can call him an *enforceable* one. The latter word, eschewed by the summiteers, applies to agreements and has a legal use: an *enforceable claim* offers a cause of action, and the essence of legality is that a contract is "enforceable in a court of law." At the center of the word is *force*, compulsion rooted in the Latin *fortis*, "strong." Mr. Reagan is familiar with the more powerful word; in his address to the nation on his return from the summit, he used it in the context of "America's commitment to a consistent, enforceable plan to reduce our deficits."

Effective—"having effect"—just does not have the strength of *enforceable*. Its width of meanings has led to a variety of offshoots: *efficacious* (applied to treatments), *efficient* (applied to the competency or ability of an agent to have an effect) and *effectual* (applied to the action and not the agent). An effective hair-splitter would say, "For an *effectual* result, get an *efficient* doctor who prescribes *efficacious* medicines."

Thus, an *effective measure*—one that will have some beneficial effect, perhaps even do the job—is a far cry from an *enforceable measure*, which would require whatever action is necessary to carry out the agreement. The first is fuzzily rhetorical; the latter involves a legal commitment. For the President and his fellow-summiteers to suggest that *enforceable* was cut out because *effective* means the same is disingenuous. (In degree of puissance, *effective* is to *enforceable* as *disingenuous* is to *lying*.)

In the same press conference that featured this obfuscation through doubtful synonymy, however, Mr. Reagan gave to the English-speaking world the imprimatur that legitimized a previously taboo phrase.

"I told you all the truth that first day," he insisted, referring to the revelations of the diversion of arms profits to the contras, "after the—everything hit the fan."

This is one of the great examples of "punchline English," along with "So who's counting?" "Ready when you are, C.B.!" "Who's minding the store?" and "Don't make waves." (Some will insist "It's your turn in the barrel" fits this category, but that line, of naval origin, is not widely enough understood.)

Until now, the presence of a scatological noun just before the familiar *hit the fan* has restricted its written use; the President's skillful substitution of the simple "everything" for the offensive word changes its approval rating from R to PG.

Lexicographers have been filing citations on this phrase for years. When I gingerly touched this subject three years ago, I did not have the courage to report that lexicographer E. W. Gilman of Merriam-Webster explained the origin in a story that "dealt with a man who mistakenly took an exhaust fan above a barroom as a suitable receptacle for defecation," following which the bartender asked the man returning downstairs the question referred to by President Reagan in connection with the furor caused by the diversion of arms profits to the contras in Nicaragua.

Mr. Gilman reported, "Even though the story was . . . based on highly improbable assumptions (for one, that the fan was working in reverse), the image evoked was vivid enough to have won itself a small place in the language."

As the text of the press conference released by the White House indicates, the President did some efficacious euphemizing in mid-sentence and thereby effectuated a change in the acceptance level of the phrase, making previous taboos unenforceable.

> I hope you will reconsider the distinction you make between "enforceable" and "effective." I believe you have the matter completely backward, perhaps a result of your immersion in political perspectives.
>
> "Enforceable," I argue, is weaker than "effective." The suffix "-able" is associated in meaning with the noun "able"—can do, but perhaps won't, or doesn't. Enforceable, but may, perhaps, not be enforced.
>
> "Effective," I argue, is productive of an effect, not merely capable (there's that suffix again) of producing an effect. Thus, an effective remedy cures the disease, an effective campaign wins the election, an effective argument (such as this one) wins agreement.
>
> Perhaps a synonym, in my sense here, would be "successful." Try it!
>
> *Joseph C. Bronars, Jr.*
> *Elmont, New York*

The Erroneous Eagle and the Cross-Eyed Bear

"Where does it say we can do testing?" President Reagan asked his advisers at the Iceland summit meeting, reviewing their draft of a United States proposal to adhere to the antiballistic missile treaty in return for reductions in offensive ballistic missiles. That draft began, I am told, something like this: "Both sides would agree to the continuance of the ABM treaty for a period of five years. . . ."

His advisers explained that the American interpretation of the ABM treaty included testing, and that testing was implicit in the draft proposal. Not clear enough, said the President; hard-liners back home would raise the roof if it looked as if the United States were avoiding the subject. On orders to put it in explicitly, the drafters chose language that illustrates (1) the leadership of our country is seeking nuclear agreement without understanding pronoun agreement, and (2) our leaders have a firm grasp on the importance of the difference between *which* and *that*.

"Both sides would agree to confine itself *[sic]* to research, development and testing which is permitted by the ABM treaty for a period of five years . . ." went the language of the first proposal on this subject submitted to the Russians, according to the text provided later by the State Department.

Wrong. *Itself* does not agree with *both sides*. To fix it, the framers could have tried "Both sides would agree to confine *themselves,*" which is correct, but the plural construction ill fits a singular "side." Another way, "Each side would agree to confine itself," matches up the pronoun with the antecedent, but makes it appear that the side is agreeing with itself.

I would like to think that we created this grammatical bind to confuse the Russians, but it is more likely that it was the result of last-minute drafting by negotiators under great stress.

By the time we upped the ante of this proposal to ten years, some cooler linguistic heads had prevailed and this sentence was recast to get rid of the problem of pronoun-antecedent disagreement. "The U.S.S.R. and the United States undertake," went the revised version, "for ten years not to exercise their [the pronoun *their* agrees with the plural subject] existing right of withdrawal from the ABM treaty. . . ."

That was the embarrassing part; the proud moment came in the *which* construction. If we had said, "Both sides would agree to confine itself to research, development and testing *that* is permitted by the ABM treaty," the emphasis would be on the limitation: *only* that testing permitted by the treaty. However, by using *which*—introducing a nondefining dependent clause concerning the treaty—the drafters emphasized that testing is an integral part of the treaty.

A *which* clause, as readers of this column have had relentlessly drilled into them, must be separated from the word or phrase it relates to, most often by a comma; that is a signal that it is not a defining *that* clause. Unfortunately, in all the excitement of the first draft, the comma was left out—"and testing which is permitted" appears in the State Department release—which surely must have discombobulated Soviet interpreters, as it fuzzed up the emphasis in a manner worthy of Clausewitz.

We are rarely permitted to see the submissions of summit proposals in their raw form, and never, to my memory, this soon after a meeting. Why the full disclosure? Because Senator Sam Nunn, Democrat of Georgia, worried about our ability to hold off the Russians in a world without nuclear arms, demanded to know if we had proposed to eliminate all missiles. To reassure him that our offer was specific about *ballistic* missiles, the texts of our first (five-year) and second (ten-year, grammatical) proposals were released.

Is there a difference between a missile and a *ballistic* missile? You bet. Although the science of ballistics deals generally with the motion and impact of all projectiles, the word when used as an adjective has come to mean "long range" or "intermediate range," but never "short range." When you're talking about *ballistic* missiles, you're talking about *strategic*, not *tactical* issues. Thus, the offer excluded the sort of short-range missile that might help offset Soviet conventional (nonnuclear) superiority.

Our hats should be off, then, to the unknown grammarian who stood tall and saved the day in redrafting our five-year proposal. (That grammarian even proposed "strictly to observe" ABM provisions, refusing to split an infinitive, which many of us would have permitted in that case.) Easy at first, tough at the end; that was the linguistic story of the Iceland summit.

Our interpreters were alert, too. When Marshal Sergei F. Akhromeyev, the Soviet chief of the General Staff, was speaking, his interpreter passed along in English the phrase "the great responsibility we bear." The American interpreter interrupted to point out to our side that the Marshal's words in Russian were more accurately translated as "the cross I bear."

This reminded some of us of the mondegreen "Gladly, the cross-eyed bear," based on a hymn lyric: "Gladly the Cross I'd bear." No wonder the Russian interpreter tried to cover it up.

Dear Bill,

Relative pronouns (which for me does not include *that*—I follow Jespersen in identifying the *that* that introduces relative clauses with the "complementizer" of *I said that I was sorry*) have introduced both restrictive and nonrestrictive relative clauses in the English of virtually all authors since before Shakespeare's time, except for those who (sic) have fallen victim to overzealous copy editors. The restriction to which you alluded is really only a one-way implication: nonrestrictive clauses must have a relative pronoun and not a *that*. Your suggestion that a *that* is needed to make a relative clause unambiguously restrictive makes me wonder whether you wear suspenders along with a belt: presence versus absence of a preceding comma is enough to draw the distinction with elegant simplicity.

Jim [James D. McCawley]
Professor of Linguistics
University of Chicago
Chicago, Illinois

Falling in Love with Luv

On Valentine's day, philologists wonder: What's happening to *love*? "O, my Luve's like a red, red rose/That's newly sprung in June . . ." wrote the Scottish poet Robert Burns in a 1794 song, deliberately using a variant spelling, *luve*. He was not the first or last to fiddle with the spelling or pronunciation of this fairly important noun and verb.

Love's root is not Latin; *amor* is what some Romans felt for each other, leading to our *amorous*. For the origin of *love*, we turn to the Saxons, whose Old English word was *lufu*, and the Gothic tribes of Central Europe, whose L- words led to our *love*, *lust* and even *libido*.

The English pronunciation began with LOO-voo, changed to LOW-vuh in Middle English, and now—as every lyricist knows—rhymes with *dove*, *above*, *of* and *shove*. People who like their language neat will frown at the inability of our spelling to convey consistent pronunciation: the same combination of the letters *ove* have an *oo* sound in *move* and *prove*, and a long *o* (like Bobby Burns's "O, my Luve") in *cove* and *rove*. We do that to make English more interesting to learn. (Actually, the differences reflect the etymology: words with Germanic roots shorten the *o* sound, as in *glove*; French roots, taken from Latin, lead you through *mouvoir* to *move*.)

The spelling variant that has gained in usage so much that it has lost its kinkiness is *luv*. This hypocorism started about a century ago, as friendly British barmaids clipped the word's pronunciation slightly to use it as a term of endearment: "What'll yer 'ave, Luv?" (You like *hypocorism*? It comes from the Greek and means "the use of pet names"; when a person calls everybody "Dahling," that word is hypocoristic. Glad to help, Guv.)

Today, *luv* is used to show affection, care or cordiality without getting serious. If you get a note signed with the dialectal form, the sender is saying, "Look, I'm being cheerfully affectionate, but this verbal embrace is no protestation of undying love; don't get any ideas." *Much luv* is to real *love* as *ta-ta* is to a serious *farewell.* A smiling "luvya!" is usually a friendly or filial equivalent to "see you soon," although it can conceal a genuine expression of love under a sassy colloquialism.

As used by the Beatles in the 1960s, the word was said almost like "loov," close to *move*; more recently, some singers have taken to pronouncing it "lewve," close to nothing else. The three-letter spelling was popularized in the 1963 play *Luv*, about pseudo-intellectuals, by Murray Schisgal, and the subsequent movie starring Jack Lemmon. The variant's popularity in the United States has been certified by its trademarking as a disposable diaper by Procter & Gamble, which advertises Luvs as "virtually leakproof," a phrase hitherto confined to the National Security Council.

Love, spelled the traditional way, covers both spiritual and personal commitments. The powerful word is unsullied by the trend toward using *make love* to mean fornication rather than courtship: In 1897, the Century Dictionary defined *to make love to* as "to profess affection for (one of the opposite sex); strive to win the affection of"; but in 1976, the Oxford English Dictionary Supplement said the verb phrase's meaning has changed: "Now more usually, to copulate" (from the Latin *copulare*, "to join, couple"). *Love*'s spelling, however, is firm and likely to last another thousand years.

Luv may also be here to stay.

Dear Bill:

No Scot would say Bobby Burns, any more than a San Franciscan would talk about Frisco. In print, it's always Robert. In camera (i.e. wherever two or three are gathered together to sample the Right Stuff, the crop, the barley wine, a wee drap) it's Rabbie.

The Beatles' pronunciation of "love" is standard North Country. It's one of the several vowel sounds that—they say—went over from Denmark—and with the German mercenaries—to the invaded North. (The Lancashire and Yorkshire pronunciation of "man" is exactly the German "mann.") Ridiculously, as you imply, this normal North Country sound—as in love, luck, mud, mother—is as difficult to transcribe in print as the sound of the schwa. It's just a touch shorter than "loov". Until the age of eleven, I heard no other sound than the Beatles' love, mother, etc., until I went to a school where the headmaster spent half his leisure time purging the barbarous Lancastrians of their native accent.

Lang may yer lum reek! Also—a wee deoch an doris!

Alistair [Cooke]
New York, New York

Fornication is sexual intercourse between a man and a woman not married to each other.

The last I heard, *making love* included married couples.

Harold D. Moses
Peabody, Massachusetts

As an old phonetician, I have an urge, which I am indulging, to point out your error in listing *of* as having the same vowel pronunciation as *love, above* and *shove*. If you will say aloud, "I didn't say *for*, I said *of*" you will notice that the vowel in *of* in an accented position is like the *o* in *cot*.

Even in an unaccented position, as in "the *days* of the *week*," the sound of the *o* in *of* is not like the vowel in *love*, etc., but is the neutral vowel, represented phonetically by the schwa (ə). Many vowels in English in unaccented positions or syllables, fall into this neutral vowel sound, as for instance, the *a* in *above*, *acute*, etc. The vowel sound in *love*, *above*, etc. is the same sound as the *u* in *but*, *cut*, etc. It is represented in the phonetic alphabet by the symbol ^.

Frances Willard von Maltitz
Weston, Connecticut

Fawn Hall's Shredding, Ek-setera

Fawn Hall, who was secretary to Lieutenant Colonel Oliver L. North at the National Security Council, appeared before the Iran-contra panel and boosted its ratings overnight. Linguists were immediately struck by her pronunciation.

Like many native American speakers, she dropped the *g* in *recognize*. " 'Reckonize' is not a recent development," reports Fred Mish, rex of lex at Merriam-Webster. "It's recorded in Webster's Third (1961) with the obelus mark used to indicate evidence of its use by educated speakers, but that pronunciation is stigmatized by commentators on usage." That means me, and other stiffs who frown on words like *ain't* in formal settings. Distinguished Americans who are in the file using "reckon-ize" include

President Carter, Henry Luce, Senators Claiborne Pell and Terry Sanford, and now Fawn Hall.

She also pronounced *et cetera* "ek-setera." This is not recorded in the unabridged Webster's, but the lexicographers are picking up many recent citations, including Senator Jim Sasser of Tennessee and Julie Nixon Eisenhower, who is author of the best seller about her mother and the wife of David Eisenhower, who is author of the best seller about his grandfather, ek-setera, ek-setera.

According to the Dictionary of American Regional English (which is a huge success, and its lexicographer, Fred Cassidy, America's Sir James Murray, is getting the recognition he deserves), "The pronunciations 'ek-setera' and 'reckon-ize' are not regionalisms. They are, in fact, very common, although you wouldn't expect to hear them from a person of high education. I would call them general colloquialisms, pronunciations that widely occur and are not restricted to a single region."

Professor Cassidy calls "ek-setera" an example of "homorganic sound substitution," and then explains: "Homorganic means 'made with the same speech organs,' such as the tongue, the lips, et cetera. *Homos* means 'same,' and *organum* is 'organ.' The letters *p* and *b*, for instance, represent homorganic sounds because they are made in the same part of the mouth; you wouldn't call *k* and *n* homorganic, though, because their sounds are made differently."

Changes in pronunciation can take place almost automatically as the sound slips over from one to the other. These sound substitutions are usually made for some physiological reason. "But if you don't hear yourself speaking and are uncritical of your own pronunciation," Professor Cassidy adds, "you can easily slip from one to another of homorganic sounds."

Sometimes homorganic sounds are added to words and are known as "intrusive consonants," as in "horspital" or "fambly." The late cartoonist Al Capp, creator of "Li'l Abner," always used this device in dialogue among members of Dogpatch's Yokum "fambly."

The difference is that an intrusive consonant adds a sound to the word. "Ek-setera" is an example of sound substitution, not intrusive consonant, because *k* is substituted for *t*, not added to the word (or it would be pronounced "ekt-setera," which was not what Miss Hall said; I was listening closely).

Professor Cassidy's enlightenment on homorganic sound substitution is firmly anchored in Hebrew and Talmudic lore.

On Leviticus 19:16 "You shall not go up and down as a talebearer," Rashi, commentator par excellence, writes:

I think because all who instigate strife and tell gossip, walk about in neighbors' houses, searching to see or hear evil to spread it in public are called "walking spies" (the word *rachil* is identical with *ragil*) . . . hence I believe that the letter *ch* is related to the letter *g*, because ALL LETTERS THAT COME FROM THE SAME PART OF THE MOUTH ARE INTERCHANGEABLE, b & p, g & ch, k & ch, n & l, z & ts.

In Tractate Eduyot IV Mishna 3 the topic is *hefker*, ownerless objects. Curiously it is spelled *hevker* (a soft v rather than a hard f). Jastrow's Dictionary of Talmud Babli, Yerushalmi, Midrashic Literature and Targumim, lists *hevker* as "Palestinian dialect."

Rabbi Shlomo Kahn
New York, New York

Dear Bill:

Apropos of "reckonize," it is interesting to note that *recognizance* in legal usage is pronounced without the *g*. It was so as well in the old Savoy Opera Company's rendering of the song in *The Mikado*, where the word occurs.

Jacques [Barzun]
Charles Scribner's Sons
New York, New York

You discussed changing the consonant (ek-setera) and adding one (fambly), but you left out leaving one out: facks, producks, insecks, et cetera. All these mispronunciations are common. While you were overly kind to the offenders, to me they indicate sloppy listening, reading and/or speaking. But I guess that kind of thing is *routine* these days.

Jerome S. Schaul
Caldwell, New Jersey

After reading your column on the usage of the word "etcetera," I felt motivated to write to you about some other verbal abuses that my ears endure every day. Perhaps you could do a column on Corporate "verbal offenses." I offer my "Top Five" in order of occurrence, with the misuses, in brackets, as follows:

1. Subsidiary (Subsidery, Subsiderary, Subsiduary)
2. Asterisk (Asterick, Asterix)
3. Oriented (Orientated)
4. Regardless (Irregardless)
5. Project (Projeck)

Steven H. Axelrad
Boca Raton, Florida

I believe that in "etc." the original "t" rather than the substitute "k" is actually homorganic with "s." Both "t" and "s" are made with the tip of the tongue against the alveolar ridge (right behind the upper teeth).

The "k" is usually made by the middle of the tongue, farther back against the roof of the mouth. What I believe happens in "ek-setera" is that the short "eh" sound is made with the tongue in about the same spot as required for the "k" sound, but rather awkwardly for a "t" sound.

It takes conscious effort to say the "eh" and then immediately get the tongue into position to say the "t," so we sometimes fudge a little. Some people use a similar sound, the "k," that the tongue is precisely positioned for already. Others of us fudge in a different way by using a glottal stop (a kind of catch in the throat) instead of clearly enunciating a "t."

Other common examples of homorganic sounds are the nonstandard forms "drownd" for "drown" and "acrosst" for "across."

William Leffingwell
Associate Professor of English
Cayey College, University of Puerto Rico
Cayey, Puerto Rico

In this region a turtle is sometimes called a turkle.

In the German orthography, you can only with difficulty distinguish between *T* and *K*.

John Jackson
Lexington, Kentucky

"Ek-setera" need not be a "general colloquialism" to which we all have to adjust. It is a display of ignorance that could be cured if Latin were required—even one year of it—in high school. I had two. I don't use this to read Caesar or Virgil, or even the more difficult tombstones. But I sure know that "et" means "and." In a world of uncertainty, such knowledge can be comforting.

Carol Becker
New Brunswick, New Jersey

As another example of a homorganic sound substitution, I submit the following: an irritating mispronunciation common to New Jersey residents, the substitution of "ck" for "tg" in saying "Rutgers." Even some graduates of the State University refer to their alma mater as "Ruckers."

Adeline Arnold
Aberdeen, New Jersey

Another example of "homorganic sound substitution" is the more and more common pronunciation of "technical" versus "tetnical." It almost seems the converse of "ek-setera" for "etcetera."

At any rate, hearing "tetnical" causes me to gnash my teeth, etc.

Muriel Phillips
Levittown, New York

That also occurs with the ubiquitous asteriks that mark a footnote, and the students in my English class who want to aks a question.

David Galef
New York, New York

How could you have missed hearing Fawn Hall's "extrenuous" for "extraneous"?

Danielle Lalime
New York, New York

Another word for your list is *jewelry*, which is often mispronounced *jew-lery*.

Alfred R. Pagan
Westwood, New Jersey

You mentioned two words mispronounced by Fawn Hall. When you did not cite a third and because I have heard so many people pronounce it that way, I went to my Webster's. I found the "L" is still in *vulnerable*. It came from her lovely lips as "vunnerable." The error does not fit into your two categories: "homorganic" or "intrusive consonant." Is it elision or ellipsis—or "elophobia" (not in my Webster's)?

You mentioned Jimmy Carter's mispronunciation of "recognize," but the most annoying to me was his "nuclear." He moved the letter "L" in that word so that to me it sounded like a tongue twister.

I wish people would not abuse or ignore the letter "L" because without it my name would be "Inch."

Rosemary Lynch
Yonkers, New York

". . . and Julie Nixon Eisenhower, who is author of the best seller about her mother and the wife of David Eisenhower . . ." This sounds as if the best seller is about two people.

Bernard E. Edelstein
Weymouth, Massachusetts

Fewer Bursts, Less Bursting

The CBS correspondent Bob Schieffer, reporting election returns on one of the primary nights, wondered aloud whether a percentage figure he was giving should be described as *less* or *fewer.* The grammarian on the spot immediately pronounced judgment: when a percentage is used to indicate an amount or quantity, it takes *less;* when used to describe a number, it takes *fewer.* Thus, you say, "His Florida percentage in 1988 was less than it was in 1984," and "Fewer voters went for him this year."

Wait a minute. This is not a simple fight between amount and number. The amount-number, less-fewer rule is clear: *Less* is used with amounts thought of as a quantity that can be measured or a singular abstraction (less ink, less time, less political power), while *fewer* is used with numbers thought of as individual persons or things that can be counted (fewer good stories, fewer minutes of airtime, fewer moments of glory). A Chinese bakery may produce 10 percent fewer fortune cookies and in each cookie use 10 percent less sugar; a primary election may turn out 50 percent fewer voters, who are 50 percent less sure of their convictions.

But here's the rub: when you use a qualifying adjective before the word *percentage*—specifically, a comparative, ending in *-er,* rather than a superlative, ending in *-est*—then *smaller* or *lower* is preferred to *lesser,* and *greater* or *higher* is much preferred to *more.* Say, "He won a greater percentage of the vote than last time, even if he got fewer votes."

(And do not equate *percent* with *percentage points,* the grammarian should have gone on to say, if he had had time, and if he had thought of it. As the style manual for *The New York Times* explains, "If an interest rate rises to 11 percent from 10 percent, it is a rise of one percentage point, but it is an increase of 10 percent.")

Consider, then, this fragment from an Associated Press dispatch about the sale of the Eastern Air Shuttle, as printed in the *Times:* "If less than 50 percent of the new company's employees chose to join the union. . . ." Consider it incorrect. It could be "less than 50 percent of the new company's work force," in which the workers are lumped together into a force, but it has to be "fewer than 50 percent of the new company's employees" because employees are individuals, no matter how plural. You would not, however, say "smaller than 50 percent"; you might say "the percentage is smaller" or that it's "below 50 percent."

Look, this less-fewer stuff worries people: the most power-intensive moment in the history of this column came when Safeway Stores was criticized here for "Express Lane—Ten Items or Less" and promptly rectified the mistake. Millions of mothers take their tots through the checkout counters at that fine company under signs that now read "Ten Items or Fewer."

In return for the grammatical steer that night, the anchorman Dan Rather slipped me an inside usage: "In this next interview, watch for a *prepackaged burst.*"

I listened, and sure enough, when a candidate was asked about one subject, he gave it short shrift and then exploded with a fifteen-second pitch about what he had come on to say in the first place.

This oratorical *burst* does not come from *outburst,* a sudden eruption of rhetoric, an uncontrolled breaking of the verbal dam; on the contrary, the etymon of this political television device can be found in the electronic *burst transmission.* The dictionaries have not yet covered this sense.

The *prepackaged burst* is rooted in spookspeak, and I turned to former Director of Central Intelligence Richard Helms.

"I'm not very up to date on communications technology," he began (the former master spy always says that, presumably to throw off listeners-in), "but I can tell you generally what is involved in a *burst.*

"Sometime back, the technicians discovered how to send a hell of a lot of words in a very quick broadcast, making it hard to intercept and decipher. Say you're an agent in a house in the center of Moscow and you want to communicate with your headquarters. You wouldn't want to be on the air long enough for the triangulation of listening bands to locate you. With a *burst transmission,* you can pass along information instantaneously, making you harder to trace."

How far back is "sometime back"? "At least twenty-five years," Dick Helms estimates, "because I've been out of this thing for ten or fifteen years now, and burst transmissions had been common practice for quite a while before I left."

Burst is a wonderful old word; a thousand years ago, the verb was busting out in "Beowulf," and Shakespeare picked it up in noun forms as "a hollow burst of bellowing" and the related "almost to bursting." (That *bursting* is a gerund, an *-ing* noun formed from a verb; but an adjective that is formed from a verb, as in "a bursting pipe," is a participle, not a gerund. When I am asked about this, I reply that Gerund was a friend of Beowulf's. When anybody challenges your grammar, hit him in the teeth with your knowledge of gerunds.)

As *cuss* comes from *curse,* *bust* comes from *burst;* the rich root word now has senses ranging from "intense activity" to "sudden emotion" to "a rapid sequence of shots from one pull of the trigger." That last sense is what the television people have in mind when a pol erupts with his pitch.

Was Gerund a friend of Beowulf . . . or was he a friend of Beowulf's (e.g., friends or relatives or some other connection, as your apostrophe implies)? I believe that you merely meant that he was Beowulf's friend, not a friend of other persons known to Beowulf.

Others have used your apostrophe but I see no justification.

Harold Newman
New Orleans, Louisiana

In the eighth grade (in 1926, when grammar was thoroughly driven home to us), Miss Newton made a strong distinction between the gerund, the noun form, and the gerundive, the adjectival form.

Thus, "Cleaning is a chore," (gerund); "My cleaning lady does it," (gerundive).

No longer? A lot of things have changed in fifty years.

C. Stanley Ogilvy
Mamaroneck, New York

Dick Helms was not a "master spy"—a secret agent of extraordinary ability, experience, versatility, and so on. No, Dick was a spy master—an intelligence officer who runs a single spy or sometimes a whole network.

Roger Hilsman
New York, New York

Finding's Losings

Gerunds everywhere are proud that one of their clan has made it big in Washington: a *finding*, capitalized when used by the National Security Council staff, is the noun that enables a President secretly to suspend a law.

(A *gerund*, called by stiffs a "verbal substantive," is a term in grammar that is forgotten as soon as it is learned. It means "a noun that is formed from a verb and ends in *-ing*"; in the sentence *Ducking a question is easy*, the gerund is *ducking*. In addition, when you hold a witness's head under water, you are giving him a good gerundy *ducking*; however, when the same word is used as an adjective, it is not a gerund but a participle: "the bobbing, weaving, ducking adviser took the Fifth." Hold your breath; count to three; you have now forgotten what a *gerund* is.)

"I hereby find that the following operation . . . is important," goes the once-secret document signed by President Reagan back on January 17, 1986, ". . . and direct the Director of Central Intelligence to refrain from reporting this Finding to the Congress. . . ." In that sentence, *finding* is a gerund (a wha'?), and that noun is dear to executives because it has since

1859 had a judicial connotation: "The result of a judicial examination or inquiry; the verdict of a jury, the decision of a judge or arbitrator." In this case, the National Security Act of 1947 lets the President act as judge of when to obey a law.

A shoemaker, holding tacks grimly between clenched lips, will wonder what all the brouhaha is about—to that person, *findings* are the small parts and materials other than leather used to make a shoe (laces, nails, buckles, etc.)—but a secret *finding* is hot stuff to congressmen planning televised hearings. (In the sentence *The President turned off his hearing aid when the hearings came on the screen,* the adjective *hearing* is a participle because it modifies *aid,* and the noun *hearings* is a gerund.)

The President and his tormentors would do well to heed this advice, using the gee-whiz gerund, in a translation of an 1829 Goethe essay: "The artist may be well advised to keep his work to himself till it is completed, because no one can readily help him or advise him with it . . . but the scientist is wiser not to withhold a single finding or a single conjecture from publicity."

The White House press office decided it would be wiser not to withhold the President's finding on Iran arms sales from publicity, because it is better to look naïve than to look crooked. As a result, we have a document and its attachments to inspect that contains what were until recently the most closely guarded words in our Government. From its own unique perspective, this department will now analyze that document.

"Because of the requirement in U.S. law for recipients of U.S. arms to notify the U.S. Government of transfers to third countries," wrote John M. Poindexter, then national security adviser, *"I do not recommend that you agree with the specific details of the Israeli plan."* His prepositional phrase beginning *because of* and ending with the comma, which gives his reason for the recommended action, would better be placed after that recommendation because it seems now to be directed toward the "I" instead of the action.

It would have been clearer to write "(recommended action) because (reason)," as I did in the previous sentence; if you disagree, try swinging the recommended action part of my previous sentence around to the beginning. It's not as good, because putting the reason before the action leaves the reader in the dark too long about what action is being talked about.

"It is their belief that by so doing they can achieve a heretofore unobtainable penetration of the Iranian governing hierarchy." In that sentence, *unobtainable* is the wrong modifier for *penetration.* The action desired is the accomplishment, or achievement, of penetration, not the *obtaining* of it; therefore, the phrase should be "a heretofore *unattainable* penetration." (Only in football backfields do you get, in the sense of "obtain," penetration.) If the writer (Oliver L. North, who drafted the document for Mr. Poindexter) wanted to put the sentence in plain English, he would have written, "They believe

that is how they can penetrate the Iranian governing hierarchy for the first time." However, that is apparently not the preferred style for official findings.

"In that we have been unable to exercise any suasion over Hezballah. . . ." Although *in that* is not slang, it is a weak and awkward way to avoid the use of *because.* It is akin to beginning a sentence with *Seeing as how. . . .*

"A dependency would be established . . . thus allowing the provider(s) to coercively influence near-term events." That *coercively* is one word too many; the phrase would better be left with its infinitive unsplit, because it is possible simply "to influence events," near-term or otherwise. The verb *coerce* means "to force or compel"; *coercively,* the usually pejorative adverb, is probably intended here to mean "more than strongly"; however, the "force" meaning of the adverb *coercively* overpowers rather than modifies the sly verb *influence.*

If the writer's intent was to emphasize *influence,* then *strongly to influence* or *forcefully to influence* would have been a more puissant intensifier, because *forcefully* does the job without meaning "using force." However, if the Northdexter intent was well beyond *influence,* the drafter should have used a verb such as *determine* or *dictate.*

"The Secretaries do not recommend you proceed with this plan." This is a confusing or deceptive construction. Does it mean that the Secretaries (of State and Defense) do not have a recommendation? In that we now know (see how weak *in that* is?) that Secretaries George P. Shultz and Caspar W. Weinberger vigorously opposed the plan, that line should have read: *"The Secretaries recommend that you do not proceed with this plan."* The misplacement of the *do not* was inadvertently or intentionally misleading.

That sort of sloppy writing would ordinarily cause most citizens to be incensed at the disservice done the President, but it turns out he didn't read it anyway. In a handwritten notation on the appendix to the Finding, Mr. Poindexter wrote: "President was briefed verbally from this paper."

Which raises the question: does *verbally* still mean "by use of words, either spoken or written," or has it come to mean "orally"? My long-held position is that usage has changed *verbal* to mean exclusively *oral,* but prescriptivists of the stature of Jacques Barzun and John Simon strongly (though certainly not coercively) disagree.

The last time I verbalized in print on this subject, biologist Lawrence P. Kunstadt of New York City put in this objection: "Many communications in the animal world are made orally, by mouth. All sorts of animals grunt, howl, chirp, bray or otherwise vocalize through their buccal cavities. Even ants communicate orally, through mutual feeding by regurgitation, a behavior known as trophallaxis, which functions in part to communicate information concerning the colony. Only one species of animal communicates verbally, with words."

That is as good a case as I have read for using *verbal* to mean "communicate with words," but I would have to side with John Poindexter in his use of *verbally*; his point would have been clearer if he had written "orally," but most people today take *verbally* to be its synonym. Purists will hate it, but that's my finding.

I wouldn't have believed it: William Safire rewrites John Poindexter's prose and makes it harder to understand. I refer to your recommendation that the *because*-phrase in "Because of the requirements . . . , I do not recommend that . . ." be put at the end. With Poindexter's original word order, that phrase unambiguously modifies the main clause, i.e. the sentence unambiguously gives Poindexter's reason for not recommending that the President agree with the specific details of the Israeli plan, which appears to be exactly what Poindexter meant. With it at the end, the sentence would be ambiguous between that interpretation and two others: that Poindexter recommends that the President agree . . . but that he has a different reason for so recommending, or that he recommends that the President have a different reason for agreeing with the details of the Israeli plan. A comma could rule out the latter interpretations, but you didn't say how you wanted the sentence punctuated.

Jim [James D. McCawley]
Professor of Linguistics
University of Chicago
Chicago, Illinois

You identify the word *hearing* in the phrase *hearing aid* as a participle because it modifies *aid*. However, it is a gerund, as it is in the sentence *His hearing was poor.*

A noun can be used to modify another noun, as in the phrase *grammar expert.* The word *grammar* modifies the word *expert*, so it is used as an adjective, but it is still a noun—a noun used attributively; it attributes its meaning to the second noun.

In the phrase *hearing aid*, the word *hearing* has the meaning "faculty of hearing" and it is functioning as an attributive noun. Since it derives from the verb *to hear*, it can be called a gerund, although many *-ing* words, including *hearing*, are so commonly used as nouns that they really have become nouns and are identified as nouns in dictionaries. For example, in *I hope I haven't hurt your feelings*, few would think of *feelings* as anything but a true noun.

In the sentence *Because the President's utterances were sometimes ill-considered, he preferred a deaf aide to a hearing aide*, the word *hearing* has the meaning "possessed of the ability to hear" and it is a participle.

Edward D. Johnson
Brattleboro, Vermont

You took Lieutenant Colonel Oliver North to task for using the phrase "to coercively influence."

"Coerce" in the intelligence business has a special meaning. Just as "terminate" is often a euphemism for "kill," "coerce" is often intelspeak for "blackmail." Since only our enemies would stoop so low as actually to blackmail someone into giving them information, our side, the good guys, uses "external coercion." (The term is actually broader than simple blackmail—threatening to expose someone's guilty secrets unless he comes across with whatever you want. It includes using people's weaknesses and mistakes against them in other ways: supplying money for the compulsive gambler, liquor for the alcoholic, sex for the lecherous, expensive goods for the materialistic, and so on.)

In this light, North's phrase clearly means "to influence events by bringing indirect pressure on the participants." Simply "to influence events" might be misinterpreted to mean doing so directly, by overt means, even legitimate ones. It is the same difference as that between "attack" and "sneak attack." The distinction, however rhetorically awkward, would be important to the intelligence and bureaucratic people reading the report.

> Richard E. Kramer
> New York, New York

Your argument that verbally is a synonym of orally is not something that is merely an anathema to purists; it is quite simply just plain wrong. While you and biologist Kunstadt are correct that most of our species usually communicate verbally, the issue that you touch only lightly upon and Kunstadt misses completely is whether the communication is in writing or is spoken, and that is the heart of the matter.

> Alan Steinert, Jr.
> Cambridge, Massachusetts

You discussed the current tendency for Americans to use "verbal" to mean oral and I inferred that you now think that this is not too bad. Just wait until you start reading in your local papers about villains who have forced women to commit verbal sex acts.

> Tom Luebben
> San Francisco, California

Flopping the Flip

"There's a *flip-flopper* over here," charged Michael Dukakis, pointing to Richard Gephardt, adding, "I'm not a flip-flopper or back-flopper." Although the Massachusetts governor unnecessarily introduced *back-flopper*—a dive in which the unfortunate diver lands on his back, also called a *back-whopper*, opposite of a *belly-whopper*—the Dukakis use of *flip-flopper* was vintage American political vituperation.

A century ago, a politician was called "the Florida flopper" by an alliterative opponent, and the word was used in its reduplicative form to mean "somersault" by George Lorimer in 1902: ". . . when a fellow's turning flip-flops up among the clouds, he's naturally going to have the farmers gaping at him."

Ridicule is one of the central goals of reduplication (which is a redundant word, but I can't fight every battle). The grammarian Randolph Quirk has noted that the technique can be used to imitate sounds (*bow-wow, ha-ha*), to intensify (*tiptop, teeny-weeny*), to signify alternation (*zigzag, seesaw*), or to disparage (*mumbo jumbo, wishy-washy, higgledy-piggledy*—and now, *flip-flop*).

The first defense of flip-flopping was put forward by my *New York Times* colleague Tom Wicker soon after the Dukakis charge: "What's wrong with a Presidential candidate changing his position—though his opponents call it 'flip-flopping'—in order to improve his chances of winning? Nothing's wrong with it . . . unless the flipper . . . denies having done it. . . ." Often, he points out, the charge is "a tortured or dishonest interpretation of an opponent's record."

Just as one man's *consistency* is another man's *rigidity*, one man's *flip-flopping* is another man's *opportunity to grow when circumstances change.* That's what Richard Nixon told me one day in 1971—"circumstances change"—and I was assigned to write a speech closing the gold window, putting on a border tax, slapping on wage and price controls—all in what was remarked as the most stunning flip-flop of the year.

Where does *flip* come from? The word was originally *fillip*, the curl of the thumb against the index finger, building the pressure to project a coin into the air. Now a *fillip* means "a snap of the finger," while campaign aides flip their lids at charges of *flip-flop*.

You were quite wrong in describing the "back-flopper" as unfortunate. This was a highly successful maneuver first used in Mexico City in 1968, at the Summer Olympics.

Viewers were amazed as a U.S. high jumper turned his back as he neared the bar and went over headfirst and backwards.

His competitors all laughed at what they called the "Fosbury flop," but the last laugh was enjoyed by Dick Fosbury as he won the gold medal.

Arthur J. Morgan
New York, New York

Mr. Dukakis is the techno-Democrat. Would not the vocabulary of electronic computer technology be second nature to him?

A *flip-flop switch*, basic to computer design, is one which has two stable states, and changes its state in response to a triggering signal. In terms of binary arithmetic (the heart of digital computer calculation), on receiving a signal the switch's output becomes 1 if it was 0, or 0 if it was 1.

You could look it up: OED Supplement Volume I, p. 1109.

Stephen E. Hirschberg
Elmsford, New York

Flip-flop is the keystone, the very heart, of the computer. A flip-flop is a bistable device that forms the elementary binary memory. Although IBM was reluctant to admit it, the punched card is really a binary or flip-flop recording system; there is either a hole or there isn't a hole.

I wrote the manual describing the BINAC, the first internally stored program computer built in this country in 1949. The first chapter of this work is a full description of the logical composition of the computer. It begins with the flip-flop and develops outward. Although that computer contained 1,200 vacuum tubes and measured 6' by 6' by 1', and could now be entirely contained in a chip $1/4'' \times 1/4''$, young computer specialists, not yet born when I wrote the BINAC manual, look in amazement that the logic of their computers today is not different from that of 1949; only the manifestation has changed. And at the root of it is the flip-flop.

Joseph Chapline
Newbury, New Hampshire

You stated, "ridicule is one of the central goals of reduplication (which is a redundant word but I can't fight every battle)."

Philologically, *reduplicate* means to repeat or to duplicate. In spite of its acceptance, the latter meaning is more than redundant, it is illogical.

For example, to duplicate 1 is to double it. To redouble 1 is to quadruple it:

$(1 \times 2) = 2$ which is to duplicate

but $(1 \times 2 \times 2) = 4$, is to reduplicate

To believe that reduplicate means to double is to say that $(1 \times 2 \times 2) = 2$ (the letter "l" in philologically is reduplicated, not duplicated).

It is easy to understand that the combination of the Latin *duplicare,* to duplicate, and re-, meaning again, led to its meaning to repeat. Moreover, its use for emphasis in non-mathematical connotations, e.g. he reduplicated his effort, is appropriate and understandable. But if one reduplicates goody, it should be goody-goody-goody-goody.

I suspect (but have no proof) that from its use "to repeat" etymologically led backwards to the illogical derivative, "to duplicate."

I propose a resolution for the next meeting of the Lexicographic Irregulars that, in spite of its currently accepted meaning, reduplicate be used to mean repeat or emphasize and that its use meaning to duplicate be discouraged, if not banned from future meetings, and literary uses.

Stewart B. Dunsker, M.D.
Professor, Neurological Surgery
University of Cincinnati
College of Medicine
Cincinnati, Ohio

Future King's English

His Royal Highness the Prince of Wales is the man most likely to become the next King of England. That archaic term is understood to include Wales and Scotland; he could also be called King of the United Kingdom, which sounds redundant, or King of Great Britain and Northern Ireland and the Commonwealth. Prince Charles came to the commemoration ceremony for the 350th anniversary of the founding of Harvard and, in a well-received speech about higher education's need to impart spiritual values, called attention to a Greek word, *metanoia,* which he translated as "knowledge that transforms." (In 1873, Matthew Arnold defined Jesus' use of *metanoia* as "a change of the inner man.")

The Prince's point: "In the headlong rush of mankind to conquer space," he said, it is important to teach our children "that to live on this world is no easy matter without standards to live by."

The intensely educated audience was willing to drink to that, but the Prince had already blown it.

"As parents you may be wondering," he had said a moment before, "like I do on frequent occasions. . . ."

Like I do? Does the royal family walk around Windsor Castle using *like* as a conjunction? As every flower girl knows, *like* is a preposition; in *like me*, the preposition *like* introduces the pronoun it uses for comparison. But *like* may not, in formal speech, be used as a conjunction introducing a clause: *like I do* is not standard English. It should be *as I do*.

It may be fine to encourage children to live on this world like metanoiacs, but it is no less than a Dover solecism to exhort them to live "like metanoiacs do"; the conjunction required is *as*.

Who says? Didn't another man who was once Prince of Wales throw out the word *wireless* and substitute *radio* in his abdication, thereby proving that the King still has something to say about what is the King's English? Shouldn't the current Prince of Wales have the *droit du seigneur* to have his way with our maidenly tongue?

No. Oh, most grammarians would not object to using *like* as a conjunction in an informal setting, when chatting with a pal: "If you drip that clotted cream on my pants instead of over the strawberries like you did last year, Sir Basil, you won't be invited to the fiftieth anniversary of the Bronx High School of Science." In that sentence, strictly speaking, "like you did last year" should be edited to "as you did last year," but few of us speak strictly when unobserved. In that circumstance, watch out for the clotted cream, but let the use of *like* as a conjunction go.

However, if you find yourself representing the English-speaking world, making a formal address at a ceremony honoring an institution of higher learning, and you choose as your theme the difficulty of living on this world without standards—never use *like* as a conjunction.

There's His Royal Highness faced with the problem of making a speech on erstwhile Empire soil—something that sounds princely but not patronizing, amusing but not facetious, informative but not pedantic. For a bit of local color, he researches the American scene— catches up on television, glances at a few magazines for the current expressions. What does he hear? "Like I said." What does he read? "Manage your body like you manage your business." "Aha," he thinks, "an American colloquialism, just the thing," and he drops a "like I do" into his speech.

But does our defender of the language appreciate this? Certainly not. You fire off a reprimand, forgetting the emphasis of British schools on the right word in the right place. Even princes can't win them all.

Camille M. Lundell
Port Washington, Long Island

Although he cautioned readers to be on their guard about using *like* as a conjunction, Porter G. Perrin, in his 1939 "Writer's Guide and Index to English," went on to say that "this construction is worth careful observation to see if *like* gains sufficient reputability so that it can be safely used in writing."

It is fitting that the time has arrived, and at Harvard, no less.

Raymond David Wheeler
Dolgeville, New York

A "breach of etiquette" is what I would prefer to define as a "social gaffe." A "gaffe" is a mistake, an unwitting mistake, so that if it is done deliberately, in order to put the company you are with at ease then it is not, by a process of contorted reasoning that I hope you can follow, a gaffe, not a solecism. This is not uncommon among the "noblesse" who are, as we all know, constantly bound by obligations. For example, for Eleanor Roosevelt to have greeted a lineup of guests at the White House by rubbing noses would have been a solecism but it was not a solecism when, dear lady, she did so in the South Sea Islands. Similarly, it was not a solecism when Edward, the immediate predecessor of the present Prince of Wales, picked up the finger bowl at the end of a municipal banquet somewhere in the Provinces and sipped from it. He had noticed that that was exactly what the mayor had done and he eased an awkward moment by doing precisely the same thing. Full marks for a charitable instinct and also for quick-wittedness.

Charles was doing precisely the same thing. One of the first things I noticed—and I am sure he did too—when I came to America was the misuse of "like" and "as": *"Winston tastes good like a cigarette should,"* "Like I said, . . ." and so on. Until I knew better, I tried to correct the way America speaks. I can remember saying to a lady who, in reply to my question as to how she was, told me she was "good," "Yes, I'm sure you are but are you *well?*" So, Charles was not committing a solecism, he was "rubbing noses" with the aborigines!

Thomas J. Bates
Berkeley, California

Surely clotted cream does not drip. And the chance of it getting on one's pants (for the second year in a row) suggests an unfortunate disregard for the normal dress code—even at a school reunion.

Nicholas Hughes
Mechanicsburg, Pennsylvania

I want everyone to talk English the way I do.

I would never say "like I do," and to hear it in other mouths always gives me a slight shudder.

On the other hand, you grammarians can never come up with any alternative save *as.*

Isn't "I want everybody to talk English as I do" just a bit stiff! "The way" is simple, idiomatic, grammatical, creates no shudders, and to my tongue at least, is the most natural solution to the problem.

Priscilla Robertson
Lexington, Kentucky

"As parents you may be wondering, like I do . . . ," said the Prince of Wales. To which your answer was: "it should be *as* I do".
Come on, Mr. Safire, you can't be serious. It should be "as I *am.*"

Gabriel Stelian
King of Prussia, Pennsylvania

It is not only because I was born in Scotland and find myself still to be a member of the Scottish nation that I take you to task for writing that "King of England" is an archaic term understood to include Wales and Scotland. For one thing there were kings of England well before the Norman Conquest and after it until the union with Scotland in 1707, and it is perfectly proper when referring to them now and not archaic to call them kings of England. For another kingship is an institution of the state and there has been no such thing as an English state since 1707. As a Scot, I am frequently annoyed by English writers who write as if England were the whole of the British state.

J. H. Aitchison
Halifax, Nova Scotia

Get Me Rewrite

An eight-cylindered bloopie award to Chrysler and its chairman, Lee Iacocca, for the following ad:

"Chrysler is the only American car maker who builds their convertibles from start to finish."

That's like saying "its front wheels are not connected to their rear wheels." In car making and sentence structure, alignment is all: a pronoun has to agree with its antecedent and a subject with a predicate, or the torque of error will twist the whole thing out of shape.

What is the subject of the sentence? Chrysler. That corporation is a legal entity, but not a human being. (Walter Chrysler is long gone.) Only the impersonal *that* will do, not *who*, a most personal pronoun; "Chrysler is the only American car maker *that . . .*" Not *who*, reserved for people, and not *which*, which is used to begin a nonrestrictive clause. (We should always say *people who*—as John V. Twyman of Hollywood observes, *"people that* has replaced *people who* to such an extent that the next 'Who's Who' should be called 'That's That.' ")

Now to the next Iacocca mistake: "Chrysler" is a word that must be expressed in the singular; no native speaker, not even a Ford dealer, would say "Chrysler are." (We construe collective nouns differently from the British, who say *the public are*; what do they know about English?)

The pronoun that agrees with Chrysler is not *their*, which would agree with "Lee and the other guys at Chrysler," a plural notion. No, the only correct pronoun for a singular, impersonal noun is *its*.

Wait. That's too impersonal, the copywriter may say. We're one big happy family here at Chrysler, marvelously diverse and individualistic, and besides, if I tried to fiddle with anything the chairman said, I'd have a tailpipe wrapped around my neck. No way you're gonna get me to change that to "who builds *its* convertibles."

Solution 1: *Drop the pronoun entirely:* "who builds convertibles." But that might not be suitable, since it fails to get across the possessiveness the people at Chrysler feel about their product. You cannot say *our* because that would not agree with Chrysler, so try Solution 2: *Change the subject to enable you to use your warm and compassionate pronoun:* "We at Chrysler are the only American car makers who build our convertibles . . ."

Straighten it out, Lee; we don't want you telling us on the Fourth of July how Miss Liberty is holding high their torch.

Readers may not be aware that, stylistic preference aside, there is no grammatical basis for opposing "people *that*"—a usage attested in the earliest records of English. As Theodore Bernstein says in *Dos, Don'ts and Maybes of English Usage,* "If Miss Thistlebottom taught you . . . that *that* applied only to things, forget it." The American Heritage Dictionary concurs in the usage note under *that.*

As for eliminating restrictive *which*, the stylistic wish can cloud the grammatical facts. Strunk and White say, s.v. *That. Which,* "it would be a convenience" if *that* were restrictive and *which* nonrestrictive, but "occasionally *which* seems preferable to *that.*" And Margaret Nicholson says in *American-English Usage,* under *that,* rel. pron., "there would be much gain" if the distinction were made, "but it would be idle to pretend that it is the practice either of most or of the best writers."

Harvey Minkoff
Associate Professor of English
Hunter College
New York, New York

Getting Whom

"The dead hand of the present should not lay on the future," I wrote in a harangue about unfair constitutional strictures denying naturalized Americans the right to become President. "Let tomorrow's people decide who they want to be their President."

That is known in the pop-grammarian trade as a *two-fer*, "two embarrassments for the price of one." In the relative clause "who they want to be their President," the first word should be the objective pronoun *whom*. My rule is "when *whom* is correct, use some other formulation," so I should have written "who is to be their President."

The other gaffe, *lay*, was circled by Elizabeth Teague, hotshot Kremlinologist at Radio Free Europe in Munich. In the sense of reclining or resting, the verb should be *lie*, which takes no object; I simply lie down.

The past participle of *lay* is *laid*, a word that can be used innocently about hens and eggs but is now giving headaches to advertising-acceptability executives in its slang sexual meaning.

The director Stephen Frears and writer Hanif Kureishi, whose film *My Beautiful Laundrette* was acclaimed by some and detested by others (my own reaction was that there should have been another *e* in "launderette"), have come up with a new movie starring Claire Bloom about a couple named Sammy and Rosie.

Its title appeared unabashedly in *New York* magazine, and could also be found in *The New York Times Magazine*. (That first *Times* use doesn't count; it probably slipped through when nobody was watching, and the arbiters of taste at the *Times* are now puzzling over how to handle it officially.) I will not print the title here because I deal with a family trade; besides, it is much more titillating to ostentatiously avoid the slang term.

The pressure to use the whole title of the movie, including the past participle, will come from those concerned about artistic integrity: nobody edits *'Tis Pity She's a Whore*, though that noun causes the easily offended to wince.

When *The Best Little Whorehouse in Texas* came to Broadway, the word was accepted for advertising in newspapers, but an ad that said "Come to the 'Whorehouse' " was banished from advertising on city buses. Editors who would normally shy away from jarring words, and who would quickly strike out sexual slang in copy, are reluctant to tell artists what they cannot name their works of art.

In this case, count me among the bluenoses. Not only would I refuse to run an ad with the full title, but also I would refer only to "Sammy and

Rosie" in the review. Why? Taste counts, that's why. If I wouldn't use the phrase in front of children (who probably use it all the time), then I wouldn't use it in a newspaper or a public speech. Realism in dialogue is fine, but its use in a title forces others to print what offends their sense of propriety. Art, shmart—the title was chosen to gain commercially by shocking, and I don't have to play along with such let's-raise-eyebrows manipulation.

No one would describe your analysis of what hens do to eggs as prurient; if anything, you err on the side of modesty. After all, the past participle is in common usage, although many males prefer to talk about getting it (the reasons are best left to practitioners of pop-psych).

Whatever the case, if your literary preference is for mere titillation, you are right "to ostentatiously avoid the slang term." But why the blatant grammatical raunchiness of a split infinitive?

This is the sort of thing that gets some of us really aroused.

Mark A. Heller
Associate Professor
Peace Studies Program
Cornell University
Ithaca, New York

Gifts for Glossolaliacs

Only two gifts are suitable for a word lover: a new word or a new lover. Let us look at ways to stimulate the ecstatic sighs of the most discerning glossolaliac.

Biz Speak: A Dictionary of Business Terms, Slang and Jargon by Rachel Stein Epstein and Nina Liebman (Watts) is perfect for the kid who was graduated from business school last June and is now making a million a year on his way to the penitentiary. The entry that caught my eye is *plug-compatibility*, a computer term for software designed for one operating system that can also be run on another. "If Burroughs machines could run IBM software," write the lexicographers, "the systems would be plug-compatible. They are not."

This book is a production of the Stein family, which is to the book world what the Wallendas are to trapezes. The economist Herbert Stein, coiner of such seminal phrases as *supply side* and *Kemp follower*, wrote *Washington Bedtime Stories: The Politics of Money and Jobs* (Free Press), the only economics book written in understandable English this year. It contains such examples of seeded-wry wit as this definition of *neo-conservatism:* "Old wine drunk by new winos." Meanwhile, the Stein scion, Ben *(Ben* means "son of"), has written a Hollywood novel, *Her Only Sin* (St. Martin's). Ben Stein's piece on Ivan Boesky appears on page 134.

The Dictionary of American Regional English has already spawned its first offspring, *American Regional Dialects: A Word Geography,* by Craig M. Carver (University of Michigan Press). This work, for scholarly types, has the most fascinating appendix of the year, examining the patterns being found in the DARE statistics and showing how usage varies from one part of the United States to another.

For example, a loosely woven cloth bag is called a *croker sack* in the lower South, a *tow bag* in North Carolina, a *grass sack* in Virginia and a *gunnysack* out West. And what do you call a worm used as fishing bait? It's an *angle-worm* in the upper North and West, a *nightcrawler* just south of there, a *nightwalker* in the Northeast, an *eace worm* around Narragansett Bay, a *mud worm* in the Atlantic South and eastern New England, a *wiggler* in the lower South and a *bloodworm* in New York City, where it isn't easy to find a worm and very hard to find a good fishing hole.

A Word or Two Before You Go . . . (Wesleyan University Press) by Jacques Barzun, the grand-master of usage, takes its title from a remark in Shakespeare's *Othello,* which he suggests was followed by the admonition "No more of *that,* I pray you, in your letters." (Professor Barzun subtly manipulates Shakespeare's words there to make his own admonishing point; that full Shakespearean passage can also be used by President Reagan to speak to memoirists at the National Security Council writing of Iranian arms shipments and his concern for hostages: "I pray you, in your letters, / When you shall these unlucky deeds relate, / Speak of me as I am; / nothing extenuate, / Nor set down aught in malice. Then must you speak / of one that lov'd not wisely but too well. . . .")

Professor Barzun is more of a hard-liner than I am and stoutly resists the use of such a term as *verbal agreement* to mean only "oral agreement." (He thinks it means both oral and written agreements, with *verbal* used to differentiate from *nodded assent;* I think *verbal agreement* and *oral agreement* are now synonymous, differentiated from *written agreement.* That's what makes usage races.)

This most persuasive of the strict usagists finds that slang, far from being the colorful source that causes so many of us to go hoo-ha, "rather preys on the straight vocabulary than feeds it new blood." He deplores the loss to the language of such standard words as *adult* and *gay,* whose meanings have been warped, and is unafraid to denounce it: "So let us cut the cackle about the wonders of the colloquial." Catnip for prescriptivist cats.

A fine companion volume to Barzun's standard-bearing for Standard English is the New Dictionary of American Slang (Harper & Row) by Robert L. Chapman. This is an updating and a revision of the classic dictionary by Wentworth and Flexner, and its weakness lies in not including dates and citations for sources. For example, "The opera's never over till the fat lady sings" is attributed to a W. T. Tyler, with no date; I have that down for a basketball coach, Dick Motta, in 1978 (who perhaps picked it up from San Antonio sportscaster Dan Cook), and don't know which is the earlier use.

The strength of a new slang dictionary, of course, lies in its additions to the language: *800-pound gorilla* is defined as "a powerful force" and *puzzle palace* as "any higher headquarters." I was unfamiliar with *bodice-ripper*, a publishing term for "a romantic-erotic novel." (But does the book have legs?) The definition of *blivit* as "anything superfluous or annoying" does not exactly blow my mind, but the citation contains the explanatory image of ten pounds of material in a five-pound bag, as every Sad Sack will recall.

A Handlist to English: Basic Terms for Literature, Composition, and Grammar (from University Press of America) by Stan Malless and Jeff McQuain is a quick, down-and-dirty way for students to understand all the terms needed to pass basic courses in English. But it is more than an extended crib sheet: the authors (Professor McQuain is the researcher responsible for every mistake in this column every week; I am innocent) use good examples to help you remember differences. *Verbal irony,* when a speaker says the opposite of what is true, is exemplified in Mark Antony's description of Caesar's assassins as "honorable men"; *dramatic irony* occurs when the reader knows that the opposite of what a character expects will happen, as when Romeo thinks Juliet is dead; *situational irony* occurs when a person is unaware that the opposite of what he expects will happen. Example: "You have studied hard for two weeks for a final exam, only to find out on exam day that you have studied the wrong notes."

A subscription to a linguistics magazine reminds the recipient with noodging regularity of your generosity. The quarterly *English Today: The International Review of the English Language* from Cambridge University looks at the language from a British viewpoint. And if British slang is your thing, try *Street Talk: The Language of Coronation Street,* a paperback based on the sort of lingo used in the British television series. The British say "Ewe wha'?" instead of our "Say wha'?"; they have also come up with *dicky bird* as rhyming slang for "word"—"I haven't heard a dicky bird from Bud since he got back from Teheran"—as well as the useful word *wuzzock,* to denote "an idle man with no inclination for domestic duties."

Know somebody who is into extended metaphors? *The Moon Pinnace* (Doubleday) is a novel by Thomas Williams that plays on the lingo of sailing. A *pinnace* is a light sailing craft; the heroine is named Dory, which is also the word for a small boat; the central symbol is the lima bean, the Latin name for which is *Phaseolus lunatus,* "a little boat shaped like a moon." Though full of beans, the novel is a good one for readers attuned to symbolism and semiotics.

The noun *present,* by the way, comes from the Latin *praeesse,* "to be before [someone]," which led to the Old French *presenter*, "to make a presentation of." *Present*, as in *Christmas present*, connotes a small thing, given with affection; the word is synonymous with, but less formal than, a *gift*, which a certain French perfumer will be pleased to learn may be rooted in the German word for "poison." (Ewe wha'?) Advertisers lure the unwary with a redundant *free gift*, but for some reason, no pitchman suggests he will present you with a *free present*.

In the many years I have worked with infernal analytical engines, I have seen "plug-compatibility" applied to hardware only, and never to software. The notion involves a third-party vendor, who makes a device that can be attached to a mainframe computer, at less cost but able to deliver the same level of service as the device of the original manufacturer. Such devices include tape drives, disk drives, and even main computer memory. The idea is, that you can just "plug it in" and it works just as well as the device of the original manufacturer. There is a long and established industry experience that this does work.

The analogous attribute in the case of software is normally termed "portability." If software can be taken from, say, an IBM computer to a Burroughs computer, and still run properly, it is termed "portable software." Your source is quite correct in pointing out that this is usually not the case. Portable software has been one of the more elusive goals of the industry throughout its life.

When speaking of interchangeable computer technology, hardware is plug-compatible, but software is portable.

Jack S. Berger
Mahwah, New Jersey

The term "bodice-ripper" refers specifically to *historical* romance novels, books featuring a great deal of historical costume description and sex tinged with a degree of violence. While modern dresses may be said to contain "bodices," the word does have an archaic ring to it. More important, the word "ripper" implies a level of force in the stripping of a heroine as a prelude to sex. Authors and readers of sensual historical novels justify the rape-like quality of such sex scenes by pointing out that, given the historical milieu of such novels, no respectable heroine would willingly comply with a man's sexual advances. Therefore, he would in all likelihood have to tear her clothing off in order to make love to her.

As the author of twenty-one contemporary romance novels, I can assure you that contemporary romances are *not* referred to as "bodice-rippers" in the publishing industry. In romances set in modern times, the heroine may well rip her bodice (or, for that matter, her sweatshirt, the bib of her denim overalls, or the jacket of her pinstriped St.

Laurie business suit), but if she does, it will probably be in the course of climbing a mountain, repairing a car, building a bookshelf or rescuing the hero from a burning house. If she and the hero make love, it will be by mutual consent, with an absence of violence and an abundance of love and respect between the partners. The label "bodice-ripper" simply doesn't apply to such novels.

Barbara J. Keiler
Branford, Connecticut

After years of chiding my friends and children for using the contemporary cliché being "into" something, you ruin it all: "Know somebody who is into extended metaphors?" If you're into contemporary clichés, I'm sure your readers could send you many.

William Cole
New York, New York

The Wallendas were, and perhaps still are, primarily and possibly exclusively, high-wire artists. No doubt you were thinking of the Concellos, trapeze artists who in the '30s and '40s were to the circus world what William Safire usually is to lexicologists.

Chase Small
Boonton, New Jersey

Gimme a Breakpoint

"We have now reached *breakpoint*," President Reagan told the nation in a televised address. The word was obviously chosen with deliberation; later in the speech, while launching a crusade to hold down the deficit, he repeated the word that is not yet in most dictionaries and added his definition: "The choice is now upon each of us—as I said, we've reached *breakpoint*; decision time."

In a darkened room controlled by Richard Wirthlin, the President's pollster, sits a panel made up of 50 demographically balanced human beings. (This advanced market research applied to Presidential speechmaking has not yet been reported in the news pages of your newspaper; I am dropping it in here because people interested in language deserve to be ahead of the news.)

Each person has in hand a small computer, called the Populus Speedpulse, which enables the panelist to register reactions to what the President is saying as he says each word. For example, if the President were to say "Ayatollah," the people would press the negative buttons, marked E or

F; if he were to say "Christmas," all but the worst misanthrope would mash down the happiness, attaboy, I-approve buttons, A or B.

"At the first mention of the word *breakpoint,*" a White House opinion-molding source tells me, "there was not much of a reaction, maybe because it was unfamiliar. But the second time, when the word was backed up by the words 'decision time,' they really hit the positive button." Asked for confirmation of this revealing tip, pollster Wirthlin replied only, "*Breakpoint* received a measurably positive response."

I next called the President's chief speechwriter, Anthony Dolan. After five minutes of ritual denial of having had anything to do with the speech, and a short dissertation marveling at the way Mr. Reagan writes all his own material (this sort of anonymity-passion befits a candidate-member of the Judson Welliver Society, a group of presidential speechwriters), Mr. Dolan agreed to entertain a question about one word in Mr. Reagan's speech.

Was he aware, and was the President aware, that his word *breakpoint* is a tennis term? It is defined in Tim Considine's *The Language of Sport* as "a situation in which the next point to be played could result in a service break for the receiver if the point is won by the receiver." The Merriam-Webster Sports Dictionary defines *breakpoint* as a situation "in which the receiving player or side will break the opponent's service by winning the next point."

The followups tumbled out: Does the President frequently use tennis terminology? Is he turning yuppie in his old age? Was the use of *breakpoint* a subtle hint of support for George Bush in 1988?

"I played second base for Our Lady of the Assumption," the stunned speechwriter insisted. "I don't deal in yuppie-isms." He recovered quickly, imputing toughness and middle-class seriousness to the formerly elite game: "You know, tennis is no longer a yuppie sport, not since television. It's a high-stakes money game. *Breakpoint* is no weenie word." He recalled that there may have been a movie with that word as its title.

Not quite; he may have been thinking of two films named *The Breaking Point,* one in 1950 starring John Garfield, and another in 1976. The term is based on an 1899 coinage meaning "the degree of stress at which a particular material breaks," which H. G. Wells in 1908 applied to human beings: "Under the stresses of the war their endurance reached the breaking point." Today the predominating sense of that phrase is "the last straw," and may have originated in "the straw that broke the camel's back."

There was also a 1959 collection of short stories titled *The Breaking Point* by Daphne du Maurier, which Mr. Dolan may have meant.

Or the speechwriter may have had in mind *Breakout,* a 1975 movie starring Charles Bronson, about an American's helicopter escape from a Mexican jail; that word is frequently heard in Washington arms-reduction salons today, meaning "a sudden change in the strategic balance in which one superpower gains a decisive advantage," probably taken from the idea of breaking out of the confines of a treaty.

Since *breakout* cannot be what the President favors, and he could not be suggesting that American malaise has reached the *breaking point*—and since he spends very little time watching the play on the White House tennis courts—only a couple of other possibilities exist.

One is computer lingo. According to Collins English Dictionary, a *breakpoint* is "an instruction inserted by a debug program causing a return to the debug program." (American programmers talk about "breakpoint logic," but I don't want to break my point on that.) The other is in accounting terminology, especially affecting income taxes; in 1975, *U.S. News & World Report* wrote: "Here are the 'breakpoints' of income on which no tax is paid, assuming deductions are not itemized. . . ."

A style note: The Reagan speechwriters use *breakpoint* as a single word; the White House press office, distributing the text, prefers two words. *The New York Times* took the text off the air and used one word; the *Washington Post* did the same and used two words. OK, everybody, here comes the final decision: one word, no hyphen.

Evidently the President is in a pointillist phase. Earlier in what lexicographers call "his breakpoint speech," he explained his reason for putting 11 Kuwaiti ships under the protection of the American flag: if we did not, he said, "we would open opportunities for the Soviets to move into this chokepoint of the free world's oil flow."

Chokepoint is the hot new synonym for the 1896 "bottleneck." Railroaders will spot a metaphoric tie to "throat," the point at which a railroad line enters or leaves a yard. The Oxford English Dictionary to this day has no citations in its files for this term, even though the 1976 edition of the unabridged Merriam-Webster's Third New International carries the entry, defined as the railroading "throat" and the more familiar "bottleneck."

The earliest citation of the term in the Second Barnhart Dictionary of New English is from *The Times* of London's 1976 account of the North Atlantic Treaty Organization's military power: "[the Soviet] access to the open seas passes through a number of choke points (such as the Bosphorus, Gibraltar, and the Greenland-Iceland-United Kingdom gap) and her freedom to deploy outside the range of her land-based fighter cover is limited. . . ." A few months earlier, *Aviation Week and Space Technology* was writing about "the control of key chokepoints throughout the world."

By 1987, the word had become almost a cliché in descriptions of the channel leading into the Persian Gulf: "[The Strait of] Hormuz is the narrowest channel in the Gulf," wrote Reuters, "and Washington says it has become a potential chokepoint because of deployment there by Iran of deadly Chinese anti-ship Silkworm missiles."

Again, the problem: one word or two. OK, everybody, we have obviously reached breakpoint, decision time in the neologism factory: *chokepoint* it is. Personally, I think of the Strait of Hormuz as a bottleneck, but am almost ashamed to use that nice old term lest it provide competing pundits with a more with-it breakout.

You seem to assume that *breakpoint,* the tennis term, is always one word. However, all the leading tennis writers separate the term into two words and for logical reasons. There are a variety of "points" in tennis and each requires a distinguishing adjective. For example, "match point" (the person who is ahead will win the match if he wins this point) and "championship point" (the person who is ahead will take the championship if he wins this point). Thus, it is grammatically necessary to separate the adjective "break" from the word it modifies —"point."

> *Burling Lowrey*
> *Washington, D.C.*

The word *breakpoint* has been used since at least the early 1940s in the field of the chlorination of water and of wastewater, to designate that dosage of chlorine at which free residual chlorine begins to appear in the treated water or wastewater, i.e. that dosage at which the reactions of chlorine with foreign substances have been completed and further additions of chlorine appear as free residual chlorine.

> *Morris Lipschuetz*
> *San Francisco, California*

Possibly the President's speechwriter had in mind the movie *Turning Point.*

> *J. Harb*
> *Hillsborough,*
> *North Carolina*

You equate bottleneck with chokepoint. The two are obviously similar but far from synonymous. The first sounds to me like an innocuous statement of fact; the latter is loaded with definitely sinister (leftist?) connotations. It makes me think of the jugular. A bottleneck merely exists; it takes an enemy to convert one to a chokepoint. The Strait of Hormuz always was a bottleneck; it took Iranian missiles to make us think of it as a chokepoint.

> *George J. Alexander*
> *New York, New York*

Glossary of a Scandal

The secret presidential finding that he destroyed, Rear Admiral John M. Poindexter told the Iran-contra committees on national television, "had been prepared essentially by the CIA as a—what we call a C.Y.A. effort."

CIA, as most Americans know, stands for Central Intelligence Agency (or, in recent years, "Casey in action"); C.Y.A. is a less familiar military-bureaucratic term that Senator Sam Nunn, Democrat of Georgia, defined in a question to another witness at the hearings. "Isn't this cable in effect a C.Y.A. cable? . . . They were covering their rear end back in Washington, weren't they?"

The senator is correct in his definition—the term means "to diffuse responsibility"—and appropriately delicate in his euphemism. The first two initials of C.Y.A. stand for "cover your," and the dread "a" word is expressed variously as *rear end, butt, behind, backside, tail, seat,* or, if you are President Reagan, *keister.* The objection to the operative word is of long standing; a new sense has evolved that uses the word for the posterior as a synecdoche for the whole person, and now to *move one's backside* means merely to move oneself quickly. Thus the initials today are an anachronism, euphemizing a meaning that has changed.

Initialese was also used by the former White House chief of staff Donald T. Regan, who thought the arms sales were conducted under a policy of N.P.H.—"no profit here." A committee member, Representative Jack Brooks, Democrat of Texas, soon recalled what he described as an East Texas expression about an eager customer: C.I.F., for "cash in fist." Businessmen are slipping into initialese, and government officials will soon be using B.P.M., "best practical means," C.O.G.S., "cost of goods sold," and O.P.O., "one-person operation." Meanwhile, bureaucrats like Admiral Poindexter have adopted *micromanage,* the boardroom synonym disparaging the sort of management that used to be criticized as *finetuning.*

"We'd been *snookered* again," Mr. Regan reported he told the President, adding, "How many times do we put up with this rug-merchant type of stuff?" Although *rug merchant* is widely understood to be a derogation for a craftily bargaining, untrustworthy tradesman (and is sometimes taken as a slur against both Persians and manufacturers of hairpieces), the verb *to snooker* is less familiar to younger Americans never exposed to pool-hall life.

Snooker is a variation of billiards played with 15 red balls, a white cue ball and six balls of other colors. The story is told of a subaltern in central

India, Neville Chamberlain, later Prime Minister of Britain, who in 1875 was playing this game with a cadet with the last name of Snooker. The cadet played so badly that Chamberlain used his name eponymously to mean "to place oneself in an impossible position."

Influenced by the earlier *to cock a snook,* a vulgar hand gesture, the verb came to mean "to cheat, swindle," not necessarily by hustlers limited to billiard parlors. (Card players prefer the synonym *to euchre,* after the name of the game in which the player making trump is prevented from winning the necessary three tricks; that has come to mean "to cheat" also; the victim is *euchred out* of what he thinks is rightfully his.)

Republican Senator James A. McClure of Idaho promptly used a card term in response to Mr. Regan's pool-hall usage: "There are a lot of *markers* down here." In context, he seemed to be referring to conflicting stories told by various witnesses. Originally a scorecard, the *marker* came to mean a promissory note, or I.O.U., accepted among gamblers. In current political usage, says Richard Perle, a former Department of Defense official and now a novelist, *to lay down a marker* means "to give an indication of concern; to put someone on notice, but not to take the issue through to a conclusion or resolution."

One linguistic error made during the hearings was in the misconception of the phrase *plausible denial.* This term of art was rightly used first by Lieutenant Colonel Oliver L. North: "Part of a covert operation is to offer plausible deniability of the association of the Government of the United States with the activity." The meaning is "cover story," as Fox Butterfield of *The New York Times* points out: "In intelligence, *plausible deniability* means that higher-ups do know, but the paper work is stopped at a lower level so that the higher-ups don't appear to know."

However, when used by Admiral Poindexter, that phrase lost its central point: instead of being a believable fiction told by a President who knew of the diversion secret, it was a truthful denial by a President who was denied any knowledge of the secret. Veteran spooks were appalled at the admiral's abuse of their term of art. (Mr. Butterfield, incidentally, noted that Richard V. Secord claimed to be a patriot and not a profiteer, and unearthed the 1928 term *patrioteer.)*

As for covert action, these hearings laid down the marker for the final switch of the pronunciation of *covert.* For centuries, *covert* sounded like *cover;* however, in juxtaposition with its opposite in spookspeak, the out-in-the-open *overt,* the pronunciation of the sneaky *covert* has been changing. Now, after these televised hearings, it's OH-vert and COH-vert. (Colonel North had some trouble with *perpetuity,* but persevered and managed to get out the correct per-pe-TOO-it-ee.)

Secretary of State George P. Shultz came up with a creative oxymoron. He described the testimony of Assistant Secretary Elliott Abrams as "a combative apology," which was a cruel kindness met with thunderous silence. However, the Shultz usage most widely remarked was the bureaucratic term *to task.* In Washington, nobody in a with-it mode *assigns* anymore; now they *task* it, thereby sounding like an old Ella Fitzgerald song. That word was originally a verb based on *tax*—"to exact tribute from"— and has now reverted to its 1483 form. Relatedly, the verb *compartmentalize* in its past participle *compartmentalized* has been clipped to *compartmented* by people who work in top-secret, sensitive, eyes-only compartments.

The alliteration prize was won by Robert C. McFarlane for his "The contras had to continue, in some fashion, to buy beans, bullets, Band-aids. . . ." Strangest euphemism: *residuals,* a word now being remaindered by television writers and arms dealers to replace the word *profits,* which had not previously been a dirty word among capitalists. And Colonel North won the synonymy award: he opened by admitting, "I participated in the preparation of documents to the Congress that were erroneous, misleading, evasive and wrong," and went on to say he knew he "would be the person who would be dismissed or reassigned or fired or blamed or fingered. . . ."

Which brings up the expression "fall guy," used by Colonel North to epitomize all the foregoing. Mr. Regan, long an amateur etymologist, said he had asked his staff (he still leans on a staff) to get the origin of that expression, and found that it originated in English wrestling: "the guy who agreed to lose." Had he called me, as he used to when in power—how soon they forget—Mr. Regan would have learned that the phrase was popularized in America by the Dutch Treat Club in New York, who invited guests to be honored with jocular insults.

Who was the linguistic star of the hearings? My vote goes to Senator William S. Cohen, who castigated Admiral Poindexter on the abuse of language in politics: "I find it troubling when you say that 'I withheld information from Congress but I did not mislead it.' Or that the Administration's support for the contras was *secret activity* but not *covert action.* . . . Or that the transfer of funds for the sale of weapons was a *technical implementation,* not a *substantive decision.*"

Later, in a colloquy with Donald Regan, Senator Cohen—the only Republican senator from Maine ever to have published a book of poems— observed that the chief of staff had "slipped the surly bonds of public service." This remark to a man who had been shoved off the pinnacle of power was an allusion to John G. Magee, Jr.'s, poem "High Flight," which begins, "Oh, I have slipped the surly bonds of earth. . . ."

Corrections

The "On Language" column in *The Times Magazine* refers incorrectly to the Neville Chamberlain who originated the term "snooker." The originator was Colonel Sir Neville Francis Fitzgerald Chamberlain (1856–1944), a career officer in the British Army, not the Neville Chamberlain who later became Prime Minister of Britain.

I was interested in the language used in the Iran-contra hearings. It seems to me that the language of the public opinion polls on this issue might be scrutinized also.

I was polled by *The Wall Street Journal*/NBC and asked if, on the basis of what I had heard so far (the first week of his testimony), I thought that Lieutenant Colonel Oliver L. North should be "criminally prosecuted."

It occurred to me that this question is poorly worded. It implies something shady about the prosecution. A more grammatical construction would be "legally prosecuted," a more objective one, "prosecuted for violations of the law." I believe that if an alternative form had been used, the results of the poll would have been somewhat different.

> *Nancy L. Cone*
> *New York, New York*

I must question your comments on the verb "to snooker." It is not "to put *oneself* in an impossible position" but to put *another* in such a position. There are no overtones of cheating or swindling. Snooker is a variation of pool, not of billiards, and the United States equivalent is to leave someone behind the eight-ball.

> *Bryan G. Reuben*
> *London, England*

It is rare that one finds inspired figures of speech ascribed to such ponderous speakers as our forthright Secretary of State, yet you credit George P. Shultz with a "creative oxymoron" in the Secretary's description of Elliot Abrams's testimony as "a combative apology." Mr. Shultz was apparently using the word "apology" in its original sense of justification or excuse, and not as expressive of regret; Shultz's phrase was more accurate than colorful. In fact, the artful oxymoron was conspicuously absent from the Iran-contra hearings, unless, of course, one counts that deafeningly silent one: military intelligence.

Gregory J. Segreti
Annapolis, Maryland

You write of a new sense evolving "that uses the word for the posterior as a synecdoche for the whole person."

New? What about "horse's a—?"

"Silly ass," of course, derives, not from the word for the posterior but from an animal that some think is deficient in intelligence.

In its other meaning the word is probably an American corruption of the old English word, "arse." Our ancestors weren't used to the way a true Britisher swallows that second letter.

Dudley Britton
Pleasantville, New York

Something for your files, re: *to task:*

"The poor child had been tasked beyond her strength . . ." Mary Mapes Dodge, in *Hans Brinker*, Scribner's, 1926.

Jeannie Willis
New York, New York

CIF is a current commercial abbreviation in the import/export trade (Cost, insurance, freight) indicating a quotation including all three, as opposed to F.O.B. (Free on board) a quotation including cost plus transportation from factory to ship.

There may be a lot of Anglo-American confusion in the following:

	AMERICAN	BRITISH
RN	Registered Nurse	Royal Navy
MP	Military Police	Member of Parliament
BSA	Boy Scouts of America	British Small Arms

There are probably a lot more it may be fun to trace.

The same thing happens in the U.S. The only case I can think of offhand is:

NCR	National Cash Register	National Catholic Reporter

Another amusing failure that does seem to have been reported anyway is the EXXON logo. It seems the company ran an expensive computer program to make sure it had no negative connotations, but the uneducated computer failed to notice the company was putting a *hex on* its own brand!

José de Vinck
Allendale, New Jersey

Peace in Our Time

Some days you can't make a nickel. In tracking down the origin of the slang verb *to snooker*, I let out a euretic "Gotcha!" and attributed the coinage to the Sir Neville Chamberlain who later became Prime Minister of Britain. A thousand umbrellas beat down on my head: the originator of *snooker* (which all those sporting a pool-hall pallor know means "to place in a difficult position") was a different Sir Neville Chamberlain, a career British Army officer who died in 1944.

The word was used by former White House chief of staff Donald T. Regan, who thought we had been snookered by Iran and wondered about who was being made the *fall guy*. Mr. Regan reported that his staff's research showed that *fall guy* was a nineteenth-century English wrestling term, meaning the wrestler was deliberately trying to lose (to "take a dive," in modern wrestling).

Comes now William Morris, who was editor of the American Heritage Dictionary's original edition, to correct Mr. Regan on the place of origin of *fall guy*—it was originally the United States, according to the Oxford English Dictionary's Supplement—and to knock down my suggestion that the phrase was popularized at the Dutch Treat Club in New York. It was the Circus Saints and Sinners Club of America Inc., founded by the fabled press agent F. Darius Benham. I shoulda stood in bed (a phrase coined by neither of the Sir Neville Chamberlains).

I wonder if anyone will catch the error in the title for this entry. Prime Minister Chamberlain returned from Munich in 1938, speaking of "peace with honor. I believe it is peace for our time." The phrase is almost always misquoted as "peace *in* our time," probably because those are the words in the Anglican morning prayer: "Give peace in our time, O Lord." People who lie in wait for that error are members of the Nitpickers' League.

Benighted he may have been, but Prime Minister Arthur Neville Chamberlain never got to be knighted.

Horace T. E. Hone
Trumbull, Connecticut

Gondoliers of Metaphor

Whenever a newsworthy event is held in a colorful place, the hounds of metaphor begin baying in the minds of headline writers.

When Venice became the focal point of color stories by a press corps drawn up in what Winston Churchill called "vast cumbrous array," we braced ourselves for quotations from Shakespeare's "The Merchant of Venice" and were not disappointed by this obvious stuff. Literary allusion watchers, however, waited for resuscitation of the phrase "Death in Venice," which was the English translation of the title of a 1912 novella by Thomas Mann.

However, with the omnipresent threat of terrorists, the word *death* was too strong for feature use in a light vein. "Dearth in Venice" was, I thought, labored. The problem was solved by Joseph Laitin, ombudsman of the *Washington Post,* in a piece about the need to assign so many reporters to the economic confabulation. His title, which wins this year's "O Sole Mio" award for zippy headline writing: "Debt in Venice."

Laitin, an old-time press agent best known for his Bible-thumping instructions to astronauts, undoubtedly took this construction from the borrowed headline for a 1936 critical review by Frank S. Nugent of *The New York Times.* Directed at the fiery playwright Clifford Odets, the headline criticized his film *The General Died at Dawn* for lacking the familiar spark: "Odets, Where Is Thy Sting?"

Good as a Mile

"I'm surprised that professors of religion haven't called you to task," writes Father George F. Mattice of the Church of St. Brigid and St. Joseph in Syracuse. "Please check up on the word *myth* and only use it properly."

Sure enough, soon after a piece appeared that I had entitled "Ten Myths About the Reagan Debacle," Professor Neil Gillman of the Jewish Theological Seminary of America wrote: "After years of trying to persuade my students that a myth is not a fiction, but rather a structure of meaning through which people read complex and elusive experiences—and that myths are therefore indispensable—you have undone all of my work. There are apparently *myths* and there are *facts*; the former are false, the latter are true."

My clerical correspondents have locked on to the original meaning of *myth*, a word clipped only in the last century from *mythology*, rooted in the Greek *muthos*, "narrative, story." To many teachers of religion, and to some psychiatrists, a myth is a legend that helps people cope—an ostensibly historical story passed on by a culture to help its members explain their practices and beliefs. On the other hand, fundamentalists believe that myths are to be taken literally, and treat what some consider a quaint folk story or instructional allegory as an article of faith.

The word has gained another sense, however, that conflicts with its original sense: "fiction, fable, old wives' tale." The philosopher Plato started this sense by treating a myth as an allegory, a story made up not to deceive but to illustrate some philosophical idea. It was sealed in modern politics by John F. Kennedy, in a 1962 speech at Yale, as meaning a frozen, unintentionally misleading mind-set, contrasting what he called "myth and reality." As Kennedy said: "For the great enemy of the truth is very often not the lie—deliberate, contrived and dishonest—but the myth, persistent, persuasive and unrealistic." J. William Fulbright later entitled a book *Old Myths and New Realities*, emphasizing the self-deluding nature of the myth.

Here we are, then, with a word having two meanings that confuse and irritate teachers who want their students to be very clear about the first sense. I must disappoint them. Sorry, but that's what the language is like. Nobody owns it. If they want to teach Mythology 101, let them use the word with their meaning and say sternly "in the original sense" or whatever modification of that first sense suits them. The rest of us will go on using the new myths and old realities.

Goons and Ginks and Company Finks

"Scab ball" was the label pinned on the professional football played by *replacements* or *substitutes* by such sportswriters as Tony Kornheiser of the *Washington Post*. The owners' use of *scab labor*—usually a union member's derogation of an employee who works during a strike—prevailed, and the players' strike was broken.

The use of the word is intended to impute disgust. From the Old Norse, *scab* means "crust that forms over a wound or sore," and is akin to the Latin *scabere*, "to scratch." Although most lexicographers had long thought that the slang term was an Americanism, the Oxford English

Dictionary's Supplement tracks the strike-related meaning to a British publication, Bonner & Middleton's *Bristol Journal* in 1777, writing about a strike in a cordovan shoe factory: "Matters are amicably settled. . . . The Conflict would not been [sic] so sharp had not there been so many dirty Scabs."

In 1792, a writer in *Early English Trade Unions* defined the term somewhat heatedly: "What is a scab? He is to his *trade* what a traitor is to his *country*. . . . He first sells the journeymen, and is himself afterwards sold in his turn by the masters, till at last he is despised by both and deserted by all." Substitute *players* for *journeymen*, and *owners* for *masters*, and you have a fairly current description of the fix some of the replacement players now find themselves in.

Other synonyms for *strikebreaker* include *blackleg, jackleg, red apple, scissorbill, rat* and the ever-popular *fink*.

"*Fink* came into the language in 1902," says the lexicographer Stuart Berg Flexner, "probably as a clipping of *Pinkerton*, with the *p* changing to *f* in pronunciation." Allan Pinkerton (Gen. George B. McClellan's Civil War secret-service chief) founded a detective agency that later gained ill fame as an organization of strikebreakers hired in 1892 to fight the workers in the Homestead strike against Carnegie Steel. As the language scholar H. L. Mencken's *American Mercury* was the first to point out, in 1926, the Pinkerton agents were then reviled by unionists as *pinks*, which may have changed in a decade to *finks*.

Or maybe not. Mr. Flexner's new Random House unabridged dictionary speculates that, in German, *Fink* is the name of the bird we call the *finch*, and also refers colloquially to an undesirable person. In German compounds, the syllable is used to impute untrustworthiness: a *Duckfink* is a sycophant and *Schmierfink* means a "sloppy writer." That's a less likely etymon than the mispronounced Pinkerton (whose symbol, an open eye with the slogan "We never sleep" under it, gave us the expression *private eye*).

My colleague in columny, Russell Baker, nobody's *Schmierfink*, was moved before Labor Day to evoke a song best known to labor skates: "Let us disturb the bottom-line dispassion of this once-famous weekend to sing an old union song crying defiance of 'goons and ginks and company finks and deputy sheriffs that made the raids.' The tune is 'Redwing.' Ready?"

I am unready as Ethelred to be sidetracked from *fink*. (*Goon* is a hired thug, perhaps derived from the 1580s English dialect word *gony*, "simpleton," and popularized by the hairy creature Alice the Goon in the cartoon "Popeye." *Gink*, a 1910 synonym for "jerk," may come from carnival usage. Back to *fink*.)

Although *scab's* slang meaning is limited to labor lingo, *fink* has broadened to include any dirty, lowdown, miserable object of scorn. As early as 1903, the humorist George Ade was writing that "Anyone who goes against the Faculty single-handed is a Fink." In a piece on corporate ethics in *Business Month* (no kin to *Business Week*), Thomas J. Murray wrote: "It is no secret, for example, that most senior executives are contemptuous of whistleblowers, labeling them 'snitches' and 'finks' and often demoting or firing them."

An example of an even more diffuse usage is in a recent William Wilson architectural review in the *Los Angeles Times*: "Only a fink would begrudge museums a useful civic role. . . ." And the *Washington Post*'s Alex Heard wrote in defense of Michael Jackson, subject of a critical cover story in *People* magazine, which had for years been Duckfinking for the singer: "Although I agree with them, I still say those finks at *People* should be tossed in a vat of boiling glitz."

Fink is also a verb—"to inform on," or otherwise to play the contemptible fink—although the current use of *out* as a verbifying phrasemaker has led to the expression *to fink out*. I would resist this latest nonce use, as it detracts from the power of the single-syllable derogation, and to use it is a form of Schmierfinking out.

> I fail to see much humor in your column. Perhaps you are not aware that Fink is also a surname—one, I might add, not always easy to live with. In the Manhattan telephone directory alone, you'll find almost 200 people listed, to say nothing of the Finck or Finke variety. Multiply that out across the United States and you've got a sizable group.
>
> Yes, my name could be Anglicized to Finch, but I am quite proud of my heritage and my immediate ancestry; I would, therefore, much prefer that the verb and noun versions continue their slow demise out of the vernacular without splashy resurrections.
>
> *George H. Fink*
> *Chestnut Ridge, New York*

> I would like to point out that there is more to *fink* and *schmier* than meets the eye. The English "canary" is about the equivalent of the German "fink"—meaning "to sing," thereby breaking the rule of ethics not to tell.
>
> *Schmieren* is not only sloppy writing, but implies a very low standard of content, akin to the English verb "to smear."
>
> *Henriette L. Israel*
> *Forest Hills, Queens*

> Re origins of *fink*: I always understood that it referred to Mike Fink, a legendary (mythical?) riverboat gambler of the nineteenth century who was considered treacherous.
>
> *J. Foster*
> *North Falmouth, Massachusetts*

I am a retired shipmaster and recall the word "Fink" being used by veteran sailors during my early sea-going days.

The old-timers told me that there was a boarding house for out-of-work sailors which I believe was located on the West Coast and which was owned by a Mr. and Mrs. Fink. In addition to serving as a temporary home for indigent seafarers, the Finks' establishment also provided a pool of men for ships' crews. Shipowners would convey to the Finks the ratings required and they would dispatch the appropriate men to the ship.

Now here's the rub. When a sailor was so dispatched from the Finks' house, he carried identification papers from the Finks on which a character reference was made including drinking habits. Perhaps a code was used; of course, if the sailor were held in ill-favor by the Finks, he might not be dispatched at all. This procedure was common before union hiring halls took over the manning requirements of vessels.

Seamen's discharge records were at that time compiled in a book issued by the U.S. Government which showed the names and voyages of the vessels in which the seaman had served. At one time these books contained a column in which the shipmaster could indicate the deportment of the sailor; they came to be known as "Fink books" and are still called that.

To those sailors the word "Fink" came to mean someone in cahoots with shipowners or the establishment who could, and did, adversely affect the lives of sailors in an underhanded way.

Is it possible that the Finks' boarding house was indeed the real origin of the scornful appellation?

Carl W. Swenson
Scarsdale, New York

Dear Bill:

Following our conversation the other night on the origins of, and distinctions between, the terms "scab" and "fink," I am enclosing a copy of novelist Jack London's definition of a scab: "After God finished the rattlesnake, the toad and the vampire, He had some awful substance left, with which He made a scab.

"A scab is a two-legged animal with a corkscrew soul, a waterlogged brain, and a backbone made of jelly and glue. Where others have hearts he carries a tumor of rotten principles.

"When a scab comes down the street, men turn their backs, angels weep in heaven and the devil shuts the gates of hell to keep him out. No man has a right to scab as long as there is a pool of water deep enough to drown his body, or a rope long enough to hang his carcass with."

> Lane [Kirkland]
> President
> American Federation of Labor and
> Congress of Industrial Organizations
> Washington, D.C.

As a source for "goon," please consider the Bengali word *goonda*, which means a ruffian, scoundrel, hoodlum: another of those words that made their way into the English language by way of the Indian Civil Service.

> Mary Lago
> Professor of English
> University of Missouri
> Columbia, Missouri

Thanks for the illumination about the Pinkerton "eye" . . . but what about the story that the term came from an abbreviation for "private investigator" ("private i.")?

> Robert C. Cumbow
> Bellevue, Washington

May I draw your attention to what I consider a somewhat mistaken interpretation of *Schmierfink*, a term used frequently for me when I got my fingers into paint and over my dress or in similar situations. It is mostly used reproachfully for the very young, like *Schmutzfink* which would be applied to a child descending from explorations in the attic which was never dusted. If the latter term were used seriously for an adult, this would imply a choice over one involving the word obscenity.

For example, I would never use *Schmierfink* for a student who writes poorly, however, my friend Professor Peter H. von Blanckenhagen, with whom I have discussed the matter, just reminds me of the past tense of the verb *schmieren* to smear, to grease, with a small but decisive prefix *hin*. *Hinschmieren* does mean writing rapidly and carelessly, something my other favorite among the writers of *The New York Times*, Russell Baker, would indeed never do. Hoping to have conveyed to you the fine overtones of *Schmierfink*.

> Edith Porada
> Professor Emeritus of Art History and Archaeology
> Columbia University
> New York, New York

My memory tells me that a fink is one who betrays a trust. Here's the background. Two young men in Old England engaged in a contest for the hand of a comely lass by daring deeds—such as shooting pewter mugs off each other's head. One young man, whose name was Fink, shot his opponent squarely between the eyes. He swore it was an accident. But his name entered the English language as a description of a friend who betrays a trust.

John L. Lowden
Tampa, Florida

At one point, you state, "fink has been broadened to include any dirty, low-down, miserable object of scorn."

That was me—until I changed my name. I was baptized in 1927 with the name of Leslie Thornton Finkelday, Jr. My parents started calling me Thornton because my father was Leslie or Les. My little friends started calling me "Fink." During one of our cowboy and indian type games one of my more literate little friends dubbed me "Stinky Finky, The Terror of the Pampas."

The nickname "Fink" followed me all the way through college. I was never too happy about it and I'm sure it gave me some kind of inferiority complex. I tried to substitute "Ted" because I had once admired a kid with that name, but that was not too successful.

When I asked the girl to marry me, she suggested that I might change my name. I thought that sounded like a good idea and we did it. Now none of my five kids would be called "Stinky Finky." My name is now officially the chopped-off Leslie Thornton. I can unashamedly introduce myself at cocktail parties as "Ted Thornton."

Apparently this never bothered my father—or my mother, either. Maybe that's got something to do with your chronology of the meaning. Even though you quote George Ade writing in 1903, the pejorative meaning probably did not come around until much later.

I feel strongly that a person's name can have an effect on his personality. Perhaps you might like to do a column on that subject.

I hope you will not consider this letter mere Schmierfinking.

Leslie "Ted" Thornton
Point Pleasant, New Jersey

Ready for This?

Watch those obscure allusions. I let a simile be my umbrella in a piece—"I am unready as Ethelred"—figuring that a few people would catch the allusion to King Ethelred II of England who reigned from 976 to 1016. Known as "Ethelred the Unready," he has stuck in my mind as an example of a ruler who believed in unilateral disarmament.

I owe His Majesty an apology; he has friends everywhere, and are they ever prepared. "Ethelred was *redeless*," writes Dr. Alan E. Van Sciver of Amherst, Mass., "which means 'without counsel,' not 'unready.' He ascended to the throne at age ten. . . . The next year the Danish invasions restarted." David J. Cope of Titusville, Pa., adds: "to be *redeless* or *unready* was to fail to need advice."

And Jacques Barzun, the great usagist who reads this column closely and has thrice retired the Gotcha! Award, observes: "Whoever coined the title that you allude to confused *rede* with *ready*, perhaps by pronouncing them almost alike. Not that anything hangs on the difference at this late date, but that, though you may be *unready*, you are anything but *redeless*."

I'm surprised that some of your readers failed to mention probably the most well known use of "rede" and that, of course, is Ophelia's counsel to Laertes in *Hamlet* as Laertes leaves for Paris, and she warns him as follows:

> . . . but good Brother
> Doe not as some ungracius Pastors doe,
> Shew me the steepe and thorny way to Heaven;
> Whilest like a puft and recklesse Libertine
> Himselfe, the Primrose path of dalliance treads,
> And reaks not his own reade.
> (*First Folio, Act I, Scene iii*)

> Roland Dickison
> Sacramento, California

The Gruntled Employee

"We ought to sit quietly and think about how we handle Mike," wrote Oliver L. North to Bud McFarlane, "so that he does not start talking out of disgruntlement (if that's a word). . . ."

Whether the National Security Council consultant Michael A. Ledeen was unhappy about the way his geostrategic dream had turned into an arms-for-hostages swap and was getting ready to blow the whistle is a matter for congressional hearings to explore, but the status of the locution *disgruntlement* is properly in this department's bailiwick.

Yes, Ollie, *disgruntlement* is a word. The noun used to mean "moody discontent," but is now almost exclusively used to describe the state of resentment, accompanied by sulking and pouting and leaking to the press, felt by employees who think themselves abused or unfairly dismissed.

Like *peevishness, disgruntlement* is always pejorative; you may think of yourself as being in a state of *resentment, anger* or *bitterness,* but you never describe yourself as being filled with *disgruntlement.* That's how the boss characterizes you if you blab about the kind of incompetent martinet you think he is.

Perhaps what Colonel North was wondering about subliminally was whether *gruntled* is a word. At present, it is not; nobody walks around the White House basement saying, "What a nice place to work, I'm feeling perfectly *gruntled* today." Centuries ago, it was in use, based on the little grunts of pleasure given when the lord of the manor patted his help on the head; like *couth, kempt* and *ept,* the root word became obsolete, remembered only in its opposite.

As we discovered last week, the computer mail unearthed by the presidential board looking into the Iranian arms affair, as well as the testimony that such mail generated, is a trove of real-life, real-time locutions.

You like your speech enlivened by a foreign phrase? The aforementioned Mr. Ledeen told investigators he received a message from an Iranian intermediary "that said, *grosso modo,* we have been very patient with you people." This is an Italian adverb phrase that means "roughly, approximately"; it is not to be confused with *quasi modo,* meaning "as if just now" in the Latin phrase *quasi modo geniti infantes,* "as newborn babes," from the beginning of a Latin introit that became the basis of the name of Victor Hugo's *Hunchback of Notre Dame;* Quasimodo was a foundling. (If I knew the Latin for "but I digress," I would insert it here.)

You dig the latest corporate-military lingo? Try this message from North to McFarlane regarding an approval from the Secretary of State of an early approach to an Iran opening: "God willing Shultz will buy onto [sic] this tomorrow. . . ."

The transcriber, thinking the slang term was in error, put a *[sic]* after the *onto.* (*Sic* is Latin for "so, thus," and is used in English to tell the typographer and reader that the mistake is to be printed and noted as a mistake.) But was North wrong?

According to Robert L. Chapman's New Dictionary of American Slang, the verb phrase is *buy into,* defined as "to accept; acquiesce in. Thought of and perhaps coined as the opposite of *sell out,* which has a more contemptuous suggestion of betrayal." However, I have often heard *buy onto,* which may be a variant of the Army lingo *to buy off on,* meaning "to agree," on the analogy of *to sign off on,* meaning "to approve."

I would treat Colonel North with greater respect as a native speaker and remove the *[sic].* Nor is that the only case in which the snickering admonition is out of order. When Graham Fuller of the Central Intelligence Agency was quoted in Appendix B as having written: "Whoever gets there first is in a strong position to work towards [sic] the exclusion of the other," the Tower Commission writer (Nicholas Rostow) ought not to have joined the Nitpickers' League: even the prescriptive Fowler-Gowers usage bible notes without disapproval that, in the prepositional form, *towards* is prevailing over *toward.*

In one instance, the appendix writer was uncertain whether to sic 'em: in reprinting a letter to General Richard Secord that Colonel North signed on behalf of Colonel McFarlane, the Tower report scratched its head: "Your discrete [sic?] assistance is again required. . . ."

Discrete means "separate, independent"; *discreet* means "tactful, prudent" and, in this case, "protective of secrecy." In the same message to Secord, McFarlane-North used the noun form of the adjective *discreet:* "You should ensure that only those whose discretion is guaranteed are involved." I have no doubt that *discreet* was meant but misspelled by North, and the question mark inside the brackets should be removed after the *sic.*

How is your mouth fixed for some previously unremarked intelligence jargon? The report identifies George Cave, who traveled to Teheran to interpret for the American team, as "a CIA annuitant and expert on Iran." Does the CIA offer annuities? In a sense, yes; in governmentese, an *annuitant* is a retired employee who receives a regular pension (from the Latin *annuus,* "yearly"). The word conveys a brisker and more inside connotation than "retired CIA employee on a pension," and is often assumed to mean "spook officially retired but still on the payroll and available."

"I guess I'm a little puzzled about the Iranian *wiring diagram,*" wrote McFarlane on the little green screen. This electrical term began to be used figuratively in the late 1960s, as *The Times* of London used the phrase to describe the nervous system. In military bureaucracies, *wiring diagram* is the flippant term for "table of organization."

Little-used but colorful words have a way of being recalled by witnesses asked for their best recollection. In testimony to the Tower Commission, the Secretary of State (apparently known as "God-willing Shultz" to the NSC staff) said: "I later learned that Vice Admiral Poindexter reportedly told Ambassador Price that there was no more than a smidgen of reality to the story. 'Smidgen' is his word."

The admiral's word has obscure roots. The latest Oxford English Dictionary Supplement speculates that *smidgen* is based on *smitch,* an 1840 term for "a particle, bit," perhaps from the even earlier *smit.* In the mid-nineteenth century, it blossomed in the midwestern United States with the concluding *n,* and is now used in the most downhome manner by copywriters for Wonder Wheat Bread: "Not just a smidgen of wheat but a whole passel!" (*Passel* is an 1835 alteration of *parcel.* Poindexter must have known there was a whole passel of truth to that story.)

Finally, the CIA's George Cave is quoted in what the Tower Commission calls "May 1986 Hot Docs" as complaining in writing that "The people we were negotiating with were a couple of rungs down the ladder.

The fact that [the Iranian official's] breath could curl rhino hide was no help either."

The rhino (from the Greek for "nose"; *rhinoplasty* can be a nose bob) is a mammal known for its upright keratinous horns on the snout and for its thick skin. The insult humor of *breath that could curl rhino hide* is formulaic hyperbole, containing a comic clause analogous to *a face that only a mother could love.* It reflects, grosso modo, the annuitant's discreet disgruntlement.

"Discrete assistance" is a request for help in a series of written memos. Discrete is typically used in engineering and military jargon to modify the noun "increments" or "packets."

The writer did not ask for a one-shot telecon but he did need a series of somethings. In context, one can assume the somethings were briefings in written format to be incorporated in CYA files.

A junior officer does not tell a senior (retired or not) to be discreet. In clandestine work the reminder would be redundant anyhow.

The antecedent for North's use of discrete goes back to Albert Einstein's 1905 paper on photo emission where he postulated that light travels in discrete packets which he called "needles" and modern physicists call "quanta".

"Wiring diagram" refers to the Iranian blueprint, schematic, plan or modus operandi. Thus, wiring diagram is the equivalent of schematic, the map of a scheme.

A Table of Organization is a list of personnel resources and does not qualify as a scheme. Perhaps you intended Organization Chart which is, in military parlance, a wiring diagram. A drawing of the central nervous system is not a TO but is identical to an electrical schematic.

The antecedent for this usage goes back to an old expression used in engineering and military circles: "in like a burglar with a blueprint" which expresses the rare joy of a plan working out.

Bernard E. Coffin
Haddonfield, New Jersey

As researchers who study television and cognition, we are sensitive to misuse of the term "subliminal" and were chagrined to see you using it incorrectly.

A *limen* is a limit of physical ability. For example, the limen of loudness describes the softest and loudest sound that can be detected by the average human being. The limen of pitch refers to the highest and lowest pitch detectable, etc. Limen is not typically used to apply to the limit of consciousness, which would be a difficult limen to establish in any case. *Subliminal* refers to stimulation below the level of one of these lower limits, and *supraliminal* refers to stimulation above the upper limit. The term *subliminal*, then, should be used only to refer to external physical stimulation below a specific limit of perception or sensation.

As such, saying that ". . . what Colonel North was wondering about subliminally. . . ." represents an incorrect use of the term. The word that comes closest to what you apparently mean would be "subconsciously," and even that is not perfect. It is doubtful that people "wonder" subconsciously. There is such a thing as subconscious processing and there are possibly memories stored in the subconscious, but active processing of the wondering sort in all likelihood transpires above the level of consciousness.

John Condry
Professor
Department of Human Development and Family Studies
Cornell University

Cynthia Scheibe
Assistant Professor
Department of Psychology
Ithaca College
Ithaca, New York

According to the research done by James Lipton in his *An Exaltation of Larks* (pub. 1967 by Grossman Publishers), the word passel was used in the fifteenth century as in "a passel of brats" and recorded as such in *The Book of St. Albans* published in 1486.

Thomasina Webb
New York, New York

May I point out that the meaning of *quasi modo* is more correctly explained by "as if in the manner [of]" or "almost in the manner [of]" and not by "as if just now."

Moreover, you (or Webster) seem to translate it as "as" only, because you cannot be unaware that *geniti infantes* is "newborn babes."

Erminio D'Onofrio
New York, New York

The phrase *quasi modo* does not mean "just now"; *modo* by itself means that. *Quasi* means "as if." It comes from the introit for Low Sunday or Sunday in White (meaning Sunday in White-off, *Dominica in albis depositis*), the week after Easter. It comes from 1 Peter 2.2: *Quasi* (or *Sicut*) *modo geniti infantes, rationabile sine dolo lac concupiscite;* that is, "Like newborn babes, seek rational milk without guile." Since little Hunch was born on *Quasi Modo* Sunday, it seemed like a good thing to name him: "Like New," or "Like Now."

Andy Kelly
Department of English
University of California, Los Angeles
Los Angeles, California

Re: roots whose negative prefixes are no longer used, I thought you might be interested in the poem I wrote years ago, about Sam Goldwyn's alleged "I want a lady—one that's couth."

A SONG OF CREPANCIES

Give me a lady, one that's couth,
　　　　Who putes the things I say;
Who's gainly in the eyes of man,
Who's imical to the things I plan,
Who parages me whenever she can,
　　Who's gruntled all the day.

Give me a girl whose hair is kempt,
Whose talk is always ane;
　　Who's ept at ridding home of dirt,
　　Who's iquitous and not a flirt,
　　Who's dignant, and whose mind is ert,
And I'll look on her with dain.

Leonard Rosenthal
Tucson, Arizona

My best guess for "but I digress" would be *sed divagare*—from the Vulgar Latin *divagari*, "to wander," from which the French *divaguer* is derived. I hope this helps.

Elizabeth Jaffe
Amherst, Massachusetts

I suggest *Sed egredior a proposito* for "But I digress." Thanks for bringing up the Latin.

Virginia S. Browne
Wayland, Massachusetts

Hail to the CEO

The most painful ad of the year appeared in business pages, headed "One Clarification of Motorola's Management Succession Announcement."

The copy explained that the company had just put out a six-page "progressive plan for top management succession." The casual reader would take that to mean that somebody new would soon be in charge. But in a curiously constructed sentence, seeming to suggest that the original announcement had been in a foreign language that had some sort of computerized interpretation program, the company said: "Unfortunately, one part of this announcement has not translated clearly."

It seems that some reporters, the sort of ghouls who shovel on the rocks before the board-room chair is cold, took the succession announcement to mean that Robert W. Galvin, chairman and chief executive officer, was "stepping down."

"This is incorrect," said Motorola. "Mr. Galvin will continue to work and *lead* [italics not mine] the company just as before . . . he relinquished one of his titles, Chief Executive Officer, so that other eminently deserving long service associates can carry this richly deserved recognition."

Hmm. I am drawing on a pad little boxes with dotted lines, with one box titled "CEO," and a line of dots upward toward a chairman. When the chairman says "hop," the line of dots quivers and the CEO jumps. In at least one company, then, *chief executive officer* appears to mean "second in command (eminently deserving of richly deserved recognition)."

A call to Galvin's office elicits this quotation from him, passed on here without translation: "The senior officership of this company, as designated by the board, is the chairman of the board, *not* the chief executive officer."

Look, when you're the boss, you can call the guy down the hall anything you like, even "boss," if it pleases you, until you fire him in richly deserved recognition of his getting uppity. But somehow this watering-down of the CEO title strikes me as too much too soon; a title should have a certain period up at the top.

"The boss used to be either president or chairman of the corporation," writes John C. Bogle, who is both chairman and chief you-know-what of the Vanguard Group of investment companies, "and no modifier was considered necessary. . . . It might be interesting to research the origin of *CEO.*"

I, too, recognize that the essence of executive leadership is to delegate the work to others, and passed the buck on to Fred Mish, editorial director of Merriam-Webster. Instead of naming his office boy chief lexicographic officer, Mish looked it up himself. The 1950 *Current Biography* included these historic lines: "B. Earl Puckett was in February 1950 elected board chairman (the chief executive officer) of the Allied Stores Corporation, one of the largest department store chains in the United States. . . . The bylaws of Allied were changed on February 14, 1950, to provide for the Chairman of the Board to become the chief executive officer, who shall, under the control of the Board of Directors, have the general management of its affairs." This is now known to linguists as the St. Valentine's Day Massacre of the Title of President; three years later, *Time* magazine was writing: ". . . but as chief executive officer, iron-fisted [Eddie] Rickenbacker is still the real boss."

Executive is rooted in the Latin *ex-*, "out of," and *sequi*, "to follow," and at one time meant "that which executes a sentence of death"; we have since differentiated between executives and executioners. *Chief Magistrate* was the coinage of Alexander Hamilton in 1788, describing the President of the United States, and *Chief Executive* was first used by John Tyler, who succeeded to the Presidency when William Henry Harrison died in 1841: "I have been clothed with the high powers which they have seen fit to confide to their Chief Executive." Showing some executive muscle, Tyler —too quickly dismissed today as "Tyler, Too"—rejected the notion of an Acting President, considering himself President and chief executive officer.

Although *exec*, for executive officer, has a naval meaning of second in command, CEO was doing pretty well until Galvin, who is not stepping down and you'd better believe it, gave the short-lived title the torpedo. CEO, according to the Acronyms, Initialisms & Abbreviations Dictionary, also means command entertainments officer in the British military, customs enforcement officer in the United States Treasury, communications-electronics officer in the Air Force and casualty evacuation officer (no source for this is given, but it would not be considered inappropriate at CBS News). CEO is an initialism, not an acronym, because the letters are individually pronounced and not made into a word.

The CEO era gave rise to the CFO (not certified flying object, as you might imagine, but chief financial officer) and, most recently, the CIO, chief investment officer, a nice boost for the bookkeeper you can't afford to give a raise, unless he is a member of the Congress of Industrial Organizations, in which case you can stick your title in your ear.

I mourn with you the CEO title's passage into ambiguity. We definitely need a term that makes absolutely clear, and without undignified questioning, which of those august personages, the "chairman," or "president" is indeed the "boss." But, I am afraid you can't blame this particular title "massacre" entirely on Mr. Galvin. There have been any number of top executives who, late in their careers, tried to stay boss while giving up the day-to-day duties of running their corporations. Most had the wisdom to keep the CEO title, but a number, like Mr. Galvin, have, for reasons not altogether clear, shifted it to their successors. Some have even tried to create new titles for themselves. Several years back, for example, William Verity, after yielding his title as CEO of Armco Steel to the company's President, coined a new title for himself: Chairman and Chief Governance Officer. But the title never took; to my knowledge no other executive ever adopted it.

Still, I believe a far more significant reason for the decline of the CEO title lies, not with people like Mr. Galvin, who gave the title to their number two, but with those who have given it wholesale to the heads of divisions and subsidiaries. To encounter an individual with the title "President and Chief Executive Officer of the XYZ Division" who is not even within hailing distance of top management is to recognize, sadly, that Gresham's Law of Corporate Titles has been at work, degrading the usefulness of yet another senior management title.

Allen R. Janger
New York, New York

CIO more commonly stands for Chief Information Officer than for Chief Investment Officer. The position is supposed to be for the executive who is in charge of all information resources (computers, records, etc.) in the corporation.

David Macfarlane
New York, New York

The number-two executive in a corporation is often called COO (chief operating officer); the accompanying title is generally "president."

> *Murray L. Weidenbaum*
> *St. Louis, Missouri*

You missed one of the earliest usages, perhaps even the first. I refer to Chief Administrative Office, or CAO, a position created when the current San Francisco city charter went into effect in 1932. The creation of the position of CAO represented a compromise between those who favored a city manager and those who opposed placing executive authority in the hands of an official not responsible to the voters; the CAO is responsible for managing those portions of the city bureaucracy that are considered to be routinely administrative and to have no policy-making implications.

> *Robert W. Cherny*
> *Professor of History*
> *San Francisco State University*
> *San Francisco, California*

I always shared Mr. Puckett's impression that it was of recent origin. Recently, however, Mr. Woloson of this office and myself were researching the matter for one of our corporate clients, and ran across the term in a Nevada Supreme Court case from 1882, *Reno Water Company v. Leete*, 17 Nev. 203, 30 Pac. 702. The case addressed the question as to whether the president of a corporation was authorized to initiate a lawsuit without express authority from the board of trustees. In its decision the court said, in part:

"This suit was commenced at the instance of the president of the plaintiff, the chief executive officer of the corporation. As such officer he was presumably empowered to commence suits in its name, and perform such other acts in its behalf as the necessities of the case demanded."

> *L. T. Jones*
> *Schrenk, Jones, Bernhard,*
> *Woloson & Godfrey*
> *Las Vegas, Nevada*

Here I Sit, No Warts at All

His back was to the wall in New Hampshire. Hot-eyed pollsters were tracking voters through the snow to detect the impact of the "Iowa bounce," the term for the influence of one state's results on the next state's election. The trend-happy media were headlining "Dole on a Roll," suggesting momentum growing for the campaign of Bob Dole, a phrase based on a crapshooter's run of luck, and not a new heroic sandwich.

Obviously, what was needed was a thematic line, some memorable phrase that would help roll back the turning tide. Vice President George Bush reached into history for a ringing battle cry.

"As Abraham Lincoln said," he evoked, on the stump and during the crucial debate, "Here I stand—'warts and all.' "

The message was clear: nobody's perfect, and George Bush was making no pretense of being a rabble-rousing orator. By admitting imperfection, he was encouraging his audience to identify with him; by asserting an inability to articulate his deep feelings, he was pointing to his possession of those feelings. Mr. Bush, in the wart phrase, presented himself skillfully as a man presented without slick packaging; what you saw and heard, he was saying, was what you got.

The message, coordinated with an attack on his opponent's record, evidently had the desired impact; the candidate touched a chord in integrity-seeking audiences that the Vice President had never reached for in previous speeches. However, as a longtime Lincoln buff, I had a nagging suspicion that Mr. Bush was harking back to the wrong Civil War.

Warts and all. Mr. Lincoln had a prominent mole on his right cheek, and frequently mocked his own face as one of the ugliest he had ever seen; that particular self-derogation was the sort of thing he might have said. But the famous phrase was never associated with him, and my run of the usual Lincoln traps turned up no specific citation; indeed, many fellow buffs said, "Wasn't that Cromwell?"

Yes. In a book written in the late 1760's by Horace Walpole about painting in England, the Lord Protector, Oliver Cromwell, was quoted as telling his portrait artist, Sir Peter Lely: "I desire you would use all your skill to paint my picture truly like me, and not flatter me at all; but remark all these roughnesses, pimples, warts, and everything as you see me, otherwise I will never pay a farthing for it." (I suspect Walpole made up that quote, attributing it to a famous man who died more than a century before, but when it comes to spicing up a biography, necessity hath no law.)

As the marriage broker said when the poor boy agreed to marry the princess, that was half the battle. Now—what about the opening, not put in direct quotation in Mr. Bush's speech, but clearly evocative of past resolve?

Here I stand. There was Martin Luther on April 18, 1521, just 467 years and one day before the New York primary, facing the Diet of Worms. (Many now think that phrase denotes a faddish sixteenth-century weight-loss regimen, but like "Dole on a Roll," the phrase has an entirely different meaning: the Diet was an early legislative body of the Holy Roman Empire, which on that day gathered at the city of Worms to pressure the reformist theologian, recently excommunicated by the Pope, to recant. But Mr. Luther would not knuckle under.)

Hier stehe ich, ich kann nicht anders. Gotte helfe mir, he was reported to have said at the conclusion of his self-defense, most dramatically translated as "Here I stand; God helping me, I cannot do otherwise."

Maybe he said it that way, maybe not; the words now engraved at the base of the Luther monument at Worms were not transcribed immediately, but were part of what is called an oral tradition; people told others that was the gist of what the father of Protestantism said. At any rate, no doubt exists that the words *Here I stand* came to be closely associated with Martin Luther's act of ecclesiastical defiance.

("Necessity hath no law," a thought held and acted upon by many desperate candidates, and tracked back to Publilius Syrus in the first century B.C., was actually written down for a 1654 speech to Parliament by Oliver Cromwell. As we see, the only "quotes" to be trusted completely are the ones recorded in writing or, more recently, on tape.)

Although it is entirely fitting that an American political figure has chosen to evoke memories of courage by using Luther's "Here I stand"—and may even switch a few voters from the Democrats' Paul Simon of Illinois, who is notably popular among Lutherans and is also a Lincoln buff—we can say, with malice toward none, that the powerful *Here I stand, warts and all* is not primarily linked with Mr. Lincoln. Mr. Bush cannot be accused of plagiarism because he attributed the quote (to the wrong man) and he used it in the sense of "Here I am, standing before you" rather than "Here is the firm position I will defend."

And where was the non-Reverend Pat Robertson when his opponent in debate unwittingly seized Martin Luther's words "Here I stand" and seemed to misattribute them to Lincoln? There he sat, missing the God-given opportunity to score a stunning debating point; had the ex-televangelist been alert, he might have changed the course of American history right before our eyes.

When I called Bush headquarters to get the source of the "Here I stand, warts and all" supposedly spoken by Mr. Lincoln, spokesman Pete Teeley dove under his desk as if one of Mr. Robertson's evanescent SS–4 missiles located in Cuba were headed his way.

The call was returned by Peggy Noonan, the former Reagan speech-writer. Within the Judson Welliver Society of former White House speech-writers, she is admired as a power hitter to the heart—one capable of rousing an audience. Ms. Noonan was called up to New Hampshire when the Bush candidacy was thought by the easily panicked to be *in extremis,* and her talents, say some reporters on the scene, contributed much to the attempt by the candidate to overcome the aloof persona and whining tone that had been debilitating his campaign.

After firmly asserting The Speechwriters' Code—just helped a little with the phrasing, the content and strategy were strictly the candidate's—the passionately anonymous Ms. Noonan manfully (I'll get mail on that ad-verb) took responsibility for the research error: "I goofed. All my fault. Must have been thinking about the mole on Lincoln's cheek. Of course, *warts and all* was Walpole's attribution to Cromwell." The *Here I stand* phrase, because it was not in quotes in the text, was therefore not attrib-uted to Lincoln and had not been deliberately evocative of anyone.

Thus did the episode turn out to be a "forward fumble," one of those minor errors that result in a major gain. If Mr. Bush succeeds in his quest, we will cock an ear to his Inaugural, waiting for "As Martin Luther said, *Here I stand,* with, as Oliver Cromwell insisted, *warts and all,* seeking what Abraham Lincoln called *a just and lasting peace.*"

For Americans the most noteworthy reference to Luther's *Hier stehe ich. Ich kann nicht anders. Gott helfe mir* is the ending of Woodrow Wilson's speech to Congress in 1917 asking for a declaration of war against Germany. The last two sentences of his peroration—unjustly forgotten now, for it is one of the noblest paragraphs of all American oratory, on a par with Lincoln's Second Inaugural—are:

> To such a task we dedicate our lives, our fortunes, every-thing that we are and everything that we have, with the pride of those who know that the day has come when Amer-ica is privileged to spend her blood and her might for the principles that gave her birth and happiness and the peace which she has treasured. God helping her, she can do no other.

The echo of Luther was deliberate; Wilson knew how deeply it would resonate in German ears.

Thaddeus Holt
Carlisle, Pennsylvania

At the risk of being relegated to the Gotcha Gang, I must point out a wart in your translation of Luther. It is true that the word order in German often seems contorted to English speakers. In this case, however, the word order should have been retained. "Here I stand, I cannot do otherwise. God help me." He implores divine assistance, does not claim that he has it.

The translation you quote may be the most dramatic but it is not correct.

Russell Hill
Medford, New Jersey

Apropos "Necessity hath no law:" agreed on the attribution to Publilius Syrus and use by Cromwell in 1654. However, the likelihood that the latter (or his equivalent of the JWS type) got it from a perfectly decent, domestic, English source—no necessity to ape Roman Republican rhetoric—is high. Edmund Plowden in *Commentaries*, his early exemplar of modern law reports for the period 1550–1580, at eighteen, trotted out *Necessitas non habet legem*. Somewhat later, Henry Hobart in his Jacobean *Reports* (first printed 1641) at 144, produced *Necessitas vincit legem; legum vincula irridet.*

Thomas G. Barnes
Professor of History and Law
University of California, Berkeley
Berkeley, California

"Necessity hath no law" was written some centuries earlier than Cromwell's 1654 speech to Parliament.

In the *Summa Theologiae*, III, Question 80, Article 8, *corpus*, St. Thomas Aquinas argues that those in danger of death from illness should be permitted to receive Communion even though they are not fasting prior to its reception as required by Church law. The law should be set aside in such cases, he writes, "lest they die without Communion, because necessity has no law (*quia necessitas legem non habet*)."

James I. Campbell
Professor of Philosophy
Rochester Institute of Technology
Rochester, New York

When did "the Diet gathered to press the reformist theologian" turn into "the Diet gathered to *pressure* the reformist theologian?" "Pressure" as a verb is no improvement over "press."

Leonard Rubin
New York, New York

Hermen Eutic's Original Intent

Hermes, the Greek god of speech and travel, commerce and thievery, who also answers to the Roman name of Mercury, zipped into my office the other day, wings flapping on his feet, with a message: he's back in the news.

The chief of the manuscript division of the Library of Congress, James H. Hutson, helped resuscitate him, making headlines. The historian was poring over handwritten documents of the Founding Fathers (that phrase was Warren Harding's nice alliteration—earlier students called the Constitution-makers "the framers") and came across a draft of the Bill of Rights in the writing of Connecticut's Roger Sherman, which had gone unnoticed for a couple of centuries.

Mr. Hutson has revised and updated the classic *The Records of the Federal Convention of 1787* by Max Farrand, and knows as much as anybody about what the framers said in the secret sessions they held in Philadelphia 200 years ago. He is also the author of a *Texas Law Review* article that challenges what some scholars call "the jurisprudence of original intention" from an original angle. He informs me "that the documentation of the Constitution is so corrupt that we cannot certainly know what the framers said; and if we cannot know what they said, how can we know what they intended?"

The historian does not flinch from controversy. Attorney General Edwin L. Meese III, he told reporters peering at the Bill of Rights draft, "has expressed the notion that judges, in interpreting the Constitution, should be close to the original intent of those who wrote it." Then he called in Hermes: "But to try to recover original intent from records that are nonexistent or not faithful to actual proceedings may be an impossible hermeneutic assignment."

Hermeneutic is a word that calls for interpretation as well as definition. The word came into English more than three centuries ago as a kind of antonym for *euretic,* which meant "inventive." (Eureka! I found it!) Wrote Richard Burthogge, a seventeenth-century theological author, "Ratiocination Speculative, is either Euretick or Hermeneutick, Inventive or Interpretative." Scholars working in biblical interpretation took up the word to denote their close examination and explication of texts, using it to distinguish that eye-straining interpretation from *exegesis,* or the practical exposition of Scripture by preachers. *Hermeneutics* became "the art or science of interpretation."

But then the interpretation dodge became complicated, and the word was used to cover more. Hugh J. Silverman, co-editor of the 1985 *Hermeneutics and Deconstruction* and a philosophy professor at the State University of New York at Stony Brook, says, "The *inter-* of *interpretation* suggests 'between.' Interpretation is the matter of determining what the basic message, meaning or context is—and that requires not only the interpreter and interpreted, but also the in-between itself."

Still with me? Hermes, the interpreter of Olympian messages, readily understands that; he has to figure out what Zeus meant, what his own translation does to the original message and how his interpretation will be understood by mere mortals. Martin Heidegger, an existentialist philosopher, used to argue that a thing is no big deal just standing there by itself, but comes into authentic being—rootin'-tootin' existence—when it has been translated and comprehended.

We are now hip-deep in the meaning of meaning. Although it seems as if we are trying to read a transparent sign in a hall of mirrors, an interdisciplinary message is trying to come through: the hot political argument about "original intent" now going on among lawyers, political scientists and historians is the latest manifestation of an argument raging for the past twenty years among linguists, philosophers and literary critics about hermeneutics and one of its subsections, *deconstruction*.

To the decon crowd (if we can call Irving Kristol's neoconservatives *neocons,* we can call Jacques Derrida's deconstructionists *decons*), this "original intent" business is a lot of hooey. (Do I oversimplify? Very well then I oversimplify; I am large, I write for multitudes.)

The decons were preceded by the New Critics, who read Romantic criticism that presumed to spell out what poets like Shakespeare and Coleridge meant in their more obscure passages, and the New Critics said: Don't tie that albatross of interpretation around our necks. Nobody can say for sure what was in a writer's mind when he wrote a line, not even that writer himself.

In Stuart Berg Flexner's superb second edition of the unabridged Random House Dictionary, *deconstruction* is defined in part as a critical movement that "emphasizes that a text has no stable reference" and a text must be studied by "eliminating any metaphysical or ethnocentric assumptions through an active role of defining meaning, sometimes by a reliance on new word construction, etymology, puns, and other word play."

Hold on, say the traditional analysts; a poet's life cannot be separated from his work; he wrote letters, talked to people, left conscious and unconscious clues to his intended meaning. To understand the poem, we should try to understand the writer and—in the vernacular of the New Critics' critics—to see where his head was at and where he was coming from.

In the same way, turning to the scrap among legal eagles, the Meese school of jurisprudence—led by Bruce Fein, a constitutional specialist at the Heritage Foundation—holds that we not only can but also ought to discover what was in the minds of the framers, and stick to that or change it by legislation rather than judicial interpretation.

It's a great fight, cutting across all sorts of philosophical lines, causing knees to jerk in strange directions. And it comes under the heading of *hermeneutics.* Watch that word; when it gets tied firmly to a concept in many people's minds, it will be taken as a sign of our times.

Many writers have claimed a connection between Hermes and hermeneutics, but the evidence is in short supply. Onions's etymological dictionary sees no connection, tracing hermeneutics back to the Greek *hermeneuein,* or interpret, and saving Hermes for the origin of hermetic (by way of Hermes Trismegistus, the author of occult science). The link in question seems more than logical, especially to those who see interpretation as somehow slippery and elusive, and I think for that reason it has come into vogue. But as you know, there's a wide gulf between what ought to be and what is.

In all other respects, I enjoyed your column.

Donald P. Spence
Princeton, New Jersey

Isn't the opposite of hermeneutic the word *heuristic,* from the Greek *heuriskein,* meaning to discover or find, rather than your *euretic?* According to Webster's Third New International, *eureka* is the first person singular perfect indicative active of *heuriskein.*

John A. Rayll, Jr.
Tulsa, Oklahoma

Exegesis—derived from the Greek verb *exegeomai* ("to lead out," hence "to explain the meaning" of a text)—does *not* refer, as you assert, to "the practical exposition of scripture by preachers." Rather, it denotes the work of "close examination and explication" that you misleadingly associate with *hermeneutics.* Exegesis is, or should be, prerequisite to homiletical exposition. In the terms of Krister Stendahl's rough but heuristically useful distinction, it deals with what a text *meant* in its original setting rather than with what it *means* for present-day readers. (Of course this is precisely the distinction that is challenged by deconstructionists and other debunkers of "original intention.") The process whereby a preacher, or any other interpreter, makes the transition from *exegesis* to contemporary appropriation of a text is the special concern of *hermeneutics.*

One further note on usage: a person who does the work of exegesis may be designated an *exegete;* regrettably, in the jargon of the seminary, this legitimate noun has spawned an execrable back-formation, the verb "to exegete," as in the sentence, "She exegeted the passage in preparation for writing her sermon." May Hermes dispatch this neologism to the netherworld!

Richard B. Hays
Associate Professor of New Testament
The Divinity School
Yale University
New Haven, Connecticut

You showed uncanny good hermeneutical sense in subsuming Ed Meese's quixotic pursuit of "original intent" under the rubric of hermeneutics. When I read about this, it seemed to me that Mr. Meese could profit greatly from taking a course in basic hermeneutics. Besides, as a law man, he should know that sticking to "original intent" has been an impossible position ever since Emperor Justinian attempted in A.D. 533 (in vain, of course) to outlaw any interpretive glosses on the *Institutiones iustiniani* ("If any should presume to do such a thing, they themselves are to be made subject to a charge of fraud, and moreover their books are to be destroyed"). The next time you see Mr. Meese you might recommend to him that he contract out with us as consultants before he makes any further hermeneutically unjustified pronouncements on "original intent."

G. B. Madison
Professor of Philosophy
McMaster University
Hamilton, Ontario

Hits and Errors

Thomas Jefferson, who preferred to be remembered on his gravestone as an author, fighter against religious intolerance and educator (not as George Washington's Secretary of State or as President of the United States), is being falsely accused of a serious grammatical lapse. I rise to his defense.

At an auction at Sotheby's, in New York City, historians and autograph collectors were able to examine an important and unpublished Jefferson letter on religious intolerance. The former President wrote the letter in 1818 to Mordecai M. Noah, a Jewish diplomat and journalist in New York, who had sent Jefferson a speech he had just delivered.

"I have read it with pleasure and instruction," the Founding Father wrote, "having learnt from it some valuable facts in Jewish history which I did not know before. your sect by it's sufferings has furnished a remarkable proof of the universal spirit of religious intolerance . . . disclaimed by all while feeble, and practised by all when in power. . . ."

Note the *it's*. Did this author of the Declaration of Independence need a copy editor? "I had assumed that the use of *it's* as a possessive was a modern aberration," writes Sidney Green of Ithaca, N.Y., a charter member of the Nitpickers' League, Colonial Era Troop. "Here is Thomas Jefferson using the word in 1818. Was it right then? Is it wrong now? Or doesn't it matter?"

All of us, Founding Fathers included ("Founding Fathers" was a coinage of Warren G. Harding, by the way; he liked alliteration), have the inalienable right to be wrong. (Big fight over *inalienable*, too, which made it into the Declaration as *unalienable*, an archaic form; this may have been the choice of Jefferson or of an irascible printer.)

It's is a contraction for *it is*, and is not and should never be confused with the neuter possessive pronoun *its*. The English language has had its fight over this, and clarity won.

The fight started about four centuries ago when some secret prefeminists objected to *his* as the pronoun for an antecedent that was not masculine. Here's how it looked when *his* was the neuter possessive: "Ye are the salt of the earth," wrote the men translating the Bible for King James in 1611 when they came to Matthew 5:13, "but if the salt have lost *his* savour, wherewith shall it be salted?"

His didn't work too well for salt. Up in northwest England, Lancashire people preferred *hit* for a neuter-gender pronoun, and used *his, her* and *hit*. A few of the far-out types used *hits*, and soon began dropping the initial *h*. Down south, around London and Oxford, *its* was the form adopted to fill the need for possessives of things like salt, and Shakespeare may have picked up the habit.

But how to spell the new word? Some said to go on the analogy of *his* and *hers*—just add the *s* and be done with it. Others held that it should be *it's*, because an apostrophe before an *s* signifies the possessive. Lexicographers flip-flopped. John Florio, in his 1598 *A Worlde of Wordes, or Most Copious and Exact Dictionarie in Italian and English*, used *its* without the apostrophe in his translation of the Italian *spontaneamente*: "willingly . . . for *its* owne sake." But in his 1611 revision, *Queen Anna's New World of Words*, he changed that to "*it's* owne sake." Somebody must have hollered at him, "Whatsamatter, you spell like those rednecks up in Lancashire?" and he panicked.

By 1818, most lexicographers spelled the neuter possessive pronoun without the apostrophe for one very good reason: That saved *its* from confusion with the contraction for *it is*. But many diehards, among them the framers of our first state papers, spelled it the old way, and could not be accused then of being in error. Thomas Jefferson was a radical in his adoption of Locke's philosophy, but he was a conservative in spelling.

There must be no *ex post facto* laws of grammar; we cannot condemn the men of the past for the accepted usage of the past. But we learn from this exercise that the language changes in order to improve itself; to be more accurate, people change the language to express more clearly what they mean.

OK, Tom, if you can hear me up there: When it's a possessive, it's *its*; when it's a shortening of *it is*, it's *it's*. That's settled; now we're working on unisex pronouns to replace *he/she* and *him/her*. Possibilities include *se* and *herm*, but those look as funny to most of us as *hits* and *it's* looked to the English-speakers of three or four centuries ago.

We cannot, however, let our sloppy founders get away with everything. In the same letter auctioned last month, Jefferson also began sentences without capital letters: "your sect by it's sufferings. . . ." When Homer nods, must we all shake our heads? In this case, yes. The man who coined the words *electioneer* and *belittle* was noted for his command of the language, and must be held to the highest possible standards. Sentences begin with capital letters. Let's try it again, Tom: "When in the Course of human events . . ." That's the way. We still uppercase the first word; these days, though, we try to lowercase the ones in the middle.

Dear Bill,

The stimulus for this letter is your statement that the spelling without an apostrophe 'saved *its* from confusion with the contraction for *it is.*' Do you really think that such a confusion is possible? Are there any instances of *it's* in Thomas Jefferson's other writings or in the huge corpus of writing that precedes the standardization of the spelling *its* in which one couldn't tell whether the contraction or the possessive was intended? The two forms are used in such different syntactic contexts that it takes considerable imagination to think of a context in which the two could be confused (indeed, the task of finding such a context would make a good exam question). Such forms as *John's* and *the king of Sweden's* likewise can represent either a contraction or a possessive, but no confusion results and I haven't heard of any prescriptive grammarians demanding that the possessive be spelled differently from the contraction, even though that would have the same rationale as is given for distinguishing *its* from *it's* orthographically. Next time you use the word 'save,' think about whether the alleged danger really exists. You don't get any credit for saving Denver from tidal waves.

Jim [James D. McCawley]
Department of Linguistics
University of Chicago
Chicago, Illinois

Oy gevolt, Safire, you have some khutsba in talking about grammar when you mean spelling or semantics. The use of an apostrophe in *its* would cause as little confusion as the use of one in *Safire's* serving either as a possessive (e.g., *Safire's arrogance*) or as a contraction (*Safire's arrogant*). If we wrote these forms using Chinese characters without apostrophes, the *grammar* wouldn't change. So it makes no sense to brand *it's* for *its* a "grammatical lapse": *its* simply goes against traditional spelling.

Edgar A. Gregersen
Flushing, New York

As a writer and copy editor who has long bewailed the misuse of "it's," I read your column on Thomas Jefferson's letter with great interest. A couple of days later I happened to be reading Margaret Drabble's "A Note on the Text" in her 1974 Penguin edition of three short works by Jane Austen. The following sentences leaped out:

Lady Susan is little altered from Chapman's version, though I have modernized most of the archaic spelling, and removed capital letters and unnecessary punctuation. ("Her's" has become "hers", for example.)

I omitted the aspostrophe which she usually places after the possessive "its", because I at least always find it confusing; on the other hand I inserted one or two possessive apostrophes when their absence made the sense obscure.

Thomas Jefferson used "it's" for "its"; Jane Austen used "its' " for "its"; and modern commentators have dared to emend them.

Now what shall we make of Drabble's very British, but nonetheless incorrect, substitution of "which" for "that" and insistence upon placing commas outside quotation marks—or, as she calls them, inverted commas?

Marcia Ringel Barman
Oradell, New Jersey

Despite what one might think about the superiority of the English language, Chinese has it beat on unisex pronouns: In Chinese, *tā* is the spoken word for *he/she/it*.

David Bernklau
Brooklyn, New York

How Strait the Gate

When a sitting judge was denied consideration for a place on the Supreme Court because he had puffed a reefer at a party years before, Professor Robert B. Reich at Harvard deplored the "moral straitjacket" implied: "That would limit our selection to only the straitlaced and the goody two-shoes."

U.S. News & World Report, the *Christian Science Monitor* and sometimes the Associated Press spell that *straight-laced;* in my book they're wrong, although the new dictionaries now accept that frequent misspelling as a variant.

The confusion of *strait* and *straight* is about five centuries old, and it's time to get it straightened out. *Strait* is from the Latin *stringere,* "to bind"; *straight* is from the Middle English *strecchen,* "to stretch."

In the King James Bible in 1611, the reader was adjured to reject the wide gate of destruction, "Because strait is the gate, and narrow is the way, which leadeth unto life. . . ." Unfortunately, this led in an 1842 hymn straight to *straight and narrow,* leaving meaning and all distinction in dire straits. The Oxford English Dictionary still holds to *strait and narrow,* but that's not the phrase in current use; it is *straight and narrow,* with the first word not meaning "tightly bounded" but being the antonym of *crooked.*

Straitlaced means "proper to the point of prudish." Charles E. Funk and his son, in *Horsefeathers,* linked the figurative use of the term to the literal: "The strictures laid upon the body through the tight lacing of the bodice were quickly seen to be closely similar to those laid upon one's conduct through what seemed to be excessive prudishness."

"The History of Goody Two-Shoes," a children's story written in 1765, was about a poor orphan girl who acquires learning to improve her lot in life. (The printer was John Newbery, although he may have had a lot of help from playwright Oliver Goldsmith, who did some hack writing on the side.)

Margery Meanwell's brother "had two Shoes, but Margery had but one." When given a new pair of shoes, little Margery (I'm gonna cry) "ran out to Mrs. Smith as soon as they were put on, and stroking down her ragged Apron thus, cried out, 'Two-Shoes, Mame, see two Shoes' . . . and by that Means obtained the Name of Goody Two-Shoes. . . ."

The name *Goody* not only suggests a sentimental goodness, but also was the term of civility used in the sixteenth century, a shortening of Goodwife. The reduplication *goody-goody* was used by Samuel Smiles in his 1871 book, *Character,* to mean spuriously saintly, and was picked up by politicians in the late nineteenth century to derogate reformers as *goo-goos,* rooted in *goody-goody* or—even more derisively—*good government.*

I Am Appalled

"It is nothing short of *appalling,*" declared Democratic presidential candidate Albert Gore, Jr., on NBC's double six-pack debate, "that five of the six Republican candidates have expressed reservations—or outright opposition—to the treaty. . . ."

"I was *appalled,* Tom," said Republican candidate George Bush to moderator Tom Brokaw a few moments later, "at the Democrats' answer—absolutely *appalled* at their concept that everything is wrong. . . ."

Toward the end of the same broadcast, the Vice President responded to a charge that the Reagan administration had not done enough to combat AIDS: "I was *appalled* again at the Democrats. We're spending a billion dollars of federal money on AIDS research." After he said that the Democrats' response made him want to switch over to another network to watch "Jake and the Fatman," which drew a laugh, Senator Gore issued a stern statement: "I was *appalled* at the treatment of AIDS as a joke. . . ."

We evidently have two men aspiring to the Oval Office who have a unique capacity to be appalled, or who have an uncommon affinity for this past participle. The term—often accompanied by a smacking of the palm on the forehead and an expression of pained disbelief or feigned outrage—is in vogue in the politics of shock and horror, and calls for examination.

Rooted in the Latin *pallere*, "to be pale," *appall* retains its kinship to *pale*: it refers to the state of shock in which blood drains from the face, and still has a meaning of "stunned and unable to act because of disgust or fear." Shakespeare was the first user of the past-participle form, and was a frequent user in other tenses: the horrified Macbeth, seeing the ghost of Banquo, describes the event as one that "might appall the devil." Hamlet, comparing himself to a passionate actor, says, "He would drown the stage with tears,/And cleave the general ear with horrid speech,/Make mad the guilty, and appall the free. . . ."

In a double play on the present-participle senses of whitening and surprising, the poet W. H. Auden wrote, "Into many a green valley / Drifts the appalling snow." The literal meaning of the word is unmistakable— "stimulating an emotion that turns the face pale"—but the question follows: what emotion?

Not *anger*; if that were the feeling, the speaker would talk of being infuriated, outraged or angered, or would sputter, "That makes me sore" or "It riles me up." Not *disgust*, a strong stomach-turning emotion; few remarks by an opponent are so repugnant as to cause a speaker to raise the possibility of retching in public view. (The Kingfish, in the radio series "Amos 'n' Andy," coined the term *regusted*, an excellent euphemism.)

And not *fright*. Can you imagine a red-blooded politician admitting, "I am frightened by" or "I am fearful of" or even "I shrink in horror from"? The people who use *appalled* today do not intend to display real fear, which would be impolitic if not wimpish. Same with *unnerved*, and a fright-rooted adjective—*aghast*—often used by Joseph Alsop. (To denounce a proposal as *scary* is different: when someone or that person's theory is called *scary*, a degree of weirdness or irrationality is imputed to the scarer, and suggests no fear in the unkooky scaree.)

Nor does the person claiming to be *appalled* mean *confused, confounded, perplexed, puzzled, bewildered* or otherwise not on top of the job of understanding everything profoundly. Although *amazed, surprised,* and *astonished* are in the ball-park, none of those emotions carry the necessary alarm and disapproval, nor do they cause the speaker to go pale.

What, then, does the word mean in current usage? One meaning of *appalled* is "struck dumb," or "dumbfounded." However, because *dumb*, in the sense of "stupid," is a slur on the speech-impaired, it is rarely used in politics (except in "That's a dumb idea, Pierre," when directed at an idea and not a person). No politician would say, "I am dumbfounded," because that would associate him with dumbness, suggesting his followers may be dummies; in the same way, "I am floored" suggests a loser, and "I am speechless" obviates the opportunity to provide a sixty-second sound bite by making a short speech expressing why one has been rendered inarticulate.

The meaning intended, I think, is *dismayed*, which once meant "deprived of courage by sudden fear or confusion," but has come to mean "struck by a piercing feeling of disappointment that carries an overlay of alarm and disapproval." Good word, widely understood, and most important, not hoity-toity.

That's the trouble with *appalled*. It's not a word that ordinary people use; there's a highfalutin, elitist connotation to the word that engenders a suspicion that maybe the person claiming to be appalled is perhaps affecting a pose of shock. When an old appall-bearer like Alexander M. Haig, Jr., leans forward and says with great sincerity, "I'm appalled," somehow I do not get the impression he has really been driven to abandon his resolution by fear and revulsion.

There's another past participle to express disapproving surprise: *shocked*. One trouble with it, however, is its most famous use in a movie, when Claude Rains in *Casablanca* tells Humphrey Bogart that he is "shocked, *shocked* to find that gambling is going on in here!" In the screenplay by Julius J. Epstein, Philip G. Epstein and Howard Koch (based on the play *Everybody Comes to Rick's* by Murray Burnett and Joan Alison), the word is used ironically; the charmingly corrupt French official, who wins in the gambling there, cannot be shocked at that, or anything else. "I'm shocked" is borderline effeminacy, as in "I'm hurt"; politicians (both male and female) are rightly leery of it.

Try *dismayed* for a while, or *amazed* or even *troubled*. Those are words voters use, and are using more and more.

You included just about every political use of "appalled." I suggest one more, this one by Adlai Stevenson. The time—September 1960. The issue—Senator John F. Kennedy's religion.

A group of prominent Protestant clergymen, led by Reverend Norman Vincent Peale, attacked Kennedy for his Roman Catholicism. Coming to Kennedy's defense, Stevenson, the previous Democratic standardbearer, took up the religious imagery. Comparing Peale with St. Paul, he said that he found Paul appealing and Peale appalling.

Leave it to one of our most eloquent spokesmen to not only use a pun, but a chiasmus as well.

Gary Muldoon
Rochester, New York

I have been thinking about "aghast" and "appalled." But why can't people any longer be "horrified," "profoundly shocked" (no Claude Raines here), or even caused to have their "flesh crawl"?

Joseph W. Alsop
Washington, D.C.

I'll Stand Alone

In the Iran-contra hearings, Lieutenant Colonel Oliver L. North testified that Director of Central Intelligence William J. Casey told him he was "interested in the ability to go to an existing—as he put it—off-the-shelf, self-sustaining, stand-alone entity that could perform certain activities on behalf of the United States."

Watching, I shook my head: Bill Casey, a careful man, would never have said that. He knew the difference between *on behalf*—"acting in another's place"—and *in behalf*—"acting for another's interest." If he had an outside operation in mind, it could not represent the United States or appear to be its agent in any way; on the contrary, the outside entity could act only *in* behalf of the United States, to its benefit or advantage, while providing plausible deniability. The distinction is eroding, but old-fashioned writers and aging spooks still make it.

Adding to my suspicion of the words attributed to the deceased spymaster (and Casey was a *spymaster*, not a *master spy*—I wish KGB interpreters would get that straight in their secret transmissions) was the North use of the compound adjectives *off-the-shelf* and *stand-alone*.

Self-sustaining was OK; Casey would use that sort of standard participial compound. But *off-the-shelf* is computerese: "All three systems will be sold off the shelf in production-line models," wrote *Business Week* in 1975, describing marketing plans for a D.E.C. minicomputer.

The phrase is like the French fashion term *prêt-à-porter*, "ready-to-wear"; it means "from stock on hand," and may have been used first in a piece about defense technology in the Encyclopedia Americana's 1950 annual volume: "Two interesting trainers were developed by American manufacturers for consideration for 'off-the-shelf' purchase for the Armed Services."

The vast Merriam-Webster files also show the hyphenated adjective appearing in the November 1963 *Technical Survey* about rocketry: "Total cost of firing this off-the-shelf, four-stage, solid-propellant Forester is under $500,000." In today's computer lingo, *off-the-shelf* is a modifier that contrasts an item with "custom-made" and means both "available from stock" and "requiring no adaptation (of software)."

Stand-alone is a hyphenated modifier derived from an independent clause (with the "you" understood in an imperative sentence), but in current use, the phrase is always attached to a noun and never stands alone. In the *Computer Dictionary and Handbook* put out in 1966 by C. J. Sippl, it is defined as the capability of "a multiplexor designed to function indepenently of a host or master computer." In this generation, as defined in Jerry M. Rosenberg's 1984 *Dictionary of Computers, Data Processing and Telecommunications,* the phrase has an additional meaning of "a single, self-contained word processor, as opposed to a word-processing terminal that is connected to and dependent upon a remote memory and processing unit."

"Stand-alone refers to a complete system," explains Oliver Smoot, acting president of the Computer and Business Equipment Manufacturers Association, and presumably no kin to the Smoot of the much-maligned Smoot-Hawley tariff. "It's like a hi-fi system that has the radio, record player, cassette player and compact disk player all in one place. The opposite of *stand-alone* would be, say, a computer that lacks a monitor or has to hook up to a network."

The figurative sense has already been extended to politics. In Congress, *omnibus bills* are often glued together so that popular segments support other elements of parochial interest. A retronym is *stand-alone bill,* used to mean "naked and vulnerable" in this sentence by the Associated Press's Matt Yancey: "Kennedy and Metzenbaum, however, opted to include the measure in the trade bill, contending there was no way they could muster sixty votes in the Senate to prevent a stand-alone bill from being filibustered to death."

The two words met in Chaucer's *Canterbury Tales*—"An emperoures doughter stant allone"—and were immortalized in the nursery rhyme "The Farmer in the Dell," with "The cheese stands alone." In modern times, before the words were taken up by hackers and their robotic ilk, they were used in fashion in this florid citation from a 1955 *Playbill:* "Elanora Garnett does it in her ensemble of mist-gray chiffon dress, stand-alone black satin greatcoat. . . ." What is a stand-alone coat (and what is she doing in it)? Fred Mish, at Merriam-Webster, wonders about that—Is the garment so stiff that it can stand by itself? Is it so dramatic that it stands alone, independent of the world of greatcoats?

My old independent-minded friend Casey might have had in mind a self-perpetuating, self-contained operation far from the prying eyes of congressional overseers and revenuers, but I cannot hear him talking about a *stand-alone* cloak with an *off-the-shelf* dagger.

> Your "stand-alone" column arouses a memory in me from about seventy years ago, when the Boston company of S. S. Pierce (pronounced "purse" by true Bostonians—a tribe to which I cannot rightfully claim to belong) put out a new mixture of coffee beans and christened it Stanzalone Coffee. I remember my father, having drunk a cup of the stuff, remarking: "Well, it can keep on standing alone, as far as I'm concerned." I would date the year as 1916, when I was thirteen years old, but I may be in error by a year or two.
>
> *John T. Edsall*
> *Cambridge, Massachusetts*

Shelf Life

Using Holmesian deduction in a column, I was able to absolve the late Director of Central Intelligence, William J. Casey, from having said he was "interested in the ability to go to an existing—as he put it—off-the-shelf, self-sustaining, stand-alone entity." (That's Lieutenant Colonel Oliver L. North quoting Casey.) My hound that did not bark was the fact that *off-the-shelf* was computerese, a lingo that Casey, a crusty old Wall Street lawyer, did not know.

Reporter Jeff Gerth of *The New York Times*, who reads Securities and Exchange Commission filing statements for fun, promptly stuck his head in my office and said, "You just hung your friend Casey—that was a securities term long before computerese was born, and he sure would know it." I corrected him on *hanged* versus *hung* and put it out of my mind.

"Perhaps William Casey did not speak computerese," writes David P. Cannon of Upper Montclair, N.J., "but as a former head of the Securities and Exchange Commission he most certainly was aware of Rule 415, a 'shelf registration,' which results in an *off-the-shelf* offering of shares to the public."

According to *Biz Speak*, compiled last year by Rachel S. Epstein and Nina Liebman, with a one-shot *shelf registration* of securities with the SEC, "a new stock issue can sit on the shelf for up to two years and come to market in slices." The purpose of Rule 415, governing such registrations, is to eliminate "the costly and time-consuming process of registering each new issue." Or, as Mr. Cannon suggests, of informing Congress of new covert activities.

Accountants and attorneys also use *stand-alone* as a compound adjective, same as computer hackers who want to refer to a PC rather than a workstation. As this corporate shell game is played, "You incorporate a number of stand-alone businesses," explains my correspondent, "that literally sit on the shelf in your attorney's office (in a Corporate Records three-ring binder that also holds the corporate seal) until you need to take one or more 'off the shelf' to divert money out of one business (usually for tax purposes) or to conduct some business transaction so as to avoid scrutiny by other partners or managers."

The old business guys evidently have a lot to teach the young hackers. Casey would be pleased to hear that his vocabulary has been ridden to shore by the wavers of the future.

In case a horde of Sherlockians haven't written to you yet, let me note that your use of "Holmesian deduction" follows a popular tendency to use *deduction* (inference by reasoning from the general to the particular) in place of *induction* (reasoning from the particular to the general), which is what the canny detective actually did.

Stanley Weintraub
Evan Pugh Professor of Arts
and Humanities
The Pennsylvania State University
University Park, Pennsylvania

I'm afraid you've cloaked the expression "off-the-shelf" with an aura of class (Wall Street, computers, etc.) it doesn't deserve.

It's merely an old merchandising designation for a product that could be purchased immediately, in contrast to something that was ordered and shipped by mail (seed, for example, or stuff from Sears, Roebuck or M/W.)

Robert A. Sestero
Assistant Professor of
Communication Arts
Iona College
New Rochelle, New York

"Off-the-shelf" has been in my vocabulary for perhaps two decades. I use it in lectures and course material to describe all readily available government/community/industry statistics—often available at no cost. "Off-the-shelf," in the sense I use it, distinguishes thus-labeled statistics (as well as other data appraisers seek) from personally compiled and analyzed information.

As I understand "off-the-shelf," it shares meaning with "off-the-rack" garments ("Confection" in Europe), and separates that class of merchandise from tailor-made, made-to-measure, or custom-tailored apparel.

Romain L. Klaasen
Victoria, British Columbia

In a Muddles

A book collecting language columns that will not get a plug in this space has this on the cover's flap copy: "He routs out . . . examples of vacuous, trendy lingo that muddles understanding."

Is that right? Shouldn't it be "examples . . . that muddle," not "muddles"? If the word *that* is being used as a relative pronoun for the plural noun *examples*, then the plural verb *muddle* is required to match it. Gotta have agreement.

But wait. Relative pronouns like *that* usually take as their antecedent (the word they are substituting for) the noun they are closest to. In this case, *that* snuggles up to *lingo*, which is singular; we are not talking about two lingoes. Therefore, the singular *lingo* calls for the singular verb *muddles*. In this case, it is the *lingo that muddles* understanding, not the *examples . . . that muddle* understanding.

Two insights emerge from this dreary analysis. First, the English language makes plurals out of verbs by removing an *s* and makes them singular by adding an *s*. This seems wrong, and had I been present at the creation of English, I would have switched it around the other way. But that's the way it is; I'm just a traffic cop, I don't paint the lines on the roads.

Second is Safire's First Law of Relative Pronoun Agreement: if it looks funny, the hell with it. The words "examples of . . . lingo that muddles understanding" look funny; so does the more defensible phrase "examples of . . . lingo that muddle understanding." Don't just stand there preparing pedantic defenses of your position—instead, solve the problem. Solution: recast the sentence.

In this case, kill *examples of.* That leaves: "He routs out vacuous, trendy lingo that muddles understanding." End of confusion. The writer owns the prose; the prose doesn't own the writer. Take charge of your relative pronouns; anything else muddles understanding.

I have never before jumped into the ring with a columnist, both modesty and a self-protective timidity safeguarding any presumption from a public swat, but this time I would be protecting generations of former students from the heartbreak that would surely result if, after reading your comments on agreement of "examples" with its verb in the sentence you quote, they remember my firm insistence that a prepositional phrase modifies a subject word—tells us more about the subject word—but under no circumstance can contain the "subject" (as if the nose could contain the face), and therefore the verb must be attached to the word being modified (i.e., the subject, a word outside the prepositional phrase).

The singularity or plurality of the verb is therefore determined by the word being modified by the prepositional phrase. In this case "examples" is the subject. "Of vacuous, trendy lingo" is the prepositional phrase modifying it, and the relative pronoun "that" refers back to "examples." Ergo, "examples" being plural, its verb is a plural "muddle." And the respect my students may have retained for me, and an "English" teacher's dictum on the matter, is preserved.

Robert Bederman
New York, New York

As you say, it is either "examples that muddle" or "lingo that muddles," though one would be inclined to favor the first and charge an error to the writer. But the author does what a lot of grammatically solid citizens do in both writing and speaking, namely, to have the verb agree, in singular or plural, not with the true subject but with the noun immediately preceding. Let me give you a few examples, all read or heard, none invented by me for the purpose of this letter.

One of five brides get married before they have to.
With this award goes our best wishes.
The exchange of ideas were one-sided.
He said some things in the past that is important.
The danger this nation and the world faces.
One must probe what the implications of any church-teaching is.
The number of drunk diving arrests have increased sharply, but the
    number of alcohol related deaths has not dropped.

In Modern Standard English (but of course not in all languages), singular, plural, and person are fully conveyed by the noun (*book, books*) or by the pronoun (*I, you, he/she/it, we, you, they*—though *you* may cause ambiguity, hence *you all* in some speeches). Hence any additional signal in the verb is semantically unnecessary (and in any event rare since it occurs only in the third person of the present indicative with its final *-s*), though grammatically required. The careful user of Standard English is obliged to obey the grammatical rule and says *he sings, they sing*, though the distinction is redundant as the person and number are marked twice: in the pronoun (or noun) and in the verb. But the redundancy is attested by the fact that, as in the examples cited, the verbal forms are used without regard to the number of the subject, and that this is done without impairment to the meaning of the phrase. What prevails over the grammatical requirement is, as it were, the short-term memory of the writer or speaker that causes him to have the verb agree with the nearest noun.

Ernst Pulgram
Professor Emeritus of
    Romance and Classical
    Linguistics
The University of Michigan
Ann Arbor, Michigan

"This seems wrong, and had I been present at the creation of English, I would have switched it around the other way." Isn't this redundant? Shouldn't the sentence end with ". . . , I would have switched it around."

Glenn Fancie
The Bronx, New York

Note from W.S.: Yes, yes.

A more teasing question of agreement than the one you raised occurs when the verb *to be* gets squeezed between a subject and a subjective complement of which one is singular and the other plural.

This was foisted on my attention in the gymnasium of a university I shall not name, where above each washbowl was a liquid soap container and a notice saying: "Treat these containers gently. A few pulls are all that is needed."

This started an argument among a number of very learned professors. The best qualified—a professor of linguistics—maintained that since the copula is tantamount to an "equal" sign, it may agree with either what comes before it or what comes after. Nobody took the line that "a few" is a singular. Most took it for granted that whatever comes before the verb is the subject but nevertheless felt uncomfortable with "are" .

The Arab grammarians have rather a neat way of settling comparable issues in their language. They ask: "What unspoken question does this statement answer?" Now anyone approaching a washbowl would be asking himself not "What will a few pulls do?" but "What is needed to make this contraption work?" On the basis of this reasoning, the true subject of the sentence is "all that is needed" even though it is placed after the verb, so the copula should be singular.

Pierre Cachia
Department of Middle East
    Languages and Literature
Columbia University
New York, New York

In a New York Minute

The attorney general of Alabama, denied the Democratic nomination for governor, was furious. He denounced the people around his opponent as "a bunch of sleaze-bags—you can see that in a New York minute."

Regular readers of "On Language" already know that *sleaze* began as an ethnic slur, unfairly derogating the linen products made by the people of Silesia, an area of southwest Poland. But many will wonder why I have not yet dealt with *in a New York minute.*

"If there was any hint of impropriety," a Dallas police official, eschewing the subjunctive, was quoted as saying in 1980, "they'd be on us in a New York minute."

In a 1983 television movie *A Killer in the Family,* someone says of the brutish father played by Robert Mitchum: "He'd kill you in a New York minute."

"Welcome to Houston," wrote *Forbes* magazine in 1983, "where lizard-skin boots go with pin stripes, and business is done quicker than a New York minute."

The phrase—evidently a Southernism used with particular frequency in Texas—was given further national currency as the title of a song by Ronnie McDowell that made the country music top forty in 1985. The song contains a second example of a place name used as an attributive noun: "I'd make love to you in a New York minute and take my Texas time doing it." But what does *in a New York minute* mean?

Consider this speculation by Chris Dufresne, a sportswriter for the *Los Angeles Times,* about a new tailback: "He plays the game as if lost in a New York minute. He zigs and zags much the way you would through Times Square at rush hour—darting, dashing, cursing. When he sees a linebacker, he just pretends he's side-stepping a taxi."

With this lead in hand, I conducted extensive field research to determine the nuances of meaning in this burgeoning Americanism. (What I did was to go into the city room of *The New York Times* bureau in Washington and shout over the non-din of murmuring terminals: "How fast is a New York minute?" This query was met with blank looks from all but deputy Washington editor Howell Raines, an Alabamian whose previous assignment was as Atlanta bureau chief; Mr. Raines replied with a snap of his fingers: "Means *that* fast." That's all I needed; I hate to go outside for field research.)

From these spoken and written contexts, as well as from extended talks with native speakers of the Suthrin dialect, I define the phrase with final authority as "instantly, without hesitation, and with overtones of freneticism; based on a derogation by Southerners of the supposed hectic pace in New York City."

T. T. Wiley, Acting Traffic Commissioner of New York City in 1951, described a "split second" as "the time it takes for the light in front of you to turn green and the guy behind you to honk his horn." Johnny Carson used that definition recently to describe *a New York minute.*

The earliest citation I've found is in the files of the Dictionary of American Regional English, quoting a sheriff in Piney Woods, Tex., in 1967. I hope that when DARE gets to the letter *N,* we will have the definitive word on the location and frequency of the expression. (Good news: DARE just received a $600,000 grant from the Andrew W. Mellon Foundation, the outfit that has led in helping serious dictionary-makers all over the continent and has put so-called "communications foundations" to shame.)

This leads us, of course, into the use of geographical locations as the source of derogatory labels. People from other places use the names of loathed or feared cities or states to describe a variety of objects. Fred Cassidy, editor of DARE, points to *Carolina racehorse*, which is a razor-back hog. *Alaska time* and *Jamaica time* are always inexact hours, early or late, aspersions cast on punctuality in those places. *Coney Island butter* is mustard; an *Arkansas toothpick* has been used since 1837 to denote a bowie knife, and an *Arkansas fire extinguisher* is a chamber pot.

The best collection of these expressions is in the hands of Robert L. Chapman, editor of the New Dictionary of American Slang, the much-needed updating of Wentworth and Flexner's work of the past few decades.

Las Vegas throat is what entertainers get from singing in smoky bars; a *Chicago piano* is a submachine gun; a *New Jersey eagle* is a large mosquito; a *California prayer book* is a deck of cards and *Mississippi marbles* are dice. A *Michigan bankroll* is a wad of singles, with a $100 bill conspicuously on the outside, and a *Mexican breakfast*, being a glass of water and a cigarette, is one of many Texas slurs on our neighbors to the South.

Jack Valenti, at a recent party (I will go outside for *some* field research), self-mockingly described *California courage* as "the confidence of a driver whose brakes have given out on a steep hill but who doesn't worry because there is a stop sign at the bottom."

Lexicographic Irregulars are invited to send their favorite locutions to this linguistic study; thanks, but I cannot use *Tijuana bible* or *Vatican roulette*. For poetic justice and sectional retribution, your attention is called to *Georgia credit card*: the length of hose used to siphon gas out of somebody else's tank. It can be done in a New York minute.

My father died in 1930 at the age of sixty-nine, when I was twenty-seven years old. I give you the statistics because age has something to do with my question. When I was a child, and later too, my father would often say, "I can do that in a York minute." I used to wonder without saying anything just what that meant, or where the expression came from. I hope you have an explanation. Otherwise I'm likely to keep on thinking that a "New York minute" is a corruption of a "York minute."

Sister Benvenuta Bras
Dominican Archives
Sinsinawa, Wisconsin

Your reference to a submachine gun being called a "Chicago piano" was wrong. It was called a "Chicago typewriter."

My grandfather lived in Cicero, Illinois, during the reign of Al Capone. In fact, he lived around the block from the Evergreen Theatre. My father, when telling stories about that era, would refer to a submachine gun as a "Chicago typewriter." Between the two, my grandfather and my father, I have never heard or read about its being referred to as a "Chicago piano."

Stanley J. Kolanowski
New York, New York

The term *California kilowatt* is used by amateur radio operators out here, especially truck drivers, to mean a grossly illegal 5,000 watts as referred to transmitter power.

Tom Luebben
San Francisco, California

For your collection of regional put-downs: "Mississippi Flush: any five cards and a .38 Special."

Dan Gray
Berkeley, California

My attention was drawn to the term "Georgia credit card." I think this term has suffered Eastern displacement (whoa—could *that* ever have possibilities!) as I have heard since childhood of Oklahoma (or Okie) credit cards, coming into vogue with the dust bowl migrations to California in the late '30s.

W. Allan Skaar
Alameda, California

In my collegiate days in Virginia, we often used another "New York" -rooted slang phrase. This phrase centered on ". . . a New York whore" and was invariably linked with "nastier than," "quicker than," etc. Forgive me for the coarseness. However, my now dimmed memory seems to suggest that a New York minute relates to or arose from how long it took with or for a New York whore.

Later, we always used "in a New York minute" as a response to a query about one's opinion of a good-looking girl. The more civilized usage of New York minute at the present time fits well with your recent article about the gentrification of coarse language and its assimilation into polite conversation.

Timothy C. Taylor
Austin, Texas

I want to mention that out here what you report as the California or Hollywood stop is known as a *Missouri stop*. There also is the

Missouri pass (passing on the right side of a two-lane highway), and a variety of other Missouri commentary.

I'm surprised that you didn't come up with the best-known version in this part of the country, the *Rocky Mountain oyster*—widely advertised in drinking establishments and as part of TGIF snacks. This is a French-fried delicacy of steer testes, culled when male cattle are castrated to make them manageable for herding, thus young and tender.

Harold L. Orbach
Manhattan, Kansas

The Piney Woods of East Texas is a region, much like the Catskills or the Great Plains. It is not the name of a specific city, town or county, and thus while there may be a sheriff in the Piney Woods region, there can be no sheriff in Piney Woods, Texas.

David L. Shapiro
Austin, Texas

Larchmont Lockjaw

A New York minute is what some Southerners call a frantic moment or a very short time; in retaliation, a *Georgia credit card* is what some Northerners call a short length of hose for siphoning gas out of a car's tank. A piece on these geographical derogations brought out additions from Lexicographic Irregulars.

A *Charleston butterfly*, writes George Loukides of Alexandria, Va., is a palmetto or water bug, "or, if one is really honest, a roach."

Seven Nights in Scranton is the put-down of a perfume, according to Andrea Barnett of Ithaca, N.Y., the derogation probably based on "Evening in Paris."

A *California stop*, frequently localized as a *Hollywood stop*, is what many readers identify as the slight slowing-down of a motorist surreptitiously jumping an octagonal stop sign.

Although *Chicago piano* was defined here as "a submachine gun," other readers in snap-brim fedoras recalled *Chicago sewing machine* and *Chicago typewriter*.

A *Carolina robin*, reports John P. W. Vest of Centreville, Md., is a smoked herring, given the nickname because "the fish, when processed according to the North Carolina recipe, takes on the color of the American robin's breast."

A *Rocky Mountain canary* is a burro, according to a January 1962 article in Western Folklore by Ed Cray, which also defines a *California breakfast* as "a cigarette and an orange." Any ethnic group to be slurred can be affixed to the poker term *straight,* then defined as "any five unrelated cards and a sharp knife."

Coney Island head is a glass of foam with no beer, reports Gladwin Hill of Los Angeles.

A *Kentucky right turn,* writes Jane Shear of Binghamton, N.Y., is "the maneuver performed when a driver, about to turn right, first swings to the left."

A *Texas T-shirt,* reports Gregg A. Stacy of Webster, N.Y., is one of those disposable "seat bibs that are found in interstate roadside truckstop bathrooms." (Texans take a lot of linguistic abuse.)

Vermont kindling is a wad of newspapers, tightly rolled, with each leaf partially overlapping the next, for use "when you are out of wood or too cheap to buy some," according to Annette H. Landau of New York City.

Larchmont lockjaw is a mysterious message left for me, with no further explanation, by my colleague Russell Baker. This alliterative geographic slur may refer to a type of speech by yuppies, but since neither Mr. Baker nor I am young or upwardly mobile, I must assume it has something to do with the accent of upper-class lower-classmen returning to suburbia from ritzy finishing schools; obviously, more research is needed on this locution.

And Frank Mankiewicz of Washington urges me to catch a gesture in the movie *The Color of Money,* with Paul Newman and Tom Cruise. Mr. Mankiewicz, movie buff and billiardist, says: "Newman is seen from time to time banging his pool cue on the floor to applaud a particularly good shot or run. . . . This action—banging the cue up and down on the floor in a vertical position—is called, believe it or not, *the Indiana accolade.*"

I read with fascination Don Walsh's column, "The Lexicology of Cue-Banging," in the *Cape Cod Times.* I was delighted to hear about the use of banging the pool cue on the floor to summon Blinky, or any other whose job it was to rack up the new game, because it explained to me something that has troubled me for some time— namely, why that gesture is called the "Indiana accolade." Obviously it is not just an accolade, or it would not be preceded by the faintly pejorative adjective, "Indiana." The presence of "Indiana" in this two-word phrase is, I believe, similar to the presence of "Georgia" in the "Georgia credit card" (a hose used to siphon gasoline from someone else's tank). In other words, what seems an accolade is in fact merely a summons to rack up a new game, which takes a little something off the praise for ending the game, which might or might not have been done with an excellent shot or run.

Frank Mankiewicz
Washington, D.C.

I was quite surprised to see "Larchmont lockjaw" mentioned. You attributed your discovery of the phrase to Russell Baker.

As Mayor of Larchmont, I am quite curious as to how that phrase arose. Actually, I had only heard heretofore of "Locust Valley lockjaw" and I hope Larchmont is not acceding to Locust Valley's undoubtedly well-earned designation.

Having presided at a fair number of Village Board meetings and having lived in Larchmont for twenty-five years, I must report to you that I have seen no signs of lockjaw-type speech here. Jaws seem to move most freely and, more often than not, interesting, thought-provoking and challenging words and ideas issue forth.

Good luck in tracking down "Larchmont lockjaw." When you find that elocutionary dragon, please slay him.

> Miriam Curnin
> Mayor
> Larchmont, New York

Locust Valley Lockjaw

It began in a New York minute after a piece about geographical derogations, the use of place names as modifiers to sneer at a trait or an occupation. My colleague Russell Baker passed along a cryptic message— "Larchmont lockjaw"—which I took to mean the pronunciation affected by yuppies. I then passed it along to the Philadelphia lawyers who read this column as the speech affected by "upper-class lowerclassmen returning to suburbia."

Came the deluge. "The correct phrase is *Locust Valley lockjaw*," insists Arthur Knapp, Jr., of Larchmont, N.Y., where the famed Larchmont Yacht Club faces Locust Valley, L.I., across the Long Island Sound barrier. He claims that locution denotes the speech of "the yacht-racing members of the highly social Seawanhaka Corinthian Yacht Club located on Oyster Bay, many of whom live in or around Locust Valley." Mr. Knapp, a prominent yachtsman, says, "You cannot pin that way of talking on Larchmont. We are too close to the 'Bronnix' for that to happen."

The rejection of elitism by residents of Larchmont can better be understood when the accent is described. "The *Larchmont lockjaw* to which you referred is also known as *Locust Valley lockjaw* and *Main Line malocclusion*," writes Eve Golden of New York City. "If you want to hear two flawless examples, look for reruns of 'Gilligan's Island' and listen to Thurston Howell III (Jim Backus) or 'The Beverly Hillbillies' and Jane Hathaway (Nancy Kulp)."

What does this speech sound like? "The term describes a manner of speaking with the mouth opened as little as possible," observes Richard P. Hunt of New York City. "The enunciation is done principally by movement of the lips, producing a nasal tone. . . . Perhaps the Latin form would be *Tetanus Pretentious.*"

From the history department of Bowdoin College in Brunswick, Me., Daniel Levine provides us with instructions for imitating this aristocratic accent: "1. Open the jaws an eighth of an inch. 2. Press the tips of the lower incisors firmly against the inside of the upper incisors. 3. Without moving the jaw, and moving the lips as little as possible, say, in a low, Katharine Hepburn sort of voice, 'I'm *terribly* glad to have met you,' while implying that you are not terribly glad to have met them and wish that they would go away."

"It involves more than just an inflection," adds Robert Rylee of New York City, "but also the machination of a somewhat extended neck and taut lower jaw and lip, involving, I am sure, several sets of facial muscles." Luli Gray of New York City suggests the accent "can be approximated, if you are not bred to it, by placing a pencil crosswise just behind your eyeteeth and talking through it. In my boarding school days this was called *boarding school lockjaw.* . . . William F. Buckley speaks this way, without a pencil, no doubt through years of practice."

Because this form of speech is too breezily associated with a more serious affliction, we turn to Frank W. Mastrola, D.D.S., associate director of the Rhode Island Hospital's department of dentistry in Providence: "This method of speaking is accomplished by clenching the upper and lower teeth together, smiling and talking all at the same time. It requires an appropriate prep school education to talk as if you suffered from lockjaw, a form of the disease tetanus, in which the jaws become firmly closed because of spasmodic contractions of the muscles of mastication."

Well, which is it to be—Larchmont or Locust Valley? Willard Espy, the wordsman whose most recent book is *Words to Rhyme With: A Rhyming Dictionary,* recalls, "In the early 1930s, the expression *Larchmont lockjaw* was generally restricted to certain upper-class females from Westchester County, and the affliction was presumably the fault of the schools they attended."

That would locate an early use of the expression on the side of the sound that lies on the North American mainland. However, recent print citations tend to place the locus on Long Island's North Shore. In a 1981 article in *The New York Times* on learning to be a preppie at age thirty-seven, Rita Esposito Watson wrote, "One lovely lady—with *Locust Valley lockjaw*—asked, 'How, my deah, are you going to manage graduate school in teeny-tiny quarters without household help?' " A year later, in the same publication, Charlotte Curtis described an effusion by Gloria Vanderbilt as coming "in that locution so redolent of *Locust Valley lockjaw.*"

The term is geographically limited. In a 1982 *Times* article on the Parisian retailers like Berteil who catered to preppie tastes, John Vinocur—now editor of the *International Herald Tribune*—wrote: "French preppiedom is essentially an Anglophile graft, rather studied, and carries a genuine class feel. If you listen to the accents in Berteil, there's a good chance you'll hear some pure sixteenth arrondissement mumbling and diphthonging, an arch but rough equivalent of *Locust Valley lockjaw.*"

After reading your article, I tried to enunciate, pressing "the tips of the lower incisors firmly against the inside of the upper incisors," but it did not work. Perhaps one needs to be a member of the Larchmont Yacht Club to get the right drawl.

I would like, however, to point out a discrepancy between the description and the illustration, which shows a protrusion of the mandible where the incisors are in a reverse situation from what is described in the article. What the illustration shows is called prognathism, whereas the members of the yacht club affect a contraction of the facial muscles that results in a sardonic laugh, also seen in patients with tetanus.

Hector Bensimon, M.D.
McLean, Virginia

Neither Am I

In a piece about Larchmont (or Locust Valley) lockjaw, I mentioned Russell Baker and observed in passing that "neither Mr. Baker nor I am young or upwardly mobile."

"I couldn't believe you would write 'neither Mr. Baker nor I *am* young,'" writes Richard Dresselhuys of New York City. "The clause has a compound subject joined by a coordinate conjunction—*nor*—and requires the plural verb *are.* Gork!"

That's what *you* say, Mr. Gork. I have long been a believer in the Rule of Proximity: in a *neither/nor, either/or* or *not only/but also* construction, the verb should agree with the closest subject. I frequently sing to myself: "If my verb is not near the subject it loves, it agrees with the subject it's near."

Neither and *nor* were somewhat racily labeled by the grammarian George O. Curme as "copulative conjunctions" because they work as a pair—together, though not adjacent—to make connections. "Most grammarians prescribe that the verb should agree with the nearest subject," he wrote in his authoritative two-volume *A Grammar of the English Language,* and gave as his example: "Neither he nor I *am* in the wrong."

Randolph Quirk and his co-authors of a more recent grammar lean toward that Rule of Proximity in determining the person of the verb, using this example: "Neither you, nor I, nor anyone else knows the answer." *Knows,* the verb, agrees with the singular *anyone else* near it, not the whole crowd in the preceding list.

But there is something strange going on here that makes the most prestigious grammarians nervous.

"Most people desire to avoid the annoying necessity of making a choice between the two persons," says Curme. Quirk acknowledges that resistance: "Because of the awkwardness of this device, a speaker may avoid it." Quirk and Curme are joined by usage superstar Henry W. Fowler, who observed the complications that arise when the person or number of the *neither* differs from the person or number of the *nor*—"Neither eyes nor nose (does its? do their?) work"—and came to this conclusion: "The wise man, in writing, evades these problems" by "putting the thing in some other shape." Thus, the sanhedrin of great grammarians agrees with the pragmatic mouse who said to his colleagues, "To hell with the cheese—let's get out of the trap."

You win, Mr. Gork. You and my old inamorata, Norma Loquendi, triumph again. The Rule of Proximity has its exceptions, and the biggest of them is this: When it looks funny, don't argue the grammar; recast the sentence.

Neither Mr. Baker nor I am young looks funny. *Neither Mr. Baker nor I are young* looks just as funny. *Neither Mr. Baker is young, nor am I* is awkward, too. Keep your cheese; lemme out: *Mr. Baker is no spring chicken, nor am I, and neither one of us is upwardly mobile. . . .*

Invasion of the Arbs

The arbs are moving in. No, I am not using a clipped version of "labor arbitrators," or trying to pronounce "Arabs" in a single syllable, or clandestinely using the acronym for Angle Rate Bombing System.

The *arbs* are the *arbitrageurs*, who have taken the place of Bet-a-Million gates in the corporate crapshoot. "A call came in to Lehman Brothers from an *arb* and was transferred to me," said Dennis B. Levine to the Securities and Exchange Commission, before being charged with insider trading, ". . . so the arb got on and said, 'Are you guys involved in Textron?' "

The first use of this shortened locution I can find is in a glossary of takeover terminology in *Business Week*, May 16, 1977. The writer defined *arbitrageurs* as "stockmarket professionals who buy up huge quantities of a target's shares at prices below the takeover bid." (Arbs apparently "buy up" rather than merely buy.) This buying is encouraged by the group seeking to take over a company, because it puts large blocks of stock in the hands of short-term speculators; the arbs are usually the natural allies of the takeover crowd.

Curiously, the glossary used the short form—*arb*—only in passing, but the clip turned out to be as hardy as the whole word. Readers of this space bought at the low such phrases as *poison pill* (a device to make takeovers more difficult) and *white knight* (a friendly suitor who will guarantee nervous management platinum parachutes); in the past decade, other Wall Street nonce phrases have withered, such as *gray knight* (an opportunistic second bidder), *smoking gun* (a mistake by the shark that gives the target company a target of its own) and *show stopper* (a smoking gun the size of a cannon, such as an antitrust ruling that sends sharks and arbs scurrying).

Although *arb* is a noncontroversial clip, a donnybrook is shaping up over the spelling of the word it shortens. *Arbitrageur* is one of the more than twenty words in English with the French *-eur* suffix. We are all familiar with *amateur, saboteur, liqueur* and *restaurateur* (leave the n out of *restaurateur*), and some will even recall the *conglomerateurs* who used to make us all *migraineurs*; nobody is trying to Anglicize any of them.

But *arbitrageur* is under attack. In *The New York Times* the spelling *arbitrager* outnumbers its French counterpart 399 to 13. Why? Here's why: At the *Times*'s news desk, in a list of dos and don'ts (one of which is to spell *dos and don'ts* without all those apostrophes), somebody once specified a preference for the Anglicized version. No special reason; no explanation; just one of those decisions that did not seem to be a big deal at the moment it was made.

I protest, appeal and demand a new hearing. Webster's New World Dictionary prefers the *-eur* suffix, taking the *-er* grudgingly. Over at Merriam-Webster, the unabridged Third New International (1961) preferred *arbitrager*, but that was typical of the anything-goes edition; the new, more sensible Ninth New Collegiate edition prefers *arbitrageur*. "Since the Third," says Merriam-Webster editorial director Fred Mish, "*-eur* has been cited almost 2 to 1 in preference, and is found in a much wider variety of sources. I think that *-eur* is clearly the preferred spelling."

Yeah (not "yea," or "yeur"). I am fiercely nationalist to the point of jingoism, and can see the value in sometimes Anglicizing foreign words. When different alphabets are used, we must transliterate; that gives us the chance to clarify as we Anglicize, as in changing the Cyrillic *kosmonavt* to *cosmonaut*, or the Greek *mekhane* to *machine*. Sometimes we have to fix a borrowed word to conform to our tongues: the Portuguese *palavra*, which calls for a nice rolling of the tongue, became our more familiar *palaver*.

But sometimes linguistic chauvinism asks too much. If we knock over *arbitrageur* for the assimilated *arbitrager*, can an insipid *enterprener* be far behind? How about sneaking around looking through the keyhole of a *voyer*? Will the *arbitragers* be driven to work by gum-chewing, bare-headed *chauffers*?

Come ye back to *arbitrageur*, and if the *-eur* is hard to pronounce, slang it up with *arb*. Otherwise, as Poe never said to Helen. "Thy Naiad airs have brought me home/To the glory that was Greece,/And the *grander* that was Rome."

In addition to the ease of pronunciation, I would argue that there exists a precedent to Anglicize arbitrageur into arbitrager. Since the activity (arbitrage) undertaken by the activist (the arbitrageur) is an English word, it seems natural to create the descriptive noun "arbitrager." Just as fighters engage in fights, lovers pursue love, arbitragers undertake arbitrage. As long as chauffeurs cannot chauff, voyeurs cannot voy and amateurs cannot amat, the future of these words of French origin is safe.

Linda Allen
Oceanside, New York

The Greek word *mekhane* passed into Latin in the form *machina* and then into French as *machine*; the French word was borrowed into English without further change. What we have is thus a case of *Gallicizing*, not Anglicizing! (This information will be found in any standard dictionary.)

Louis Jay Herman
New York, New York

Arbitrageur, to my French ear, would be as much a barbarism as *arbitrager* to his. The real word is *arbitragiste*. Amateur, *saboteur, liqueur, restaurateur*, yes; *arbitrageur*, no.

The *arbitragistes*, in the old precomputer days, used to buy a stock on a certain stock market and sell it on another one. As you might imagine, having to deal in two different currencies, it required quite some skill. All the arbs of today have to do is to cash in on some indiscretion, free or bought.

Our old *arbitragistes* did not make as much money, but they were *clevereur*.

Jacques Lindon
Paris, France

Jiminy Cricket Sings Again

In 1970, the nation's campuses were erupting with demonstrations against the war in Vietnam, the best-selling novel was Erich Segal's *Love Story*, the most popular film was *Patton* and the top song was Simon and Garfunkel's "Bridge Over Troubled Water," and throughout the eastern United States you could hardly hear yourself think because of the chirping of the male cicadas.

Like Richard Nixon, the cicadas disappeared and made a comeback. Brood-10 cicadas—1987s variety of the inch-long winged insects wrongly referred to as "seventeen-year locusts"—were hanging from the fruit trees and dropping by the millions on cringing suburban passersby.

Cicada, pronounced si-KAY-da, is one of those words you need only once every seventeen years, and then you need it badly. It is not a locust, which destructively chews, whereas the cicada harmlessly sucks (I fully expect bumper stickers announcing "Cicadas Suck" on teenagers' cars in my neighborhood), and furthermore this all-too-reliable visitor, with the longest developmental cycle of any insect, is better than Halley's comet for marking eras.

You need an understanding of this word if you intend to cook out. Urban guests will say: "What's all that racket? And should the flames shoot up that high?" The asbestos-gloved host, unperturbed by having to wear earmuffs in June, will reply: "That's the mating call of the male *cicada*, and this is the way I barbecue."

The Latin name *cicada* is echoic, which means "imitative of the sound made by the thing it denotes," sometimes called onomatopoeic by the crowd that prefers longer Greek derivations. (Greek-speakers will call the same insect the *tettix*, because that's the way the call of the cicada or tree cricket sounded to ancient Athenian suburbanites; that ticking sound hardly resembles the whirring buzz of the Latin term. Perhaps an unpopular Brood-10 leader once said: *"Tettix, tettix* doesn't attract females for me anymore—what if I try *cicada?"*)

I don't know why the word is classified in dictionaries as echoic. Today the noise made by the insect does not sound like si-KAY-da to me; the disturbance squawk sounds like BRA-A-ACK; the congregational song, BUZZ-AYE-EE, and the mating call I am reluctant to commit to print lest the unsuspecting reader say it aloud and be swarmed over.

In newspaper stories and television broadcasts about this visitation, the definition is likely to be "a homopterous tree cricket," although crickets are of a different order of insect. People often use a scientific word like *homopterous* without a definition because it sounds pompously technical, as if to say: "I looked it up, and that's what it says in the dictionary; don't bother me with the meaning."

In the tribe of invertebrate animals called *arthropods*, there is a class labeled *Insecta*, within which we find an order called *Homoptera*. Entomologists know that the key element of this name is *pter*, from the Greek *pteron*, meaning "wing"; this type of winged insect is of an order with sucking mouthparts, which is why thoughtful teenagers would affix the bumper stickers to their cars as a useful mnemonic. (*Entomon* is Greek for "insect"; *etymos* is Greek for "true," particularly "the literal meaning according to origin." An annoyed etymologist says, "Buzz off, entomologist," when he wants to be onomatopoeically offensive.)

Ready for some heavy erudition to lay on back-seat barbecuers? Poetry lovers will note that poets prefer the Italian word *cicala*, pronounced si-KAH-la, to the Latin *cicada*. Byron, in "Don Juan," wrote of "the shrill cicalas, people of the pine," and Tennyson noted, "At eve a dry cicala sung."

That was the spelling also used by W. Rhys Roberts in translating one of my earliest predecessors, a Greek philologist named Demetrius Phalereus, who wrote his work on prose style, now known as *De Elocutione*, around the third century B.C. I tripped over this book, published in 1902 by Cambridge University Press, while browsing at Booked Up, a bookstore in Georgetown owned by Larry McMurtry, the novelist. (Owning a bookstore gives a writer an edge.)

Demetrius was impressed with allegorical language, and found delight in the brevity and force of messages that took advantage of widely known allusions. One example he gives is that of the defiant message of the Lacedaemonians to the threatening Philip, which read simply: "Dionysius at Corinth." As Demetrius puts it, "If they had expanded the thought at full length, saying 'Dionysius has been deposed from his sovereignty and is now a beggarly schoolmaster at Corinth,' the result would have been a bit of narrative rather than a taunt."

The Greek rhetorician again used Dionysius the Younger, tyrant of Syracuse, as an example of the suggestion of irony in what is called "covert allusion." (What has this to do with the damned noisy insects? Stick around.) "Great lords and ladies dislike to hear their own faults mentioned," writes Demetrius. "Accordingly, when counseling them to refrain from faults, we shall not speak in direct terms. We shall, rather, blame some other persons who have acted in the same way. For example, in addressing the tyrant Dionysius, we shall inveigh against the tyrant Phalaris and his cruelty. . . . The hearer is admonished without feeling himself censured." In modern times, this covert allusion has become known as the Adulatory Admonition of the White House Counsel.

Demetrius has a final example of the Lacedaemonians' natural turn toward the powerful use of language. "Brevity is, indeed, more forcible and peremptory," he writes, "while prolixity is suited for begging and praying. For this reason, symbolic expressions are forcible, as resembling brief utterances. We are left to infer the chief of the meaning from a short statement, as though it were a sort of riddle."

He cites the saying of the menacing Dionysius that the despot made before he was deposed and became a poorly paid teacher of rhetoric in Corinth: "Your cicalas shall chirp from the ground." Comments Demetrius on that allegorical threat referring to the crickets that live in the trees: "The saying 'Your cicalas shall chirp from the ground' is more forcible in this figurative form than if the sentence had simply run, 'Your trees shall be hewed down.' "

Put that on your outdoor grill and let the sparks fly upward. The summer song of the cicada has been sung for thousands of years. Not only did it provide the ancients with allegorical ammunition to deride former big shots reduced to miserable teachers of rhetoric, but also the damned recurrent chirping down the corridors of time has provided suitable allegorical material for writers on language.

I commend the ancient word picture to our arms-control negotiators in Geneva; when the Soviet statements resound with Dionysian rodomontade, come right back with a cool "Your cicalas (or cicadas) shall chirp from the ground." Let the decoding computers at the KGB figure that one out.

There are several ways of pronouncing Latin words, all of them justifiable, *unless* one is talking about echoic words. In that case, one should try to stick to the original sound that was imitating the real life sound.

In the case *cicada,* back in Vergil's day it was pronounced kih-KAH-dah, presumably because that's what they thought the bug sounded like. But within a couple of centuries, certainly by St. Augustine's time, they were saying *chih-KAH-dah,* not because the bug or their ears had changed, but because *c* was "palatized" when it came before *e* and *i.* This is the way the Italians still pronounce Latin (and so do most English speakers when pronouncing the Latin liturgy), but other countries adapted Latin to their own tongues: the Spanish said first *see-KAH-thah* and then *thee-KAH-thah* (a very foppish kind of tree-cricket), the Germans said *tsee-KAH-dah,* and so on. The Italians in their own language liquidized the *d* and came up with *chee-KAH-lah.*

In English, back in Chaucer's day, they said *sih-KAH-dah,* but by Shakespeare's time the great vowels had done their shifting and they were saying *suh-KAY-duh,* as many of us still do today; but I seem to hear a lot of Chaucerian accents for that particular word.

There is, in fact, quite a falling away from the English (Shakespearian) form for pronouncing Latin. Many persons insist on the classical (Ciceronian), but it seems rather affected to say for vice versa *WEE-kay WEAR-sah* rather than *VIGH-see VUR-suh;* however, it also seems affected in the case of exempli gratia to use the English *ex-EM-pligh GRAY-she-uh.* The Italianate *eggs-EM-plee GRAH-tsee-ah* seems most natural; the Chaucerian is about the same, except that the second word would be *GRAH-see-ah.*

A lot of Americans learned the Chaucerian pronunciation by being taught in the Jesuit high schools and universities of the Midwest and West, though they called it the Continental system.

Andy Kelly
Department of English
University of California, Los Angeles
Los Angeles, California

"Cicada" is not echoic; however, Mexicans (and some Southwestern North Americans) do come echoically close with *their* pronunciation. They use the word *chicharra* (chi-CHA-rrrra), strongly emphasizing the double "r," instead of "cicada."

Chicharra colloquially means: an extremely talkative woman; a kazoo, or a plaything. *Cantar la chicharra* translates as "to be scorching hot." The verb *chicharrar* is a "shortening" of *achicharrar* which means "to fry too much." *Chicharron* is fried pork rind which makes a loud sizzling noise while frying.

Rudy Leal
New York, New York

1. You used the word "tribe" to describe the Arthropoda. This is wrong. Arthropoda is a phylum. Zoological classification has a strict hierarchy as follows:

Kingdom
Phylum
Class
Order
Family
Genus
Species

Tribes are an optional subdivision between family (actually subfamily) and genus.

2. You state that "It is not a locust, which destructively chews, whereas the cicada harmlessly sucks." We've enclosed an excerpt from the book Eastern Forest Insects which contains some information regarding the physical damage to trees and shrubs caused by cicadas. While it's true that cicadas suck, this clearly is not a method of feeding that causes no harm.

We also thought you might be interested in the fact that "homo" in the name Homoptera refers to the fact that the front and hind wings are similar.

Ann E. Hajek, Ph.D.
Visiting Fellow

James K. Liebherr, Ph.D.
Assistant Professor of Entomology
Cornell University
Ithaca, New York

The Juddering Juice Shtick

"Britain's steadily growing prosperity," boasted Nigel Lawson, the British Treasury Minister, "is not some short-lived boom, which could come to a juddering halt at any moment." Only a year before, the leader of Britain's Labor Party, Neil Kinnock, expressed the hope that America's policy toward Nicaragua would be "brought to a juddering halt."

Juddering is an arresting modifier for *halt.* I had circled that participle in a Mercedes-Benz ad: "In place of juddering tires comes an unflustered negotiation of the road's flaws." My own car—a 1969 Cougar on its way to becoming a classic if it doesn't judder itself to an early junkyard—shakes and rattles and, let's face it, becomes hopelessly flustered when negotiating the road's flaws, which it calls "potholes."

The word is often used to knock engines that knock. Marshall Schuon, writing in praise of the Corvette in *The New York Times* in 1980, cautioned that the stiff suspension, so road-gripping on smooth terrain, "goes into its oh-wow frenzy" on rough roads, "juddering and slewing and causing the plastic body to creak and slam. . . ."

This is an 1800s English dialect word from Suffolk and Somerset that is now making it in the United States. Although *quivering halt* is still the preferred cliché, *juddering* is filling a need for a noisier modifier. In 1902, the verb *judder* appeared in the English Dialect Dictionary as a variant of *jouder,* defined as "to rattle, shake, jar," with an 1892 citation defining the sound resulting from it as "such as is caused by machinery 'knocking' when some part is not going smoothly." In his first novel, *Hatter's Castle,* A. J. Cronin in 1931 wrote of a train "juddering in every bolt and rivet of its frame as the hurricane assaulted. . . ."

When to use it? *Jolting* and *bumping* connote a series of shocks. *Vibrating, oscillating, shaking, shuddering, trembling* and *quivering* call up movement back and forth, with *joggling* the slightest of shakes and with *quaking* and *quavering* most closely associated with fear. *Bumping, knocking* and *rattling* are used to show how noisy the shakiness can be. *Juddering* carries both the bumpiness of *jolt* and the shakiness of *shudder,* and may have been coined by combining the two words.

Judder is also a technical term for the big wave in the voice of an aging singer who can no longer emit a clear single note. The word is used in this sense more frequently in England than over here, but it is not an isolated Britishism.

Apropos of your treatment of the word in the primary sense, there is also the phrase "come to a shuddering halt." I haven't looked it up, but it may be that the *sh* and *j* are variants.

Jacques [Barzun]
Charles Scribner's Sons
New York, New York

Re "Juddering": there is another use of the word, also very British. When I was covering motor racing in the golden years of Jaguar at LeMans, etc., juddering was something brakes did when not well adjusted. I believe the term applied particularly to drum brakes, before the coming of discs. Drivers would screech into pits and announce that the brakes were "juddering"—i.e. that they were not smooth when applied, that they had a washboard feeling. This use of the word juddering would seem to work better with the phrase "juddering halt" than with some of the others. I always thought of it as quite onomatopoetic.

Charles N. Barnard
Cos Cob, Connecticut

On a recent trip to Australia and New Zealand, I discovered that the folks down-under do not employ the common U.S. road-building term "speed bumps." The Aussies call them instead "road humps" and the Kiwis call them "judder bars."

Herbert B. Landau
New York, New York

In New Zealand, "judder" is in common, rather than trendy use. Those long, low mounds to slow cars called here traffic bumps or speed bumps are there called judder bars on the official warning signs. I have heard of their being called sleeping policemen, I believe in the Caribbean.

Margaret Holton
Seattle, Washington

You call *quivering halt* "the preferred cliché."
But what about the recurrent combinations *a grinding halt* and *a screeching halt* as in *to come to a grinding/screeching halt?*

Morton Benson
Philadelphia, Pennsylvania

Just Routine Tests

"It's time we knew exactly what we were facing," said President Reagan, mistakenly using the past tense *were* to parallel *knew* in a speech about AIDS, "and that's why I support some *routine* testing."

He did not explain what *routine* would mean in connection with federal testing of immigrants, inmates of federal prisons and patients at veterans' hospitals, but the word was central to his approach: "I encourage states to offer *routine* testing for those who seek marriage licenses. . . . And I encourage states to require *routine* testing in state and local prisons."

The question immediately arose: Would *routine* mean "mandatory, compulsory"? And if so, why didn't he use one of those hard, clear words?

First to the ordinary meaning of *routine.* Rooted in the French *route,* "traveled way, regular course," the noun was adopted into English by Samuel Butler prior to 1680 in this sentence: "The general Business of the World lies, for the most Part, in Rotines and Forms."

Then the noun was used attributively, modifying another noun. *Routine task* was born in 1817 (the label, not the action), and the word was officially dubbed a full-fledged adjective in the Oxford English Dictionary Supplement in 1982 with the meaning "mechanical, unvaried," the sort of activity that drives imaginative types bananas. A frequent synonym is *hum-drum,* an irregular reduplication of *hum* that epitomizes boredom. Teenagers' slang still uses *baw-RING* to describe routine tasks.

Is that what the President meant? Of course not; *routine* has gained another sense in its adjectival state, more mollifier than qualifier. The phrase *routine tests* is used by people going into hospitals to cover both ordinary periodic examinations and treatment for ailments. It is a soothing phrase, which seems to add "nothing to worry about."

That soothing connotation is what the President and his writers sought in using a word for a policy that means *mandatory,* "commanded," or *compulsory,* "forced." Gary L. Bauer, the President's domestic policy adviser who knows what Mr. Reagan has in mind, told me plainly enough that "routine testing at the federal level does not include the right to opt out." (*Opt out* is an academic-bureaucratic vogue term meaning "choose not to," obliterating the useful distinction between the thoughtful *choose* and the impulsive *opt.*)

The feeling the President and his advisers wanted to get across is that the mandatory testing is to be applied in the regular course of human activity, part of what seems a *normal, customary, usual, regular* process. Immigrants are normally tested for communicable diseases; patients being admitted to federal hospitals are regularly given blood tests; prisoners are periodically checked for evidence of disease.

The compulsion is not out of the ordinary in these instances; hence, it can be called *routine.* It is doubtless mandatory, but the harshness of its unavoidability is tempered by the assurance that it is being done all the time as part of something else. The point being made by the use of the mollifying word is that the populace is not being told to line up next Tuesday at noon for testing for this specific purpose—or else.

A further confusion was introduced by officials of the Justice Department who said that they were considering *random* testing of prisoners. That word, rooted in "run," means "haphazard, aimless, purposeless"; Bennett Cerf and Donald Klopfer wanted "to publish a few books on the side, at random," and named their company Random House. The word has become a term of art in the polling field, as a sampling technique in which each element has an equal probability of occurrence. Such testing is almost always voluntary, but in a random sample of federal prisoners or members of the armed forces, better not try to opt out.

In the medical profession, the phrase "routine test" often refers to studies done on patients who do not exhibit any specific symptoms or sign which would otherwise indicate a need for those tests. A blood count (CBC) or serum potassium might be ordered on all patients scheduled for surgery and not due to any suspicion of anemia or electrolyte imbalance.

Perhaps that is the sense intended by the advocates of routine

AIDS (HIV) testing. Requiring the test "routinely" would not imply any association with known risk groups (other than the human race).

Dennis E. Novak, M.D.
Forked River, New Jersey

Speaking as an academic who teaches about bureaucracy, I must object. An opt-out provision refers to a situation where something will happen unless specific action is taken to avoid that event. Book and record clubs provide an example. Members are informed about the selection of the month, which is sent (and billed) unless the member acts affirmatively to decline the book or record. (This is called a negative option plan.) Many books and records are sold in this manner to club members who do not want them. (Indeed, that is how owners of book and record clubs make money.) Computer people refer to what happens in the absence of an opt-out decision as the default settings. Computers do all sorts of things in the absence of contrary instruction.

My area of special expertise, the regulation of depository institutions (banks, thrift associations, and credit unions), provides a good example of an opt-out provision. A 1980 federal law preempted certain state usury laws, subject to an opt-out provision that permitted a state to negate the federal law by the adoption of legislation to that effect. See S. Huber, *Bank Officer's Handbook of Government Regulation*, paragraph 15.07 (1984). (The default settings on my computer do not include a paragraph symbol, and I do not know how to opt out of this choice.) The federal law governs in the absence of subsequent state opt-out legislation. The federal law changed the status quo in a major way. It made a choice and then offered the states a route to making a different decision. Opting out may be easy in principle but it is difficult in practice, and few states have done so.

Normally when a person is presented with a choice, the status quo remains in the absence of specific action, whether thoughtful or impulsive. An opt-out provision arises in situations where change occurs in the absence of contrary action. The choice not to purchase the monthly selection of a book club is different from the choice not to purchase a book after browsing in a book store. The phrase "opt out" captures that difference.

Stephen K. Huber
Professor of Law
University of Houston
Houston, Texas

The term "opt out" is used in the legal fraternity largely with reference to class actions, where a notice is typically sent to the members of the putative class advising them of the action filed on their behalf, and of their right to be excluded from the class if they give notice to the court by a specified date. This latter process is what lawyers refer to as "opting out," again a choice to be exercised after thoughtful consideration and not impulsively.

The only context in which I sense even a smattering of impulsiveness in the world of options is in the option play in football, where the quarterback sometimes thrusts the ball to a tailing running back in what seems an impulsive manner. However, it is the suddenness of the lateral which gives the appearance of impulsiveness; in fact, the quarterback's choice is based upon his reading of the reaction of the defense, and not on impulse (in the sense of a spontaneous impetus not based upon rational considerations).

Raymond F. Zvetina
Haskins, Nugent, Newnham, Kane & Zvetina
San Diego, California

Teenagers in this part of the country use "Bow-ring" or, better yet, "Boar-ring."

Usually, it is the teenagers' slang which is boring. Particularly odious is the constant use of the verb "go" to describe all manner of narrative forward motion.

For example, "I go 'What a hunk.' Then she goes 'Oh no what a clod! You gotta be kidding.' Then Roger goes 'Why don't we just get on with the assignment?' But Jennifer goes 'Oh, yech, boar-RING.' "

Stephen P. Smith III
Jacksonville, Florida

Know Ye by These Presents

No gift at Christmastime reflects better on the giver than the gift of gab. Here are books about words that will enliven debates, illuminate issues, prop up little kids at the table and prevent doors from slamming shut.

New Big Guy

The Random House Dictionary of the English Language: Second Edition-Unabridged is the big book for word mavens. At 2,500 pages, 315,000 entries—50,000 of them new—it weighs more than 13 pounds.

A good new unabridged delivers a deep draught of the language as it stands today. If you're waiting for the Fourth New International edition of the unrivaled Merriam-Webster unabridged, don't hold your breath; I suspect we won't see it until the late 1990s. The R.H.D. II is here now, when we need it. The usual controversy about whether the work is too permissive is a phony: it should report the language as used, and it should also specify when usage is considered slang or substandard. That's what the R.H.D. II does with the acceptable *hopefully* and the hopeless *irregardless.*

You might expect a dictionary edited by Stuart Berg Flexner, the world's leading slanguist, to be deep into dialect. He will feed you a *hero sandwich* overstuffed with delectable regional variations: *hoagie, poor boy, sub, grinder, wedge* and *torpedo.*

Thanks to the pioneering work by Fred Cassidy's Dictionary of American Regional English, an entry such as *pancake* has more than the usual differentiation of *griddlecake, hot cake* and *flapjack*; Southerners use *battercake* for what some Northerners call *flannel cake,* and someone driving from the Northeast to the Southwest is likely to encounter *johnnycake, corncake* and *hoecake.* (Now you're talkin' *dictionary.*)

Pronunciation notes are a useful new feature. Look up *junta*; after informing us that the word was Anglicized to JUN-tuh in the 1600s, the lexicographer points out that in the twentieth century we have seen "the gradual predominance of the pronunciation HOON-tuh [*oo,* as in *book*], derived from Spanish HOON-ta [*oo,* as in *boot*], through reassociation with the word's Spanish origins. A hybrid form HUN-tuh is also heard."

On *exquisite* and *harass,* the R.H.D. II goes with the more common accent on the second syllable, which will evoke petulant scowls on the faces of traditionalists; however, Flexner & Company takes pains to point out that the controversy exists, which is all a reporter should do. If you find the pronunciation shift lamentable, you will be pleased that the R.H.D. II still calls that LAM-en-ta-ble, although most people I know say la-MEN-ta-ble when they pull a long face.

The illustrations are usually put in for a semantic purpose, not just to pretty up the page: the *Rhodesian Ridgeback* is a dog with a funny-looking spine, and is so shown. I don't know if I would have put in the whole dancer when showing her *leg warmers,* but was glad to see a picture of a *havelock,* that flap of fabric that hangs down the back of a hat to protect the neck.

New words? *Zap,* that exciting imitative verb from World War II, made it as "to kill or shoot," with the additional modern sense of deleting television commercials by pressing the fast-forward button on the videocassette recorder. The Britishism *dishy,* "attractive," has a second meaning of "gossipy" that was news to me, while the slang Americanism *ditzy,* "flighty," is analyzed by an astute etymologist as having perhaps been influenced by *dotty* and *dizzy.* The meanings of *networking* as a noun are nicely split between "supportive system of sharing information and services among individuals and groups having a common interest" and the design of a computer network.

To nitpick ("to be excessively concerned with or critical of inconsequential details"), I wonder whether one alphabetical entry for all uses makes it harder to find the meaning you want. The word *eye,* for example, is both noun and verb, so the R.H.D. II has one long entry including forty-nine senses of the noun followed by the transitive and intransitive verb forms; it's easier on the eye not to run them together that way.

And some characters are chosen oddly: *Laertes* is listed as the father of Odysseus in classical mythology, but most of us know him as the son of Polonius in *Hamlet*. (That's a cheap shot; is *cheap shot* in? Yop: "a covert, unsportsmanlike and illegal act of deliberate roughness." Is *yop* in? Nope: only *yep* and *yup*. Get with it, Flexner; in New Yorkese, it's *yop*.)

"It may be too blue-eyed for anyone to believe," says lexicographer Flexner, "but we did this not for profit but for the sake of producing the finest dictionary that was in us." *Blue-eyed?* There it is, the second and nonliteral meaning: "having or representing childlike innocence."

In My Cozy Morris Chair

When Barbra Streisand was singing Irving Berlin's "All by Myself," she came across the lyric "in my cozy Morris chair" and interjected, "And what is a Morris chair?"

The answer can be found in the Facts on File Encyclopedia of Word and Phrase Origins by Robert Hendrickson. William Morris (not the co-author of the Morris Dictionary of Word and Phrase Origins, and not the theatrical agent) was a nineteenth-century poet and pamphleteer who helped establish England's Socialist Party. He was also a furniture manufacturer who led the arts-and-crafts movement, which changed the Victorian tastes of his time: "Among the furniture made by the company was the *Morris chair*, a large easy chair with an adjustable back and removable cushions."

This feast for phrase detectives also corrects us on *Tinkers to Evers to Chance*, the double-play specialists of the Chicago Cubs in the early 1900s. Not only was their fame suspect (the trio averaged only fourteen double plays a year from 1906 to 1909), but also the name of the short-stop is continually misstated. He was Joe Tinker, not Tinkers, enshrined at Cooperstown's Hall of Fame, and you can win a bag of peanuts on his real name every time.

The compiler of this compendium also saw fit to include this estimate of "the three major administrative problems on U.S. college campuses" by Clark Kerr, the California educator: "sex for the students, athletics for the alumni, and parking for the faculty."

You were in error when you cited Irving Berlin's "All By Myself" as the source for Barbra Streisand's interjection, "And what is a Morris chair?" It actually occurred in her 1963 recording of "My Honey's Lovin' Arms," a tune by Joseph Meyer with lyrics by Herman Ruby.

Mr. Ruby used the allusion to "a cozy Morris Chair," in referring to his honey's lovin' arms as "a place to nestle when I am lonely." The song was written in 1922. Berlin's "All By Myself" was written a year earlier. (I just thought I'd throw that in.)

Bob Allen
Long Island, New York

The Iscious Factor

onfusion Reigns is subtitled *A Quick & Easy Guide to the Most Easily Mixed-Up Words*, by James S. Harrison with mind-tickling illustrations by Kimble Mead. This paperback (St. Martin's Press) offers us needed differentiation, as in *"Equable* means steady, even. *Equitable* means fair and square, evenhanded." I am especially grateful for *obelisk/odalisque:* "A pillar with a pyramid-shaped top is an *obelisk.* An *odalisque,* once a female inhabitant of a Turkish harem, is now seen only in paintings, usually reclining on her side in a sultry pose." Tip for hostesses: "Canapés are always served on toast. . . . *Hors d'oeuvres* . . . usually appear by themselves."

Grammar Girl

n *Quiddities: An Intermittently Philosophical Dictionary* (Harvard University Press), by W. V. Quine, the teacher often called a *polymath*, or "person of encyclopedic learning," offers a gallimaufry of high-intensity linguistic musings.

Among them is this etymological gem: *"glamour* and *grammar* are in origin one and the same word. . . . There were secluded stretches of eighteenth-century Scotland in which the grammar school, or its master, came in the shepherd's mind to epitomize learning. Through hyperbole and liveliness of imagination the word then came to connote magic, and it was with this connotation that the word, distorted by then to *glamour,* was insinuated into standard English by Sir Walter Scott."

Let It Snow

"Do you suspect," asked Cable News Network's Bernard Shaw of President Reagan, "that Gorbachev thinks he can do a snow job on the American people?" The President ducked the question, but the phrase came up again during summit week, this time as a verb in a comment by Malcolm Forbes, who had been in a meeting with the Soviet leader: "The fact that he mixes a little venom with the candor—he unloaded on the press people he met—to me, it lends credence to the fact that he's not trying to snow-job us."

A *snow job* is a line of patter intended to persuade or deceive. The noun phrase first appeared in the *American Mercury* of November 1943, in the article "Service Man's Slang" by Albert A. Ostrow. According to Ostrow, when a G.I. meets a woman at a dance, "he tries a snow job on her (hands her a line) and if she falls for it she's been *snowed under*." Where did it come from? Perhaps the 1880s term *snowed under*, which means "overwhelmed" (and why that phrase should not be *snowed over* I don't know). Other theories exist, including *snow* as a slang synonym for cocaine, also a white substance.

The phrase has evidently filled a void in the language. Its most popular synonym, *line*, was born in the early 1900s: "Are you handing me a line of bogus conversation?" asked a character in Hugh McHugh's 1903 novel, *Out for Coin.* A more famous use is in F. Scott Fitzgerald's 1920 novel, *This Side of Paradise:* "Lordy, Isabelle—this *sounds* like a line, but it isn't." However, this sense of *line* has competed with the 1890s sense of political party line, especially the *general line* of the Communist Party.

In the lingo of ingratiation, *spiel* is still with us, from the German *spielen,* "to play, gamble," which led to a meaning of "glib talk" among grafting politicians around the turn of the century.

But neither *line* nor *spiel* has the wide usage of *snow job.* The verb is being clipped to a simple *snow,* as in "Surely Mr. Gorbachev wouldn't be trying to snow us with this bill of goods in Krasnoyarsk."

When, in 1933, '34 and '35, I was on the staff of *The Dartmouth,* the student daily of Dartmouth College, the denizens of our ski-tracked Hanover, New Hampshire, campus spent a lot of their time "snowing" Smith girls, and others. "Snow job" was common in our lexicon and on our pages. Among the paper's off-campus readers who were fascinated by undergraduate parlance was B. P. Schulberg, the Hollywood producer and father of not-yet-novelist Budd, my 1936 classmate and competitor for a top job on the daily. (We called this rat race "heeling" for the paper). Around the time Budd told staffers of B.P.'s interest, the lexicographer Wilfred Funk wrote a magazine article that found college kids a strong force for change in the language. Since Budd knew many film writers, several of us—including Maurice Rapf '35, the son of M-G-M studio boss Harry Rapf—put together a short list of zippy Hanover locutions for his ink-stained wretches to insinuate into films. (We held the list to three or four; the only one besides "snow job" that I remember was "to put on the tear-bag," or just "tear-bag," v., i., to whine or weep copiously.) For a couple of years we waited and watched, catching many a stinker at the Nugget, Hanover's one-screen cinema complex, in the process. "Snow job" made it into one B movie, its title lost to posterity.

Frank K. Kappler
Ardsley-on-Hudson, New York

As an erstwhile ticket taker (Wilbur, Boston) I can hear thousands of theater people all over saying, "Come on." Snow means paper. "Good crowd tonight," I say to the manager. "All snow," he replies. The house has been papered: free passes to fill seats and mask big trouble. Snow and papered are interchangeable.

Earl Hills
Saugus, Massachusetts

I jumped at Malcolm Forbes's saying: "lends credence to the fact . . ." *Credence* is believing, and only a person can lend it or possess it. He meant "lend credibility," after which *he* could lend credence.

Why do you think the phrase should be snowed *over?* Surely the image is "buried in snow = snowed *under."* You might launch *blizzarded.* Why don't you?

Jacques [Barzun]
Charles Scribner's Sons
New York, New York

Let Us Distance Ourselves

D on't crowd me; I'm distancing myself from the hottest cliché in Scandalville.

"The distancing of himself from Administration actions," wrote Helen Thomas of United Press International, "puts in question the role of Secretary of State George Shultz. . . ."

Robert Craig, a political scientist at the University of New Hampshire, said Vice President Bush "wants to distance himself from the Administration but he can't do that," U.P.I. reported.

A *New York Times* report concerning White House chief of staff Donald T. Regan read: "The National Security Council 'does not report to me,' Mr. Regan declared Nov. 26 in an apparent effort to distance himself from the scandal."

Although the verb phrase *keep one's distance from*, as well as the more loyal *go the distance*, is in most dictionaries, and *distance* as a transitive verb is listed as meaning "to place at some distance," lexicographers neglect the reflexive verb form, which is outdistancing every other use of the word in the general lifting of skirts and tiptoeing-away.

Even the sports pages have adopted the vogue usage: George Raveling tried his best, wrote the *Los Angeles Times* about the basketball star, "to distance himself from all the emotions of coming back to Pullman and coaching against his former team."

That takes distancing oneself too far; the transitive *deny* or *suppress* would work better on emotions, though if you're determined to be intransitive, you could *separate yourself from* them.

Leave the self-distancing to people worried about the taint of scandal. "H. R. Haldeman," wrote Peter Goldman in *Newsweek* in 1975, "professed continuing loyalty to Nixon and yet seemed at moments almost eager to distance himself from him."

A related phrase is *out of the loop,* which is the condition you are in when all your colleagues have distanced themselves from you. "A lot of the people he cut out of the loop are gunning for him," a White House aide was quoted as saying about Donald Regan. The *loop* was a term in electrical circuitry that was adopted by automation theorists to describe operations in which a *closed loop* provided the machine the feedback to control itself. Now to be *in the loop* is to be in the circle of power, and to be *out of the loop* is not to have to worry about a special prosecutor coming after you.

The long self-distancing runners of today find their patron in the prophet Isaiah, who coined a memorable phrase in quoting the non-kosher incense-burners who distanced themselves from him: "Stand by thyself, come not near to me; for I am holier than thou."

> "Distance him/herself" is perfectly normal usage in public German *(sich distanzieren)* and also, I think, in French *(s'éloigner)*. This reminded me, in turn, of other clear and present Germanisms that have somehow turned up here in recent years including "oversight" in the sense of supervision *(Aufsicht)*, "time frame" *(Zeitrahmen)* or the ubiquitous "point in time" *(Zeitpunkt)*.
>
> David Schoenbaum
> Professor of History
> The University of Iowa
> Iowa City, Iowa

Long Time No See

When Jewish leaders met at the Vatican with church leaders to prepare a joint communiqué to be issued at the close of a meeting with Pope John Paul II, Rabbi Marc H. Tanenbaum of the American Jewish Committee noted a surprisingly informal construction in the Catholic draft. The document referred to the president of the Commission for Religious Relations With the Jews as "Cardinal John Willebrands."

"Shouldn't this read 'His Eminence, John Cardinal Willebrands'?" asked the rabbi, referring to the ancient, formal style stemming from the time the nobility put the Christian name before the title, as in "William, Duke of Norfolk."

"We don't do that anymore," said Cardinal Willebrands cheerfully, and into the historic communiqué went a couple of references to cardinals using the title before the first name.

The statement read: "On Tuesday morning, the Jewish delegation met with Cardinal Agostino Casaroli." That was how the text appeared in *The New York Times*, but the accompanying news story clung grimly to the old ways: "This morning the Jews met with Agostino Cardinal Casaroli." In some matters, *The Times* thinks in terms of centuries.

The Associated Press Stylebook goes with the new form, and most newspapers are adopting it. "There has been no formal decree to change the placement of *Cardinal* from its traditional use after the first name," says a spokesman for the National Conference of Catholic Bishops in Washington. "It has become an informal option."

Mebbeso, but priests who want to get in tune with the latest Vatican usage will probably take this communiqué as their keynote. Personally, I hate to see the archaic usage go—we have few enough reminders of our linguistic heritage—but the adoption of the modern form will simplify matters for those outside the church who wondered why so many church leaders had the same middle name.

An interesting choice of a verb in the statement suggested that men of good will found an acceptable euphemism to paper over a problem: "Regarding the state of Israel, the Cardinal [Casaroli] stated that while diplomatic relations have not been 'perfected,' there do exist good relations on many levels." The Vatican has resisted establishing normal diplomatic relations with the State of Israel perhaps out of fear of reprisal against Christians in some Moslem states. The use of *perfected*—from the Latin *perficere*, "to make complete, finish, accomplish"—subtly suggests that the matter is in the process of completion. The decision to put the word in quotation marks indicates that it was a word used by Cardinal Casaroli that the Jewish leaders wanted directly attributed to him.

Sharp eyes reading the text of the communiqué in *The New York Times* noted that the word *state* in "state of Israel" was not capitalized. In *Times* style, one does not capitalize *state*, for example, in "the state of New York," unless the reference is to the state's government, as in "the State of New York's suit against. . . ." Was the Vatican trying to slip around recognizing the existence of Israel's government in its lack of capitalization? No; a tracking of the text back to the source shows that "the State of Israel" was the original reading, with the capital *s* lost in the transcription. (You think nobody reads this kind of writing closely? Read on.)

"It was also noted," read the communiqué, "that Nazi ideology was not only anti-Semitic but also profoundly demonic and anti-Christian." *Demonic* is an adjective that has special resonance for theologians, who take demons seriously; a synonym is *satanic*. The Jewish drafters were aware of millenarian cosmology, which holds that the Christ and Antichrist will do battle at some future Armageddon; for centuries, many priests identified the Jews with the Antichrist, and icons often pictured Jews as demonlike. In this statement, the use of *demonic* to describe Nazism breaks the libelous link between Jews and demons, placing Christians and Jews on the same side against the satanic Hitler.

Another significant usage: "The agenda for the meeting included the Shoah (Holocaust)." *Shoah* is a Hebrew word for "catastrophe," also described in some Hebrew-English dictionaries as "destruction, ruin." It was used soon after World War II to describe the attempted extermination of Europe's Jews. (If anybody has early printed citations, send them along.) In Hebrew and Yiddish, *churban,* "destruction"—specifically, the destruction of the Temple in Jerusalem—was often used to describe the death of six million. In English, the word *holocaust* (from the Greek *holokaustos,* "burnt whole") first appeared in the language around 1250, in a biblical song telling the story of Abraham's willingness to sacrifice his son, Isaac, as a burnt offering to God. In its application to the Nazi era, the capitalized word was used first in this specific sense in the title of a 1965 book of memoirs about the Warsaw ghetto by Alexander Donat, *The Holocaust Kingdom.*

However, the word *holocaust,* even when capitalized to refer to the specific Nazi era, has been used to encompass more than the murder of Jews. From the casualties in our Civil War (then described as "a holocaust of lives") to the wholesale murder of gypsies in World War II to later genocide in Cambodia, the coverage of the term has not been limited to any single group; hence, Jews sought a term for their particular tragedy. *Shoah,* a Hebrew word, has filled that need; Claude Lanzmann used the word to title his powerful 1985 documentary, a nine-hour oral and visual history of the killing. The Catholic Church's use of *Shoah* in this context in recent years shows its willingness to acknowledge the uniqueness of Jewish suffering.

"Citing the Exodus of the Jewish people from Egypt as a paradigm. . . ." The Pope used the word *paradigm* in his meeting to show how "evil can be overcome in history, even the awesome evil of the Shoah." Some of the Jewish leaders took *paradigm*—"model, example, pattern, archetype"—as a word they could apply to the aftermath of the Pope's reception of Austria's Kurt Waldheim, a member of a unit that deported Jews to their deaths. These leaders held that out of evil could come good, and saw in the Pope's use of *paradigm* an oblique hint at what good could follow the widespread dismay of Jews at that much-criticized papal audience. That strikes me as stretching the word a bit, evidence of Talmudic overinterpretation, but not every brother can paradigm.

That was a pun, as is the title of this piece. In the phrase *Holy See,* the word *see* comes from the Latin *sedes,* "seat"; the Holy See is the throne, or seat of power, of Catholicism. A *Washington Post* editorialist, seeking a pithy headline a few years ago for a piece about Washington's decision to establish full diplomatic relations with the Vatican, suggested "Long Time No See." It was rejected lest it be construed as irreverent, but the unwritten headline's consideration should not go unrecorded.

Loop the Loop

W hen George Bush explained that he was *out of the loop* on Iran-contra matters in 1985, he used a Washington expression of disputed etymological origin. Some say the *loop* began as a term for a conference or network—"the Big Ten Loop"—drawn from a circle formed by a rope. Others point to a term in electrical circuitry, later adopted by automation terminology, in which a closed loop enables a machine to munch on its feedback and thereby regulate itself.

Written citations before 1970 would be of help. Meanwhile, we find the latest loop-to-do in Hedrick Smith's *The Power Game: How Washington Works*, under the heading "Are You in the Loop?"

Test of loopmanship: being on the short list of distribution of secret stuff. My idea of being in the loop has always been to be a recipient of the *NID*, the *National Intelligence Daily*, a précis of the overnight take of the intelligence community. That's limited to the 200 people in government who have to be in the knowiest know.

"Even more rarefied, however," writes Rick Smith in this most inside new book, "is another, smaller intelligence document: the 'FTPO'—'For the President Only.' White cover . . . likely to have inside tips on the health of a foreign leader whom the President is meeting . . . often contains 'SCI'—Secret Compartmented Information—circulated only on a 'need-to-know' basis. . . . Only about twenty people qualify to see it—the President, Vice President, their chiefs of staff and the innermost of the national security circle."

That's your loop of loops. And the Veep is inside.

   Let me be one of the first ten thousand to tell you that "The Loop" is the heart of Chicago. So called because the elevated railway conducts a loop around the principal stores, like Marshall Field, the principal hotels, like the Palmer House, and also the largest banks and financial institutions.

   So to be in "The Loop" is to be in the center of what's going on. I am not a Chicagoan, but New York businessmen of my acquaintance all refer to The Loop as the place to be in. How do you like that preposition?

                                                              Edward Greeman
                                                              Bay Harbor Islands, Florida

Madam, I'm Adam

Nothing beats catching a great editor in an error. Howard Simons, former managing editor of the *Washington Post* and now head of the Nieman Fellows program at Harvard, teamed up with (he would cut the *up*) Haynes Johnson, the columnist, to produce an edge-of-the-seat page-turner of a novel about Nazi sabotage and assassination in Washington during World War II called *The Landing* (Villard Books).

Here we are in a tense and steamy scene, which is not indicative of the rest of this well-researched book, but keeps you on your toes. The Nazi is having his way with a Washington prostitute named Odessa, cries out in German and must then kill her. His murder weapon is a knotted watch chain.

"He quickly slipped the chain around Odessa's neck," write Simons and Johnson. "He gripped the watch and T bar tightly and pulled sharply. The knot caught her Adam's apple. Odessa tried to scream, but managed only a gurgle. . . ."

I tried to scream, "Women don't have Adam's apples!" but managed only a gurgle: "It's a secondary sex characteristic." After finishing the chapter, I looked it up to chastise the editor whose previous experience with throats was during Watergate.

Adam's apple is taken literally from the Hebrew *tappuah haadam.* The *apple* is a round projection, and *Adam* is a man. The legend associated with the phrase is that in the Garden of Eden, Adam took a bite of the forbidden apple, and part of it stuck in his throat. The projection is the largest laryngeal cartilage in the front of the throat and is found mainly and most pronouncedly in men.

Although the characteristic is thought to be male, research shows that many women have Adam's apples, too, some of them—usually in those with skinny necks who gulp a lot—pronounced. The authors are not in error. Rats.

According to your column, "Adam's apple" is taken from Hebrew *tappuah haadam.* I find the same error in my 1970 American Heritage Dictionary. We biblicists attempt, often in vain, to convince people that the fruit eaten by Adam was not specified by the Hebrew author of the second and third chapters of Genesis. Readers of the Vulgate Bible probably supplied the apple because of the similarity between Latin *malus* "bad" and Latin *malum* "apple." My O.E.D. does not list a citation for "Adam's apple" earlier than the eighteenth century. As correctly noted in the authoritative *Hammillon Hehadash* (New Hebrew Dictionary) compiled by Abraham Even-Shoshan (Jerusalem, 1975: Kiryath Sepher Publishers), Hebrew *tappuah haadam* is a modern expression derived from English "Adam's apple."

S. David Sperling
Hebrew Union College
New York, New York

Discussing Adam's apple in the same column with *blush* and *pink* is more appropriate than you probably realized. After all, *adam* first meant red or ruddy, being related to Arabic and Ethiopian roots "to be fair, handsome"—much like what you called "the ruddy glow of health." By extension the word came to mean man (this is the word used in the famous phrase "the son of man"), human being, mankind, and in particular, the first man. Since God formed man *(adam)* from dust *(adamah)* (Genesis 2:7), it's not surprising that these two words are so similar. The further connection is that *adamah* (dust, earth, and by extension soil, field, ground, region) may refer to the reddish or tawny color of soil.

Tappuah does not mean a round projection. In the Song of Songs, *tappuah* is the apple tree (2:3 and 8:5), so called from its scent (7:9, or 7:8 in the RSV). In Proverbs 25:11, *tappuah zahav* probably refers to the fruit rather than the tree.

My reference for most of the foregoing is pages 13, 14 and 871 of *Gesenius' Hebrew-English Lexicon to the Old Testament* as translated and compiled (in 1846) by Samuel P. Tregelles, Wm. B. Eerdmans Publishing Co., Grand Rapids, Michigan, 1952.

In modern Hebrew, *tappuah zahav* means orange—a less poetic interpretation than Ray Bradbury used in his title "The Golden Apples of the Sun."

Tappuah adamah isn't Adam's apple, but the lowly apple of the earth. And just as in modern French and Dutch, so also in modern Hebrew the apple of the earth is the potato.

Amos Roos
San Francisco, California

Marxian Plagiarism

Ran into Bea Kristol on the Pan Am shuttle. I try to take that carrier when bopping between Washington and New York, because the New York City Traffic Department tries with suspicious intensity to make it impossible for taxis to get to Pan Am's terminal at La Guardia Airport, and it is in my perverse nature to resist such manipulation.

Mrs. Kristol is a professor of history at the City University of New York, who teaches and writes under her maiden name, Gertrude Himmelfarb. Her book *The New History and the Old* is the subject of hot intellectual discussion in the historical dodge. In a mischievous way, she shot a quick query at me: "Who coined the metaphor about religion being the 'opium' of the people?"

I was ready for that, having recently participated in a Commie-trivia quiz. "Karl Marx used *Opium des Volkes* about religion while he was knocking Hegel," I replied.

"Gotcha," she said, a locution popular in academic circles. "It's been variously attributed to Ludwig Feuerbach, Bruno Bauer and Moses Hess, but it was probably current among all the Young Hegelians before Marx used it in his *Critique of Hegel's Philosophy of Right* in 1844."

With less certitude, I wondered why all the Young Hegelians had been kicking the phrase around, and was informed that the Opium War of 1839–42 made the drug famous and such a figure of speech likely. However, lexicographers insist on written citations, and the phrase coinage cannot be denied Mr. Marx until hard copy of earlier use comes to hand. Did the father of Communism lift any other expressions, for which he is now famous, from people who wrote down the words first?

She ticked off a few: "*Cash nexus* was used by Carlyle; *proletariat* was popularized by Proudhon; *dictatorship of the proletariat* was attributed by Marx to Blanqui." (That's Thomas Carlyle, the British author; Pierre Josef

Proudhon, the French social theorist, and Auguste Blanqui, the French revolutionary.)

How about the famous line from the 1848 Marx-Engels Communist Manifesto, "The proletarians have nothing to lose but their chains"? According to one historian that Professor Himmelfarb does not altogether trust, that figure of speech may have been used earlier by Jean Paul Marat, the French revolutionary, but more research is needed on that.

However, she attaches more authenticity to the origin of another well-known declaration associated with Marx: "From each according to his ability, to each according to his work." That was from the Saint-Simonians, followers of Claude Henri de Rouvroy, Comte de Saint-Simon, in 1829, and Marx changed the last word from *work* to *needs*.

Oh, there'll be mail on this. Gotcha! Gang of the world, unite! You have nothing to lose but your postage.

> Re: A source for Marx's "From each according to his ability, to each according to his needs,"
> I'd like to cite the following passage from the Bible:
> "And all that believed were together, and had all things common; And sold their possessions and goods, and parted them to all men, *as every man had need."* Acts 2:44–5
>
> Jan Goldstein
> New York, New York

I noticed your use of the term "maiden name" to refer to Mrs. Kristol's work as Gertrude Himmelfarb. Doesn't that phrase strike you as hopelessly obsolete, and possibly offensive? (What is the equivalent term for a man whose name changes?) I haven't seen any examples in print, but I have begun to hear "birth name" or "original name" used in conversation.

> Kee Malesky
> Washington, D.C.

Means Test for End

Supporters of (more accurately, believers in) Lieutenant Colonel Oliver L. North hold that, in his case, the noble cause of the freedom fighters in Central America provided the good *end* that justified his use of tawdry *means*, such as lying to Congress and shredding documents.

"At the risk of drawing the attention of a special prosecutor," writes Jim

Newton, formerly of *The New York Times* foreign desk, "I'd like to call attention to the origins of the phrase *the end justifies the means,* which the Iran-contra investigative committee appeared eager to attribute to Karl Marx."

I recalled the often-quoted use of the phrase by Thomas Jefferson, after he slipped around Congress and the Constitution to acquire the vast Louisiana territory. "To lose our country by a scrupulous adherence to written law," said the nation's third President, "would be to lose the law itself . . . thus absurdly sacrificing the end to the means." But Mr. Newton tracked *end vs. means* to a translation of the forty-eighth letter of St. Jerome, written circa A.D. 400. "The line, often adopted by strong men in controversy, of justifying the means by the end . . ." wrote St. Jerome, the church father who translated the Bible from Hebrew and Greek manuscripts into Latin texts that formed the basis of the Vulgate.

"However eager, and correct, the congressmen must be to cast Colonel North as adopting the methods of the Marxist 'enemy,'" concludes my recent colleague, now at the *Atlanta Constitution,* "surely they didn't have St. Jerome in mind."

Or Sophocles, either; in *Electra,* written circa 409 B.C., the Greek playwright used words that translate into English as "The end excuses any evil." Bad philosophy, but certainly a provocative thought; it does not, however, have the specific *end-means* juxtaposition, so until a Lexicographic Irregular comes up with an earlier citation, St. Jerome gets the credit.

Meet My Whatsit

If Jessica Lange attends, wrote "Personalities" columnist Chuck Conconi in the *Washington Post,* speculating on the appearance of movie stars at a glittery premiere, "then her significant other, Sam Shepard, who is also in the film, won't be far behind."

On the NBC sitcom "Night Court," in an episode written by Reinhold Weege, a man introduces his pregnant girlfriend to the judge with these words: "This is my significant other, Babs Townsend."

Dr. Shepard G. Aronson of New York City, who keeps me informed on the latest hospital-chart lingo, writes: "*Significant Other* now appears on admission forms of many hospitals. Since there is another heading, *Spouse,* should *Significant Other* be regarded as a substitution or addition to *Spouse?*"

We are witnessing the trendy trivialization of a useful psychological term. Harry Stack Sullivan, a psychiatrist who died in 1949, defined "personality" as a "relatively enduring pattern of recurrent interpersonal situations," especially involving relations with "significant others." For a child, those "others" could be parents; for gang members, the leaders; for students, influential teachers; for business executives, mentors. In Dr. Sullivan's teaching, a *significant other* had power over a subject, and helped shape values, norms and behavior. He avoided the obvious completion of the phrase—significant other person—perhaps anticipating confusion with the acronym, SOP.

Lovers, mistresses and the people who write about them glommed on to the psychiatrist's phrase as a vogue variant of *live-in* (was too often confused with domestic help), *live-together* (never caught on) and *roommate* (does not connote a sexual relationship). The Census Bureau, seeking a neutral, non-intrusive term for the makeup of a household, played with *cohabitee* for a while and then settled on *POSSLQ*—Persons of the Opposite Sex Sharing Living Quarters—which is pronounced "Possle-Q" by lascivious census snoops who pretend not to want to know if the couple is a-he-in' and a-she-in'.

We have failed to come up with a satisfactory term for an unmarried, long-term sexual relationship that does not convey moral disapproval. *Tootsie* is hopelessly outdated, *concubine* never made it in the Occident, and *cookie* has crumbled. *Gigolo*, from the French *giguer*, "to hop or dance," is directed, always contemptuously, at a well-supported male companion.

Lover should logically apply to both sexes, but it still connotes the male because *mistress* is invariably female; unfortunately, *mistress* still carries the suggestion of financial support, and is thus rejected as sexist. Nobody thinks of the *mistress* paying the *lover's* rent, although antisexists would argue that it is a perfectly sensible idea.

Paramour, from the French *par amour*, "by or in love," has the advantage of applying to either sex, like the married *spouse*. In addition, it seems to go along with the popular *para-* prefix (*paralegal*, *paramilitary* and I need not mention *paraleipsis*), but the word connotes an arch illicitness. The Italian-derived *inamorata* implies less sneaking around, and has a masculine form in *inamorato*, but will never fly here.

Some people try the old *fiancé* or the archaic *betrothed*—in "Say hello to my betrothed," the word has three syllables—but that implies impending marriage, and the speaker may not want to make the commitment. A *friend* is what a fella or gal needs, but many consider that great word inadequate: "I hate that word *boyfriend*," writes Kristine Brower, an attorney in Lexington, Ky., "but I can't think of a better one—*significant other* is even worse." In current use, *boyfriend* and *girlfriend* can either mean a platonic relationship (exemplified in the cool "We've agreed to be friends") or imply a romantic attachment that could lead to marriage.

The latest entry in the "We live together, we're not married and we're not ashamed of it" sweepstakes is *convivante,* coined by Carl-Magnus Fallenius of Strangnas, Sweden, in 1979, from the Latin for "live together"; *convivere,* "to carouse together," led to *convivium,* "a feast," and the adjective *convivial.*

I wish hospital chartists would offer *spouse,* followed by *next of kin* and, finally, *sweetheart.* That last word is on the poetic side, but it does not draw leers, and we could all use a little romanticism in describing romances that exist without benefit of clergy. Leave *significant other* to the psychiatrists.

Introductions can become clumsy, family members uncomfortable and business associates confused when asking the inevitable. Indeed, there are many choices: roommate, co-habitee, boyfriend or girlfriend, significant other, POSSLQ, etc. However, in this day of business megadeals, corporate acquisitions and mergers, we choose to buck the trends and feel completely comfortable as *partners.*

> *James Reichert*
> *Stacy Keelor*
> *St. Louis, Missouri*

The term I prefer is *place-mate,* which my sister coined in 1982, as far as I know. Besides distinguishing the relationship from marriage by grounding it in place and conveying no moral disapproval, *place-mate* sounds friendly, as much a term of endearment as a definition of status. It's close enough to *placemat* to conjure up domesticity, close enough to *playmate* to ring of affectionate camaraderie. So it's exactly the blend of realism and lightheartedness that the best place-mates share.

> *Jody Gladding*
> *Lancaster, Pennsylvania*

Your collection of alternatives to the commonplace but immature-sounding introduction "This is my boy/girl friend" omits one, of neutral gender, that I suggest should head the list:

"This is my consort, Mary (Charles) Robin."

In view of "consort's" primary definition, it is a regal-sounding introduction: "A husband or wife; spouse"—being most often used in the context of royalty.

But that may not be what was implied—particularly if the last names of the introducer and introducee do not match.

So fall-back is had to the second definition in Funk & Wagnalls Standard College Dictionary (1963): "A companion or partner; mate."

Isn't that beautifully ambiguous—involving no commitment, as intended?

But it does indicate to the host that, if the two are to be overnight guests, they will share the same room.

Charles C. Trelease
Livingston, New Jersey

The term we came up with when we needed labels for each other was "homemate." This word captures the fact that our relationship involved creating a home together. It reflects the closeness, intimacy and long-term nature of such a relationship, without overemphasizing the sexual aspect. It is also handy because it is gender-neutral, carries no implication of impending marriage, or any other unwanted connotations, and could just as easily refer to married people who still live together as to unmarried people who live together. Besides, it's nice and simple.

Michael Sancilio
St. Paul, Minnesota

I think you're talking about *my old lady*. From 1966 to 1984 I lived mostly in the East Village of New York City. Nearly everyone I knew in Lower Manhattan said things like "he's my old man" or "she's my old lady." Boyfriends and girlfriends were for teenagers.

Thomas R. Haskett
Red Bank, Tennessee

For those who persist in this title search, I suggest "life partner" (my preference) or "personal partner" (his).

Rita Waterman
Fairfield, Connecticut

I shouldn't expect you to know that "companion" was used for decades by anarchists and others who lived in companionate marriage because they refused to recognize the authority of church or state, but I should think you'd know that *The New York Times* has been using "companion" for some time. At any rate, that gender-neutral term is by far the simplest and clearest.

Phyllis F. Calese
New York, New York

The term I use is *main squeeze*. My husband loves it.

Kate Bailey
New Orleans, Louisiana

I was very amused by your piece "Meet My Whatsit" especially as my son in his latest letter from New York referred to someone's "significant other," which I misread as "significant otter." The fact that I felt no surprise at this shows how I react to American vocabulary and usage!

Joan Harrisson (Mrs.)
Avon, England

My mother has solved the problem of what to call the family of one's sweetheart: the out-laws. She casually remarks that a client might have to have her out-laws cosign the contract (Mom sells real estate), or that a friend's son is going to his out-laws' for Thanksgiving. The term hints of disapproval, in the sense of the Old West, but is funny enough to imply my mother's acceptance. In my case, I think she would be happy if my out-laws became my in-laws.

Karen Falk
New York, New York

I introduce my son's girl (who is nice but certainly not significant) as my affair-in-law.

Philip H. Cohen
New York, New York

A wise, older woman at our church, who happens to be the wife of a retired minister, told me her daughter returned from Europe in order to be close to her "special friend" (emphasis, mine; friend, daughter's). What could be more clear and yet tasteful? This phrase implies no morality judgments nor bendings-over-backward to avoid the same.

Bill Davis
East Windsor, New Jersey

Why not use the word "mate"? This has established usage and is short, simple, and maybe even elegant. "This is my mate, Jane (or John)" sounds better than "my significant other." Nonsexual mates will not be confused since they are prefixed by "room," "house," etc., e.g., "roommate." True, the British use "mate" to mean "friend," but the context can make the distinction clear.

Fred E. Foldvary
San Francisco, California

Maybe the French do it right: When a man introduces someone to his bed-mate, he calls her *mon amie*; otherwise she is just *une amie à* (or *de*) *moi*. Another example of French nicety is the word *baiser*; as a noun it means a kiss. But as a verb, *baiser* means to kiss sexually, in all forms and places, while to kiss platonically is *embrasser* (*bras*, "the arm," which "embraces.")

[Name withheld]

On a recent trip to South America, I was studying my Spanish colloquialisms and came across the expression *media naranja* for "side-kick" or "better half." Literally *media naranja* means "half of an orange" which I think is a colorful, somewhat poetic way of suggesting sweetness and *equality*. It's an ideal term for two people involved in a sweet, loving relationship, the seeds of which have yielded or might yield new fruit.

And speaking of oranges, maybe this Spanish colloquialism is the real origin of the hip Black expression "main squeeze"?

> *Ed Lucaire*
> *New York, New York*

I thought you would enjoy the Scottish word for live-in lover: "Bidey-in" (presumably from the verb abide). As in: He/She is bringing his/her bidey-in along. Genderless, uncensorious and deliciously archaic!

> *Paula E. Ardehali*
> *Kendall Park, New Jersey*

The best term coined to date is *"mari-novio(a)."* To my knowledge it was coined in Puerto Rico and it is a merging of two words in Spanish—*"Marido(a)"* (the words for husband and wife) and *"novio(a)"* (the words for fiancé(e) or boy/girlfriend).

> *M. D. Taracido*
> *New York, New York*

Our Canadian cousins have faced this phenomenon more forthrightly than we have. Revenue Canada, the Canadian version of the IRS, solicits family information on its tax form with the inclusion of a box for "spousal equivalent."

> *Stanley A. Zuckerman*
> *Counselor for Press and*
> *Culture*
> *Embassy of the United States of America*
> *Brasilia, Brazil*

Contrary to what a psychologist might say, the issue is *not* what the person in question means to his or her companion ("significant other"), but the role that he or she plays. The term is "spouse-equivalent." I realize that in order for it to be grammatically correct, it would have to be "spousal equivalent," but that is too cumbersome to gain popularity.

> *K. Jill Kiecolt*
> *Baton Rouge, Louisiana*

I wondered why you had not considered the use of "cohabitant," a word that is legitimate and one that describes the situation exactly.

Dorothy Powers
Ocala, Florida

There has been a word in the English language for many years to cover "a man who lives with a woman without marriage." It is *tally*, and can be found in the Century Dictionary & Cyclopedia (1896 edition). It also appears in the expression *to live tally* "to live together as man and wife without marriage." Both are labeled "Provincial English."

The O.E.D. labels it *slang: to live (on) tally* "to live in concubinage, to cohabit without marriage." The earliest citation given is 1887. The O.E.D. also cites *tally-husband* "a man who 'lives tally,' " *tallyman* "one who 'lives tally' with a woman" (1890), and *tallywoman* "a woman who 'lives tally' with a man."

As the words and the verb phrase already exist, why all the fuss?

Larry [Laurence Urdang]
VERBATIM
Essex, Connecticut

Why try to coin a new word for a live-in companion of the opposite sex when there is an old word which means exactly that? The word is *leman* and O.E.D. says it was in use about a century ago. My dictionary calls it "archaic" and perhaps it can be prevented from becoming obsolete in view of the present need for it.

The only trouble with it I see is that it almost rhymes with what so many lemans turn out to be: lemons.

Warren H. Goodman
Ossining, New York

I enjoyed your article on "significant other." Can you now find an alternative to "sexual intercourse"? The four-letter word is best but not acceptable. "Sleeping together" is worse than a euphemism because it is often untrue. Do what you can!

Esther M. Doyle
Huntingdon, Pennsylvania

Miss Feasance of 1987

I call a source to get some information. A secretary answers who has orders not to put a caller through without first learning my name and number (reasonable enough) and asking, "What is this call in reference to?" (Never the simple "about"; always the highfalutin "in reference to.")

I don't like to tell other people what I am calling about, nor do I like to let the targets on the other end of the line know in advance what I am going to ask them about, lest they prepare some innocuous response or shift me to some smooth-tongued aide trained to obfuscate.

So I always tell the secretary of the public official, "Tell him I want to speak with him about malfeasance in office." That usually gets a call back. On one occasion, a Cabinet member not easily intimidated by a pundit had his deputy assistant amanuensis call back to ask, "The Secretary wants to know whether you meant *malfeasance* or *misfeasance?*"

I had to work that out slowly. *Feasance* in all its forms usually has to do with official conduct, action taken by those who hold public office or some form of public responsibility whether in government or not. *Mis-* means "badly, wrongly," but *mal* is the French noun for "evil." Obviously, those who blithely say that "a miss is as good as a mal" do not understand the gulf of difference here.

Misfeasance is a transgression, perhaps inadvertent; it is wrongdoing that may not be a crime. "*Misfeasance* involves doing what one may do," says Kevin Driscoll of the American Bar Association's Washington office, "but doing it incorrectly or illegally. For example, if there are guidelines for a certain tonnage of waste allowed to be dumped, and someone dumps more than the allowed amount out of ignorance or not with evil intent, that would be *misfeasance.*"

What about the toxic creep who knows full well what the law is, and goes ahead and dumps a ton of garlic in some mountain brook? The executive of that company, which has a public responsibility, is engaged in *malfeasance*, lawbreaking with evil intent, and it is to the hoosegow with him.

Now let's get to an example that offers more satisfaction: abuse of power by public officials.

The New York City Landmarks Commission issued a warning against any proposal to redevelop the seedy park behind the Forty-second Street Public Library that might obscure the back of the building. But they were commenting in advance on a quasi-judicial matter about to come before them; *The New York Times* promptly condemned such prejudging "A

Landmark of Misfeasance." That was an accusation of recklessness that raised questions about the fitness of the commissioners to serve, but not an accusation of corruption.

An official guilty of *misfeasance* should be tossed out on his or her ear— but only an official guilty of *malfeasance* should be tossed in the jug.

Irving Howe, the editor of *Dissent* magazine and a frequent contributor to *Partisan Review,* recently expressed anguish at the contretemps around the latter magazine's planned publication of an article by Michael A. Ledeen, who was one of the originators of the Reagan administration's arms-for-hostages dealings. "I felt it was like finding out a cousin was involved in public malfeasance," he said of the Sturm und Drang at *PR.* "It's still a cousin." (*Public malfeasance* verges on the redundant.)

Supporters of President Reagan in the Iran arms affair say they are unworried by charges of *misfeasance* (political partisans have been calling him unfit for years) and are also not worried about *malfeasance* because they think it unlikely that the President will be shown to be consciously breaking the law (he signed a "finding" that suspended a law). What concerns them most is *nonfeasance.*

That word is used half as often as *misfeasance,* one-thirteenth as often as *malfeasance. Nonfeasance* means not doing what you are obligated to do— failing to act when your specific responsibility is to act. In civil law, a tort case could be brought when nonfeasance is involved if failing to do something caused harm; in criminal law, some states have laws involving "affirmative obligation" to aid strangers in peril: according to the Vermont rescue statute, under some circumstances a fine may be imposed for nonfeasance if one does not aid a stranger. Perhaps the best-known examples of nonfeasance are taxpayers' failures to file tax returns and landlords' failures to make repairs.

To recap, *misfeasance* is doing something very badly; *malfeasance* is abusing official office, perhaps corruptly, and *nonfeasance* is failing to carry out one's responsibility.

In the case a few years ago that occupies the minds of White House watchers, nobody may have been guilty of anything, but it seemed to me that former chief of staff Donald T. Regan was in danger of being charged with acts of misfeasance, the boys in the National Security Council basement may have been charged with acts of malfeasance and the man in the Oval Office risked accusations of nonfeasance. That was early speculation; of course, as a scandal develops, any feasance is feasible.

Bill:
"The New York City Landmarks Commission issued a warning. . . . But *they* were commenting in advance. . . ."
Have I caught you committing one of my bêtes noires, the disagreement in number? I tell you, when it slouches off the subway ads and

the news radio into Safire's language column, I'm taking my rifle and chain saw and heading for my cabin in the woods."

Best,
Steve [Pickering]
The New York Times
New York, New York

The Modifiers of Mother

"**M**y colleagues at *U.S. News & World Report* and such learned journals as *The New York Times,*" writes David E. Pollard, "keep referring to Mary Beth Whitehead as the *surrogate mother* of Baby M. I hold that she isn't a surrogate anything. I say she *is* the mother. As in real, actual, honest-to-God mother. For hire, maybe. But mother, nonetheless.

"And if society is going to insist that Mrs. Whitehead is the *surrogate mother*, then whatever shall we call Mrs. Stern, the wife of Baby M's father? Please give us a ruling."

Surrogate, the noun derived from Latin, means "one who takes the place of another." In the seventeenth century, it was the name given to the deputy of an ecclesiastical judge; the bishop would let the surrogate handle the issuance of marriage licenses. That led to its use in admiralty law courts: a surrogate was appointed to act in place of a regular judge. This substitute judge stopped being a second-class judicial citizen when he was given jurisdiction over the probate of wills; an additional meaning was given to the judge in that field when he was considered to be acting as surrogate for, or in place of, the deceased parents of a minor.

The Russian novelist Ivan Turgenev liked the term, criticizing a colleague's book: "In his eyes, art is (as he himself expresses it) only a surrogate for reality, for life, and is essentially fit only for immature people."

Surrogate became a learned, bookish substitute for *substitute*, and was picked up by psychologists. A *mother surrogate* is one who takes the place of the mother in the child's mind: a female schoolteacher or older sister often takes on this role in the child's early life. The two words turned around in sequence when the psychologist Harry Harlow referred to the wire and cloth dolls that he used in the studies of maternal attachment in monkeys as *surrogate mothers*.

The word then hopped to politics. In the Nixon campaign of 1968, we were looking around for an important-sounding word for the person who was asked to stand in for the candidate on occasions not important enough for the presence of the candidate himself. *Substitute* was pejorative; *pinch-hitter*, too informal; *stand-in*, too theatrical. But *surrogate* sounded vaguely legal and dignified, and we went with it. It caught on; people seemed more satisfied with "one of Mr. Nixon's team of surrogate speakers" than with a miserable *substitute*.

On June 5, 1978, *Time* magazine wrote about a new idea of implanting a fertilized egg or embryo in the womb of a woman different from the one in whom conception took place: "The demand for surrogates remained strong. . . . Despite potential legal problems, some have already opted for surrogate mothers." Thus the phrase, with this new meaning, was started, and the potential legal problems soon became real.

The Supplement to the Oxford English Dictionary took that *Time* usage as the basis for its definition: "A woman whose pregnancy arises from the implantation in her womb of a fertilized egg or embryo from another woman." But that, of course, does not apply to the case of Mary Beth Whitehead, whose own egg was artificially inseminated.

The meaning of *surrogate mother* changed with the increase in frequency of the new practice. No longer was the woman who provided the uterus the only one given that label; the woman providing the egg was also referred to as the surrogate, or substitute.

That was an anomaly, promptly objected to by opponents of the procedure; they held that Mrs. Whitehead, who was present at the conception, was the mother (or *natural* or *genetic* or *biological* or *real* mother), and that the woman who with her husband had contracted to adopt the child was the child's *surrogate* (or *foster* or *adoptive*) mother.

The Vatican, in a statement, condemned all such end runs around infertility: "Surrogate motherhood . . . offends the dignity and the right of the child to be conceived, carried in the womb, brought into the world and brought up by his own parents . . ." Rome did not differentiate between the process of implanting a fertilized egg in a rented or borrowed womb and the process of impregnating the hired childbearer by fertilizing one of her own eggs.

That exemplifies the linguistic confusion. *Surrogacy* is now most often taken in its most inclusive sense, seen and spoken of to mean "the business of arranging for a baby to be produced in the body of a woman other than the female partner in a marriage." The crucial difference made by the place of the egg's fertilization is usually overlooked; wombs for rent and eggs for purchase, quite different situations, are lumped together in the whole field, or issue, called *surrogate motherhood.*

What, then, does the person who wants to be linguistically precise call the woman who is the genetic female parent and also the bearer of the child? Logic suggests the answer to be, simply, *the mother,* but strict logic does not rule the language. In current use, that woman is part of the surrogacy movement (or trade, if you disapprove), and as such is called the *surrogate mother.*

If enough people write angrily to media outlets to protest the use of this phrase in this sense, and claim that the phrase has a built-in bias against their cause or beliefs, perhaps writers and broadcasters will be intimidated or stricken with logic; in that case, some other phrase would be coined that engenders less controversy.

It's too soon for a "ruling"; current usage is clearly on the side of calling the hired carrier the *surrogate*, but a backlash may be developing. I would stick to the facts: if you mean the woman who provides the egg alone, use *genetic* mother; if she provides the uterus without the egg, try *uterine* mother; if she provides both egg and uterus, try *genetic, childbearing* mother or, if you want to sneak in a little propaganda, *natural* mother.

As for the other woman, the one contracting for the child's delivery, if she provides no egg, she is the *adoptive* mother, and would probably prefer that more recent modifier to *foster* (from Old English for "food, nourishment"). If she has custody, she can also be called the *legal* mother.

Least desirable is *stepmother*, which still carries the unfair "wicked" connotation: as Mary Beth Whitehead said in her failed custody attempt, "I do not want to be known as a stepmother. I want to be a legal mother." In Merriam-Webster's Ninth New Collegiate, *stepchild* is defined as "1: a child of one's wife or husband by a former marriage 2: one that fails to receive proper care or attention." *Step-* is related to the Old High German *stiufen,* "to bereave," following the death of a parent; with the increase in divorces, death no longer determines step-status. Also, *step-siblings* may be considered to refer reciprocally to children of a later or former marriage, and *step-* is more inclusive than *half-*, which requires being related by blood through one parent.

In the proliferation of modifiers for *mother*, we have been dealing here with adjectives used by observers and participants in controversy or complexity. However, from the point of view of the language user on the receiving end of maternal devotion from any source, it is still *Mother's* Day.

I have a suggestion which would satisfy the scientist—namely "host mother." I feel the term cannot be misunderstood—it simply means that the fetus is the "guest" of a person without the intent that it stay with her.

Liselotte K. Fischer
Amherst, New York

Your reference to Mary Beth Whitehead as the one "whose own egg was artificially inseminated" can best be described as muddle-headed.

Her egg was not inseminated, it was fertilized in the normal biological way: therefore, Mary Beth was inseminated. The only artificial aspect was the manner of introduction of the semen, which is what "insemination" means. Insemination and fertilization are not identical; one refers to semen, the other to spermatozoa.

S. E. Liverhant
New York, New York

"Surrogate" is derived from *subrogare* "to name as an alternate."

The SOED definition of surrogate is "a person or thing that acts for or takes the place of another; a substitute."

Thus, a women whose own ovum is fertilized and implanted and who bears her own infant is the child's mother; another person who acts in any other maternal capacity cannot be the mother, but may be a surrogate mother. A woman who had another's ovum implanted would be a true surrogate mother to the child she bears. In the recent media attention the "surrogate" mother (who apparently carried her own ovum) was in fact the true biological mother. Your soapbox is as good a place as any to continue to ask for correct usage of terms, especially with such emotionally and legally wrought issues as motherhood.

Mark C. Steinhoff, M.D.
Associate Professor
Department of International Health, and
Department of Pediatrics
The Johns Hopkins University
Baltimore, Maryland

You quote Mr. David E. Pollard as asking, "And if society is going to insist that Mrs. Whitehead is the *surrogate mother*, then whatever shall we call Mrs. Stern, the wife of Baby M's father?"

After your very informative history on the evolution of the term "surrogate," it was surprising to see that you didn't come up with the most obvious answer to Mr. Pollard's question. In Christian mythology, Mary conceived through the "good offices" of the Holy Ghost, leaving dear husband Joseph in a tight spot. Since Joseph wasn't the real father of Jesus, he came to be known as his *putative* one.

According to the Webster's New Collegiate Dictionary, "putative" (ME, fr. LL *putativus*, fr. L *putatus*, pp. of *putare* to think) means "commonly accepted or supposed." Therefore, Mrs. Stern would become *ipso facto* Baby M's putative mother. And, come to think of it, Mary would be the first surrogate (in the current, all inclusive meaning of the word) mother "recorded" in history. So much for "surrogate motherhood . . . offends the dignity and the right of the child to be conceived, carried in the womb, brought into the world and brought up by his [oops, sexism raises its tail] own parents. . . ."

Miguel Falquez-Certain
Sunnyside, New York

Gotcha! I am unsure of the exact origins of the word *surrogate*, but am quite sure that there were never "admiralty law courts." For the English-speaking world, the word *law* has always been tricky, this one word often being used where other languages would more readily use two (e.g., Latin with *jus* and *lex* or German with *Recht* and *Gesetz*). This observation aside, England long distinguished between Courts of Law (or, as they are commonly called, common law courts) and, among others, Courts of Admiralty. The framers of our U.S. Constitution continued this distinction; in the second section of Article III of the Constitution, they wrote: "The judicial Power shall extend to all Cases, in Law and Equity . . . [and] to all Cases of admiralty and maritime Jurisdiction. . . ." In short, while there may be admiralty law, there were never admiralty law courts, only law courts or admiralty courts.

C. Peck Hayne, Jr.
New York, New York

Mr. Bonaprop

A *malapropism* is a word or phrase that is amusingly off the mark. For example, a recent pamphlet circulated by the Department of Health and Human Services dealt with "inpatients" but stated that "hospital insurance covers impatient hospital care." *(Inpatient* is a retronym based on *outpatient;* used to be, a person receiving treatment in a hospital was merely a *patient,* and only the hatchet-faced head nurse was *impatient.)*

The eponymous *-ism* was formed from Mrs. Malaprop, a character in a 1775 play by Richard Brinsley Sheridan who used *reprehend* for *apprehend* and *oracular* for *vernacular.* Today, the word applies to any goofy linguistic mistake, like the unintentional irreverence in the simile "drunk as the Lord."

Sheridan formed the name from *malapropos,* originally meaning "inopportune, unseasonable." The French formed the term from *mal,* "badly"; *à,* "to"; *propos,* "the purpose." This idea is expressed in English as *inappropriate,* the bureaucrat's all-purpose excuse for not doing anything. ("Sorry, it's not our policy to comment on that." Why? "It would be *inappropriate.")* The English version of *mal à propos* is intended to convey the illusion of "wrong," but *inappropriate* is rooted in the more manipulative "not suited to the purpose."

Which brings us to *bonapropism,* a coinage touted in this space for the past few years to describe happy mistakes: words or phrases that are seemingly off the mark, but unintentionally hit the mark right on the button.

For example, a disk jockey in Los Angeles named April Whitney who posed seductively in *Playboy* magazine reported her reaction to a subsequent invitation to fly to Dallas: "I'd be worried that I'd get off the plane and never be seen from again." At first glance, her comment appears to be a garbling of "heard from again," but the visual element of the story leads Don Shannon of the *Los Angeles Times* to suggest, "Mrs. Whitney may be the long-sought replacement for Sam Goldwyn, somebody who gets it wrong but with just a fraction of something that sounds right."

Mr. Goldwyn, the Hollywood producer, was famed for the mistakes created for him by the press agent Lynn Farnol, such as "A verbal contract isn't worth the paper it's written on" and "Include me out." In later years, Mr. Goldwyn decided he wanted a more statesmanlike image, fired his press agent and claimed he never said any of those funny things. That left a void: who would become "Mr. Bonaprop," the person who would be a natural source for the attribution of such constructions?

Casey Stengel, the baseball manager, filled that role for a time—he is usually cited as the source of the Thurberism "You could look it up." Walt Kelly's cartoon character Pogo was heavily quoted for "We have met the enemy and he is us," usually by self-flagellating foreign-affairs writers, but this was his only major contribution to the language. The real person in our time who is most often credited with, or stuck with, bonapropisms is former Yankee star Lawrence (Yogi) Berra.

I have long been searching for the origin of "The opera ain't over till the fat lady sings." Coach Dick Motta of the Chicago Bulls, who popularized the phrase in 1978, has been noted here as a possible coiner, but Daniel S. Knight of Philadelphia, who styles himself spokesman for the "Fat Lady Sings Society," cites the Concise Oxford Dictionary of Proverbs: In 1975, Ralph Carpenter, information director of Texas Tech, told a contingent of sportswriters in the Austin press box that "The rodeo ain't over till the bull riders ride." Dan Cook, a sports editor for the *San Antonio Express-News,* responded with "The opera ain't over till the fat lady sings."

In searching for the origin of this gem, I came across the simpler and even more frequently cited "It ain't over till it's over," which I presume is a shortening (and philosophic extension) of the adage "The ball game isn't over until the last man is out."

Did Yogi Berra actually say that, or was it a concoction of some anonymous attributer? Reached at his Montclair, N. J., home, Mr. Berra acknowledges the coinage: "Yes, I said that. It was during a pennant race for the Mets."

And what about "Thank you for making this night necessary"? The substitution of *necessary* for *possible* broke the cliché and added a note of honesty to an otherwise insipid statement. "Yes, I said that too," confirms Mr. Berra, "in St. Louis."

Such pinpoint sourcing of proverbial statements is as rare as it is useful to lexicographers yet unborn. What about the recent "It's *déjà vu* all over again," so often attributed to Mr. Berra? "Nope, not true, I never said that." Or the advice, "Always go to other people's funerals—otherwise, they won't come to yours"? That too is disclaimed; not an authentic bonaprop by Berra.

"That place is so crowded," Mr. Berra was supposed to have said, "that nobody goes there anymore." Properly sourced? "Yes, Yogi said that," said his wife, Carmen, on a telephone extension, "about a restaurant."

One bonapropism I have especially admired for its ultra-subjectivist, post-neodeconstructivist quality, is—it can now be confirmed—not that of the Land-of-the-Nihilist critic Jacques Derrida, but of New Jersey's Yogi Berra: "If I hadn't woke up, I'd still be asleep."

If you ever again speak with Yogi Berra, please find out if he said my favorite Yogism. It is asserted that one September afternoon, as the shadow crept toward home plate, he said: "It gets late earlier this time of year."

> Gene Shalit
> "Today" Show, NBC
> New York, New York

After many years as the Yankee catcher, Yogi played a couple of seasons in left field. As you may know, left field at Yankee Stadium is a tough position during day games because the sun sets behind home plate. Accordingly, the shadow of the stadium slowly advances across the infield toward the left field stands.

After Yogi's first game in left, a reporter asked him how he liked it. Yogi's reply: "It gets late early out there."

And how about a new one?

While in L.A. on our shoot, the subject of Joliet, Ill., came up. (I forget why.) The following dialogue ensued:

YOGI: Joliet? I know Joliet. I have a lot of cousins who live on farms around Joliet.
ME: Yeah, huh? Gee, that's interesting, Yog.
YOGI: Yeah. They grow a lot of baked potatoes out there.

There will never be another Yogi. We all loved working with him.

> Anthony J. Oestreicher
> New York, New York

Your "Mr. Bonaprop" column referring to Yogi Berra reminded me of a classic Berra story told to me over twenty years ago by the Cleveland Indian great, Al Rosen.

While on a road trip to New York, Al and his wife ran into Yogi as they were exiting a hotel. It was a hot summer day and Al's wife remarked to Yogi, "You look so cool in that seersucker suit, Yogi."

Yogi cheerfully replied, "Thanks, Mrs. Rosen, you don't look so hot yourself."

Saul Isler
Cleveland Heights, Ohio

The hatchet job you did on head nurses by your description of the "hatchet-faced head nurse" is unfortunate. I have known more head nurses than you, Mr. Safire, and I have yet to see one who was "hatchet-faced," whatever that is.

More likely the Lord made *His* face to shine upon our head nurses for their devotion and dedication.

Harvey N. Mandell, M.D.
Medical Director
The William W. Backus Hospital
Norwich, Connecticut

You too quickly dismissed Pogo as a source of "bonaprop" wit. What about "Suspicion is nine points of the law"—a pronouncement made by a character that looked remarkably like John Mitchell?

John Hellegers
Jenkintown, Pennsylvania

Historical correction: your invariably entertaining column said that Goldwynisms were created by Goldwyn's press agent, Lynn Farnol. Oh no, no. I worked as gofer-copywriter for Lynn during his time as Goldwyn's publicity man in New York in the late 1920s and was off and on in touch with him after he went to the Goldwyn office on the Coast. I'd have known if he fathered any such. To make sure, I've checked with an old friend retired from *Variety* who says: "I knew Lynn long ago on both coasts. My distinct recall is that he never liked the Goldwynisms and that Goldwyn was not amused." He suggested I check further with another *Variety* old-timer still active. I did so and he says: "Lynn Farnol was a fine fellow, but his sense of humor did not run to Goldwynisms—he would have hesitated even to repeat one. To the best of my recollection they sprouted from Howard Dietz. I can't give you chapter and verse, but I'm quite certain Howard was the originator. Alva Johnson, I'm sure, contrived several in his *New Yorker* profile, 'The Great Goldwyn.' "

It would be fun for me to believe I was a fly on the wall when "A verbal contract isn't worth the paper it's written on" was born. But it won't wash.

J. C. Furnas
Lebanon, New Jersey

I must commend you for eschewing one of America's favorite journalistic customs—the quoting of Yogi Berra without any attempt to determine that the quote is really his—and actually checking with our good friend Yogi about these issues. Congratulations.

Another favorite may fit in your file somehow:

"You can observe a lot just by watching." Yogi said this, partially swallowing his words, at the press conference in which he was named Yankee manager in the fall of 1963, succeeding Ralph Houk, who had been promoted to general manager and therefore remained Yogi's boss. It had come out that the plan to make Yogi manager had been in the works for some time and that Yogi, as a player-coach during 1963, was being "groomed." Asked about his inexperience in managing—he had been considered, by all around him, as only a player and quote-machine—and why he thought he could handle the job, he replied with the above remark.

A major dispute broke out among my colleagues about what it was Yogi had misstated. Did he mean "learn by watching" or "absorb by watching" or "observe and learn"? I argued that he meant exactly what he said, and that "observe" and "watch" weren't identical. But I was prejudiced in his favor.

> Kop [Leonard Koppett]
> Palo Alto, California

Dear Bill:

In *Malaprop,* the *mal* is an adverb, not an adjective, so its opposite should be *bien,* not *bon.* BUT if you had followed this logic you would have been unintelligible to 9½ out of 10 readers. When such a situation occurs (and it's frequent), what does the conscientious writer do? Does one follow your bold example every time?

> Jacques [Barzun]
> Charles Scribner's Sons
> New York, New York

Ms.-ing Word

"If the word *emasculate* means 'to deprive of virility and vigor,' " writes Nathan Mitchell of New York City, "would you know the corresponding word for the removal of feminine attributes?"

I would but I don't. The question is worth examining because it seeks a co-respondent, to use divorce-court lingo, for the extended meaning of the word. The *mas* in *emasculate* is the first syllable of *masculine,* and the original meaning of *emasculate* was "to remove the capability of reproduction." The extended meaning is as Dr. Mitchell states: to strip of manly or virile attributes, as in taking the punchiness or savagery out of prose. (Editor: this is not a complaint.)

The word we're looking for is not directed to the removal of a woman's capacity to reproduce; it is the metaphoric counterpart we're after. Nor is *sterilize* suitable, because that is not limited to women, and *barren* has no current verb. We seek a term for the extended meaning, for the removal of qualities associated with women. Those "feminine" qualities—I'm getting in trouble, I know—include sensitivity, softness, beauty and the range of activities that now come under the heading of *nurturing*. (I have left out *passivity* because I don't want to get slugged by Jane Fonda.)

In short, what is needed is a synonym for *defeminize,* a word coined in 1900 that doesn't cut the mustard; *-ize* is too common a method of manufacturing verbs.

So let's build one now. We naturally turn to *fem* to match the *mas.* We can also begin with *e-*, as *emasculate* does, because that is a shorter form of the prefix *ex-*, which means "out of." And *-ate* is a good verbifier, if we're trying for parallelism.

That gives us the verb *efeminate.* But hold on: the Romans beat us to it, with the Latin *effeminare,* carrying the opposite meaning: "to make womanish." Although that verb is rarely used in English, we already have the adjective *effeminate,* meaning "weak and decadent" to some, plain "girlish" to others.

What to do? First, forget the verb to *"efeminate"* as the logical opposite of *to emasculate* because another word is already there, and it is not the object of coinage to confuse. Erase that entire blackboard and reformulate. Lexicographic Irregulars are invited to try their hands, but here's my candidate: *toughen.*

Coinage Dept.

Potholes exist in the language. We try to fill them in here.

In the past, note was taken of the absence of the female form of *avuncular,* "like the relationship of an uncle." What about an aunt? After examining the spidery *tantular* and the hesitant *tantative,* and rejecting the archaic *materteral,* we took the root from the Latin for "father's sister"— *amita*—and settled on *amital.* Nobody has used it yet, but it's there, which is a comfort.

Now the tidying-up aims at answering the question: "What's the feminine for *emasculate?*" When the manliness—the strength, bravery and resolution—is taken out of prose, it is said to be emasculated; when the womanly qualities—compassion, sympathy, tenderness and gentleness—are stripped from prose, what verb do we use? (*Manly* and *womanly* are adjectives—they may look like adverbs, but they function more often as adjectives—used in admiration; *mannish* and *womanish* pejoratively liken one sex to the other.)

The verb that is supposed to do the job is in some dictionaries as *effeminate*, but that word is confused with the adjective *effeminate*. I coarsely put forward *toughen*, but Lexicographic Irregulars have responded with other choices.

Using the Greek root *hustera*, "womb," from which we already have *hysterectomy* and *hysteria*, the suggestion of *hysterectate* has been put forward. No; makes me want to scream. Dr. Stewart B. Dunsker of Cincinnati, using the combining form *gyne-*, from the Greek *gune*, "woman," also offers *gyneclate*. Other suggestions on that line are *degynify* and *exogynate*. Close, but no slim cigar.

"Might I suggest the word *spay*?" writes Dr. David C. Brooks of the Harvard Medical School. "It works quite well for dogs and cats and might be quite appropriate applied to humans." Sorry; animal lovers would object to *spay*, which is the feminine version of *geld*.

The unfamiliar word *muliebrity* exists, meaning "the soft characteristics of womanhood," the opposite of *virility*; John E. Winter of Victoria, B.C., uses the root of that word to recommend *demulierize* as the feminine equivalent of *emasculate*. Sorry; that *mule* syllable conjures an image of stubbornness.

Several readers found the answer in Shakespeare: "Unsex me," said Lady Macbeth, girding herself for deeds not associated with womanliness. It worked for her, as would have *unwoman*, a locution that would not have worked for a male character.

The overwhelming choice (twenty-eight letters) of the Irregulars: *defeminate*. Simple, direct and an apposite opposite to *emasculate*. If an editor chooses to defeminate this copy, all the tender quality will be cut out.

Glad that's all settled. Relatedly, in a recent piece on pronunciation, I expressed my preference for GUY-necologist over GONE-ecologist; some heavily defeminated letters came in from doctors who call themselves JIN-ecologists. They have a great case in the etymology: the soft g was the earlier pronunciation, and a gynecocracy—government by women—is still pronounced JIN-ecocracy. But in today's world, where pronunciation is dictated by usage, a JIN-ecologist would sound to many like the name for a highly specialized bartender. Go with GUY-.

Murder Board at the Skunk Works

"**B**ork shunned 'Murder Boards' and Prepped Alone" was the headline in *Legal Times*. Before the Senate hearings into the confirmation of Judge Robert H. Bork began, according to the Washington weekly for lawyers, the White House held a session with the President's nominee to the Supreme Court to help him anticipate likely questions. "He did one *moot court* over at the White House," a Bork friend was quoted as saying, "but after that he canceled all the rest."

Wrote Aaron Freiwald, the reporter: "A senior White House official acknowledges that the 'murder boards,' as the moot-court sessions are known to Administration officials, did not prove effective with Bork." Apparently the judge knew his own mind and needed no coaching from White House aides, but many of us need coaching about the business of coaching.

A *moot court* is a hypothetical arena, a mock court set up for students; the phrase was recorded in the 1788 writings of Thomas Jefferson: "He gives lectures regularly, and holds moot courts and parliaments wherein he presides." As a noun, *moot* came from the Old Norse word for "meeting," and from this legal usage gained a connotation of "debatable," which has come down to us as an adjective meaning "abstract, purely academic."

But *moot court*, even as a hyphenated modifier, lacks zip and sparkle. A term was needed to describe a more hectic, hostile affair. *Murder board* is Pentagonese, though some say the phrase originated in the interrogation methods used by intelligence analysts seeking to establish a defector's bona fides. The original meaning was "rigorous examination of a proposed program" or, more specifically and less bureaucratically, "a group charged with the responsibility to slam a candidate or proposer of an idea up against the wall with tough questioning."

Thus, as *Aviation Week & Space Technology* wrote in 1976: ". . . so-called 'program murder boards' have been established to insure that the concept is structured properly and that its test and logistics implications are considered and defined in its initial stages." In 1980, the Joint Chiefs of Staff received a report from Admiral James L. Holloway criticizing the absence of an "intervening scrub-down or murder board of the planning product."

Scrub-down did not make it outside the naval bureaucracy, perhaps because of its closeness to *shakedown*, but more likely because *murder board* was more colorful. In 1982, *The Economist* of London used the Pentagonian term in a more specific reference: "A so-called 'murder board' was set up to test Air Force witnesses with hostile questions they might encounter from committee members." Although the military continues to use the phrase to cover all tough-minded review boards, civilians have narrowed its use to the no-holds-barred preparation of witnesses for hearings or of politicians for press conferences.

We are indebted to the defense community for another colorful phrase, recorded first by the *Harvard Business Review* in 1976: "Lockheed Aircraft Corporation's 'skunk works' is an example of this kind of highly productive approach. . . . Before a dollar is spent, a skunk-works staff is indoctrinated to ask, 'Will it contribute to short-range profit?' " A year later, *Newsweek* wrote that the U-2 aircraft of the 1950s had been "fashioned by ace designer Clarence (Kelly) Johnson at Lockheed Aircraft's California 'skunk works.' "

Within months of the attribution of the phrase to Lockheed, the Jet Propulsion Laboratory went a step further and dubbed a special office "the planetary skunk works." The phrase was picked up by the author Thomas J. Peters in his best seller, *In Search of Excellence*, as a technique shared by innovative companies in which small groups are encouraged to break out of establishmentarian habits to come up with new technologies, marketing strategies or products.

At the Random House Dictionary, lexicographers took note and decided the phrase was being used too often over too long a period for it to be dismissed as a nonce phrase. Hence, in the new Random House Unabridged, the informal *skunk works* is defined as "an often secret experimental division, laboratory, project, or the like, for producing innovative designs or products, as in the computer or aerospace field."

The etymology is clear: ". . . after Big Barnsmell's *Skonk Works*, where the illicit liquor Kickapoo Joy Juice was made, in Al Capp's comic strip *Li'l Abner.*" (The cartoonist and satirist Capp spelled the first word with an *o*; usage has returned the word to its original spelling and pronunciation, and dropped the capitalization.)

Envision Lonesome Polecat, about to hold a news conference in Dogpatch to explain the contents of Kickapoo Joy Juice to assorted environmentalists, health officials and revenooers, being prepared for the most hostile questions by a murder board at the Skonk Works. There sits Senator Jack S. Phogbound, flanked by Hairless Joe, stern Mammy Yokum, the evil Skraggs, unlucky Joe Btfsplk and the unforgettable Moonbeam McSwine. . . .

In his autobiography, Kelly Johnson says that "Skunk Works" came from stirring up a brew; thence, the Li'l Abner connection.

Another version I've heard suggests that Johnson's first building (at the Burbank airport) was coincidentally located next to a plastics plant, which stank; thus the name.

Who knows. My own introduction to the name is embarrassing. In

Search, I wrote of "Skunkworks" (one word) and referenced Xerox's East Rochester operation—I honestly didn't know of Johnson, but was only later informed (by someone from Northrop); in *A Passion for Excellence*, my second book, I credited Kelly—and used his two-word version. I also got into a small legal battle with Lockheed over using the noun—they had let it languish until we brought it back into the language, at which time they resurrected it and began to use it in recruiting ads, etc.

So it goes.

Tom Peters
Palo Alto, California

The Random House citation correctly attributes the etymology of *skunk works* to the *Skonk Works* in Al Capp's *Li'l Abner* comic strip. It then states, "where the illicit liquor Kickapoo Joy Juice was made." The lexicographers should have quit while they were ahead.

The *Skonk Works* was the joint enterprise of outside man Little Barnsmell, and inside man Big Barnsmell. Little B dealt with the public from a respectable distance. Big B, in charge of manufacturing, never left the confines of the establishment and was caricaturized only in print, due presumably to his pervasive aroma, a whiff of which was deemed fatal. The precise nature and purpose of the *Skonk Works'* product, as well as those who trafficked in it, remain a mystery.

Conversely, Kickapoo Joy Juice, the communal product of Hairless Joe and his bosom buddy, Lonesome Polecat, was distilled in the proximate environs of Hairless Joe's cave and for a well-defined purpose—getting hammered. The lexicographers probably confused the noxious odor of the *Skonk Works* with the corrosive nature of the Kickapoo Joy Juice mash. Anvils were customarily dissolved in it to test its maturation. I trust that Random House will correct the etymology at next printing.

Verner J. Trees, Jr.
Missouri City, Texas

No, they didn't make Kickapoo Joy Juice in the Skonk Works. They did make it in Dogpatch, yes. But the whole point of the Skonk Works was that one couldn't guess what went on there. Somebody (at one time, Li'l Abner) was "inside man at the Skonk Works," but to guess what that could have entailed meant tuning your imagination to Apocalypse. Al Capp, who intuited the power of the Black Hole, was subtler than mere lexicographers who trace him.

Hugh Kenner
Baltimore, Maryland

Narcissus, Absorb Thyself

T he lingo of looking inward is in, especially among reviewers.

In the movie *Nothing in Common*, a girl in a singles bar looks longingly at a handsome adman, played by Tom Hanks, and asks, "Are you involved with anybody?" He volleys the reply: "Does *self-involved* count?"

The *New York Times* film critic (formerly movie reviewer) Walter Goodman observed of the interestingly conflicted character: "He's simultaneously outer-directed and *self-absorbed.*"

Vincent Canby of the *Times*, also steeped in cinema syntax, wrote in 1981 that Federico Fellini's gifts were "entangled with his *self-absorbed* excesses," and Janet Maslin wrote in *Newsweek* in 1976 that Jeanne Moreau's directorial debut was "a sweetly *self-absorbed* look at four Parisian actresses." In the *Washington Post*, the critic David Remnick opined, "*Rocky IV* may be the most *narcissistic* film since, well, *Rocky III*. Stallone . . . is far too dense and *self-involved*. . . ."

The art critic Michael Brenson borrowed a couple of the most popular examples of inwardese in hailing Leon Golub's work at the New Museum of Contemporary Art in 1984: "*introspective* without being *self-absorbed.*"

And an actress who was herself involved with Woody Allen complained to the *Ladies' Home Journal* that the writer-director-star was "very much of a womanizer, very *self-involved.*" (If anyone knows the noun for the feminine counterpart to a *womanizer*, send it in.) In a Rodney Dangerfield film, the comic says his wife is so *self-involved* that "when we make love, she calls out her own name."

This is not to suggest that only reviewers use inwardese. A media moralizer, castigating the young corruppies of Wall Street, wrote: "These are the insiders with nothing inside, status-worshiping members of a flossed generation, whose *self-absorption* is complete. . . ." (I thought that *flossed generation* was pretty good; nobody got it.)

Both *self-involved* and *self-absorbed* first appeared in the 1840s. In 1842, Alfred, Lord Tennyson, wrote in "The Day-Dream" of "the pensive mind . . . all too dearly *self-involved.*" Five years later, Sir Arthur Helps got the absorption sponge working in a dialogue on social issues.

Sigmund Freud's early work on what he called *narcissism,* taking the word from the poet Samuel Taylor Coleridge's evocation of the myth of the youth who died of longing for his own reflection in the water, pulled the psychology crowd into the field. More recently Erik Erikson, the identity-crisis man, used *"generativity* versus *self-absorption"* to describe the seventh of his eight stages of man.

"Self-absorption involves narcissism," explains the Washington psychotherapist Stephen H. Shere, "while *generativity* is the acting out of one's responsibilities to the world, such as feeding the starving." Narcissism, within bounds, is not bad: an infant is wholly narcissistic, but, "in secondary narcissism," he says, "we are aware of being separate and learn to invest in ourselves."

And so, movie reviewers, look inside yourselves before wallowing in trendy inwardese. Is everyone *self-involved, self-absorbed* and *narcissistic,* in ascending order of intensity, or might a few characters and directors be merely *ruminative, meditative, pensive* or just *thoughtful* or *preoccupied*? If the point is that the wretch is concentered all in self, would *self-engrossed* do for a change? The answer can be found through a search inside, when in vacant or in pensive mood.

Vamping Till Ready

It all began with an innocent parenthetical remark. In a piece about the language of self-involvement, I quoted a girlfriend of Woody Allen as having described the actor as "very much of a womanizer, very self-involved." Then this afterthought: "(If anyone knows the noun for the feminine counterpart to *womanizer*, send it in)."

Evidently a great many men and women have been brooding about this for years. Suggestions began coming in at a brisk trickle. Punsters always get in the act—*male-factor, man-ipulator* and *man-iac* are typical—but serious linguists have had their say as well.

"I would like to suggest the neopaleologism *gumanizer*," wrote Dr. Nancy A. Porter, one of the editors of the Dictionary of Old English being compiled at the Center for Medieval Studies of the University of Toronto. "I have a vested interest in reviving Old English words that have not survived into Modern English," she confessed, "and would welcome a compound built on Old English *guma, guman,* 'man.'"

That's a nice neopaleologism. (Which is a word not to be looked up, but to be figured out: *neologism* means "newly coined word"; *paleo-* is the Greek-derived prefix for "ancient." By infixing *paleo-* in the middle of *neologism*, Dr. Porter has made use of a satisfying coinage for "new ancient word.")

In turning to Old English for the feminine counterpart to *womanizer*, we avoid the obvious word-building based on the Latin *homo, hominis*—identifying man as distinct from beast; as opposed to *vir*, man as distinct from woman—which would give us *hominizer*. That is unacceptable because it sounds like a girl having an affair with a barbershop quartet.

I began to build a nice, respectable file on this subject, when suddenly the word at issue became a streamer headline the width of the tabloid page in the *New York Post*. "Straight from the Hart" was the lead-in line, then the big black block letters: "Gary: 'I'm No Womanizer.'" A tiny subhead summed up the story: "Dem blasts rivals over sex life rumors."

Did presidential candidate Gary Hart really say those words? Of course not, no more than President Gerald R. Ford said "drop dead" to New York City, although that was what the *Daily News* wrote in its damaging headline in 1975: "Ford to City: Drop Dead." That is a manufactured quote, a nefarious journalistic device that puts in people's mouths what the headline writer thinks they should have said pithily. (First rule of denials: never use a colorful word, because it legitimizes the charge, viz. "I am not a wimp" or "I am not a crook." Deny only hard-to-remember charges, as in "I am not an insider-informed arbitrageur engaged in market manipulation.")

What Mr. Hart did say, after *Washington Post* reporter Lois Romano informed him that other campaigns were passing along rumors that the former senator was a "womanizer" and asked him frankly how he planned to deal with that, was that candidates who try to spread such rumors are "not going to win that way, because you don't get to the top by tearing someone else down." That was a sensible, even gracious reply to the sort of question that causes less experienced candidates to strike poses of rectitude and make strangled noises of outraged virtue.

But the word in the question, escalated by the *New York Post* headline, certainly placed the need for a feminine equivalent of *womanizer* center-stage and enlivened this column's correspondence.

First, the meaning of the male word: a *womanizer* is a man who seeks frivolous and frequent relations with a variety of women. Although the verb *womanize* originated in 1590 to mean "make feminine, emasculate," that sense has atrophied; in 1893, Farmer and Henley's slang dictionary equated the word *womanize* with the merry *go wenching.* The first Oxford English Dictionary citation for *womanizer* in its modern sense was by John Galsworthy in *The White Monkey,* the 1924 installment of his Forsyte novels.

Now the term is always pejorative, replacing the mock-heroic *Lothario* (after the rake in a 1703 play) or *Casanova,* suggesting the disapproval of promiscuity expressed in the slang *makeout artist* or *operator.* The essence of the word's disapprobation is in casualness and insincerity; it stops short, however, of *lecher,* one who is interested only in sex, and is far from *satyr,* one whose interest in sex is uncontrollable.

Now, to the counterpart: a female *satyr* is a *nympho,* the clipped form of *nymphomaniac,* and a female *lecher* is a *lecher*; that last word, from the Germanic word for "lick," is ungendered, and in current use is often clipped to *lech,* pronounced "letch." The noun has formed a verb: "Did you see that slut lech after that mere womanizer?"

Slut, perhaps derived from the Low German for "mud puddle," is gaining popularity; after substituting for *whore* in genteel publications, it has maintained its vigor despite the wider acceptance of the word it euphemized. However, these words—along with *harlot* and *strumpet*—are too strongly contemptuous to be suitable equivalents of *womanizer*; something less commercial and more callous is called for.

Seductress picked up a few votes, as did *temptress,* but they have a connotation of old-fashioned wickedness; the word sought must treat liaisons as too casual and cool for all-out temptation. *Vamp,* a pre-1920s slang term for a woman who would drag a man down to her level of delicious depravity, got some play despite its etymology from *vampire.* David Galef of New York City submitted the innocent and obvious *flirt,* but admitted that it "doesn't include the idea of consummation."

The most frequently submitted suggestion by far was *man-eater.* "Whether the reference is culinary (South Seas cannibal style) or to sharks, deponent knoweth not," wrote R. J. F. Knutson of Rockville Centre, N.Y. Added reporter Stuart D. Bykofsky of the *Philadelphia Daily News*: "The feminine equivalent of *lady-killer* would be *man-eater,* as recently repopularized in the Hall and Oates song."

Few dictionaries are up to date on this sense of the word. But the superb Thorndike-Barnhart World Book Dictionary has included for a decade this figurative meaning: "a woman who is very aggressive toward men." And it cites this usage in *Time* magazine: "He is half-heartedly fighting off the advances of a man-eater named Margaret."

In current usage, then, we have to say that the feminine equivalent of *womanizer* is *man-eater*, though the female form seems deadlier than the male. But I would like to put in a pitch for a fine old word derived from the Greek *philo-*, "loving," and *andr-*, "man": a *philanderer* has long been "a lover without serious intentions." We have applied it exclusively to men, for no reason; women can philander, too, and it has a more respectful ring than *flirt* or *slut*. Better than finding a gender-counterpart is coming up with a term that is sex-free. When a woman next becomes a candidate for President, she can say, "I am no philanderer," without fear of sexism or, for that matter, of manufactured quotations in headlines.

In your industrious quest for an adequate term by which to describe an enchantress able to exercise to an exceptional degree that sweet spell which all members of the fair sex cast on men deserving or fortunate enough to win their attention, I wonder that you have not noted Max Beerbohm's description of Zuleika Dobson as "the omnisubjugant." In a moment of tranquility in the residence of the Warden of Judas College, Oxford, reflecting on her many triumphs, she asks even so: ". . . would she ever meet whom, looking up to him, she could love—she, the omnisubjugant?"

And of course, not long after the tranquil moment of reflection, looking out on the green lawns, the entire undergraduate body of Oxford University drowned themselves for unrequited love of Zuleika, who could love no one who loved her. Among the deceased was the thirteenth Earl of Dorset, *fin de ligne.*

Daniel P. Moynihan
Senator, New York
United States Senate
Washington, D.C.

The female equivalent of a "womanizer," as every schoolboy knows, is a "Donna Juana."

The gender-neutral form of the term is "bedhopper."

John Hellegers
Jenkintown, Pennsylvania

Regarding Gary Hart and his hypothetical female counterpart: The word you are looking for is "promiscuous." Sally Quinn's usage of "philanderer" for the male and "slut" for the female, is pretty close, but rude to women. The word "randy" has always been a favorite of mine.

Evan M. Camp
The Bronx, New York

The opposite of "womanizer" has always been "cock-teaser." It is derogatory, as all epithets applied to women in a sexually non–socially acceptable position are. But at least it's not vicious, or recently coined, like your "man-eater."

Julia W. Loomis
New York, New York

You suggest "philanderer" as a substantive for a woman who chases men; if we have "bibliophiles" and "pedophiles" (whom I tend to confuse with people who are overly attracted to feet), why not "androphiles"?

Several other possibilities arise as well: "paleoandrophile," a woman who likes older men; "gumalogist," a man who coins words; "neologophile," someone who likes new words; and "nymphodemomaniac," a woman who is crazy about Democratic politicians.

Timothy P. Ryan
Zürich, Switzerland

If you are going to discuss words of the English language, why not discuss *why* awful words such as "slut" and "whore" exist for women and *not* for men. When a man is overly sexually "active," we call him a "stud," which for most people has a *positive* connotation.

Joanne Cross
South Bend, Indiana

Dear Bill:

You wrote "a girlfriend of Woody Allen." The sense is clear, but whenever I come upon that construction I can't help wincing a bit. I want: "of Woody Allen's." You would certainly write "a friend of mine," not "a friend of me." Yet "of Woody Allen" is exactly parallel to "of me."

I hasten to add that current usage is overwhelmingly on your side. What's more, the greatest English and American writers have done what I'm jibbing at, though not invariably. They wobble without apparent reason. You may ask, Does it make any difference which form is used? the answer is, Yes; for there is no other way to distinguish "a portrait of Sargent" (his face and figure) from "a portrait of Sargent's," the face and figure of Mrs. Thingumbob painted by Sargent.

By the way, the phrasing I advocate is an idiom, not a use of the possessive, such as might imply "one of many"; e.g.: "a friend of mine" meaning "among all my friends." The proof of this is that we say "that nose of his," where there is no suspicion of a plurality of noses.

Any resistance to such an apostrophe-s nonpossessive can often be satisfied by using a different preposition: "a letter *from* Lincoln," "a drinking song *by* Calvin Coolidge." It is interesting that the older English playwrights always wrote in their cast of characters: "cousin to the king," "sister to Rosalind," instead of "cousin of the king's," which would produce a string of *'ses* down the line.

Jacques [Barzun]
Charles Scribner's Sons
New York, New York

Nine Yards to Imbroglio

The news about the nomenclature of the arms scandal is that *-gate* is dead as a combining form.

In European newspapers, *Irangate* was tried, but Americans did not pick it up; doves here tried to shift the focus to Nicaragua by calling it *contra-gate*, but hawks resisted; *Northgate*, after the Marine colonel in the center of the mess, was too specific and limiting. *-Gate* just did not fly, and it may turn out that the last linguistic echo of Watergate died with a whimper, in a minor flap about expense accounts a few years ago that I tried to label *doublebillingsgate*.

What catchy moniker should be applied to the crisis? Suggestions, mostly facetious, ranged from *Iranamuck* to *Gipperdämmerung*; it is as if a scandal without an agreed-upon label lacks the identity that turns a story into history. However, the grand tradition of Credit Mobilier, Teapot Dome and Watergate, and corruption's lesser symbolic tradition of Deep-freezes and vicuña coats, had been interrupted. Perhaps because there were too many suggested names, or because the scandal had not found a locus (Arms-for-hostages? Secret dealings wrongly withheld from Congress? Diversion of funds?), the business of naming the scandal was in more disarray than the Reagan administration, which is saying plenty.

Worse, grisly grammarians in the media were having trouble getting universal acceptance for a noun to describe the state of affairs. *The New York Times* had a series of pages devoted daily to what it called the White House *crisis*, a neutral term; some political observers with memories of Truman days preferred the most descriptive but less objective *mess*. Nobody turned to *caper*, the original brush-off of the Watergate break-in, because that word was too lighthearted.

Blunder stumbled on the scene, had a brief moment at the start, but was soon replaced by the more resounding *fiasco*. That ringing term may come from the Late Latin *flasco*, meaning "bottle," which was associated in slang with the actions taken in drunkenness, and came to mean "a grandiose plan that flops." *Fiasco* became the only acceptable vogue term for the aborted invasion at the Bay of Pigs, but the noun was soon replaced; the switch to *scandal* took place when the story of ransom payments was given a new dimension by the disclosure of the diversion of arms profits to the contras.

Friends of President Reagan are still clinging to *imbroglio,* an Italian word meaning "confused, noisy embroilment," from the Old French *brouiller,* "to broil," which meant "to be in disorder." It long meant a confused heap: "I keep my prints an imbroglio, Fifty in one portfolio," wrote the poet Robert Browning; now the metaphor has been extended to mean any complicated dispute from which extrication is difficult. However, the idea of embroilment carries neither the drunken stupidity of *fiasco* nor the venality of *scandal,* which is why Mr. Reagan's defenders like *imbroglio.*

The President chose an Americanism of obscure origin to give a less serious, more high-spirited connotation to the activity. In a radio address, he asked rhetorically: "Were we engaged in some kind of *shenanigans* that blew up in our face?" That word, first spotted in an 1855 San Francisco publication—"Are you quite sure? No shenanigan?"—has a jocular cast of kidding around, perhaps to the point of madcap skulduggery. Only the President has suggested it applies here.

> You gave the derivation of "fiasco" as possibly having come from an association in slang with drunkenness.
>
> I had always heard and, in fact, also was told the last time I was in Venice that the derivation is from early Italian rather than Late Latin. The story told me is that the Venetian glassblowers tried to make every bottle they fashioned a masterpiece. Frequently, however, there was a flaw in the glass or the bottle didn't turn out as expected. So, rather than a piece to be proud of, the flawed bottle was utilized as an ordinary piece of kitchenware, called a "fiasco," from the Latin "flasco." The term fiasco thus came into English as something flawed, a failure.
>
> This explanation, even if flawed, seems more pertinent than an association with "drunkenness," with all due respect.
>
> M. B. Dolinger
> Cleveland, Ohio

> "Fiasco," in the sense of a "laughable failure," comes from the Italian *far fiasco,* which itself comes from the central-Italian practice of blowing wine bottles with a round bottom. These bottles, unless stabilized by a straw jacket with a flat bottom, e.g., the familiar Chianti bottle, immediately fall over. Italians normally use the word "flask" (old German *flaska;* cf. modern German *flasche),* rather than *bottiglia* (Latin *butticula,* French *bouteille,* whence English "bottle").

These flasks, unless they are sold in stores or are for export, never have the straw jacket. As a student in Florence, I remember buying wine in the various neighborhood wineshops. None of the flasks had straw, and they could not be set down except in a wooden case. Also, for those bottles that did have straw, perhaps the straw deteriorated and the bottles reverted to their original naked state.

In any case, for the Italian having to deal with a round-bottom flask that immediately fell over, the expression *far fiasco* became proverbial as an expression of failure. And so it has spread to our language.

Gerald Kamber
Loch Arbour, New Jersey

No Excuses

Miami model Donna Rice (*Miami model* is a bogus title, like *former candidate*) decided to use her celebrity to push a line of denim clothes named No Excuses. In a caption under her photograph in *New York* magazine, she was quoted as saying: "I have no excuses. I just wear them." Under the identical picture in *Time* magazine, she was quoted slightly differently: "I make no excuses. I only wear them."

It happens that the *New York* magazine version was the line in the printed advertisement, and *Time*'s version was a transcription of the line of copy she delivered in her television commercial. This divergence in coverage gives us the opportunity to compare the choices available or not available to copywriters.

The No Excuses ad came from the Kirshenbaum & Bond agency in New York City. The executive creative director, Richard Kirshenbaum, copywriter for the ads, explained: "We were under a number of constraints in using Donna in terms of what Donna wanted to say. She felt more comfortable saying, 'I make no excuses. I only wear them.' But she thought 'I have no excuses' was less of an affront in print." Interesting.

"I *have* no excuses" and "I *make* no excuses" both use transitive verbs, taking the object "excuses." *Have* connotes mere possession, in this case the lack thereof; in using the phrase in ordinary speech, I prefer the stronger *make*, which implies action. *I have no excuses* is a flat confession of guilt, but *I make no excuses* can also convey defiance, suggesting no feeling of guilt at all—instead, feeling no need to offer an excuse, which the speaker may or may not have. However, in the ad, Miss Rice should have said, only, "I *have* no excuses," because to say *make* implies she was the manufacturer, not the model, of the No Excuses line.

I just wear them or *I only wear them?* As adverbs, *just* and *only* can be synonyms; the sense intended in this sentence is "merely." But watch out for the power of the word *only:* it is a severely limiting adverb; its placement in a sentence is tricky ("I wear only them" would mean she wore nothing underneath, and Brooke Shields got in trouble with that); its meaning too easily strays from "merely." (To some of the more suspicious of us, *I only wear them* implies *I don't wash them.*)

On the other hand, *just*—not the adjective meaning "honorable" or "fair," but the adverb whose meaning can hop from "exactly" to "narrowly" to "simply" to "possibly" to the "merely" we want here—is a softer, less decisive modifier. In this case, intending to suggest no apologies in the wearing, I would choose the mild *just*, allowing greater emphasis on the verb that follows. (I dunno why I distrust Donna Rice and her alibi-free pants; I just do.)

> You missed a chance to deal with the grammar problem of the Donna Rice campaign. The jeans are labeled "No Excuses"; therefore, the phrase "No Excuses" is synonymous with the product. Ms. Rice doesn't manufacture the product, does she? Therefore, to be accurate, the copy line should read, "I don't make No Excuses. I just wear them." This would give Mr. Safire a whole column on the double negative and would give even more play to an ad campaign that seems to be fraught with public-relations opportunities.
>
> *Mary Lois Timbes*
> *New York, New York*

> How about "I don't make No Excuses; I only wear them"?
> Not only is this version equally correct in a grammatical sense, but it makes for a stronger, more active advertising statement. The apparent double negative makes one stop and think twice—just the thing you'd want an ad to do.
>
> *Bruce Cramer*
> *Guaynabo, Puerto Rico*

> I must take exception with your use of the preposition *of*. You write, ". . . (To some of the more suspicious *of* us, *I only wear them* implies *I don't wash them*)." There are some, I am sure (myself included), among your regular readers, who share your suspicion. To be just about this, you might have written, ". . . To some of the more suspicious *among* us, not *of* us (of whom there are only a few). No excuses.
>
> *I. Siraj Jamall*
> *Jamaica, New York*

No Heavy Lifting

"Say it ain't so, Joe," moaned the dismayed supporters of Senator Joseph R. Biden, Jr., the Democratic presidential hopeful, in tones echoic of the fans of baseball's Shoeless Joe Jackson when it was discovered that their idol had faithlessly sold out to the gamblers in the 1919 World Series.

The cause of the Biden followers' dismay was what members of the Judson Welliver Society, the organization of former White House speechwriters, call "heavy lifting": borrowing at length and without attribution the rhythms, thought patterns and sometimes the words of another orator.

"Why is it that Joe Biden is the first in his family ever to go to a university?" asked the candidate in a rousing finale to a debate at the Iowa State Fair. "Is it because our fathers and mothers were not bright? . . . Is it because they didn't work hard, my ancestors who worked in the coal mines of northeast Pennsylvania and would come up after twelve hours and play football for four hours?" These rhetorical questions were answered with a ringing "It's because they didn't have a platform upon which to stand."

That was a killer-diller of a peroration, warming egalitarian hearts, until Maureen Dowd, a reporter for *The New York Times*, printed excerpts from a speech by Neil Kinnock, leader of Britain's Labor party, made several months before:

"Why am I the first Kinnock in a thousand generations to be able to get to university? . . . Was it because all our predecessors were thick? Was it because they were weak? Those people who could work eight hours underground and then come up and play football? Weak? . . . It was because there was no platform upon which they could stand."

As an old hand at the speechwriting dodge, and a longtime specialist in its Thrilling Peroration Division, my first reaction was to wince at the formalistic *upon which* construction. Although it enabled the speaker to conclude with the strong word *stand,* the ostentatiously careful grammar conflicts with the common-man point; a more forceful conclusion would be "no platform to stand on," with spoken emphasis on *stand.*

Focused on this particular tree, however, I missed the forest of moral outrage that sprang up to deride the heavy lifter. "I'm going back to Gary Hart," said one embittered Democrat. "At least he didn't steal that girl from some far-lefty in England."

Maybe my familiarity with rhetorical borrowing has left me insensitive to the shock of recognition. I remember listening to John F. Kennedy's inaugural, with its stirring line "In your hands, my fellow citizens, more than mine, will rest the final success or failure of our course." I had to admire the way writer Ted Sorensen evoked the rhythm of the line in the Lincoln first inaugural: "In your hands, my dissatisfied fellow-countrymen, and not in mine, is the momentous issue of civil war." (Kennedy subtly corrected Lincoln's redundancy of *fellow-countrymen*; that was especially astute.)

What's wrong with such evocation? Winston Churchill, writing his ringing 1940 speech about defending his island by fighting on the beaches, in the streets, etc., recalled Georges Clemenceau's defiance in 1918: "I shall fight in front of Paris, within Paris, behind Paris." (Clemenceau, in turn, was paraphrasing Marshal Ferdinand Foch on Amiens.)

That sort of boosting—a less pejorative term than *lifting* and certainly far from *plagiarizing*, rooted in the Latin for "kidnapping"—is done all the time. Time for confession.

I always admired Franklin D. Roosevelt's use of the repeated *I see* construction, begun in his 1937 "I see one third of a nation ill-housed, ill-clad, ill-nourished. . . ." Working with writers Samuel I. Rosenman and Robert E. Sherwood in 1940, F.D.R. collaborated on a speech that used *I see* to frame an inspiring vision: "I see an America where factory workers are not discarded after they reach their prime. . . . I see an America whose rivers and valleys and lakes . . . are protected as the rightful heritage of all the people. . . . I see an America devoted to our freedom. . . ."

Working as a speechwriter for Richard Nixon in 1968, I thought: Why not lift it? Adlai Stevenson had already adapted the pattern to a series of paragraphs that began with *I look forward to*, which President Kennedy had lifted in 1963: "I look forward to a great future for America, a future in which our country will match its military strength with our moral restraint. . . . I look forward to an America which will not be afraid of grace and beauty. . . . And I look forward to a world which will be safe not only for democracy and diversity but also for personal distinction." Always a slam-bang format for a peroration.

So Richard Nixon told the Republican convention: "I see a day when Americans are once again proud of their flag. . . . I see a day when the President of the United States is respected and his office is honored because it is worthy of respect and worthy of honor. . . . I see a day when our nation is at peace and the world is at peace and everyone on earth—those who hope, those who aspire, those who crave liberty—will look to America as the shining example of hopes realized and dreams achieved."

After that speech, I felt a little pang of guilt—some spark of conscience had not been totally extinguished in the peroration dodge—and I called Judge Rosenman to fess up to using the *I see* construction he and Bobby Sherwood had written for Roosevelt.

"Check Robert Ingersoll about ten years after the Civil War," replied the man F.D.R. called "Sammy the Rose." With the help of the Library of

Congress, I tracked down the speeches of the orator who coined the sobriquet "The Plumed Knight" in the rousing nominating speech for candidate James Blaine. There was the source of F.D.R.'s *I see*'s in an Ingersoll speech in 1876:

"I see our country filled with happy homes. . . . I see a world where thrones have crumbled. . . . I see a world where labor reaps its full reward. . . . I see a world without the beggar's outstretched palm . . . and, as I look, life lengthens, joy deepens, love canopies the earth; and over all, in the great dome, shines the eternal star of human hope."

That is the sort of ending to a speech that Demosthenes would have considered a grabber. I never credited Sam Rosenman, and Rosenman never credited the guy who wrote it for Ingersoll; why should the Biden speechwriter give a public pat on the back to the hack who pounds away for Kinnock?

The answer is that times have changed; you can't get away with borrowing anything these days—not even an oratorical technique, much less a phrase or paragraph—unless you are willing to give the attribution. So my advice to candidates like Joe Biden is this: Do justly, love perorations and walk humbly with thy speechwriter. (I forget where I got that, but it has a nice ring to it.)

In 1976, during the Vice Presidential debates, Robert Dole was asked why he was seeking the post. "It's indoor work," Dole replied, "and no heavy lifting."

Gary Muldoon
Rochester, New York

Most people share much more in common than they realize. Our aspirations for ourselves, our families, our associates and our countries are usually not too different. It is only natural, therefore, to have common ways of expressing these aspirations.

I am not as much concerned with Senator Biden's borrowing freely from Neil Kinnock as I am with his association with this source. His use of Kinnock could mean that Mr. Biden shares many more of Mr. Kinnock's views than he might want the public to perceive. Certainly, if Mr. Biden had credited Mr. Kinnock, it would have had a rather chilling impact on many Americans who clearly do not share Mr. Kinnock's views. That is the real mischief in the political arena of borrowing so heavily from the words and thoughts of another without giving credit. Even so, I still think the reaction to Mr. Biden's "borrowing" was too severe.

James P. Duffy III
Lake Success, New York

I suspect that the exhortation with which you ended the column, and with which you were clearly pleased, is a screened memory of the ending to the epistle for the Third Sunday after Easter in the old (1928) American [Protestant Episcopal Church] *Book of Common Prayer:* "Honour all men. Love the brotherhood. Fear God. Honour the king."

It comes from the First Epistle General of St. Peter, chapter 2, verse 17.

Heavy lifting indeed!

Michael Dawson
Cambridge, Massachusetts

Your immediate source may be irretrievable; but for what most people would regard as the original source you could prophetably turn to Micah 6:8 in the King James version of the Old Testament (1611):

He hath shewed thee, O man, what is good; and what doth the Lord require of thee, but to do justly, and to love mercy, and to walk humbly with thy God?

But *is* this the *original* source (i.e., of the sentence pattern; the combination of ideas must go back—at least!—to the Hebrew text)? Before deciding, we should remember these words, which appeared on the title page of the King James text: "Translated out of the Original Tongues and with the former Translations diligently compared and revised." Now the former translations could include those—partial or complete—in Old English, Middle English (Wycliffe), several sixteenth-century versions; outside English (but probably known to some of the scholars who made the 1611 text), the authoritative Vulgate as well as the "Old Latin" predecessor; and the Septuagint translation of the Old Testament from Hebrew into Greek (about 200 B.C.). An examination of all these, including the Hebrew, would be necessary before one could venture on even a *probable* conclusion. For any one of these predecessors, successively repeated, may be partly responsible for the marvelous felicity of the verse in the King James Bible.

John C. McGalliard
Dictionary of American Regional English
Madison, Wisconsin

Nothing to Lose but Our Keynes

Can you imagine the delight of a pop lexicographer when presented with a new four-volume dictionary of economics? If there is one thing the world of words has long needed, it is an "Oxford English Dictionary for Economists," a place where we can take some delight in what is too often derogated as the dismal science.

Learned students of the economics dodge—once called "political arithmetic"—have reviewed these tomes (named for the British banker Robert Harry Inglis Palgrave,) in terms of substance and ideas. Herbert Stein (who coined the term *supply-side economics* in criticism of the school, but is better known for his espousal of the school he calls *the old-time religion*) says: "*The New Palgrave: A Dictionary of Economics* is the best comprehensive picture of economics we are likely to see in this generation," so the editors (John Eatwell, Murray Milgate and Peter Newman) need no blurb from me. I went through it for the fun terms.

Kuznets swings immediately caught my eye. This is no stern or admiring comment on the moral laxity or playfulness of Simon Kuznets, who died only a few years ago, but a description of his variation on economic growth cycles.

Nor is *the golden rule* what it seems to most outsiders. To Bible readers, this is "Do unto others as you would have them do unto you," and to political hatchetmen, it has been changed to "Do unto others before they do it unto you"; in economics, it is *the golden rule of capital accumulation,* which, according to the new Palgrave, "states that the steady-growth state that gives the maximum path of consumption . . . is the one along which national consumption equals the national wage bill and thus national saving equals 'profits.'" How does this relate to Christ's maxim? "The choice of the rights to assert is subject to a reciprocity or cost constraint, which is a useful thing, for otherwise one would demand the most extreme sacrifices of others."

Not light stuff, but try this other archaic reference: *beggar-thy-neighbor.* Joan Robinson, one of the relatively few female economists who make it big in this dictionary (she's the coiner of *bastard Keynesianism,* a defense of Lord Keynes from those who would twist, or bastardize, the meanings in his murky writing), wrote "Beggar-My-Neighbor Remedies for Unemployment" in 1937. This is a description of trade policies during the Depression, under which one country would try to improve its lot at the expense of others.

Beggar-my-neighbor was a children's card game in the 1700s; the earliest written citation is in 1734, applied to adults: "The Lawyers play at beggar my Neighbour." It's often used in association with the more current *zero-sum*, the economics game at which nobody wins except at the expense of somebody else.

The etymologists labored mightily over *free lunch*—derived from "there ain't no such thing as a free lunch"—but could not spot the origin. Milton Friedman popularized it in our time, but when I asked him where he got it, he shrugged (a body movement gaining frequency among economists).

I have two comments about the phrase "There ain't no such thing as a free lunch." I believe that the "free lunch" in the expression refers to the practice of taverns in the 1890s to have bread, cheese and other items available as a "free lunch" for patrons who also bought a beer (for five cents?—I'm not sure of the going price of beer at that time). Since the cost of the lunch was built into the price of the beer, this was truly an example of a "free lunch" which was not, in truth, free. While I believe that this is the origin of the phrase, I cannot produce a citation to support my claim.

The first literary use of the phrase that I have been able to find is by Robert Heinlein in his novel, *The Moon Is a Harsh Mistress* (New York: George Putnam's Sons, 1966). Edwin Dolan borrowed the phrase for the title of his book on environmental economics, *TANSTAAFL (There ain't no such thing as a free lunch): The Economic Strategy for the Environmental Crisis* (New York: Holt, Rinehart, Winston, 1971). My colleague Peter Aranson researched these two citations for his textbook, *American Government*.

Leonard A. Carlson
Associate Professor of Economics
Emory University
Atlanta, Georgia

When I was studying economics at the University of Vienna in 1931, I was told a story about an encounter between Pareto and Schmoller at a conference of economists in Munich in the early years of this century. Schmoller belonged to a school of economists who maintained that there were no general laws of economics and that the economic system of any country was determined by its institutions. After Schmoller had expounded these views at one session, Pareto said to him, "You know this town well. Can you tell me of a restaurant where I can get a good lunch free?" Schmoller replied, "There are no such restaurants." Pareto then said, "There is a general law of economics for you."

Michael Lindsay
Chevy Chase, Maryland

Notional Timeline

Daniel Schorr, senior news analyst for National Public Radio, was the first to notice it. The phrase was buried in one of the duller reaches of the Senate Intelligence Committee report on its preliminary inquiry into the Iran mess.

"A memorandum from [Lieutenant Colonel Oliver L.] North to [Vice Admiral John M.] Poindexter contains a 'notional timeline,'" noted the Senate committee, which marked in quotes but carefully avoided defining the phrase. Later, the writers of the report came back to the phrase of Colonel North's, in his January 24, 1986, memo, and used it confusingly: "North's 'notional timeline' for the Iran arms sale program provided for a funding mechanism. . . ." Did the *timeline* provide for the mechanism? Or did an item described in it do that trick? I have a hunch the person writing the Senate report did not know what a *notional timeline* was and did not want to admit it.

Notional—consisting of *ideas, concepts,* or the more trivial *notions*—is a word in grammar to denote what happens in the real world, as against *relational,* what happens in the land of syntax. For example, "sex"—the real thing, garter belts, nostrils stretched wide, huffing and puffing, post-coital remorse, the works—is *notional,* while "gender"—the category that tidy linguists use for words—is syntactic, or relational. That sense does not help here to figure out what Oliver North had in mind, so forget it.

Notional is an adjective that also means "fanciful, speculative, imaginary"; could that be what one military man was saying to the other? For help in understanding its application in this context, I turned to Bernard (Mick) Trainor, military correspondent of *The New York Times,* who was a general before he went straight. He recognized the usage immediately: "for illustrative purposes" was the meaning in the Pentagon.

When a bunch of the brass hats are noodling around a contingency, they're being notional: "A notional task force," said General Trainor, "is a hypothetical one—containing so many ships, so many planes, so many troops. It exists only on paper." Some strategists use it as a highfalutin word for "typical."

Now we're getting somewhere. What about the noun *timeline?*

Only the Oxford English Dictionary (as well as its Supplement) carries the term, which was used by the psychologist William James in 1890 to mean a line "of which each undulation or link stands for a certain fraction of a second." The O.E.D. Supplement's most recent sense of *timeline* is "a schedule, a deadline."

The term appears in Nexis, the electronic morgue, as the trade name for a project-management package owned by a company that calls itself Breakthrough Software, and in many references to plans made by the National Aeronautics and Space Administration and to timetables of computer companies.

Schoolteachers may be familiar with the word as it is used today in history assignments: For tomorrow's lesson, draw a timeline of the seventeenth century with all the battles, inventions, deaths of kings and openings of plays at the Globe Theatre.

Mick heard about the military use of *timeline*, too, in his fruit-salad days: it is a series of events in sequence, some of which may overlap, within a general *timeframe*. For example (mine, not his), in a timeframe of a month, you could have a timeline consisting of one day's bombardment of a target area, a two-day invasion, a week's resupply to secure the area and three weeks of visits by selected correspondents to designated areas for reporting on the victory.

Thus, a *notional timeline* can be a hypothetical series of events, or an imagined sequence, or a reconstruction for illustrative purposes of what could take place over a given period.

Subtly, without hinting at my purpose, I tried this on a White House aide familiar with the most arcane geostrategic jargon. Did the expression *notional timeline* mean anything in his world?

The ultra-insider responded immediately: "You mean Ollie's cockamamie chronology?" He's my candidate for the next notional security adviser.

I thought you might be interested in the story of the "Notional Timeline" that was cited in the Senate Intelligence Committee report of the Iran affair.

The original report was drafted by the staff director, Bernie McMahon, and myself during the last part of December 1986. Our version (never published, but parts of which appeared in *The New York Times*) included reprints of key documents. One of these was the January "Notional Timeline" prepared by Oliver North. I think we learned of it from Bob Gates, who thought it was flaky. (We did, too.)

North titled his memo "Notional Timeline," and we referred to it as such. As I recall, we always wrote it with quotation marks.

Contrary to your column, we knew exactly what a "Notional Timeline" was—a "tentative," "proposed" or "strawman" schedule; it sounds like Pentagon jargon. In this case, though, "Notional Timeline" was "Ollie North's fantasy."

Government reports are supposed to be sober, reserved and objective, so we couldn't really say (as Weinberger said about the draft NSDD), "This is absurd." So, instead, we left it as it was—and the jargon, the silliness, all spoke volumes about North, without any commentary.

The committee voted against the report, I was fired (partisan politics sharpened by the argument over the report) and the staff began writing a new report around the investigation we had conducted. But good phrases die hard, and "Notional Timeline" survived. Dan Schorr later asked me about it at a lunch at the Brookings Institution, and he passed it on to you.

Incidentally, the report Bernie and I wrote wasn't much different from the one later released (our conclusions would have been just as appropriate). But, I might say with just a little immodesty, ours was written better—Notional Timeline and all.

Bruce D. Berkowitz
Alexandria, Virginia

The word *notional* has a special meaning in Spookspeak, one somewhat different from the definition and explanation you offered in your column. It is used in reference to the fabricated details of a cover story, or "legend." Thus, for example, the State Department official to whom a covert intelligence officer under State cover ostensibly reports is his or her *notional* supervisor (as contrasted with the real one, e.g., the chief of station).

Like many other Spookspeakisms, the use of the word in this sense has been borrowed from British intelligence. Writing about World War II counterintelligence operations, former British naval intelligence officer Ewen Montagu defined it thusly:

NOTIONAL. Term used to denote something imaginary, other than the actual object of the deception, which the Germans were led to believe. For instance a notional job; or a double agent notionally went to Bristol and notionally saw a ship (which may or may not have been there).

This is from *Beyond Top Secret Ultra* by Ewen Montagu, Coward-McCann, 1978, p. 181.

Henry S. A. Becket, in his *Dictionary of Espionage*, says that the term has expanded in American usage, that a *notional* is approximately the same as a *proprietary company*, and that the FBI uses the term *notional organization* to designate several types of devised or imaginary organizations established for clandestine purposes.

G. J. A. O'Toole
Mount Vernon, New York

The people who used the word *notional* most effectively were the British (with some input from the Americans after 1942). I refer specifically to the work of Section 17M of the Naval Intelligence Division and Section B1A of M.I.5 who reported to the Twenty Committee; it was also written in Roman numerals as the XX Committee, and soon, and quite appropriately, it became known as the "Double Cross" Committee.

They created a whole raft of notional agents who reported to the Abwehr about notional war plants, notional ships and even a notional army group (FUSAG, which stood for First United States Army Group). Notional was a "buzz" word in those days, which has only now reappeared in a similar context forty-five years later.

William M. McCulloch, LCDR RCN (Ret.)
Hamilton, Canada

Not to Mention *Prolepsis*

O ne of the last of the leading personalities of World War II arrived for a visit to Taiwan. Madame Chiang Kai-shek, then eighty-six years old, was asked by her stepson, President Chiang Ching-kuo, to issue a statement endorsing his political reforms, which included toleration of an opposition party.

She made her statement, but *The Economist*'s reporter in Taipei wrote: "The language was so arcane that it baffled interpretation."

Madame Chiang (I don't care if the stylebook calls for "Mrs."; she'll always be Madame to me) said this: "I am fully cognizant of a prolepsis of malicious misreading of my thought given to you here."

Prolepsis means "an anticipating." In the expanding language of media-bashing, it means the false description of an event before the event has taken place; a crooked theater critic will write a proleptic review of a play that has not yet had its first performance. In rhetoric, *prolepsis* is the anticipation of your opponent's argument, summarizing what he is likely to say in a slanted fashion and demolishing his point before he has a chance of advancing it himself.

It's a super trick and I do it all the time; thanks to Madame Chiang, I now know the name for it. In return, let me edit and repunctuate her sentence for those who find it arcane (from the Latin *arcanus*, "shut in, hidden"): "I am fully cognizant [better to use *well aware*] of prolepsis—the technique of maliciously misreading my thoughts—that has been given to you here." That could be followed by quoting Edward VIII's abdication speech opening: "At long last I am able to say a few words of my own."

I, too, was perplexed by her statement because *prolepsis* is easily confused with *paraleipsis*, which means "the technique of pointing something out while denying you are pointing it out." In a recent piece about the prefix *para-*, I parenthetically referred to *"paralegal, paramilitary* and I need not mention *paraleipsis."* That was an arch way of using the word in a way that defined it, but only to those who already understood it, and I ought to cut that out.

She was unafraid to use unfamiliar words, and my hat is off to her on that. In a speech during her visit, after referring to a column of mine about the defeat-from-victory meaning of Yalta, Madame Chiang deplored the way the free world had offered victory "as corban to whet the voracious appetite of the bear." *Corban* is from a Hebrew word for "sacrifice" and can still be found in unabridged dictionaries meaning "offering."

She noted with disdain the "prevalent prevarications" of some commentators. It goes without saying that Madame Chiang thought the media should be ashamed of its liberal bias. (In that last sentence, the *prolepsis* is the unfair assumption of her likely argument, and the *paraleipsis* is the saying of what is said to go without saying.)

Nyet Problemy on Snow Jobs

Brush up your Russian; détente is back. When Ronald Reagan and Mikhail Gorbachev signed the treaty in Washington on medium-range missiles, the world television audience witnessed what seemed like a nice bit of byplay between the two leaders. Mr. Reagan recalled a Russian maxim: "Though my pronunciation may give you difficulty, the maxim is *doveryai no proveryai.* 'Trust but verify.' "

According to the interpreter, Mr. Gorbachev replied amiably: "You repeat that at every meeting." Mr. Reagan smiled, "I like it," and the spirit of good will was all over the place.

However, a former refusenik who heard the Russian phrase before the English translation writes to set us straight: "The General Secretary used the Russian verb *boltaete,* which does not mean 'repeat,' but means 'drivel.' He said, 'You always drivel that,' which sounds in this context rather rude. Most of my Russian friends were flabbergasted; even in Soviet schools they teach people not to use such rude words when speaking to older and respected people, let alone Presidents."

I turned to a second, perhaps more objective, source. Eugene Beshenkovsky, information manager at Columbia University's W. Averell Harriman Institute for Advanced Study of the Soviet Union, says: *"Boltaete* [pronounced bol-TA-et-yeh] does not quite mean 'to drivel,' which suggests nonsense. It is closer to 'to talk about just for the sake of talking.' " It does not mean, as the interpreter softened it, *repeat*, the Russian verb for which is *povtoriat'*.

Well, was it rude? "It is not considered a very polite expression," said Mr. Beshenkovsky, trying to be diplomatic, but he then had to be straight about it: "Yes, rude."

The perfect translation, I think, would have been: "You do run on at the mouth about that," or more politely, "You always go on and on about that." That might have wiped the smile off the President's face.

I, too, have my translation problems. In a piece about the way the presence of the American media turns Gorby-Jekyll into Gorby-Hyde, I used the term *nyet problema* to mean "no problem."

A problem: I used the nominative case, *problema*, but after a negative, the genitive case is called for in proper Russian. Louis Jay Herman of New York City advises that the correct form is *nyet problemy* (pronounced pro-BLEM-ee), adding parenthetically, "assuming, of course, that a Russian would attempt a literal translation of this particularly American colloquialism."

The fact is that Russians do use this expression: I have heard them with my own ears, and it comes out *nyet problema*, which we can all agree is grammatically wrong. Could it be that this is an idiom, in which case all rules of grammar are suspended? ("It's me," says the idiomatic American; *"Nyet problema,"* replies the idiomatic Russian.)

The phrase appears in Serbo-Croatian as *nema problema*, and may be traveling along the route taken by the world's most widely adopted Americanism, *OK*. "On a trip to Kenya this past September," writes Bill Abbott of Westport, Conn., "we were astonished to hear the American phrase from a Masai warrior when our van stopped at a village to take pictures and bargain over beads and spears. But there it was in reply to my offer of half the asked-for shillings: 'No problem, Mister,' spoken with minimum accent."

In current use around the world, the phrase's sense seems to be broadening from its literal meaning to "Glad to help," "You're welcome" and the ubiquitous "OK." Let's keep an eye on this, but in a relaxed way; otherwise, we could be said to run on at the mouth, or to have *logorrhea*, or *boltaete*.

The perfect rendering of Mr. Gorbachev's *boltaete* would of course have been "There you go again. . . ."

> Lu Fenton
> New York, New York

As for your assessment of "nyet problema" as an emerging idiomatic expression in Russian, you can be assured that this is not yet likely. I, too, have heard the words "nyet problema" from the mouths of native speakers in Russia. It is to be heard, in my experience, only among those speakers of Russian, both educated and not, who spend considerable time with foreigners, especially English-speaking foreigners. It will be said most certainly tongue-in-cheek, almost deprecatingly, because "no problem" is indeed such an exclusively American idiom.

One of the most striking characteristics of the language of these groups is the use of English words and Americanisms. The extreme is to be found among that part of the Soviet criminal society that does the dangerous by seeking "commercial" contact with foreigners, the blackmarketeers and speculators. The slang of Anthony Burgess's *Clockwork Orange* heroes is uncannily inverted in their jargon. "Gyrleez," "shoozy," "fakovat'" (by adding the suffix "-ovat'" to almost any English word you can produce a corresponding verb; that's what they do with "gyrleez" who wear nice "shoozy"), and "okay" are all words found in the vocabulary of these people.

"Nyet problema" is not colloquial Russian. It is a specific collocation used jocularly or "cutely" by that tiny section of the Russian population who for whatever reason comes into regular contact with English speakers. Perhaps it derives from mocking the inability of Americans to deal with an inflected language. This is especially likely since the idiom itself derives from English. "That is not a problem" in Russian would be "éto nee problema." It is highly unlikely that it will become widespread because the genitive case is far from loosing its hold in Russian and in fact seems to be growing in many negative constructions. The word "nyet" is certainly in no danger of losing its genitive government.

Nathan Longan
The Russian School
Norwich University
Northfield, Vermont

The *problema* is that the genitive case of *problema*, viz., *problemy*, is not pronounced pro-blem-ē, which could never be mistaken for pro-blem-ə. The final vowel is a muted (ĭ) sound, which can be easily mistaken for (ə).

In udder woids, there is no idiomatic *nyet problema*. Russian speakers don't mix up their case endings, ever. Not these endings anyway.

Marshall D. Berger
Orangeburg, New York

When I was in the U.S.S.R. in 1985, I noticed that the phrase for "no problem" was *nyet problem*. This may sound as though it's lifted straight from English, but actually *problem* is the genitive plural of *problema.* The literal translation into English, therefore, would be "no problems."

Dianne Goldstaub
Minneapolis, Minnesota

Your delightful piece led me to the original Greek word το προβλημα. The Greeks consider all nouns ending with the syllable "μα" as of the neuter gender: dogma, anathema, dilemma. The Germanic languages invariably assign it to whose *ma* nouns that they have adopted. Often the final *a* vanishes in order to spare their euphonious sensibilities: e.g., *das Problem.*

The Romance languages, on the other hand, not having the neuter, supply the masculine gender to the *ma-* ending nouns, maybe because in Latin the declension of the neuter nouns is very similar to that of the masculine nouns. Unlike the Germanic, the Spanish and the Italian languages keep the final vowel, although it grates on their ears: *un problema.*

The geographical neighbors of the Greeks—the Bulgarians, the Serbo-Croats and through them the Russians—have apparently more fidelity to their euphony. They opted for the feminine gender.

We have *odna* (not *odno*) *problema* on our hands.

Chaim Zemach
New York, New York

When I was in Guilin, in southeast China, in 1987, "no problem" seemed to have taken over the teen-aged population. In our hotel, which was brand-new and indeed had some problems (the Li River, for example, rose periodically into the lobby), any and all questions were answered by the young staff with a wide smile and a courteous "no prob-lem." Often this meant that they didn't understand the problem or weren't in a position to do anything about it, but it was delightful to hear so far from home, nevertheless.

Annette H. Landau
New York, New York

Grovel, Grovel, Grovel

First off, I owe an apology to Mikhail Gorbachev, author of *Perestroika,* whose book tour included a stop in Washington. (Why *first off?* Why not just *first?* Because I am being determinedly colloquial, and it's better than the awkward *firstly.*)

With a loud "Ah-hah!" I quoted an anonymous refuse-nik catching the

Soviet General Secretary using a Russian word that was kind of an insult to President Reagan. When Mr. Reagan used a Russian maxim, *doveryai no proveryai,* Mr. Gorbachev replied, according to his interpreter, "You repeat that at every meeting." Got a laugh, no hard feelings.

According to my source, however, the Russian word used was not *povtoriat',* "repeat," but *boltaete,* correctly translated as "drivel," and I twitted the Soviet leader for his impertinence.

Wrong. My source misheard Mr. Gorbachev, as legions of Russian-speaking Lexicographic Irregulars pointed out. I sent the tape of the interchange to an impartial observer, Professor Vera Borkovec at the American University in Washington, who reported, "I've listened to the tape twenty-five times, and I'm confident that Mr. Gorbachev used the verb meaning 'repeat,' *povtoriat.*"

So I'm sorry, although this changes nothing about my feelings toward the treaty-breaking, phrased-array battle-management radar at Krasnoyarsk. As recompense, let me pass along a zingier response, suggested by many readers who recall Mr. Reagan in debate: "There you go again!"

That was not my only recent failing. In a piece about the character *issue,* a phrase first used in *Newsweek* about Senator Edward Kennedy's presidential soundings in 1979, I described his attempt "to wrest the Democratic nomination away from President Jimmy Carter."

"*From whence* and *wrest away* sound similarly redundant," wrote Barbara Goff, on the copy desk of the *Washington Times,* a precinct captain for the Squad Squad. She was right; when *wrest* is followed by *from,* no *away* is needed; a case can be made that the *away* is an intensifier, as in *run away from,* but that's a cop-out. If you're talking about twisting something out of somebody's hands, stay away from *wrest away,* as I will henceforth.

And that's not all, as the copywriters say. This communication from Marvin Kalb, Edward R. Murrow Professor of Press and Public Policy at Harvard's Kennedy School of Government (named after JFK, who wrested the nomination from LBJ, and not Teddy, who is wresting on his laurels):

"There I was at breakfast," wrote my friend Kalb. "Six degrees. The Charles River looking like a frozen white snake on the horizon. Cereal and Safire. And then what am I reading? 'That's a triple MEGO, more stupefyingly soporific than sipping a glass of warm milk while watching the Democratic six-pack lob marshmallows at each other.' "

The professor lets me off the hook on the counting of candidates, since six-pack is a useful grouping, but takes grammatical issue with my *each other.* "I remember from Miss Draddy in high school (she taught English) that *each other* refers to two people. Each and the other. Above two, she said, the proper phrase is *one another.* Now is Miss Draddy correct?"

Miss Draddy is losing that fight, but it's not one I want to win. According to Fowler's *Modern English Usage,* "Some writers use *each other* only when no more than two things are referred to . . . but this differentiation is neither of present utility nor based on historical usage." However, The New York Times Manual of Style and Usage goes along with the Draddy-Kalb differentiation, and I like the hair splitting —reminds me of the distinction between *among* and *between* and among *repeat, reiterate* and *you do go on.* But now for the trap:

"What a piece of work is a man!" I quoted Shakespeare's Hamlet in a piece about *piece of work,** a phrase used to express wonderment and suspicion, as in "That Gorbachev, he's a piece of work." The Danish prince continued, in my quotation, ". . . how like an angel in apprehension! how like a god!"

The trap baited, I awaited the Gotcha! Gang quarry. "Your inaccuracy is so glaring," wrote Mohan S. Kalelkar, an associate professor of physics at Rutgers, "that I predict your volume of mail may set a record. Your quotation seriously misrepresents the actual passage [II, ii, 303–307]. It really reads '. . . in action how like an angel, in apprehension how like a god!' "

Yes, that's almost the way it appears in the First Folio of Shakespeare. (That's also the way most actors render the lines, and the way they appear in such modern editions as the Oxford Shakespeare.) *Folio* is the name of a size—usually the biggest book, about 12 by 15 inches, the size of a printer's sheet folded in two, making four pages in a book; folded again it becomes a *quarto,* then an *octavo,* and finally what the experts call a little itty-bitty book.

The First Folio refers to the earliest publication of the collection of Shakespeare's plays, published in 1623, some seven years after the playwright's death. However, his plays were printed twenty years before that in quarto. Shakespearean scholars refer to the First Quarto as "Q1," and describe this transcription, perhaps from the memory of an actor, as a "bad" quarto. This was before the blessed era of copyrights, and pirated editions of scripts were frequent; they are now derogated as "memorially reconstructed."

In 1604, another quarto appeared, about twice as long as the first; this was put out, perhaps by Shakespeare's company, to replace the "bad" quarto. Its title page announces: "The Tragicall Historie of Hamlet, Prince of Denmarke. By William Shakespeare. Newly imprinted and enlarged to almost as much againe as it was, according to the true and perfect Coppie."

In the 1974 Riverside edition of Shakespeare's plays, Harvard's G. Blakemore Evans comments: "Since the pioneer work of J. D. Wilson in 1934, the position of Q2 as basic copy-text for a critical edition has never been seriously questioned. Wilson was able to show with near certainty that Q2 was printed from some form of Shakespeare's autograph, probably the 'foul papers.' " Those smelly-sounding "foul papers" are drafts or

* See "Piece of Work," pages 261–62.

working copies with corrections marked, as opposed to "fair copies," pages made after those corrections are incorporated.

Here lies the point. In the Second Quarto, which may have had Shakespeare's approval, the passage reads: "What peece of worke is a man, how noble in reason, how infinit in faculties, in forme and moouing, how expresse and admirable in action, how like an Angell in apprehension, how like a God."

Subsequent readers and printers and actors fiddled around with those words; in the First Folio, printed in 1623, a clarifying article was inserted between the words "What peece," making it "What a piece." That was good. Then the punctuation was changed as well: "What a piece of worke is a man! how Noble in Reason? how infinite in faculty? in forme and mouing how expresse and admirable? in Action, how like an Angell? in apprehension, how like a God."

I make no apologies for setting this trap, because the Gotcha! Gang makes no apologies for hooting at my ignorance, and it's good to get even. Feel free to use this riposte whenever anybody corrects your Shakespeare: "Are you using the First Folio, or have you been quoting from the Second Quarto?" As Hamlet never said, "Trust but verify."

> You inform us that after the octavo, we are left with the smallest book, "and finally what the experts call a little itty-bitty book." Could this be a case for the Squad Squad? I think the phrase would be more effective and less cluttered if it read, "what the experts call an itty-bitty book."
>
> *Geoffrey Morrow*
> *Brooklyn, New York*

> Your comment on "phrased-array" refers to your area of expertise, not mine, which you intended.
>
> A phased-array radar can track or search for objects without a moving antenna. It relies on wave interactions among signals from a multitude of small antenna elements to steer the beam. Technology has replaced the turning radar dish. Gotcha! Or, did I fall into a trap?
>
> *Mike Spataro*
> *New York, New York*

> I'm sure you'll emerge unphased, if not unphrased, from this one.
>
> *Frank S. Stein*
> *Kokomo, Indiana*

Of Baths and Garters

Sir Anthony Acland decided to leave his job as head of the British diplomatic service to go out in the field as Her Majesty's Ambassador to the United States. At State functions, when decorations are worn, he will be sporting his G.C.M.G., which everyone in the protocol dodge knows means Grand Cross of the Order of St. Michael and St. George. Do not confuse this with the lower-level C.M.G. (Companion of the Order of St. Michael and St. George) or the middle-level K.C.M.G. (Knight Commander of the Order of St. Michael and St. George).

If these abbreviations are hard to remember, do as the British do, and use this mnemonic: the ascending orders are Call Me God and Kindly Call Me God, with the Grand Cross remembered as God Calls Me God.

Of Ducks and Men

"In case you may have wondered," said Peter Jennings on ABC-TV (his variation on John Chancellor's "We just thought you'd like to know"), "in this country the phrase *lame duck* appears to derive at the time of the Civil War from duck hunting. A wounded duck, or a lame duck, isn't very effective either as a duck or a hunting trophy."

The anchorman was blind-sided on that canard, and not just in the active voice of *to derive* rather than the passive *to be derived.* In 1761, the British author Horace Walpole, who had just discovered some delicious new stock-exchange terms, wrote to Sir Horace Mann: "Do you know what a Bull, and a Bear, and a Lame Duck are?" The O.E.D. later defined the term to mean "a disabled person or thing; *specifically (Stock Exchange slang):* one who cannot meet his financial engagements; a defaulter."

Mr. Jennings has manfully helped me schlep suitcases through the airport at Islip, L.I., so I will be careful to note how he modified his statement with "in this country"; however, when *lame duck* was imported here from England in the mid-nineteenth century, the term still carried its slang meaning of bankruptcy. Soon it was applied to politically bankrupt officeholders, and by 1863, Francis Blair's *Congressional Globe* sneered at the Court of Claims for being "a receptacle of 'lame ducks' or broken down politicians."

The duck has an honored place in American slang. Mr. Reagan once told supporters he would be no lame duck; previously, Jimmy Carter used the Southernism *like a duck on a June bug* to call up the image of a persistent fowl pecking away at a hardshelled beetle. We also have *strange duck* (or *queer duck* or *odd duck*) for an eccentric person, *sitting duck* for anyone vulnerable and *dead duck* for someone whose chances are considered meager.

The best use has to do with political semantics. Not so long ago I complained about an editorial correction of a reporter who labeled the Sandinista Government in Nicaragua "communist"; the editors felt that the Central American regime was not set up on the Soviet model, and "Marxist-Leninist" would be a more accurate description. To me, this called up labor leader Walter Reuther's advice. Explaining how to tell a communist, he said, "If it quacks like a duck, and waddles like a duck, then it just may be a duck."

When I was studying civics in high school, we were taught that a lame duck is an elected officeholder whose successor has been elected but has not as yet taken office. According to that definition, which I believe to be authentic, Mr. Reagan was a lame duck President from election day 1988, or the day after, until noon on January 20, 1989.

Julian S. Herz
Indianapolis, Indiana

The "Southernism" *like a duck on a June bug* used by Jimmy Carter does not mean "persistently." This phrase, a favorite of my father's, is always used by him to mean quickly and with enthusiasm. If you have had any acquaintance with ducks, you should know that a duck swallows a June bug (a slow and stupid creature) whole and with no trouble at all. The fact that June bugs have "hard shells" is no deterrent whatsoever. Ducks are always enthusiastic when they eat, and I suspect that they find June bugs to be particularly choice morsels. By the way, my father is an Oklahoman, born and bred, and Oklahoma is not part of the South or the Midwest.

Ann Boulton
Washington, D.C.

Ducks do go lame. Otherwise healthy ducks, usually drakes, limp about as though they were arthritic, for a couple of months, and then recover. However, if a duckling is born lame, as sometimes they are, it won't survive longer than a couple of months.

Over fifteen years of keeping ducks, I've observed this a number of times.

Chloe A. Hudiburg
South Plymouth, New York

Off the Flaw

"I regret more deeply than I can express," stated presidential candidate Alexander M. Haig, Jr., "that the current proposed arms-control agreement is seriously flawed."

I give Al credit for that: he avoided the most crashing cliché of treatymanship, that ringing triumph of alliteration, *fatally flawed.* (He went on to say, "I cannot support the proposed agreement, however much that may be the politically popular thing to do." Where did I hear that before?)

Fatally flawed was Ronald Reagan's characterization of the SALT II treaty negotiated by the Carter Administration, because he said it would not bring about reductions in large Soviet land-based missiles. The phrase worked well for him; in 1987, he told an interviewer that the plan put forward by Costa Rica's President Oscar Arias Sanchez in Guatemala was *fatally flawed. The New York Times*, in rebuttal, editorialized: "The Guatemala plan, whatever its weaknesses, is not fatally flawed." The editorialist knew that, in the game of treaty flaws, to be *seriously flawed* is to mean "Look, this isn't so hot, but with a few big fixes, I could live with it," but to be *fatally flawed* is to mean "This is one I want to run against."

Mopping the flaws with fatality has resulted in a waxy buildup of bromide. "He said my résumé was fatally flawed," wrote a job-hunter in *Dun's Review* in 1975, "because it failed to tell a prospective employer what I could do for him." In 1983, United States Ambassador to UNESCO Jean Gerard said that the organization was "so skewed, so far off course, so fatally flawed" that the United States had to get out.

Indiana Senator Richard G. Lugar, observing a fraudulent election in the Philippines in 1986, refused to accept its legitimacy because the balloting was flawed in the way we have all come to know and love. Nor is the phrase limited to political righties: a spokesman for the Union of Concerned Scientists called Mr. Reagan's Star Wars proposal too costly to put up and too inexpensive to shoot down, therefore "fatally flawed."

First use? Merriam-Webster has a 1916 citation from Sir Arthur Quiller-Couch's *On the Art of Writing*, in which the famed stylist criticizes a work for "the one fatal flaw that it imports emotion into a theme which does not properly admit of emotion." The lexicographer Fred Mish thinks the phrase goes back much further (not farther): "Normally, the noun phrase would be constructed first—*fatally flawed* would come out of *fatal flaw*—and my guess is that *fatal flaw* is much older than 1916." Lexicographic Irregulars who want to top the O.E.D. and Merriam-Webster have their work cut out for them, a cliché dating to I don't know when.

It could be that *fatal flaw* is rooted in *tragic flaw*. According to Stan Malless and Jeff McQuain's *A Handlist to English*, that tragic flaw, called in Greek *hamartia*, is "a fatal weakness in a tragic hero's character. In tragedy, *hamartia* causes the tragic hero's downfall or death. . . . Having too much ambition is one of the most common examples."

Which brings us back to Presidents and candidates for President, who search for fatal or at least serious flaws and eschew *hubris*, the excess of confidence that is another of the banana peels set in the paths of heroes.

The first candidate to criticize a treaty, any treaty, without the use of the dread term, gets a laurel wreath from this department. Yes, when a noun phrase ("That treaty has a fatal flaw") develops into an adjective modifying a noun ("That is one fatally flawed dish of oatmeal"), it becomes known to grammarians as a participial phrase. Knowing that leads to hubris.

Oh, Fudge

H ere is a man who would fudge when it suits his purpose." So said Australian Justice Philip Powell, with scorn, of the Secretary to Margaret Thatcher's Cabinet, in connection with the trial concerning the attempted suppression of a book about "the fifth man" who may have infiltrated Britain's spy service.

"Kinnock Fudge Over Nuclear Pull-Out Date" was the headline in *The Times* of London, over a story about the way Neil Kinnock of the Labor party had backed away from naming the day he would toss American nuclear weaponry out of Britain.

The Foreign Affairs Fudge Factory was the title of a 1971 book about the United States State Department by John Franklin Campbell. It popularized a term that has identified that building in Washington much as "Puzzle Palace" has become the informal moniker for the Pentagon, although it also signifies the National Security Agency (previously known as "No Such Agency").

Around the English-speaking world, the use of the word *fudge* is evidently on the rise. The word is ascendant because it is used to describe three actions of government officials: 1) hemming and hawing (a single action); 2) hedging with such qualifiers as to make a position meaningless, and 3) shading truth in a way that approaches deception but cannot be called outright lying.

Fudge was a word beloved by the American poet James Russell Lowell. In 1848, he wrote of Edgar Allan Poe: "There comes Poe, with his raven, like Barnaby Rudge/Three fifths of him genius and two fifths sheer fudge." Almost four decades later, Lowell provided the motto of the American Copyright League: "In vain we call old notions fudge,/And bend our conscience to our dealing;/The Ten Commandments will not budge,/ And stealing *will* continue stealing."

Fudge is one of those words (like *bother* and *fiddle*) that can be used as three different parts of speech: interjection, verb and noun. The interjection was first provided by Oliver Goldsmith in 1766, describing a character in *The Vicar of Wakefield* who "at the conclusion of every sentence would cry out Fudge!"

The noun, in the sense of "nonsense," appeared a generation later— "That is all fudge to frighten you"—but its meaning gained a more lying connotation in the next century. Ralph Waldo Emerson denounced the "riot of mediocrities and dishonesties and fudges." In mathematics today, the *fudge factor* is a quantity introduced illegitimately into a solution by corrupt mathematicians to arrive at a desired result.

The origin of the verb *to fudge* is lost in the mists of the seventeenth century: some say it derives from the archaic *fadge*, "to agree" or "to fit pieces together"; others point to the chance of echoic variation of the German *futsch*, "gone, ruined"; Isaac D'Israeli, Ben's father, speculated that *fudge* is an eponym of one Captain Fudge, known widely as "Lying Fudge."

How did this word, usually connoting hoaxes, cheating and things in general disrepute, become associated with sweetness and candy? Nobody knows; in 1896, a Michigan publication defined *fudges* as "a kind of chocolate bonbons," and six years later, in England, the journal *The Queen* reported that "The greatest 'stunt' among college students is to make *Fudge*," including "Nut Fudges" and "Fruit Fudge."

In the 1983 Dictionary of American Food and Drink, John F. Mariani reports speculation that the hoax meaning might have come from the way that college women (Wellesley Fudge and Vassar Fudge were early citations) used the making of candy as an excuse to stay up late, and the fudging of curfews led to the making of fudge, a semisoft candy of grainy texture made of sugar, butter and flavoring such as chocolate.

AUNT TOOTS'S LOW-SODIUM CHOLESTEROL-REDUCED, CALORIE-CONSCIOUS NUT FUDGE

4	tablespoons margarine
1½	cups skim milk
3	cups sugar
⅔	cup cocoa
⅛	teaspoon cream of tartar
1	cup chopped pistachio nuts in 2 teaspoons aged rum

1. In a saucepan, melt the margarine in the milk over a low flame. Add the sugar, cocoa and cream of tartar. Cook over a medium flame, stirring constantly until the mixture comes to a boil.

2. Simmer the mixture, without stirring, until it reaches the soft-ball stage (234 degrees on a candy thermometer). Remove from heat and cool to 110 degrees.

3. Stir in the rum-soaked nuts and continue stirring until the mixture is thick. Pour into an eight-inch-square greased pan, cool and cut into squares.

Serve with brio. (*Brio* is not a side dish; it is an Italian word for "enthusiasm, heartiness, flair" that was adopted by composers of music and is now a vogue word in American English.)

Remember: *fudge*, the political practice of dodging, does not mean "sweetener" and is not derived from the candy; it means a gentle form of delusion or hoax, and has given its name to the fattening confection.

Natural scientists and engineers use mathematical methods and notation to model the real world. More often than not the real world resists full explanation in those terms. Enter the fudge factor, chosen in a way to make the formula/model conform to reality, at least in those cases where experimental evidence is available. Implicit is the hope, often justified, that the formula will also be useful in predicting the behavior of the real world under conditions not yet tested. The fudge factor is an expedient, somewhat self-consciously introduced in the interest of practical results. Deceit or intellectual dishonesty is not at issue.

Peter Korndorfer
West Caldwell, New Jersey

"Fudging" is used by engineers and scientists in the sense of *altering* rather than *hedging*. The expression "fudge factor" is not necessarily a "bad" word; it can be perfectly legitimate.

Engineers and scientists introduce fudge factors into a theoretically derived mathematical expression in order to bring the results of the mathematical theory into agreement with observed facts. That is, they alter the mathematical relation. This is equivalent to deriving an empirical law to fit the known facts. Engineers use such pragmatic procedures to get the work done; that is, to design and build a piece of equipment within time and budget constraints. The scientists cannot be satisfied with this makeshift and try to develop a better theory which gives a closer fit to the observations, but this may not happen for many generations.

Of course, fudging (i.e., altering) the observed data is forgery, and is illegitimate, incompetent, dishonest and possibly illegal. But even here subtleties arise which make the situation much less clear-cut. Differences between scientific observations and theoretical predictions are often ascribed to the difficulties and uncertainties in the observation. We are so certain of the validity of the theory and so biased and prejudiced that we lose scientific objectivity and fudge the data. Examples abound; for example, the deviation in the motion of the planet Mercury from that predicted by Newton's gravitational laws, a deviation which is now explained (partially, not fully!) by Einstein's theory of relativity.

Gerald Weiss
Jamaica, New York

You have been sitting, in a manner of speaking, on one of the interesting applications of the word "fudge."

Newspapers in years gone by had a pressroom arrangement called a "fudge press." I'm not sure of the technics, but it was a supplementary printing module, using hand-set type, that made possible the insertion of very late news, like sports scores, in a box on page 1 without replating the page—without even stopping the press, I think. "Fudge" may have come from the loose type they had to deal with.

The expression "We can fudge it in," meaning sort of to shoehorn or vamp, was common. My father, who worked on the *Times*, the *Evening Sun* and the *Commercial Advertiser* around the turn of the century, told me about it.

> Glad [Gladwin Hill]
> Los Angeles, California

On the antiquity of "fudge": see Viola's concluding speech in Act 2, Scene 2, of Shakespeare's *Twelfth Night*.

> Peter J. Price
> Katonah, New York

Nowhere in your directions for making fudge do you mention that after cooling the mixture, you should not merely stir, but *beat* it with a wooden spoon "until fudge loses its glossy appearance" (Fanny Farmer) or "until thick and no longer glossy" (Betty Crocker) or until your arm falls off, whichever comes first. This step is classic advance atonement for such outright indulgence in the first place, and should never be left out of the recipe.

> Dorothy D. Dunlap
> Tucson, Arizona

Operation Not-So-Staunch

"Operation staunch" was the name of the Reagan administration's policy to deny arms to Iran. *Staunch* is a verb meaning "to stop a flow," rooted in the Latin *stagnare*; water that has stopped flowing becomes stagnant.

Vice Admiral John M. Poindexter, the national security adviser, used the verb in that sense when asked about what Secretary of State George P. Shultz had told the Arab League about an arms embargo in the Persian Gulf. "I suspect [Shultz told the league] that we were still working to staunch the flow of arms into Iran," said Admiral Poindexter, adding, "Now, the reason that we're trying to staunch the flow of arms into Iran is to stop the war."

The Administration was embarrassed at the revelation in Iran that the arms flow had not been staunched—indeed, that arms had been secretly shipped by the United States to Iran—contrary to "Operation Staunch." Secretary Shultz was embarrassed at the way a secret White House operation, which he opposed, had made him look like a hypocrite. Most important of all, grammarians were embarrassed at the confusion between the verb *staunch,* spelled *stanch* in *The Times* and many other publications, and the adjective *staunch,* which means "loyal, steadfast, trustworthy."

Should the verb be spelled *staunch* or *stanch?* Both spellings have been used for hundreds of years, so neither is incorrect, but in an effort to put some daylight between the verb and the adjective, usagists and stylisters have been urging writers to spell the verb *stanch* and the adjective *staunch.* That makes sense to me; I have even taken to pronouncing the verb *stanch* to rhyme with *ranch* and the adjective *staunch* to rhyme with *raunch;* for example, "Ed Meese is a staunch defender of those who try to stanch the flow of raunch." (*Raunch* is a slang noun back-formed from *raunchy,* or "sexually explicit," and Feds turned off by certain language are seeking to get rid of it root and braunch, and how did I get on this subject?)

The connection between the seemingly unrelated branches of *staunch* is naval. When leaks are staunched, or stanched, a boat becomes dry, watertight and sound. "Our ship was *stanch,"* wrote Jonathan Swift's Lemuel Gulliver, "and our crew all in good health." From seaworthy to trustworthy is a short hop in meaning, and the poet William Cowper could soon assure his students, "You are *staunch* indeed in learning's cause."

The adjective and verb still have a metaphoric link: *staunch* supporters of the President do not leak information to the media about the apparent duplicity behind "Operation Staunch."

We come now to another pair of words thrust into the news by the charges and denials of a deal of arms-for-hostages. Was the Administration *duped* or was it *duplicitous?* In other words, was it dopey or too clever by half? And does a connection exist between those two derogations, *duped* and *duplicitous?*

"I see the direction you were headed," said Admiral Poindexter to pundits in trying to avoid a trap, "as to whether Secretary Shultz was being *duplicitous."* That adjective means "deceitful, sometimes cunningly hypocritical," directly from the French *duplicité,* rooted in the Latin word that also gave us *duplex;* you say one thing downstairs, its opposite upstairs. The best synonym is "double-dealing."

Dupe is a noun with no connection to *duplicity. Dupe* is from the Old French *duppe,* based on the Latin *upupa,* a genus of bird thought to be unusually stupid, sometimes called the *hoopoe.* From this comes the verb *to dupe,* which means "to fool," as in pretending to make noises like the upupa and causing it to want to mate with you. Although the *oop* sound in *stupid* may have influenced the meaning of *dupe,* the upupa has been unfairly disparaged because of its erratic flight, its odd crest (that flaps open and shut when the bird is upset) and its imitative name—even after flying up into a tree, the bird will continue to cry, "Up, up!"

The adjective that is married to the noun *dupe* is *unwitting*. On rare occasion, there can be a *witting dupe*, one who is willing to be fooled or kept in the dark, but let us not cast aspersions in the direction of Foggy Bottom in a nonpolitical column.

Is a *dupe* a *dope*? No; an intelligent person can be duped, as the National Security Council staff has just proved. *Dope* came into American English around 1800 from the Dutch *doop*, "sauce"; opium was a thick, treacle-like substance that took the name *dope*, and addicts were *dopey*—drugged, disoriented, out of it. By the mid-1800s, *dope* also became the synonym for a simpleton.

Who duped us? A carefully chosen word in this context is the one being applied to those unnamed high officials in Iran who are our contacts. A questioner asked Admiral Poindexter about *our guys* over there, and A Senior Official speaking on background cautioned that "we are not characterizing Rafsanjani as 'our guy.'"

How, then, to refer to the people we were trying to do business with? Not *partners* or *friends*, certainly, and *negotiatees* is strained; nor would *adversaries* do when we're trying to make friends. The admiral reached back into Kissingerese for the right word, one that carries no connotation of friendliness or enmity. That word is *interlocutor*. He refused to help "identify who the interlocutors are."

The Latin *interloqui* is "to speak between," and *interlocutors* are those engaged in a conversation (now almost exclusively referred to as a dialogue). *Interlocutor* is the diplomatically correct word; a second meaning in dictionaries, "entertainer in a minstrel show, one in the middle who acts as a foil for the end men," is not to be applied here unless you are casting more aspersions.

Relatedly, the pronunciation of *Iranian* is now a problem for announcers and interviewees. Robert C. (Bud) McFarlane, on television denying he ever carried a cake shaped like a key into Teheran on his mission there, referred to the country as "ih-RAHN," which is correct, and its people as "ih-RAHN-ians," which is not the preferred form; most Americans say "ih-RAY-nians" (although, in Alabama, Alabamians are more likely to say "ih-RAN-ians" because they are influenced by "ala-BAM-ian," which they prefer to "ala-BAME-ian").

One locution from the man in civilian clothes who replaced Colonel McFarlane as Assistant to the President for National Security Affairs (a title that is usually and informally shortened to "national security adviser"), and who ran the unstaunching, reveals an old salt at work. "We have had countries in the Middle East advising us in the past that we ought to see if we can develop some sort of a relationship with Iran," Admiral Poindexter observed, "to be able to carry on a dialogue there that might be helpful in ending the war. We've taken that aboard."

We've taken that aboard, in that context, means "We have incorporated that idea in our thinking," or, in another vernacular, "We bought that pitch." (Sighted *subsume,* sank same.) To all the jargonauts in the basement of the White House, depressed at their failure to staunch the derision of "Operation Staunch," let me offer the battle cry of the upupa: "Up, up!"

On *stanch/staunch:* you missed (or elected not to cite) the most familiar instance of the word to American readers of the past century: The little toy dog is covered with dust, But sturdy and stanch he stands. . . .
—Eugene Field (1850–95), "Little Boy Blue"

Jacob Wainwright Love
Washington, D.C.

Just in case you didn't know, the *upupa* sighs. At least that is what librettist Antonio Somma says in his libretto to Giuseppe Verdi's *Un Ballo in Maschera,* Act 1, Scene 6: *"Omai tre volte l'upupa/Dall'alto sospiro"* ("Three times now, the upupa from on high has sighed").

David Ambrosiana
Afton, Virginia

Outside the Quoteway

Peter Norton, the California computer-software genius and utilities in-fielder, has applied for Lexicographic Irregular status. He qualifies because he sent in a clip from *The New York Times* with a quotation that ended with the period within quotation marks.

I have long grappled with this issue. What do you do with the period at the end of a sentence that includes a quoted sentence? Example: He looked at the keyboard and said, "I wish I knew how to open a window."

"The period really belongs to the sentence and not to the quoted text," notes Mr. Norton, "but the usage I was taught puts the period inside the quotes, which I hate. Judging from *The Economist* [in his letter, the name of the publication appears in boldface, which I could do, too, if I knew how to work this machine], British usage would put that period outside the quotes, a lot more sensibly. What do you say on the issue?"

Allan M. Siegal, a stylish *New York Times* editor, asked for his opinion, writes: "British usage uniformly places the adjoining punctuation wherever logic dictates; in the example you cited, the period would go outside the quotes. American usage, sanctioned by all the major stylebooks, places all commas and periods inside the quotes and all colons and semicolons outside; in American usage, only the placement of exclamation points and question marks is governed by logic". (Note how I put the period ending his sentence not at the end of his sentence, but at the end of mine, illogically.)

Why do we do it this silly way? "I can only assume," says Mr. Siegal, "that somewhere along the way, American printers decided that periods and commas looked odd when separated from the adjoining words". (Shh-h, I put the period outside the quotes, just to show it can be done; maybe nobody will notice.)

I say: let logic and reason be our guide. Americans must not let our punctuation be paralyzed by the dead hand of some confused Yankee printer. The disposition of the concluding punctuation mark should be determined by what makes sense.

Dear Mr. Siegal,

I note your remarks as quoted by William Safire in his column (copy enclosed) on the problem of "American style", and I would like to have your help in stamping out that abomination.

In my book, *Bookmaking: The Illustrated Guide to Design/Production/ Editing* (R. R. Bowker)—which has been, since 1965, a standard text-book in most courses on publishing practice in America and is the primer used by a large percentage of beginners in book publishing—I use the logical British style throughout. In twenty-three years I have received not *one* comment about this "error" one way or the other— although the book has been very favorably reviewed in many profes-sional and scholarly publications, and hundreds of publishing profes-sionals have praised the book to me. Further, I have used this style in many of the books I have written, edited, and produced during the past twenty-five years with no complaints.

The only negative reactions have come from editors to whom I have *proposed* this usage. Their responses are remarkably emotional, considering the utter absence of complaint noted above. When I ask why they object to this reasonable method they usually say it is "ugly". I believe that I am legitimately entitled to dispute that opinion as one of the leading American typographic designers.

Like you I have tried to discover the origin of "American style" but without much success. It seems to be a case of the casual, accidental spread of a weak proposition put forward by a mid-nineteenth-cen-tury printer or grammarian. I've heard it argued that in metal typeset-ting it was better to have the wider quote mark at the end than the thin period or comma. However, unless the punctuation came at the very end of a line it would be followed by metal spaces of sufficient width to prevent any problem. In any case, the argument lost its validity with the advent of linotype (about a century ago), and it certainly has none today, when photosetting is the rule.

There is really no reason to continue this absurd, confusing practice, and I think it would not be difficult to get rid of it. Obviously, there is no likelihood of any outcry from the reading public if the change is made, and editors would fall in line if their authority sources were to sanction the change. This would require nothing more than acceptance of the change by [the publishers of] a few leading style manuals: University of Chicago [Press], *The New York Times*, etc. Teachers of editing would quickly adopt the new rules, and beginners would be taught properly thenceforth.

If you will undertake to get the *Times* to agree that it will make the change if Chicago will, I will ask Chicago. If both the *Times* and Chicago announce their intention to change, I believe the others will follow. After all, there is no vested interest in "American style". The timetable for the change can easily accommodate any technical or procedural problems. (I do anticipate a transition period in which copyeditors, typists, and typesetters will automatically use the old method, but this would not last too long.)

This is one of the few cases where it is possible to actually change something for the better—let's do it!

> *Marshall Lee*
> *New York, New York*

Dear Mr. Lee,

My compliments on your pluck in crusading against American punctuation style—but compliments only. I can't join you, because we disagree.

I think the American style produces a pleasing uniformity of typographic color (comparable, say, to the current Madison Avenue fashion for hung punctuation). I also think transparency of style, when attainable, is desirable in so utilitarian a vehicle as a newspaper. And because American style is (in America) prevalent, it is close to transparent: readers don't notice it, and they remain focused on content.

But those are secondary concerns. Primary ones, for a daily newspaper, are efficiency and accuracy. Typesetters and proofreaders disappeared ten or twenty years ago from daily newspapers in the industrialized world, victims of time pressure, cost and technology. Copy now moves directly from a writer's computer terminal to an editor's and then to a phototypesetting machine. The more time an editor must spend on style mechanics, the less time will remain for accuracy, fairness, clarity and logic. If you have felt the frenzy of a newsroom at deadline, you will understand that the price is real.

And at deadline, fine points suffer. Question marks and exclamation points, their placement still dependent on logic, regularly wind up in print on the wrong side of the quotation marks. Periods land on the wrong side of closing parentheses. Why should an American daily newspaper editor want to adopt British style, with its myriad of further opportunities for error?

Good luck, Mr. Lee. But not, I hope, too good.

A. M. S. *[Allan M. Siegal]*
The New York Times
New York, New York

In discussing what to do with the period at the end of a sentence that includes a quoted sentence, you consider the merits of two alternatives—placing it inside and outside the quotation marks. Why not a third alternative: using two periods, inside and outside? Thus: I agree with your advice that "The disposition of the concluding punctuation mark should be determined by what makes sense.".

Wouldn't that usage make more sense than the either/or choice? Where is it written that you can't have three punctuation marks strung together?

Sidney Shapiro
Chevy Chase, Maryland

Dear Bill,

In the relevant examples there are two punctuation marks doing the work of three: both the quoted sentence and the quoting sentence end at the point in question, but each of the various typographical conventions explicitly marks only one of the two ends-of-sentence. Statements such as "British usage uniformly places the adjoining punctuation wherever logic dictates" are inaccurate for two reasons. First, strictly speaking, logic by itself doesn't dictate anything about punctuation: only the combination of logic with a system of typographical conventions will yield dictates, and logic is equally much involved in dictating consequences of each of the various typographical conventions. (You will remember, I hope, that I am the author of a textbook of logic; I get annoyed when I see logic being held responsible for things which it is at most an accessory to rather than a sole perpetrator of. For example, I am shocked at the frequency with which otherwise literate authors will speak of a "logical order of presentation"; such locutions reflect confusion between the ordinary sense of the world *follow* and the technical sense that it has in logic, which has to do with the relation between conclusions and the premises from which they are inferred, not to the order in which conclusions or premises are stated.) Second, if I charitably interpret these references to logic as really referring to the desideratum that form be related in a transparent and direct way to content, "logic" would dictate neither of the two popular conventions but rather one in which the ends both of the contained and containing sentences are marked, the one with a punctuation mark before the quotation mark and the other with one after it, e.g.:

He said, "I wish I knew how to open a window.".
He asked, "Do you know how to open a window?".
Did he say, "I wish I knew how to open a window."?
Did he ask, "Do you know how to open a window?"?

(Note how craftily I choose to display the above examples rather than quote them in the text, which would have multiplied punctuation marks far beyond normally accepted limits and also made it disconcertingly hard to separate the quoted material from the frame in which it is quoted.) The two conventions differ from the one "dictated by logic" by having a convention to omit one of two sentence-end markers that would otherwise flank a quotation mark. Neither convention gives logic a significantly greater role in the division of labor than does the other.

Jim [James D. McCawley]
Department of Linguistics
University of Chicago
Chicago, Illinois

I was pained to read your piece on terminal quotes with punctuation—whether a comma or a period should precede or follow a closing quotation mark.

You have your own colleague's, Allan M. Siegal's, testimony on *New York Times* style on this matter. He is following your paper's style manual, the national standard for newspapers. As retired director of the University of Wisconsin Press (and, incidentally, friend and sometime publisher of your consultant, Frederic G. Cassidy), I point out that the Chicago Manual of Style, the book publishers' standard guide in such matters, concurs—a rare degree of agreement among editors of all kinds. Although in this country we do not agree with British opposite numbers, still, we have the thing pretty well settled. I beg you not to upset something that is working.

Thompson Webb
Waunakee, Wisconsin

If we "let logic and reason be our guide," shouldn't we use more end punctuation? Mr. Norwood asks, "What do you say on the issue?". My sentence telling what Mr. Norwood asks logically requires a closing period, in addition to his question mark. I'm not asking a question, but making a statement. My rule would be that if a sentence-closing quotation requires punctuation of its own, the sentence should still have its own ending punctuation after the quotes even if we have to end up with " ." ." . (The first period comes from a quotation, the second from the illustration of an ending period, and the third period closes my sentence.) In some styles, my middle quotation mark should be a single quote. Maybe this is why people end with the first punctuation mark.

Frederick Mosteller
Cambridge, Massachusetts

Did you study with Professor Larry Siegfried at Syracuse?

I can recall that gentleman dealing with the question. He said letterpress printing, after as well as before the advent of hot-type composition, made it easy for a period or comma, when falling at the end of a line, particularly if the line were shorter than the column width, to become "lost."

The paper, I guess, could be pushed lower than type-high where there were no longer any raised characters—lifting the paper ever so slightly away from the bottom of the line. The already tiny period or comma would then make an even spiderier impression, or none at all.

I can't really argue for this, but I thought you might receive notes from several "generations" of Siegfried Syracuse students and I might as well be one of 'em!

Robert F. Cramer
Windsor, California

I quoted the *Times* as quoting Ross Perot saying "$1 million." My claim is that that is a *written* form that's (to be cute about it) *unspeakable.* Fine and dandy if you're not fastidious. But it's my impression that the *Times* prides itself on fastidious accuracy. If so, isn't it a bad idea in a quotation to transform spoken English into written English? "$1 million" is a good written form, but it's not a good transcription of whatever Perot said (unless he knows how to say it, clever man).

Peter Norton
Santa Monica, California

The Penumbra of Desuetude

As always, televised hearings churn up new uses of old terms. As the Senate deliberated the nomination to the Supreme Court of Judge Robert H. Bork, logophiles weighed the words of the solons and the nominee.

Penumbra nearly shadowed all. Because the rights of privacy interested lawmakers who hoped the courts, rather than the Congress, would handle that persnickety issue, Justice William O. Douglas's opinion in *Griswold* v. *Connecticut* was often quoted. He had written that "specific guarantees in the Bill of Rights have penumbras, formed by emanations from those guarantees that help give them life and substance."

An *emanation*, from the Latin for "flow," is something "emitted from a source," like a gas belching from a pool. A *penumbra*—from the Latin *paene*, "almost," and *umbra*, "shadow"—means literally "almost shadow." It was first used in 1604 by the German astronomer Johannes Kepler, and a half century later made it into English: "The Moon was not at all obscured by the true shadow, but entered only a little into the *Penumbra.*"

Astronomers used the term to describe the area of faint light, or partial shadow, that surrounds the total shadow in an eclipse. The word crossed over to general use in a figurative sense of the gray area between black-and-white issues. The British novelist Maria Edgeworth wrote in her 1801 story "Angelina" that "I will defend him, madam, . . . against every shadow, every penumbra of aristocratic insolence." T. S. Eliot gave the hazy area more currency in drafts of his poem *The Waste Land* in the early 1920s: "Within this penumbral consciousness . . ."

Thus, Justice Douglas—a good and careful writer—chose an apt word to describe what he believed to be a shadowy area, slightly illuminated by light coming from parts of the Constitution, that formed a "right of privacy." A word of similar meaning, though not a synonym, is *fringe*; the noun *penumbra* can also mean "area of obscurity" or "part shaded by doubt." When *penumbra* is confused with a different noun also formed from the Latin for "shadow," *umbrella*, semanticists take umbrage.

Although many modern lawyers and jurists have placed great weight on Douglas's penumbra of privacy, none can claim the dimness to be clear or black and white; that would be a contradiction in terms.

Discussing the anticontraceptive law struck down as unconstitutional in *Griswold*, Judge Bork told senators he had described the statute as "nutty," challengeable on many grounds, but had criticized Judge Douglas's reasoning that led to the creation of an undefined and potentially confusing penumbra. "The law . . . was an utterly antique statute. Nobody would ever have enforced it. I think you'd have a great argument of no fair warning, or sometimes what lawyers call—and I hate to use a word like this —*desuetude*, meaning it's just so out of date it's gone into limbo."

The judge hated to use a word like that because it was unfamiliar to the general public, and the use of sixty-dollar words made the speaker seem intellectual or professorial. However, there are those of us who embrace *desuetude* as an old friend in political history.

The word is rooted in the Latin for "disuse" and means the same today. It first appeared in Henry Cockeram's 1623 English Dictionarie, or An Interpreter of Hard English Words, defined as "lacke of use," but made it big in politics when President Grover Cleveland in 1886 sent a message to Congress that touched on the disuse into which the once-controversial Tenure of Office Act had fallen: "After an existence of nearly twenty years of almost innocuous desuetude, these laws are brought forth."

The word's pronunciation in most dictionaries is DES-wi-tood, but perhaps because of the influence of the second-syllable emphasis of in-NOC-u-ous, most people I know pronounce it de-SUE-i-tood.

Former Speaker of the House Champ Clark, writing in 1920, recalled this famous Cleveland coinage, even more memorable than his "public office is a public trust," which had been the creation of a ghostwriter. "His most exquisite phrase," wrote Clark about Cleveland, "and entirely original, so far as I know, was 'innocuous desuetude,' still frequently quoted and perhaps to be quoted as long as our vernacular is spoken by the children of men."

I agree; the phrase has the same adjective-noun ring as the historian Sir

James Mackintosh's "masterly inactivity" or Winston Churchill's "terminological inexactitude." Where is such phrase-making today? Fallen into you-know-what.

Phantom of the Phrases

High up in the scenery of language, in his lair among old mental sets, lurks the Phantom of the Phrases, ready to hurl down a chandelier on some speaker who dares cross his purposes.

In the second act of *The Phantom of the Opera*, the smash-hit musical drama by Andrew Lloyd Webber and Charles Hart, the Phantom enters disguised as Don Juan and sings a song titled "The Point of No Return." Like a fate defied, he warns of going "past the point of no return—no backward glances: the games we've played till now are at an end. . . ."

The novel on which the musical is based was written in 1911. Ready for the chandelier? Look out below!

Point of no return is an aviation phrase and came into use long after the era of the Phantom or any of his terrified friends. It is the best example of *anachronism* now on Broadway, and bids fair to rival Shakespeare's line in *Julius Caesar*, spoken by Cassius, "The clock hath stricken three," set in Roman times, probably before the invention of clocks that struck the hour. (I say "probably"; debate rages on this point for which I have no time.)

My *point* means "the place in an aircraft's flight at which it will no longer have enough fuel to return." The first use so far spotted is from the 1941 *Journal of the Royal Aeronautics Society*, which puts the term in quotation marks, always a hint that the writer thinks it was used earlier: "This three-engined operation data is used to determine our so-called 'Point of No Return.' Laymen are inevitably intrigued by this fatalistic expression. As a matter of fact, it is merely a designation of that limit-point, before which any engine failure requires an immediate turn around and return to the point of departure, and beyond which such return is no longer practical."

The first figurative use of the phrase is in Eric Hodgins's 1946 novel *Mr. Blandings Builds His Dream House*, in which the author wrote of the delight of dying of old age in a rented apartment, "but he had reached and passed the crucial mark known, in the poetic language of the air navigator, as the Point of No Return."

The colorful, doom-laden phrase now means "the critical moment or point in a course of action at which commitment has become irrevocable." It sounds as if it might have been rooted in a previous century, and I forgive the lyricists and Andrew Lloyd Webber, but they have enshrined themselves in Anachronism's Hall of Fame.

> You have (rather unfairly, I think) held Andrew Lloyd Webber to a higher standard than the Royal Aeronautics Society.
>
> The article from the *Journal of the Royal Aeronautics Society* that you quoted states that the "point of no return . . . is merely a designation of that limit-point, before which any engine failure requires an immediate turn around and return to the point of departure. . . ."
>
> There are occasions when continuing on to one's destination would be a safer bet. Depending on such factors as available fuel and prevailing winds, the "point of no return" of an aircraft may be several hours from its "point of departure" but only minutes from its destination. Under those conditions, an immediate turn around after an engine failure may be unnecessary—and even a bit dangerous.
>
> In its definition of "point of no return," the Royal Aeronautics Society confused that point with the less romantic "equal time point." At the "equal time point," the time required for the aircraft to reach its destination is exactly the same as the time required for it to return to its point of departure.
>
> An engine failure before the "equal time point" would, therefore, require an immediate turn around and return to the "point of departure"—unless, of course, the aircraft has already passed its "point of no return."

John W. Troller
Barrington, Illinois

The definition you quote from the 1941 *Journal of the Royal Aeronautics Society* is correct. However, the writer kept on explaining instead of quitting when he was ahead, reflecting a very common layman's confusion of PNR with "Equi-Time Point." This is the point in an over-ocean flight where the *time* back to the point of departure and the *time* to the destination are the same—not necessarily halfway, since strong head and tail winds are often involved. A well-planned flight should always arrive at the ETP well before the PNR, because of reserve fuel that must be carried. It follows that an engine failure *after* the ETP but *before* the PNR would dictate continuing to destination, not "an immediate turn around" (as the JRAS writer puts it), since all hearts and minds are bent on getting the beast safely on the ground in the shortest possible time (before another engine quits, for example).

Edward A. Drew
Captain, Pan American World Airways (Ret.)
Sea Cliff, New York

You said that in Act II, Scene I, of *Julius Caesar*, Cassius's statement "The clock hath stricken three" is an anachronism because the Romans did not have clocks that struck the hour." Wrong! The reason that statement is anachronistic is this: The way the Romans told time was by starting the day at 6 A.M. and calling it "prima hora," the "first hour." If a Roman clock struck three, it would be 9 A.M. in our time. This particular scene in *Julius Caesar* is supposed to take place in the middle of the night, and the Romans divided the night into four watches, or "vigiliae," so that 3 A.M. would fall into the second or third watch. (The third watch, "tertia vigilia," is more likely.) In that same scene, I believe Brutus says something about "the eighth hour," meaning 8 A.M. That, too, is anachronistic.

Karen Byrne
Westfield, New Jersey

Piece of Work

In *Veil*, his book about William J. Casey's CIA, Bob Woodward climbs inside the head of Bobby Ray Inman, who had been our deputy chief spook and was apparently a key source for the newsman. "After a year," writes Woodward, "Inman had come to regard Casey as a 'piece of work,' a term that Casey often applied to the oddballs in their midst."

Although I never sought to penetrate the dying Bill Casey's heavily guarded hospital room, I can attest to my old pal's frequent use of the term. "He's a *piece of work*," the Director of Central Intelligence would murmur, referring to a tempestuous legal client or kooky foreign leader, shaking his head in a mixture of wonderment and either disapproval or grudging admiration.

The phrase, as Casey used it, had a built-in ambiguity, which has not always been the case. The first citation in the Oxford English Dictionary's Supplement is under *nasty*: "a nasty piece (or bit) of work (or goods)." The mystery writer Agatha Christie preferred "nasty bit of goods," but the novelist Monckton Hoffe in 1928 described a villain as "really a rather nasty piece of work."

Even without the qualifying *nasty*, the British term *piece of work* long had a pejorative connotation. In a 1965 collection of short stories, Abioseh Nicol had a character think "what an obstinate and unpleasant piece of work the fellow was." This negative sense followed the phrase to the United States: in an interchange between famous novelists in 1978, after Gore Vidal dismissed Norman Mailer with "He reads nothing at all—he's never read me," Mr. Mailer shot back, "He's really such a corrupt and unpleasant piece of work when you get to know him."

Was it always thus? The phrase first appeared in a circa 1540 interlude written by the dramatist John Heywood: "Here is an eye-tooth of the Great Turk./ Whose eyes be once set on this piece of work,/May happily lese part of his eyesight." In that context, the phrase seems to convey admiration, but a half-century later, a new meaning of "hard task, difficult business" was given the phrase in the author and translator Richard Carew's "It were an infinit peece of worke." This meaning of "strained effort" gained a figurative extension of "ado, commotion" in Charles Dickens's novel *Martin Chuzzlewit*: "What are you making all this piece of work for?"

During this development, a parallel phrase appeared in slang: *piece of trade*, "prostitute," derived from *piece of tail*, a derogation of a supposedly promiscuous woman. This has been clipped to the sexist slur *piece*, and is not to be confused in its meaning with *piece of work* in either the admiring or put-down sense.

Along the way, between the early coinage of *piece of work* to denote an intricate job and its later adoption (apparently throughout our intelligence agencies) as applicable to assets or targets who are "oddball, eccentric, weird," the phrase was immortalized by William Shakespeare's Hamlet:

"What a piece of work is a man! How noble in reason! how infinite in faculties . . . how like an angel in apprehension! how like a god!"*

He was not suggesting man is some kind of flake. Consider Prince Hamlet himself: a man tortured by doubt, driven by dreams, trusting nobody, burdened by his bloody secrets, half-crazily pretending to be demented. There was a piece of work.

The Player's the Thing

This is to report the promotion to field-grade officer of a locution that had previously been a mere vogue word in the ranks.

Player—in the sense of "a participant, rather than an observer"—has served time in grade and is now *major player*. Like *inextricably* and *linked*, *major* and *player* have become inextricably linked; the modifier has fused itself to the noun, joining such indissoluble marriages as *key aide, brazen hussy, blithering idiot* and *unmitigated gall*.

"You can find several hundred entries of *major player* in the past few

* See also "Grovel, Grovel, Grovel," pp. 237–40.

years," advises my *New York Times* colleague Irv Molotsky, sending along a sheaf of citations, "mostly in business, and lately more in politics."

My colleague is right. (Because this is a piece about clichés, I am leaning heavily on *colleague*; nobody says *associate, co-worker* or *confrère* in the media-biggie set anymore. It was Henry A. Kissinger who in 1969 brought *colleague* to Washington with him from Cambridge, and we haven't been able to shake that academic locution since. Henry's collegial phraseology lasted, but his *concrete proposals* and *conceptual frameworks* sank without a trace.)

"[John F.] Akers's other great drive," went a *New York Times* profile of the boss at International Business Machines, "has been to finally make IBM a *major player* in applications software. . . ."

"Governor Cuomo is a *major player* in this," warned a New York State assemblyman critical of his handling of the garbage mess, now called the waste-disposal problem.

A decade ago, the game being played was often included in the figure of speech: "Sadat's introduction to world affairs," wrote Thomas W. Lippman in the *Washington Post*, ". . . gave little reason to think he would later be a *major player* in the game of nations." The metaphor is still sometimes completed: "Hearst is already a *major player* in that league," said Howard Kaminsky, a publisher of blockbuster books who found a new home away from Random House, using the cliché in its original sports or game sense. But more often than not, *major player* stands alone.

We are getting carried away with these wedded words. "Zinnias are the *major players*," goes a gardening story in the *Los Angeles Times*, although "a low hedge of perennial candytuft (Iberis) does the job year-round. . . ."

Almost completely missing from the language are minor players. Then again, we never see an aide who isn't key or a partially mitigated gall.

Plug That Nickel

"T hose 'old' greenback hundreds," wrote the polemicist, urging the recall of $100 bills to discombobulate the drug peddlers, "will not be worth a plug nickel."

I was that plug-ugly polemicist. "Because you are considered to be something of a guru when it comes to the English language," writes Diane Culbertson, an editorialist for *USA Today*, "I stumbled badly over your use of *plug nickel*. Surely it is *plugged nickel*, as in shot, and something is as worthless as a plugged nickel because a nickel with a hole through the middle has no value. Please feel free to correct me if I'm wrong. (I'm sure you will.)"

We are both wrong, Ms. Culbertson, but I am the wronger. The idea behind the "plugging" of a coin is not merely to put a hole in it, but to substitute an inferior metal in the hole. The first use was in a 1694 tract of the Massachusetts Historical Society explaining to would-be counterfeiters that "If a piece of eight be plugged, it will not pass." This was followed by *plugged quarter,* the alliterative *plugged peso* and, finally, *plugged nickel*—all devalued, and all with the past participle of *plug* used as an adjective, as in this Carl Sandburg 1936 use: "He seems to think he's the frog's tonsils but he looks to me like a plugged nickel."

I'm an old-fashion guy who drinks ice tea, so I wrote *plug nickel.* I won't do it again. (And I will follow that *iced tea* with an *Old-Fashioned.*)

Poetic Allusion Watch

A new department is being created here. We call it the Poetic Allusion Watch (PAW).

"The space agency will spend $9.5 billion for next year's space show," complained a *New York Times* editorial. "Instead of reaching to stretch man's grasp, NASA's engineers plan more plumbing."

The poetic allusion that gives the editorial more resonance than the usual muttering is to Robert Browning's 1855 "Andrea del Sarto"—"Ah, but a man's reach should exceed his grasp,/Or what's a heaven for?" (That poem is also the source of "less is more," which not only editorialists but also columnists should remember.)

Many writers try to enliven and enrich their copy with poetic allusions. Readers who do not catch the allusions are not misled; they just go along not missing what they do not recognize. A reader who does catch the allusion thinks, "How apt! What a good writer to choose a turn of phrase that only a few of us well-educated types are familiar with. God, those years in that dreary English class are finally paying off." Thus, both reader and writer are served.

The problem, as I see it, is that too many allusions go unnoticed. As a result, writers get discouraged and readers go unenriched. This has caused the allusion rate to fall; prose is losing its poetry. Where can the reader turn for a fast survey of editorials and Op-Ed commentaries that are studded with the echoes of long-dead but immortal voices? Where is the clearinghouse for writers whose best allusions have gone unnoticed?

Right here. I am aware that the Nitpickers' League (Nitpicker's League?) will insist that a poetic allusion is an allusion, often to mythology, made within a poem, and that what is being referred to here is a hidden reference to poetry, but I like PAW.

Another example to prime the thinking pump: Norman Podhoretz entitled an article about anti-Semitism in *Commentary* magazine "The Hate That Dare Not Speak Its Name." This was a play on the phrase "the love that dare not speak its name," from Oscar Wilde's 1894 poem "Two Loves," the same phrase that Wilde used a year later as a euphemism for homosexuality in his trial for sodomy.

How come "the love that *dare*" and not, as you might expect, "the love that *dares*"? Step out to the grammatical woodshed: The words *that dare not speak its name* form an adjective clause, so called because it has the subject and verb to make it a clause and because the whole thing works as an adjective modifying *love*. Within an adjective clause, the verb is usually in the indicative mood—*love*, the singular antecedent of the pronoun *that*, would ordinarily call for the indicative *dares*.

But Oscar Wilde was a poet who knew his moods, and the indicative mood was all too straight in this case; the subjunctive mood, introduces a note of wishful thinking or iffiness, and that feeling of contingency was what he was after. The point he made was that love between men, which most of society thought perverted, was so taboo that it *would not dare* speak its name. Hence the subtle "love that [would] dare not speak its name."

Either that or he made a mistake, as the unreconstructed deconstructionists would say. Happens to all of us, even in making poetic allusions, as I did recently in remarking here that the First Folio of Shakespeare was no longer considered the final word on the text of the Bard but " 'tis enough, 'twill do." Edward R. Curtin of New York City, a PAW founding member, points out: "Well, 'tis not so deep as a Klong, nor so wide as a Gotcha; but 'tis enough, 'twill *serve*."

When you spot an especially sensitive and subtle poetic allusion in some piece of copy, perhaps inserted by a hack speechwriter or group journalist with a yearning to send a message to the movers and shakers via this intellectual fortune cookie, circle the allusion. Then cite the poem (no other type of literary allusions, please; that was in another country, and besides, the wench is dead) and send it to me.

Movers and shakers, of course, is from an ode by Arthur O'Shaughnessy in his 1874 collection *Music and Moonlight*:

> *We are the music-makers,*
> *And we are the dreamers*
>   *of dreams . . .*
> *Yet we are the movers and*
>   *shakers*
> *Of the world for ever, it*
>   *seems.*

I object to the "of course" phrase in your "movers and shakers, of course, is from an ode by . . ."

The implication of "of course" is that the information is so well known that it ought not to need stating. For example, one could use "Summer, of course, is usually hotter than winter." Using it with a piece of information that is probably little known by your readership is contemptuous.

Jan R. Harrington
New York, New York

Love That Dare

You have been grievously misinformed about *the love that dare not speak its name.*

I wrote that the famous phrase came from the poem "Two Loves" by Oscar Wilde. Right poem, wrong author: it has been pointed out to me by the Pulitzer-winning poet Peter Viereck that "Two Loves" was "not by Wilde but by his lover and destroyer, Lord Alfred Douglas."

Why did I think it was by Wilde? Because at his trial for sodomy, Wilde was confronted with the line that angered the Marquis of Queensberry, father of Lord Douglas. "The Marquis believed," writes John G. Bilotta of San Francisco, "that the corrupting influence of the older writer had led his son to pen it." Wilde denied that the line referred to homosexuality, but nobody believed him; furthermore, the line became associated with him and not with the real author.

That's the easy fix. Much lengthier letters came in about my explanation of why the poet wrote *love that dare* rather than *love that dares.* It seems that it has nothing to do with the subjunctive, and that the verb *dare* is one of the trickiest words in the English language.

"I find it a bit odd to be defending Oscar Wilde, who was pretty good at defending himself," writes W. Nelson Francis, emeritus professor at Brown University and textbook authority on the history of the English language.

Professor Francis explains that "Wilde was using *dare* as a modal auxiliary rather than a full verb," the modals being "those little verbs we use to qualify or hedge a statement in one way or another."

Among the many modern modals are *can, may, must* and *shall,* with *dare* and *need* on the fringe of the group. "What is important for this discussion," lectures the professor, whose tract "Modal *Daren't* and *Durstn't* in Dialectal English" has never been successfully rebutted, is that modals "do not have the *-s* suffix in the third-person-singular present—we do not say 'he cans,' 'he mays,' etc."

Let us now get very subtle. The word *dare* in its modal state has a different meaning from the same word acting as a normal verb. "*Dare* the modal," explains the professor, "means there may be unhappy social consequences of doing the act, while *dare* the full verb simply means being brave."

Durstn't we ask for an example showing the difference between *dare* as full verb and *dare* as timid modal? Professor Francis offers one from T. S. Eliot's "The Love Song of J. Alfred Prufrock," a landmark modern poem: "Note that Eliot's Prufrock says, 'Do I dare to eat a peach,' not 'Dare I eat a peach?' He was not sure he would be brave enough."

Those of us who measure out our lives with coffee spoons welcome this nice differentiation. Poor, deferential, politic, cautious *dare*: in the mists of antiquity, it began to lose its nail-nibbling modal form to the dominant and brave verb *dare*.

"But it still bears signs of its great history," writes Jay H. Jasanoff of Cornell University's department of modern languages and linguistics. "When we say *I daresay* rather than *I dare to say*, we are using the syntax of the preterito-present (or modal auxiliary if you prefer). If Wilde had really wanted a one-word way of saying what you said he said, I think he would have used the fine old past subjunctive *durst*. This, I am willing to bet, is what underlies the substandard contraction *dasn't*, which I used to see in comic books in the 1950s."

So Wilde's lover did not use *love that dare not* in the subjunctive, as I guessed, to express wishful thinking; instead, he used the modal form, or third-person-singular indicative, without the *-s* on *dare*, to emphasize tentativeness. There is much more to this can of worms, illustrating the glorious intricacy of our tongue, but I dasn't go on.

John Sholto Douglas, father of Lord Alfred Douglas, held the title Marqu*ess* of Queensberry. "Marquis" is a Continental title; "marquess" is its British equivalent.

Since it was the marquess who promulgated the rules of boxing that are known by his title, it would seem that he also had strong feelings about "low blows" in another context.

Steven D. Price
New York, New York

Oscar Wilde was not tried for sodomy. Actually, he was tried for "gross indecency."

The distinction is an important one. As late as 1861, sodomy remained a capital offense in England, and executions for sodomy were actually carried out as late as 1832, long after nearly all of Europe had abolished capital punishment for the offense and after France had decriminalized consensual homosexual activity altogether. When the death penalty was abolished in England in 1861, the penalty for sodomy was reduced to penal servitude for life or for any term not less than ten years, while attempted sodomy was punishable by a maximum of ten years' imprisonment.

The offense of which Wilde was convicted, an act of "gross indecency" not amounting to sodomy, became illegal in 1886, when the Criminal Law Amendment Act of 1885 took effect. The maximum penalty for this offense was two years' imprisonment at hard labor, the sentence that Wilde actually served.

Although the evidence indicated that Wilde was guilty of sodomy, he was probably charged with "gross indecency" rather than with the more serious offense because of the greater difficulty of proving the latter, which required evidence of penetration, and perhaps because of the reluctance of the prosecutors to subject the Draconian British legal system to the glare of European publicity certain to be occasioned by the trial (and possible life sentence) of so prominent an author.

Wilde's prosecution resulted as much from his own folly and penchant for self-dramatization as from the viciousness of his persecutors. But he ultimately became the scapegoat for his society's sexual and moral insecurities, the victim of the bigotry and hypocrisy of a society that he had ridiculed yet could never completely reject. The cruel punishment imposed on Wilde for private sexual activity (actually mutual masturbation) ought to remind us of the danger implicit in allowing the state to regulate private consensual sexual conduct, as affirmed in the U.S. Supreme Court's regressive ruling in *Harowick* v. *Bowers,* a case that did involve sodomy statutes.

Claude Summers
Dearborn, Michigan

The PAWs That Refresh

Thomas B. Morgan is a classy writer. His novel *Snyder's Walk* is about a crusty magazine writer's confrontation with the peace movement in the mid-1960s, and critics have hailed it for all the right reasons, but I know he is a classy writer because he makes a poetic allusion the way it ought to be done—cold turkey, no hints, and if the reader gets it, fine; if not, not.

"But then, there was Snyder still at it," he writes of his hero, plugging away on the front lines of the magazine craft, "when long since he could have been managing editor, or exec. . . . Who says Buffalo Bill's defunct?"

I got it. The allusion is to "Portraits," by e. e. cummings:

> *Buffalo Bill's*
> *defunct*
> *who used to*
> *ride a watersmooth-silver*

>   *stallion*
>   *and break onetwothree-*
>   *fourfive pigeonsjustlike*
>   *that . . .*

Edward Estlin Cummings, who decapitalized his name, conjured that image in 1923 of a hero who defied mortality, and its use in Morgan's 1987 novel is perfect.

That is a poetic allusion. It is not a specific citation, but a seemingly offhand pass at an image created by another, directed by a literate writer to a literate reader. To encourage this delightful pastime, this department has begun the Poetic Allusion Watch, or PAW, aided by Lexicographic Irregulars around the world.

The best newspaper columnists do it all the time. In a piece about poet Gene McCarthy, James J. Kilpatrick wrote, seemingly in passing, "Along the meandering way through these remembrances of times past . . ." No accident: the allusion is not merely to Marcel Proust's memoirs, translated into English as *Remembrance of Things Past*, but to the source of that title in Shakespeare's Sonnet 30:

>   *When to the sessions of sweet silent thought*
>   *I summon up remembrance of things past . . .*

In the same way, William F. Buckley opined, "The Reagan administration has miles to go before it sleeps." That, of course, is an allusion to the familiar line in Robert Frost's "Stopping by Woods on a Snowy Evening," and can be paraphrased with impunity; however, when Massachusetts Governor Michael Dukakis, announcing his presidential bid, used that poem from that poet (perhaps to evoke recollections of the J.F.K. inaugural, at which Frost spoke), he cited the poem directly but said, "*We* have miles to go before we sleep." He was properly zapped for that; an allusion is not a misquotation for political purposes.

My colleague Anthony Lewis uses poetic allusion in headlines above his column. For example, he titled a piece about the Administration's failure to keep up with Soviet spying "While Zealots Slept"; although many readers thought that was bottomed on John Kennedy's first book, *Why England Slept*, PAW members turned quickly to Longfellow's 1858 "The Ladder of St. Augustine":

>   *The heights by great men reached and kept*
>   *Were not attained by sudden flight,*
>   *But they, while their companions slept,*
>   *Were toiling upward in the night.*

Art Buchwald, too. In a piece from Hollywood, he explained that the AIDS scare had caused film stars to give up sex entirely and replace it with late-night television-watching; the headline in the *Los Angeles Times* read "When the Kissing Had to Stop." The phrase is Robert Browning's, from "A Toccata of Galuppi's":

> *What of soul was left, I wonder, when the kissing had to stop?*

I hope that headline was Art's, but if the phrase was chosen by the local headline writer, that would not be a surprise. Headline writers are big on poetry these days. In New York, "Ice Is Nice, and Will Suffice" was a *Daily News* headline over a picture of skaters at the Rockefeller Center rink. That was derived from Robert Frost's 1923 "Fire and Ice" (no, Virginia, that was not originally the name of a lipstick):

> *Some say the world will end in fire,*
> *Some say in ice.*
> *From what I've tasted of desire*
> *I hold with those who favor fire.*
> *But . . . for destruction ice*
> *Is also great*
> *And would suffice.*

"Someone There Is Who Does Like the S.E.C." is the heading of a piece by George Melloan in *The Wall Street Journal,* based on American Express chairman James D. Robinson III's fervent remark, "Thank God for the SEC." We're back to Frost, in this case the opening line of "Mending Wall"—"Something there is that doesn't love a wall. . . ."—with a nice internal play on Wall Street.

"Going Gently Into That Good Night" is a headline in the *Washington Post* about people angered at a power outage. Not every allusion is apt; Catherine Reef of Gaithersburg, Md., points out that Dylan Thomas, in "Do Not Go Gentle Into That Good Night," was raging about fighting for life, and "using these words to describe coping with a power failure seems ludicrous." The poet chose "gentle" rather than "gently," too, for a reason that eludes me but must have been plain to him.

The largest-type PAW was sent in by Abraham H. Lass of Flushing, N.Y. The *New York Post* headline about "How dapper don spent first weekend of freedom" after being acquitted read "Gotti's Days of Wine and Roses." Though this phrase may be routed through a popular song, its origin is in an 1896 poem by Ernest Dowson, and the *Post* headline writer was sending a subtle message to all reputed Mafiosi:

> *They are not long, the days of wine and roses;*
> *Out of a misty dream*
> *Our path emerges for a while, then closes*
> *Within a dream.*

A more likely place to look for poetic allusions is in *The New York Times Book Review*. In a review of a book by Sana Hasan on the Middle East, David K. Shipler wrote in praise: "If this book were not any of that, if it were merely Ms. Hasan's observations of Israel, it would be enough." Bernard J. Kabak of New York City notes the Shipler allusion to the song "Dayenu" from the Passover Haggadah; Rabbi Stephen Listfield of Englewood, N.J., noticed the review's headline, "Uneasy in Zion," and caught the allusion to Amos 6:1—"Woe to them that are at ease in Zion." (But let us steer clear of biblical allusion, which is a whole nother ballgame. You don't like "a whole nother"? It's called an infix, and is used for emphasis. I digress.)

The fashion field is not to be left out. In *The New York Times Magazine*'s Men's Style pages, a headline over a story on the latest rubberized raincoats is the innocuous "Waiting for Rain," but is known to T. S. Eliot fans as an allusion to "Gerontion":

> *Here I am, an old man in a dry month,*
> *Being read to by a boy, waiting for rain.*

Buffalo Bill may be defunct, but the Eliot-Marlowe wench is not dead: "This brilliant novel has many cunning passages and secret chambers," went a *Newsweek* review in 1983 by David Lehman of Umberto Eco's *The Name of the Rose*. Same poem by Eliot:

> *History has many cunning passages, contrived corridors*
> *And issues, deceives with whispering ambitions,*
> *Guides us by vanities. . . .*

I have not touched on Shakespeare's plays, greatest source of poetic allusion in the hundreds of submissions by sensitive Irregulars; the candle is too brief. But a familiarity with poetry undergirds the work of many good writers today, and pops up in the most unexpected places, as underground language lovers send secret messages to kindred spirits. You thought allusion was dead, or limited to literary elitists creeping around their contrived corridors? How do you like your blueeyed boy Mister Death?

Dear Bill:

The only biblical reference in your piece is to Amos's animadversions against a complacent and well-armed Israel, many generations later. Don't blame that on Moses. "Uneasy in Zion," indeed! We—he, I mean—never even got over the river. "Ye have been rebellious from the day that I knew you; yet ye are my people. The Lord was angry with me for your sake and said that I must not go over Jordan, I must die in this land; but ye shall go over."

> *Best, as ever . . .*
> *Chuck [Charlton Heston]*
> *Beverly Hills, California*

With respect to the origin of the phrase "days of wine and roses," is it not possible that Ernest Dowson was unconsciously echoing William S. Gilbert, who has Nanki-Poo sing in the second act of *The Mikado*: "We welcome the hope that they bring, tra-la/Of a summer of roses and wine."

The Mikado was premiered in 1885, thus predating Dowson's poem by eleven years.

> *Robert Finn*
> *Music Critic*
> *The Plain Dealer*
> *Cleveland, Ohio*

Going Gentle on My Mind

"It is more than *passing strange to me,*" Robert C. McFarlane told the Iran-contra investigating committee, "that we cannot aspire to a policy which is more effective to deal with terrorism."

Few of the solons caught the poetic allusion. In all probability, the speaker used it unconsciously. In the first act of Shakespeare's *Othello,* the Moor explains his initial attraction to Desdemona, when she asked him to tell her the story of his life. Othello recalls: "My story being done,/ She gave me for my pains a world of sighs;/ She swore, in faith 'twas strange, 'twas passing strange;/ 'Twas pitiful, 'twas wondrous pitiful."

Shakespeare liked to use the word *passing* as an adverb modifying adjectives (*passing fair, passing strong, passing gentle*), meaning "surpassingly, exceedingly." Today the term is familiar only as *passing strange,* even in the most wondrous pitiful testimony.

The Bard is also the underlying source of many obvious allusions. Erica Abeel wrote in *The New York Times Magazine* about country homes: "A final irony: in our passion for a getaway, we are killing the thing we love." That is, of course, a reference to "The Ballad of Reading Gaol," by Oscar Wilde: "Yet each man kills the thing he loves. . . ." The trick in the allusion dodge is to get to the original, in this case Shakespeare's *The*

Merchant of Venice, in which Bassanio asks Shylock: "Do all men kill the things they do not love?"

That double take can also be applied to a *Times* Op-Ed piece by Matthew Gurewitsch of *Connoisseur* magazine, writing about the Metropolitan Museum of Art's much-admired statue of the Egyptian cat that is suspected of being a forgery: "Within the Gallery of Illustrious Fakes that I envision, beauty will be truth, truth beauty."

PAW (Poetic Allusion Watch) enthusiasts will catch that reference to John Keats's quotation of a Grecian urn, which revealed to him, "Beauty is truth, truth beauty"; that was supposedly all we needed to know. Keats, however, was answering the question posed almost two centuries earlier in the first stanza of George Herbert's poem "Jordan": "Who says that fictions only and false hair/ Become a verse? Is there in truth no beauty?" John Keats did not think that unheard melody came under his need-to-know rule, but the PAW disagrees.

Nor do I join the disapproving chorus (almost as famous as the Anvil Chorus) at the verbification of nouns with *-ize.* We should lie back and see if such coinages turn out to be useful, or are merely bureaucratic pomposities. Poetic allusions can make the difference: in *Life & Death on 10 West,* a gripping account by Eric Lax of medical heroism at the UCLA Medical Center, the author recalls a fistfight that broke out between two surgeons during an operation, with "the patient etherized upon the table between them." This is an allusion to the beginning of T. S. Eliot's "The Love Song of J. Alfred Prufrock": "Let us go then, you and I,/ When the evening is spread out against the sky/ Like a patient etherized upon a table. . . ."

This department is not infallible and sometimes misses even primary allusions. In a piece searching for the female equivalent of *womanizer,* written with eerie prescience on the eve of Gary Hart's downfall, I reported that most readers cited *man-eater,* a term in use for the last decade, meaning "a woman who treats sexual relations frivolously." Geoffrey Stokes, the Press Clips columnist of *The Village Voice,* calls my attention to "Ariel," a poem by Sylvia Plath published posthumously in 1965 (its title is from the sprite in Shakespeare's *The Tempest),* in which the poet concludes: "Out of the ash/ I rise with my red hair/ And I eat men like air." This popularized *man-eater* in its present promiscuous sense; the origin may have been in Aldous Huxley's 1928 *Point Counter Point:* "Marjorie isn't the only bore. Nor Lucy the only man-eater."

The aftermath of the Hart story brought forth this lead from T. R. Reid in the *Washington Post:* "Former Presidential candidate Gary Hart is making it clear to his friends and supporters that he will not go gentle into that political night."

The allusion is to Dylan Thomas's 1952 poem "Do Not Go Gentle Into That Good Night." In a recent PAW, I made a passing remark (*passing* the

ordinary participle used as adjective, not *passing* the strange adverb) that
the Welsh poet had a reason for using *gentle* rather than *gently*, but that it
eluded me. That was a fishhook observation, designed to elicit instruction
from the Lexicographic Irregulars, and it worked: "If Thomas had said
gently," writes Marianne Fridell of Custer, S.D., "he would have been
modifying *go* and telling how one goes. Instead he says *gentle*, which refers
back to the understood 'you.' " "*Gentle* is an adjective referring to the
understood subject," explains Marilyn V. van der Velde of Ann Arbor,
Mich. "Were one to substitute *naked* or *speechless* for *gentle*, it would be
more obvious."

In grammatical terms, though, is *gentle* necessarily an adjective? Although it is almost always used as an adjective, it has also been used as an
adverb since the early 1600s. "If you have a grammatical problem with the
use of what appears to be an adjective after a noncopulative verb," writes
Allan J. Curran of Boston, "I sympathize: so many of our memorable
English teachers damned the analogous 'Go slow.' Jacques Barzun, with
good sense, encourages the use of the 'short form of the adverb' after verbs
of motion."

Let's go quick to Professor Barzun, who covered this subject in 1986 in
A Word or Two Before You Go . . . He says predicate adjectives follow
copulative, or linking, verbs, such as *be* or *become* ("Be gentle"; "Become
famous"). Beyond that, however, Professor Barzun tells me: "Verbs of
motion and sensation take adverbs that do not have the *-ly* ending—'Go
slow,' 'Think fast,' and so forth. Even though they lack the *-ly*, these words
are not predicate adjectives but adverbs. And there are many examples of
such adverbs. You would tell someone, 'Sleep sound,' not 'Sleep soundly';
'sound' is correct as the adverb's short form."

I disagree with the professor, and agree with most of the readers who
wrote in: the poet was using the adjective *gentle* to describe the condition
he hoped his dying father would not be in, rather than to describe the
method of his going, or dying. He chose to modify the person, which
called for an adjective, and not to modify the action, which would usually
have called for the adverb ending in *-ly*.

That triggers another question: do poets and other writers, as they do
their thing, knock themselves out worrying about predicate adjectives versus adverbs?

In most cases, no. Interpreters use these grammatical explanations to
show what the writer had in mind. If I go to a wine tasting and write,
"They taste *good*," the reader can tell I'm talking about the wines; if I
write, "They taste *well*," in the sense of the adverb *goodly*, I am talking
about the expert way the tasters are slurping up the booze. Understanding
grammar helps us figure out where the emphasis lies.

The writer, who knows what he is thinking and what he is modifying,
need not go through these interpretive gyrations. Consider John Hartford,

writing the 1967 song "Gentle on My Mind," who knows that "your door is always open," which is what "keeps you in the back roads by the rivers of my memory/ That keeps you ever gentle on my mind."

In this case, as in Dylan Thomas's poem, what is being modified or described is not the action—not the keeping—but the person. Thomas did not want his father to be gentle; similarly, if contrariwise, Hartford liked his woman gentle. Nobody had to tell them to use an adjective instead of an adverb. They knew what they were describing.

Apropos of adverbs without -ly: you and your correspondents disagree not just with me but also with Fowler. See his entry "Unidiomatic -ly." I believe that your determination to regard those words as adjectives confuses two situations. In "the conflict looms large, the offer seems good," the verbs are equivalent to *is* and the modifier is indeed an adjective that harks back to a subject, conflict, offer.

But in the much more frequent "drive slow, sleep sound, think fast," it is surely the verb that is modified, and the qualifying word is accordingly an adverb that happens to have the same form as the adjective. Consider "hit hard"; you cannot say "hardly" without confusion, and the very fact that the temptation to use it occurs shows that it is the verb *hit* that you mean to characterize.

Your contrary mode of analysis requires a subject to be "understood"—some hitter or sleeper not visible in the sentence. Even supposing "(You) hit hard" to be the implied meaning, how does "hard" apply to "you"? This kind of "understanding" is bad business; it will justify many solecisms. For instance, in Texas the road signs read: "Drive careful," which is detestable. But under your scheme the driver would be "understood," and "careful" would be the adjective that attempts to modify him. Shall I then add: "You should take me serious"—adjective modifying both you *and* me?

Jacques [Barzun]
Charles Scribner's Sons
New York, New York

Professor Barzun and Mr. Curran are right to point out that Thomas's use of "gentle" to mean "gently" is grammatically correct. But there is another, overriding reason for the poet's choice of word: the sound and rhythm of the line. "Gentle" simply sounds better. The second syllable of "gently" in common usage carries a slightly, but noticeably, stronger accent than does the second syllable of "gentle" and takes a fraction of a second longer to say. It is audibly more distracting than is its counterpart in "gentle." The strongest syllable in the line is meant to be *gen*, and it is meant to stand alone, as unencumbered as possible by its neighbors. Much of the beauty of the poem lies in the rhythm of a correct reading. Change "gentle" to "gently" and the rhythm is disturbed—ever so slightly, but such differences separate the good poets from the great ones.

David Groisser
Coram, New York

The association of Ariel with the sprite in Shakespeare's *The Tempest* might be tangentially appropriate, but as Sylvia Plath's own annotations to the manuscript of "Ariel" show, she had in mind the Hebrew meaning of the name, which is "Lioness of God."

Jack Folsom
Professor of English
Montana State University
Bozeman, Montana

Your Plath citation this week switched some of her finest lines from one poem to another. The lines you quote end "Lady Lazarus," not "Ariel."

Jon Swift
Arlington, Virginia

Please believe I go gentle when I suggest that the last line of your column should have read: "They knew *whom* they were describing."

Francine Flisser Helfman
Schenectady, New York

Politicians' Main Squeeze

The political times, they are a-changin'. Only a decade ago, in my favorite political dictionary, the definition of *juice* was "political power," and the observation added, "The word appears to be squeezing out *clout.*"

That was then. In current usage, the word has taken on the added meaning of "money." Martin and Susan Tolchin, in their book *Buying Into America: How Foreign Money Is Changing the Face of Our Nation* (Times Books, $18.95, well worth the juice), a chapter is entitled "The 'Juicing' of California."

A legislative bill that causes lobbyists on both sides to loosen the purse strings is known as a *juice bill*—"so named," write the Tolchins, "for the hundreds of thousands of dollars that could be squeezed from it." In one case, a tax bill was delayed for a couple of years because legislators did not want to act too soon on an issue that attracted so many contributions on both sides.

Dan Walter, a columnist for the *Sacramento Bee*, is quoted as first saying, "There's enough grease to fry a dinosaur"—using a venerable political Americanism, *grease*, for "money"—and later commenting, "If you want to play in the arena politically with a juice bill, you've got to play with juice."

"Juice" is also the ten percent penalty a losing bettor pays his bookie. This ten percent is the bookie's profit margin, since the betting "line" he establishes ensures an equal amount bet each way.

> Betty Tyler
> Fayetteville, Arkansas

Pre-Option Play

In the course of campaigning, all candidates make language mistakes; as Martha Taft, wife of Senator Robert A. Taft, said of her husband's favorite target, "To err is Truman." Some solecisms, however, are positively creative.

George Bush, rejecting a comparison by Bob Dole about the value of Congressional experience over appointive office, said he had served in the House "long enough to understand how it works, but not long enough to get kind of *pre-opted* by the situation there."

A *pre-option* was used in 1666 to mean "an option before any one else; right of first choice." This could not have been what Mr. Bush, who has been running a long time but not that long, meant. He obviously intended to say *co-opt*.

There's a verb with a political history. Three centuries ago, it meant "to elect into a body by voting." The earliest citation, from James Howell's 1651 *A Survey of the Signorie of Venice*, was "He sufferd himself to be co-opted into the Colledg of Cardinalls." Over the years, the meaning evolved to "to take as one's own," as so often happens when a local figure gets sent to Washington and falls in with national elements. Frank Cormier of the Associated Press said in 1979 that Lyndon Johnson was always trying to "co-opt reporters into becoming part of his team."

Mr. Bush's creative confusion comes from a voguish verb with a similar meaning, *pre-empt*. That is rooted in the Latin *emere*, "to buy"; *pre-emere* was to buy beforehand, or to exercise a right of first option. When a labor union anticipates a runaway-plant maneuver by management and walks out first, that could be called a *pre-emptive* strike.

The distinction between the current meanings of *co-opt*, "to absorb," and *pre-empt*, "to hit first," is worth preserving; we must not permit *pre-opt* to take hold, lest both meanings be co-empted.

Quants Ain't Quaint

Most studies of college-campus slang, including the excursions into the world of *horror shows* and *power boots* in this space, focus on the argot of students. We know what a *ding* is—a rejection ("One more ding and I'll never call her again")—because we have spent long hours *tooling*, or studying, the patois of undergraduates. I am indebted to Michael Moffatt, associate professor of anthropology at Rutgers, for the definition (originally published in the Dartmouth newspaper in 1982) of the mysterious *sproutsy:* "Anyone known to be a vegetarian, or to act, dress or think like a vegetarian." This was a word that was coined to fill a linguistic need, since *veggie* is short for *vegetable*, a person not on the *qui vive*.

Little work has been done, however, in the field of faculty slang. Several professors, demanding anonymity because a confession of ignorance is career-threatening, have written to ask for the definition of *quant*.

At first, the answer seemed obvious: a shortening of *quantum jump*, which most people think means a huge leap, as in "from teaching courses in Corp Fin to cutting actual throats on Wall Street is a quantum jump." Physicists grumble about this, holding that the phrase means the sudden emission or absorption of an atom's energy, coming from *quantum theory*, which argues that energy is transmitted jerkily and only in multiples of indivisible units called *quanta*. Strict constructionists would say that a quantum is very small, hence a quantum jump is no big deal; they are fighting the problem. The meaning is not what the Big Brains think, it is what all the Little Brains think, and a quantum jump is over a brook too broad for leaping.

On-site inspection offers a surprise: although a *quant* comes from the clipped *quantum jump*, its meaning is taken from the second word. A *quant* is a *rocket scientist.*

No, a *rocket scientist* in faculty slang is not a scientist who works on rockets. Wernher von Braun was another kind of rocket scientist entirely. "A *rocket scientist,*" I am informed by Rav Healey, Jr., of *Forbes* magazine, "is an academic superstar, especially in math or the physical sciences, who is lured away from the hallowed halls to work on Wall Street." By putting their number-crunching genius to work on less academic pursuits, these former theoreticians devise stratagems for making money in great bundles. "Apparently, zero-coupon bonds are an example of a new investment vehicle created by a *rocket scientist,*" Mr. Healey said.

Thus, *quants,* or *rocket scientists,* are great brains drained off campus by the business world. The coinages are exciting; if any faculty lounge lizards want to reveal the secret language spoken behind closed doors—especially about students—their confidences will be kept. I am ready to go to college to protect my sources.

I spent many years on the buy side as a closet quant. I seem to remember an article on this topic published in the late '70s by *Institutional Investor,* if you want an early citation. The only reference I could locate quickly was in an *I.I.* article ("Is Beta Dead") dated July 1980, an excerpt of which is enclosed. It's clear from the context that "quant" is a familiar form of "quantitative analyst," and has nothing to do with jumping. (The article reports two quants sniffing, which these days would probably lead to an involuntary drug test, but 1980 was an innocent time.)

Michael F. Wilcox
New York, New York

Other faculty slangsters will surely have written by now to say that the origin of *quant* is not "quantum jump" but rather "quantitative," as in those who use and teach courses called Quantitative Methods 101. This is mostly B-School slang—over here in Econ, statistically oriented students study *'metrics* (from "econometrics"), while mathematically inclined students with a more theoretical bent study *mathecon* (for mathematical economics). The most subtle and sophisticated of these study game theory, which has a language of its own—but since you strategically misunderstood the phrase *strategic misrepresentation* some years ago, I won't get into that.

Alvin E. Roth
Mellon Professor of Economics
University of Pittsburgh
Pittsburgh, Pennsylvania

Re "quantum jump" and "quantum leap": It is not the *size* of the jump or leap to which these expressions call attention, but rather the *discontinuity* that is involved.

For centuries, scientists accepted Leibniz's dictum that "Nature takes no leaps." In the early twentieth century, alas, it was discovered that sometimes there is no smaller flea to bite 'em. The state of a particle can go from quantity A to quantity B without traversing any of the points in between.

This was, and still is, a profoundly disturbing revelation, which implies that in the very heart of matter there is something not unlike [oops] a Kierkegaardian "leap of faith."

Hence, the expressions in question provide a means of emphasizing that something is more than an incremental augmentation of what previously existed: it represents a real "quantum leap."

Gerald Hull
Binghamton, New York

You described quantum jump as "a huge leap . . . over a brook too broad for leaping." As I understand it, the essence of a quantum jump, whether at eye level or atomic level, is that something moves instantaneously from one point to another without passing through the intervening space.

You describe career quantum leaps, as from the campus to Wall Street. That would be called a quantum jump, not just because it is a huge leap, but because it skipped the expected intervening career steps. When people make quantum leaps in logic, they leave you thinking, "What?!? . . . Now how did he reach that conclusion?" People make a quantum jump in understanding when they have been wrestling with a problem, and all of a sudden, they say, "Aha! Now I see the solution!" This intuitive leap seems like a quantum jump in physics. I have heard people talk about a quantum leap in performance. I picture a smooth upward trend in performance over time, then all of a sudden a discontinuity, a surprising upward surge in performance.

So I would define "quantum jump" colloquially as "a sudden, unexpected, discontinuous movement or shift, not predictable from prior behavior—especially as it is perceived by an outside observer." It may make perfect sense to the one doing the leaping, but it leaves the rest of us scratching our heads.

Mike Van Horn
San Rafael, California

One of the debates carried on among different schools of linguistic thought has been: does knowing the meaning of a word suffice to let one use it properly in a sentence? Your column contributes a bit of evidence that knowing meaning does not suffice for syntax. "Tooling" indeed means "studying." (The Massachusetts Institute of Technology has long borne a name based loosely on a nearby factory sign: THE MASS. TOOL OR DIE WORKS.) But it is an intransitive verb; you cannot "tool" any particular field.

Wayles Browne
Associate Professor of Linguistics
Cornell University
Ithaca, New York

Recuse My Dust

R ed lex alert! That dread signal is flashing through the world of lexi-cography. Writers of dictionaries are punching out the Nexis databank to find out why one word-missile got through the citation-slip defenses; editions on the press are being held up and remade to include the new verb or, more accurately, the rarely used old legal term in a new mood now flooding the American discourse.

A news clerk pokes his head in my office to call out: "Ed Meese has *recused* himself!" Sure enough, the transcript from the Justice Department has the Attorney General saying: "Because of my long association with Mr. Deaver that goes back almost twenty years to California, I have deter-mined to recuse myself in any proceedings in this matter."

Go try to find *recuse oneself* in a dictionary. Merriam-Webster's Ninth New Collegiate has a related noun, *recusancy,* "refusal to accept or obey established authority"; in Webster's New World, the verb *recuse* is labeled "[rare]" and defined as "to challenge as prejudiced or otherwise incompe-tent to act," similar to the definition in the Random House College and World Book dictionaries.

But it is no longer rare; and in current usage, the term is usually used reflexively: *to recuse yourself* means "to disqualify yourself," usually because of an apparent conflict of interest or perception of bias. Today's *recusants* are not Roman Catholics who refused to attend Church of England services between 1570 and 1791 (precursors to Russia's *refuseniks*) but are judges and prosecutors taking themselves out of the line of fire from plaintiffs and observers who think they may be less than disinterested.

"It is the court's duty to recuse itself," said an IBM attorney to a glowering judge in 1979; "Attorney General Benjamin R. Civiletti had to recuse himself . . . ," wrote a *Washington Post* reporter in 1980, and another *Post* reporter wrote a year later, "During his Senate confirmation hearing, [James] Watt promised to 'recuse' himself from decisions that might affect companies . . . in which his foundation had been involved."

But newscasters and newswriters hate to use the word. The *New York Times* headline writer, on the story reporting the Meese recusal, preferred "removes himself"; the *Washington Post* chose "disqualifies self"; *The Wall Street Journal* used "withdraw from 'any dealings.' "

One reason *recuse* is so often refused is that it is easily confused with *refuse*, to which it is etymologically similar: in Latin, both *recusare* and *refundere* mean "to refuse," as in "to pour back." (If a judge recuses himself too often, he should refund his salary to the taxpayer.) The *recusal-refusal* confusion is not the only problem: *recuse* is also mistaken for *excuse* (after recusing himself from the case, the prosecutor excused himself and went to the bathroom; he was a man who refused himself nothing).

That's not the worst confusion. Between the time *recuse* enters a typewriter and the time the word comes out in a newspaper, it more often than not gets changed to *rescue*. Somebody is always trying to fix it. During the Carter era, in an investigation of White House shenanigans, Attorney General Griffin B. Bell brandished a clipping of a column I had written and told a Cabinet meeting: "It says here I *rescued* myself, and come to think of it, that's exactly what I did."

In current usage, then, *to recuse* means "to remove oneself from a position of judgment to avoid the fact or appearance of bias or personal interest." It has a more legal connotation than *disqualify*, is more pointed than *excuse* and contains a reason that is not available in *remove* or *withdraw*. Use it; stick it in your dictionary, but expect a typo.

Your column today revolves around the word "recuse." You try to establish some mystery around it, especially in your electing several minor-league dictionaries as your authorities. May I respectfully suggest that you make greater use of the Century. My own seven-volume, leatherbound 67-pound edition does not fail in this case. The word gets a full definition, both lay and legal. As usual, the Century provides two citations, of which I repeat one: "A judge may proceed notwithstanding my appeal, unless I recuse him as a suspected judge. (Ayliffe, Parergon)."

Charles F. Gill
Williamsburg, Virginia

Redundadundadundant

In *The Patient Has the Floor,* the book of sparkling essays by Alistair Cooke, this one-man English-speaking Union bravely draws a conclusion: "When all is said and done . . . much British writing about America, and American cogitations on the nature of England, spring still from the deep desire not to be unduly impressed by each other. . . ."

One of the ways that too many English academics try unduly to impress Americans, and each other, is by the use of *litotes.* This Greek-rooted word, pronounced LIGHT-o-tease, once meant "negation of the contrary" but has come to mean "overweening understatement." My pen pal Alistair and I would have not a few regrets to see the not unarch practice disappear.

Brother Cooke recalls a British sportswriter who was always emptying his litotes bag with "Hogan played the back nine in 32, which on a windy, wet day was no inconsiderable feat." When pressed by people who wondered if, since he spent so much time in America, he planned to become a citizen, the sportswriter would coyly reply, "No, but I am a citizen of no mean country." (This is rooted in Acts 21:39, in which the Apostle Paul said, "I am . . . a Jew of Tarsus, a city in Cilicia, a citizen of no mean city." When he used it, the locution was fresh and the technique not hackneyed; that was long ago.)

Good writers have used *litotes* to get across a shade of meaning—*not unkindly* and *not incorrect* do not mean *kindly* and *correct*—but most often it is used to strain for stylistic effect, as Jane Austen did in *Pride and Prejudice* with *not unseldom.* Remember George Orwell's prescription—"One can cure oneself of the *not un-* formation by memorizing this sentence: *A not unblack dog was chasing a not unsmall rabbit across a not ungreen field.*"

The most straightforward use of litotes I can think of is in the title of a book by Mark and Diane Kender Dittrick, *No Uncertain Terms;* it plays on the worn-out phrase with a twist on "terms," making clear the difference in such terms as *speed* and *velocity.* (They say *speed* is the distance an object travels during a unit of time, *velocity* is the distance it travels in a specified direction during a unit of time. Not incorrect, but too technical.)

Tautology is similar to litotes in its unnecessary use of repetition, although the litotist is consciously being coy and the tautologist doesn't know what he is doing. Mr. Cooke has just won the Squad Squad's Yet-Again Another Redundancy Award for spotting this rare quadruple-tautology specimen from Larry Speakes, the White House spokesman: "The President *is watching* the *current* situation, which is *ongoing* at *this moment.*"

What started me on this item, however, is the expression *when all is said and done*. Have you noticed the way it is being replaced by a vogue term, *at the end of the day?* We are not talking about dusk, or the time for happy-hour free-lunching, but the conclusion of a metaphoric day. George Washington first used the figurative phrase *too late in the day* in a 1797 letter, but Latin American newsletters pioneered the current usage in the 1970s, writing of "foreign investors, who are not so much interested in seeing their money back *at the end of the day* as in acquiring permanently an asset. . . ."

The Economist picked up this usage in 1976: "*At the end of the day*, people may still be healthier in King's Lynn than in Liverpool." A clear difference exists between that broad use and this specific use, in *Business Week*, quoting a Middle Eastern executive saying, "*At the end of the day*, I sit here with my head on the desk, all wrung out, wondering whether it is really worth it." The new use has been picked up by geopoliticians, and Zbigniew Brzezinski and Edward Luttwak sprinkle their conversations with it.

At the end of the day is hot. But you'll see, when all is said and done. . . .

I was also grabbed by (an earlier form of "I flashed on") your reference to a current phrase "at the end of the day." More interesting to me is the older phrase *early days*, to mean "premature." A young woman responding to a young man's request might say flippantly, "Oh, it's early days for that."

Charles Newton
Pasadena, California

The statement "The President is watching the current situation" is a tautology, not a double tautology. Adding two more unnecessary repetitions does not change a (single) tautology to a quadruple tautology.

If golf usage were followed, where two under par is an eagle and four under par is a triple eagle (not a quadruple eagle), Mr. Cooke's find would be a *triple tautology*.

Arnold M. Malasky
Washington, D.C.

Your column on "litotes" reminded me of how shocked I was a couple of months ago when there popped up all over town a wall poster with a blood-red hammer and sickle over the headline KATO (= "down with") LITOTES. A peek at my Modern Greek dictionary reassured me. The party was not taking a line in regard to figures of speech, *litotes* having retained in Modern Greek what was its primary meaning in classical Greek, "austerity." So the posters were protesting not the rhetoric but the economic policies of the Greek government.

Sam Abrams
Rochester, New York

Right Stuffing

Here's lingo to cage your eyeballs: the latest vocabulary of the naval aviator, compiled by Commander Richard Shipman and Derek Nelson in a recent issue of the *Proceedings of the United States Naval Institute*.

Hit the burner is understandable to landlubbers: "Draw on inner resources to overcome a crisis." To be more busily occupied than usual is to be at *warp one* or at the *speed of heat*.

To give it a thumb check is a nice locution, not limited to people who can land on a pitching carrier deck in a storm; it describes "a quick glance at a thick document," and may soon challenge the slang verb *eyeball*.

Someone who is incompetent is called *frequently outwitted by inanimate objects*. "Evidence that you have struck a responsive chord with a listener" is described as stimulating *involuntary hip movements*. Verbal appeasement of higher authority is called *singing gospels out in front of the big house*. Evidence that our naval aviators have a solid grounding in English folklore is their term for "unquestioning compliance": *yes, sir, yes, sir, three bags full*.

Cage your eyeballs, by the way, is the expression to describe "any extreme physical experience." It is like the feeling lexicographers get when crashing the slang barrier.

On "caged eyeballs," I wasn't sure in reading your definition just how naval aviation uses the term today, but it's certain the meaning has changed. For what it's worth, here's the term's origin. I was air force but expect "caged eyeballs" crossed service lines.

When a gyro-operated flight instrument—the artificial horizon for example—went out of true, because the gyro had been inoperative for a time, or "tumbled" because the instrument's limits had been exceeded in an unusual flight attitude, the pilot would return it to true by pulling a knob on the instrument that would recenter it—cage it.

The language carryovers: At military attention, an aviation cadet's eyes were to remain riveted dead ahead on infinity. If they drifted, the commander's instant order was to "Cage those eyeballs!" On a pass to town, getting a visual on the female population, one flier might kid his buddy that he was likely going to get slapped, maybe locked up, if he didn't cage his eyeballs.

Ben Spencer
New York, New York

"To give it a thumb check" has been around for a while in education circles (among education squares) as "thumb test," the thing too many teachers do when evaluating and then deciding whether to adopt a new and possibly superior textbook. The ritual usually consists of a sub-one-minute thumbing through the text, with the teacher perhaps pausing to see whether a particular pet topic has been done the way the teacher has always taught it.

David Bernklau
Brooklyn, New York

Rooms with Words

While listening to television (in the morning, you don't have to watch—you just listen) in a hotel room in 1985, I heard Arthur M. Schlesinger, Jr., author of the spellbinding *The Cycles of American History*, use a word I didn't know: *sclerotic.*

A traveler cannot schlep around the college dictionary that contains that sort of word. A hotel offers only a Bible, placed in the room by the Gideons; that good book defines the meaning of life but doesn't help on hard words. And all the freebie bottles of bath gel, mouthwash samples, sewing kits and plastic shoehorns that nobody uses but everybody steals cannot meet the need for meaning. What to do?

"Why doesn't some hotel chain lay in a stock of dictionaries," I wrote, "placed lovingly on the pillow, instead of a fattening chocolate? I would gladly forgo a bottle of fabric rinse, whatever that is, for a dictionary."

Some hoteliers care. Bill Marriott, a good egg, dropped me a note to say he'll lend me a dictionary next time I stay at one of his hotels. In London, if I needed all thirteen volumes of the Oxford English Dictionary, I would call downstairs to Ronald Jones, general manager of Claridge's, and get action; in New York, I know that the last of the great guest-service agents, Alex Van Maarseveen at the St. Regis-Sheraton, stands ready to spell anything in five languages.

But what of the guest who is not known to be a word maven? In San Francisco, the president of the Stanford Court, James A. Nassikas, has taken up the challenge in grand-hotel style. "We've done it," he reports. "Every one of his 400 guest rooms now has a new dictionary: "On your next visit you will find over 160,000 entries in your room dictionary with clear, precise definitions coupled with more than 30,000 new words and meanings to help you keep pace with the expanding language of today's world." (I think he is reading from the blurb on the jacket of Webster's New World.)

Lucky visitors to San Francisco! On my next trip, I will check in and look up *hotel*, and note with concern that word's common heritage with *host*, *hospital* and *hostage*, all from the Latin *hospes*, "guest." Never again will an early-rising historian bedazzle me with his nonchalant *sclerotic*, which I will be able to find out immediately means "brittle."

I know now how the Gideons, facing approximately 2.5 million American hotel and motel rooms, must feel. Today, one great hotel equipped with a dictionary in every room; tomorrow, the world.

> Of all the great crusades of the twentieth century, "a dictionary in every hotel room" undoubtedly is the most humane. May your dream be realized in the language of every country of the world!
>
> Only one possibility alarms me: some hotelier may select the dictionary you used—the dictionary that defines "sclerotic" as "brittle."
>
> All my life I have thought sclerotic meant 1) "hard" or 2) "pertaining to hardness," and it still does in 1) my unabridged Random House Dictionary of the English Language and 2) my Oxford English Dictionary. Seems to have come pretty directly from the Greek *"skleros,"* meaning "hard."
>
> I know some things that are hard are also brittle, but *skleros* seems too solid to be stretched that far.
>
> *Anne N. Timmerman*
> *Mamaroneck, New York*

> Unless the last word in your "On Language" column was a typo, you missed a great opportunity for a bonaprop. I was expecting "today . . . a dictionary in every room, tomorrow the word."
>
> *Irving Kittay*
> *New York, New York*

Lexi-Klepts

In Victor Hugo's *Les Misérables*, which is getting a big ride these days, hero Jean Valjean is pursued by the relentless Inspector Javert in effect for stealing a loaf of bread to feed a starving child.

I identify with Javert. That is because this Reuters dispatch has come across my desk: "San Francisco's posh Stanford Court Hotel has never lost a Bible but since it put dictionaries in its 402 rooms last month, forty-one have been swiped."

That dream of a dictionary in every hotel room was my big idea. I saw myself as the Johnny Appleseed of linguistics, persuading hotel owners to put dictionaries in rooms everywhere, enabling weary travelers to look up the meanings and spellings of words used in late-night X-rated movies. (Go look up *lubricious* in the middle of the night with nothing but a Gideon Bible in the room.)

And what happens when a high-class hotelier sensitive to the needs of literate guests stocks his rooms with dictionaries? One out of ten guests turns out to be a lexi-klept. At this rate, all the dictionaries will have been stolen by the end of a year. What a sad commentary on the human condition; it is as if somebody is following me around, pulling up apple-tree seedlings.

The managing director of the Stanford Court, John Cameron, offers this excuse, probably because he doesn't want to knock these thieving guests: "I guess everybody has a Bible at home but a lot of people would like to have a dictionary."

Wrong. People think that if they steal a Bible, the very inappropriateness of the act will cause them to be struck by lightning; but if they lift a dictionary, they assume God won't care. As a result, departing guests leave The Word and grab the words. The Stanford Court management, a bunch of softies, is now putting stickers on the remaining lexicons: "Love is leaving our dictionary here when you leave."

If that namby-pamby stuff doesn't work, try Safire's Curse: If you steal a dictionary, there will come a day when your child will ask you for the meaning of a word, and you'll feel too guilty to look it up in the stolen book and will misinform him, and he'll be on a quiz show with a chance of winning Vanna White as a prize and will repeat your mistake and will then sue you for parental malpractice and pick you clean.

Patronize hotels with dictionaries. Use the dictionary as needed (*lubricious*: slippery, or wanton; see *lecherous*). Then leave the dictionary in the room.

The fact that 10 percent of the good books are missing after a month does *not* mean that one of ten guests is a lexi-klept—unless all guests stayed for the full month. Assuming room turnover every three days (and full occupancy), only about *1 percent* of guests help themselves to the dictionaries.

Unfortunately, this correction casts an even darker cloud over the problem, as you can see how rapidly the books will disappear even though only a small proportion of guests are taking them. I'm afraid the Safire Curse will not deter this hard-core group, and more effective procedures are needed. Say, Dictionaries by Room Service?

Charles C. Baum
Baltimore, Maryland

Ruling the Jet Set

"**K**eep your eye on *ruling,*" advised Maureen Dowd, a reporter for *The New York Times.* She said that *ruling,* long used by Soviet propagandists to derogate American democracy in the term *ruling circles,* was now being used here as a participle to mean "advanced, with-it, avant-garde" or "in." Two quite different senses are in use, confusing the incognoscenti: the first is "doing well, going along fine," as in "My day is ruling"; the second sense is "socially dominant," as in "Jackie O. rules."

I hesitated; Miss Dowd is a certified Lexicographic Irregular, but the only written citation for this locution was in a piece she wrote that appeared in Part 2 of *The New York Times Magazine* on November 9, 1986. That article was about a social phenomenon called a *celebutante* (a combination of *celebrity* and *debutante),* in particular the suddenly well-known Lisa Edelstein of New York City, who was cutting a swath through New York society for reasons obscure to most.

A message left on Miss Edelstein's telephone-answering device by one of her gentlemen friends said, "I'm in a tizzy, um. It's my day and it is not ruling." Transcribing this cryptic message, the reporter explained: "*Ruling,* once part of the street argot of the 1960s, is the current chic word for being cool or powerful, for controlling a situation." In this case, *not ruling* meant "proceeding in stress-causing manner, upsetting one's cool."

Could I risk the vast authority of this column on a single use by one slightly confused young man, perhaps just coming out of a deep sleep— especially the sort to use *tizzy,* an outdated slang term perhaps derived from *hysteria* and related to the British *tiswas?* The chance of being lured into accepting as genuinely trendy a mere nonce usage was too great; I resolved to watch and wait.

Comes now a new magazine called *In Fashion.* "IN" is printed in big letters; "Fashion," writ small. Very short names are de rigueur for fashionable magazines. I'll bet this publication soon changes its name to a simple IN, perhaps with a picture of Errol Flynn on the cover, making its title only twice as long as Fairchild Publications' *W* and *M,* which the cognoscenti know signify "Women" and "Men."

There on the cover picture of Charlie Sheen and Charlotte Lewis, apparently known as "Hollywood's Hottest Couple," is the headline: "Ruling Style," subheaded "Fashions on the cutting edge." The Dowd early warning was accurate; from now on, I will trust my sources more, and I have launched a search for citations of *ruling* in the '60s, perhaps in black English.

Here we are in the language used in *nouvelle society*. That is a term coined by John B. Fairchild, publisher of *Women's Wear Daily* and of the aforementioned single-letter magazines; it updates *café society*, which was the term used in the '20s to separate the merely celebrated from the old-line, old-money, "real" Society, often broke but always capitalized.

In Cleveland Amory's 1960 *Who Killed Society?*, the coinage of *café society* was pinpointed to an evening at New York's Ritz in 1919, when the first "Cholly Knickerbocker"—columnist Maury Paul—noted that Society figures were dining out on Thursday nights (maid's night off), and concluded that a new night life was dawning, which he dubbed *café society*.

Now we are titillated by *nouvelle society*. The use of the French adjective *nouvelle* was probably inspired by *nouvelle cuisine*, which in turn was rooted in *nouvelle vague*, a phrase used by film directors in the late 1950s meaning "new wave."

The feminine adjective *nouvelle* matched the feminine noun *société* (though in France, leaders of the big-money establishment and their debutante daughters are called *le beau monde*, "the beautiful world," I am informed by *Women's Wear*'s Patrick McCarthy). *Nouvelle* contrasted suitably with the masculine *nouveau*, which called up *nouveau riche*, a label that the longtime snooty hang on the recently snooty; these moneyed pretenders are also sniffed at as *social climbers* by those to the manor born who know how to wield a lorgnette (eyeglasses attached to a handle, once defined as "a dirty look on a stick").

In societese, *nouvelle society* is New York-based and freshly wealthy or newly notable. "It's not to be confused with the *jet set*," I am told by Claudia Cohen, Eyewitness News reporter with New York's WABC-TV, whose beat includes these freshly celebrated newsmakers; "those *beautiful people* are much more international than *nouvelle society*."

Beautiful people, a phrase possibly rooted in *le beau monde*, is attributed to *Vogue* editor Diana Vreeland in the 1960s, though some say it was the coinage of copy chief Rosemary Blackmon; however, the term is passé today. So is *jet set*, which first appeared in print in 1951 to describe the fashion-conscious group that used jet aircraft to take them to the world's watering spots in passionate pursuit of pleasure. (I spent a weekend with that crowd in Acapulco once, and a fellow named de Portonova was constantly giving champagne toasts. It's a way of life.) The term is analogous to *smart set* (the *smart* part was applied to the dandies in London in 1718). Later, *Smart Set* became the name of an American magazine edited by George Jean Nathan and H. L. Mencken.

According to Liz Smith, today's premier gossip columnist, the term *jet set* is a victim of technologically induced egalitarianism: "These days, everybody's in the 'jet set' who wants to go anywhere. There's no other way to go, so the elitist connotation disappeared." She sees the term *nouvelle society* as *nouveau riche* with the sting taken out: "People who've been designated as 'in' are usually delighted; they don't realize they are being made fun of, in a way." (Full disclosure requires me to say I was designated by *W* as "in" one year, and columnist Art Buchwald was "out"; Art cut me dead the next time we met, but with this new, profound understanding of the term, we can be read in the same circles again.)

Glitterati has fallen into disuse; this 1940 coinage, like the more recent *celebutante,* is what Lewis Carroll called a *portmanteau word,* after a suitcase that opens into two parts. It is based on *glitter* (from the Old Norse *glitra,* "sparkle, shine") and *literati* (from the Latin for "learned, scholarly people").

A locution to watch—I'm sensitized now—is *brat pack,* based on Frank Sinatra's Hollywood *rat pack.* This applies mainly to young authors who write what is called *hip lit,* often dealing with *nouvelle society* characters.

Attention is paid by copywriters who must stay on the cutting edge of *au courant:* a recent fashion advertisement by Bloomingdale's (featuring short skirts, high heels and a color called "poison green") was headlined "Bright Nights Big City/The Rules of Attraction." Ann Elise Rubin of *The New York Times* alerts me to the allusions to *Bright Lights, Big City,* a novel by Jay McInerney, and *The Rules of Attraction,* a novel by Bret Easton Ellis. Both men are successful *hip-lit* authors.

What sort of lingo do these people speak? Apparently they are influenced by movie-industry talk. Sally Quinn, author of *Regrets Only* and a valued Lexicographic Irregular, reports a new term raging through this crowd that is synonymous with "get to the point," or "bottom line," or "here's what I'm getting at." It is *cut to the chase,* from the movie habit of cutting, or switching, to the chase, usually the most exciting scene.

Example:

"Look, I'd like to hear all about it, but I'm late for the hairdresser and the decorator is already waiting in the new apartment."

"OK, cut to the chase—de Portonova lifted his glass, but the place was clean out of champagne!"

I ran *cut to the chase* past Maureen Dowd, who had not yet heard it, but bid me toodle-oo with the words, "Dissolve, dissolve, dissolve." That is at the end of a scene in a movie script, and I suspect is a way of saying, "I'm leaving now," or, "I'm history."

You, too, can swing with the swelegant and heat up with the hottest couples. If your day isn't ruling, cut to the chase, pack up your troubles and dissolve, dissolve, dissolve.

"Brat pack" must go back at least to 1983! It was originally applied to the group of actors then in their early twenties such as Rob Lowe, Judd Nelson, Emilio Estevez, Demi Moore, Ally Sheedy, etc., who acted and socialized together in a way that invited attention—rude or otherwise—from the press, especially *New York* magazine.

Robert Bookman
Creative Artists Agency, Inc.
Los Angeles, California

Thirty-five minutes into a repeat episode of *Hill Street Blues*, "Captain Furillo" used the phrase "cut to the chase" to get one of his people to come to the point.

While this relatively early use of the phrase "cut to the chase" clearly demonstrates it is "movie-industry talk," (and the writers' sense of humor in having a cop say it), it also suggests that millions of Americans first heard the expression more than four years ago. It hardly seems fit for nouvelle society.

T. Andrew Finn
Somerset, New Jersey

While "Bright Lights, Big City" may have been used by Bloomingdale's copy writers as an allusion to the novel by Jay McInerney, Mr. McInerney must have been alluding to the song of the same title, written by Jimmy Reed. The song deals with the bedazzlement of a small-town girl, from the point of view of the small-town boy she left behind. I don't have a date for the songwriting handy, but I have a 1973 recording of it by The Persuasions (an a cappella R&B group just popular enough to survive for the past couple of decades). The song is on the album "We Still Ain't Got No Band," MCA-326. . . .

The expression was in use in the rural South not long after electric lights were widespread in Southern cities; I suspect the song is almost as old.

David Pinckney
Piscataway, New Jersey

"Ruling the Jet Set" reminded me of college days in England in the sixties. Every other piece of graffiti gracing toilet walls (which is how we English gracefully refer to bathroom walls) seemed to be of the form "So and so Rules, OK?"—examples follow. My impression is that the phrase was first made popular during the Skinhead era of the mid to late sixties, and spread from the daubings of the boot boys themselves to the sometimes more intellectual musings of the college-educated elite.

Thus, "Fulham Rules, OK?," "Liverpool Rules, OK?," which are simply soccer slogans, were joined by:

Procrastination will rule one day, OK?

The Rubaiyat rules, OK?

Scots rule, och aye?

Potassium Exthoxide rules, C_2H_5, OK?

Skeptics may or may not rule, OK?

Jargon rules, ongoing agreement situation.

Typographers rule, OQ?

French diplomats rule, *au quai?*
And thousands of others.

> *Philip Rowland*
> *New York, New York*

Ruling:
Isn't it from astrology? (As in, Jupiter is in the ascendancy and Mars is *ruling*—your life; having control.)

> *Louise Kennedy*
> *Marblehead, Massachusetts*

Although visually a dissolve can simply be a way of smoothing out the transition from one scene to another, it has long had a very specific meaning in the language of film. A dissolve signifies a passage of time. In that respect, a good translation of your friend's "Dissolve, dissolve, dissolve" might be "Later, later, later."

A dissolve, it should be noted, is not an ending. As one scene disappears, another comes in on top of it. It is, therefore, both a "Goodbye" and a "Hello"—a filmic *aloha*. For those occasions when a very definitive farewell is required, try "Fade out."

Another grammatically equivalent device is the "wipe"—a more eye-catching (but old-fashioned and now a bit campy) way of marching the movie forward in time. In the not-too-distant future (if not last week), when the hip lit tire of saying "Dissolve, dissolve, dissolve," we could start hearing "Wipe, wipe, wipe." Then again, maybe not.

> *Mark Block*
> *Film Editor*
> *Editing Concepts*
> *New York, New York*

To the Jet Set Born

The Gotcha! Gang is out in force. "William Safire refers to the phrase *jet set*," writes Richard H. Rosichan of Miami Beach, one of many readers who pounced on this, "as having 'first appeared in print in 1951 . . .' However, the world's first commercial jet route . . . was not operating until 1952–53. Hence, these pioneer jet-setters would have had to have been either test pilots or combat aviators in the Korean War."

Hence, schmence. Another reader skeptical of the origin of *jet set* is Gwinn Owens of the *Baltimore Evening Sun*: "I am concerned with the number of times that you authoritatively note that a word or expression 'first appeared . . . ' How do you know?"

The phrase appeared in the *San Francisco Examiner* of August 5, 1951:

"You're strictly jet set . . . if you stake your claim in the dunes . . ." Nobody can argue with a hard citation in the Oxford English Dictionary Supplement; in this case, that's how I know. Maybe it appeared even earlier; if so, send it in, and the world's lexicographers will be happy to revise the dictionaries.

According to Edward H. Phillips, business flying editor of *Aviation Week & Space Technology*, "The first military jets flew in 1942, and the Comet I in Britain was tried in 1952. The public knew about jets." And Cynthia A. Barnhart of Barnhart Books sends along a clip from the June 16, 1951, *Science News Letter*: "The present jet-propelled airliner known as the Comet is now flying the [London–Rome–Cairo] route as the first stage in route trials. . . ."

(In the job title used above, "business flying editor," the word *flying* is a gerund, in this case a noun used attributively; it must not be confused with a participle, because it is not an adjective describing what the editor is doing. To understand gerunds, keep the mnemonic in mind: Gerund was a buddy of Beowulf's.)

It is always a pleasure to scotch the Gotchas. However, to all who have hooted derisively at my "to the manor born," I have no retort; those jet setters of the Elizabethan era were, in Shakespeare's spelling, to the "manner" born. Ya got me.

What slows me down is a line in Chaucer's description of the Pardoner in *The Canterbury Tales:*

> But hood, for jolitee, wered he noon,
> For it was trussed up in his walet.
> Hym thoughte he rood al of *the newe jet;*
> Dischevelee, save his cappe, he rood al bare.
> (General Prologue, 11. 680–83, Robertson ed.; emphasis mine.)

Robertson glosses the word "jet" as "contrivance; fashion, mode." He also lists the variant "get," which looks to me as though it were related to the modern phrase "get-up" (in the sartorial sense). Chaucer's jet seems not to be related to our kind of jet, since the latter looks to be short for jet-propelled, the manner (still mind-boggling to me) in which those big silver things go through the air. The nagging question remains, does Chaucer's foppish Pardoner, riding about hoodless in the new jet of the 1380s, have anything to do etymologically with the jet-setters who were riding about in the new jets of the 1950s?

Frank G. Hoffman
Philadelphia, Pennsylvania

Running the Traps

The language of clearance—specifically, the lingo of obtaining prior approval—has never been examined by scholars. That vacuum in philology will be filled now.

Check him out is the command gruffed by top executives to aides before an appointment is made or a nominee is announced. "Will he pass a *full field?*" asks an assistant, who much prefers to be described as a "key aide."

This is a shortening of what the Federal Bureau of Investigation calls a *full field investigation*, an inquiry that is run on all Presidential appointments and on people permitted to see classified information. It can occupy agents in all fifty-nine field offices and take up to a month, is in contrast to one of their quick looks, which is called a *name check*, and is run for some federal agencies as well as state and local governments that require such criminal checks by statute.

Let us assume the intent is to check political, rather than security or criminal, considerations. When Frank Mankiewicz, then a key aide to Democratic candidate George S. McGovern, was asked to check out Senator Thomas F. Eagleton, he did not say, as reported, "Are there any *skeletons in the closet?*" Instead, he asked, "Have you done anything that you think could give us trouble?" (a procedure he described as *casting a cold eye*).

Mr. Mankiewicz reports that the phrase he now hears is *scope him out*, perhaps derived from a radar screen. (John Ehrlichman, in the Watergate hearings, said "he went off my screen"; in journalism, to be "off the screen" is the same as "out of pocket"—that is, not to be reachable by the desk editor. Conversely, *to scope someone out* means "to examine someone closely on the screen.")

In advertising, *pretesting* (redundant) was described as *running it up the flagpole to see if it salutes*, presumably meaning to see if the emblem rated a salute. And in bureaucratese, the standard verb phrase for absolute prior approval is *sign off on*, with which one's keister is safely covered.

In politics, however, one colorful slang phrase, used frequently by insiders, rarely sees the light of print: *run the traps*. It has a general meaning of "survey those in the know," and when I asked then Navy Secretary John F. Lehman, Jr., if he had heard of some development, he said, "Beats me, but I'll run the traps and get back to you."

The phrase is filling a void in clearance lingo. In the *Washington Post*, David Hoffman and Lou Cannon wrote about a hasty selection of a press officer by Nancy Reagan and United States Information Agency Director

Charles Z. Wick; when the appointment stirred controversy, the reporters quoted "a senior White House official" as saying, "It was done quickly and without running the usual traps."

A search by computer of all the newspaper files putting together the words *run* and *traps* turns up only an unrelated football term, "running a trap play," which is seldom defined on sports pages but means "the technique of letting an opposing lineman penetrate the line and then blocking him from the side as the running back goes through the place the charging lineman vacated."

For key aides concerned with clearance, then, *run the traps* means "check for opposition and support," with a second meaning of "vet this potential appointee's résumé for exaggerations and errors."

The origin is from hunting and trapping: a trapper, checking the traps in the morning to see if any animals were caught, is said to be *running the traps,* in the sense of running over, or examining, their status. The political usage is a natural extension of the metaphor.

A caveat: do not use *running the traps* when you mean *rattle the cages.* The latter trope, taken from a zoo term, means "ask him something controversial to see how he reacts."

I hope this doesn't reflect badly on radar, but the expressions "scope him out" and "scope it out" originate in the lingo of hospital interns.

Instead of trying to diagnose an illness from the outside, a doctor may decide to take a look inside, and "scope" a patient both fore (bronchoscope) and aft (cystoscope and sigmoidoscope. I think it's safe to say that not even Clarence Darrow would look forward to this scopes trial.

Clark Whelton
Assistant to the Mayor
New York, New York

Could the expression "running the traps" come from the British Victorian slang for "traps" meaning the police? The expressions "set the traps on" and "get the traps to run over someone/something" had to do with police action rather than trappers and hunting. The American expression may be quite different in which case I'm sorry I opened my trap.

Joe Cleary
Jacksonville, Florida

I think there is another source of *scope it out:* submarine warfare, in which the term is used to describe the practice of approaching a subject warily (and, often, without being observed) in order to determine its nature and status. The *scope* is, therefore, *periscope* and not radar scope. This usage, which I have seen in countless books on submarine warfare, surely predates the other that you cited.

Donn C. Neal
Chicago, Illinois

Big game hunters often carry rifles fitted with telescopic sights (commonly referred to as scopes) to accurately sight and shoot their quarry at long range. To avoid the added weight and bother of carrying another optical device, these hunters often use their scopes in place of binoculars to scan the countryside for game and, once found, to evaluate the animals for their trophy potential. For forty years that I know of, this practice of evaluating game through the scope has been expressed *to scope him out.*

Robert Socha
Sparta, New Jersey

In 1978 I was attending Michigan State University and living in a coed dormitory. At mealtimes, the women would sit at strategically located tables in order to *scope out* the men. It struck me as a reference to a periscope—i.e., one could observe others and remain unseen.

Laura A. Voss
Brookline, Massachusetts

Full field investigation. I suspect the origin of this phrase is from the military "full field inspection." If memory serves, a full field inspection was (perhaps still is) an extremely thorough inspection which included not only each soldier's personal equipment (the subject of routine inspections), but also all of the unit's field equipment. Such inspections were especially dreaded because no amount of preparation could insure success. There was really no way of applying the same intense spit and polish to all those truckloads of stuff as was expected of one's own rifle, shoes, etc. Therefore, passing or failing inspection was determined almost entirely by how far the inspecting officer wanted to look for something about which to complain. The well-established meaning of the military phrase is so close to what is intended by *full field investigation* that it seems more than probable that the word *investigation* may have been substituted simply to make the phrase more understandable to civilians.

G. L. Andrews
Chicago, Illinois

If I'm not mistaken, the expression is more commonly "run it up the flagpole to see *who* salutes." Alternatively, "put it on the 5:15 and see if it gets off at Westport."

John W. Palmer
San Francisco, California

I once heard this in a Madison Avenue think-room while ideas were being tossed out: "Let's shrapnel that one and see who gets hit."

Irv Shapiro
Chevy Chase, Maryland

Running to Daylight

The most coveted invitation on a Sunday in Washington is to the Lombardi Room, behind the owner's box at Robert F. Kennedy Memorial Stadium, where pols, power brokers and media biggies munch hot dogs—nobody calls them "tube steaks" there—and speculate on the fortunes of Jack Kent Cooke's Redskins. (No thought is being given to changing the name to Native Americans.)

The owner Cooke is a linguistic conservative; that is, he sticks to certain pronunciations, no matter how the accents of the rest of the world are changing.

"I bet we won't be seeing Michael Deaver here," a wise guy said to him at one of the season's early games, spearing and applying a late hit to the formerly mighty assistant to the President.

"I hope you will," retorted the redoubtable Mr. Cooke. "I invited him because I refuse to treat him as a *pariah* is treated."

That snapped a few well-coiffed, blow-dried heads around. Everyone else in that room would have pronounced *pariah* to rhyme with "They Call the Wind Maria" (ma-RYE-uh), emphasis on the *i*, but Mr. Cooke made it sound more like *carrier*.

My media confrères looked to me to confront the owner with his mis-pronunciation; correcting that, they figured, was my responsibility, not theirs, and they wanted my seat in the box at the next home game. Mr. Cooke rotates the invitations, and the fewer to be invited means the greater the number of invitations left for the sycophants.

"I notice you said, '*as a pariah* is treated,'" I said, as the rest of the crowd stuffed hot dogs into their faces so as to avoid being drawn into the discussion. "I admire the way you use *as* rather than *like* a pariah—too many people use *like* as a conjunction."

I offhandedly pronounced *pariah* pa-RYE-uh, correcting the owner's pro-nunciation in an exquisitely subtle way, maintaining my language maven's integrity without jeopardizing my shot at a seat at Superbowl XXI.

"You mean PAR-ee-uh," he said. The munching around us grew deafen-ing. Sam Donaldson edged toward the door. Leslie Stahl started for the chicken wings.

I knew what I had to do. "Do you say LAM-entable or la-MENT-able?" I asked.

"LAM-entable, of course," said the crusty old gentleman. He knew what I was getting at. "And DES-picable, not des-PIC-able, and HOS-pitable, and. . . ."

He is consistent, prescriptive and certain; the way Jack Kent Cooke pronounces words is reminiscent of Slingin' Sammy Baugh—with assurance that his way is the right way. And he has the unwavering support of fans who spoke those words that way a couple of generations ago.

The Oxford English Dictionary, finished in 1933, pronounces it PAR-ee-uh (explaining afterward that the word comes from the Hindus of India whose caste was so low as to be outcaste). And Webster's New World Dictionary grants that a secondary pronunciation, chiefly British, is PAR-ee-uh.

But the Oxford Paperback Dictionary says to pronounce it pa-RYE-uh, and all the American dictionaries agree. In India, the word is still pronounced the old way, which makes PAR-ee-uh correct in India, but here in America we use the new pronunciation—except in the Lombardi Room.

Mr. Cooke is more consistent than the NBC Handbook of Pronunciation. That guide to the silver-tongued has the new pa-RYE-uh, but the old LAM-entable, HOS-pitable and DES-picable. The BBC Guide agrees, and for those words most dictionaries prefer the accent on the first syllable.

But most people who say those big words (and that is very few people) accent the second syllable. Note that I do not say that these lovers of the second syllable mispronounce those words; the pronunciation is changing—to be precise, the emphasis is shifting to the right—and what was incorrect when Ace Parker was jump-passing for the Dodgers is not incorrect today. It's not "correct," but it is uncorrectable.

That does not make me a permissive descriptivist, a moral relativist or a Cowboys fan. *Nuclear* is not pronounced nuke-u-lar, nor *judgment* judge-a-ment, nor *liaison* lay-i-zon, no matter what Presidents Eisenhower, Ford and Reagan said. If someone asks you for the name of a good "gone-acologist," you should recommend a GUY-nacologist; if somebody offers you a kruh-SAHNT, don't go for the phony French; ask for a KRAH-sant. And for God's sake, don't say DAY-ity when you refer to the Deity (say DEE-ity).

But on the inexorable move to the right of pronunciation, I resist at first, continue to use the old pronunciation myself, correct only by precept and learn to go with the flow in others.

I will sit here in the front row with my fellow freeloaders, and if one of my colleagues says, "That was an exquisite execution of the Statue of Liberty play," you will not hear me say, "Not ex-QUIZ-it, stupid, you mean EX-quiz-it." The wise language maven does not always run to daylight.

I refer to your column on the "inexorable move to the right of pronunciation": Of course, the words are easier to say. Yet I can think of at least two examples where the accent has shifted to the left, making the words less easy to say (in my opinion). I learned Carib-BEEan. I must be the last holdout; the universal pronunciation seems to be CaRIBbean. Likewise HiroSHEEma has become HirOshima.

> William H. Herder
> Somerville, New Jersey

I don't agree with you at all about *deity*. Think for a moment; it comes from *deus* and you know how to pronounce that, don't you.

> Thomas J. Bates
> Berkeley, California

You write, "If someone asks you for the name of a good 'gone-acologist,' you should recommend a GUY-necologist . . ." I always thought the latter was acceptable, but that the preferred pronunciation was "JIN-ecologist," as in "misogynist." That's the way it is in my 1970 Merriam-Webster New Collegiate, anyway.

> Frank McNeirney
> Arlington, Virginia

You wrote that "in India, the word is still pronounced the old way, which makes PAR-ee-uh correct in India, but here in America we use the new pronunciation. . . ."

This is very odd. I have lived in India, off and on, for some five years, and I have never heard such a pronunciation. Much of my time has been in Tamil Nadu and Kerala (the area where the caste is found), and I have studied Tamil. PAR-ee-uh will not be heard. There are no accented syllables in Tamil, but the common pronunciation comes out pa-rye-uh. The Tamil word for the caste is *paraiyan* (singular).

> Robert L. Hardgrave, Jr.
> Austin, Texas

Your recent column about the origin of the word "pariah" prompted me to go to a dictionary produced in India that surely stands as one of the most unusual of its kind, and one of the most impressive. It is called "Hobson Jobson," a glossary/dictionary of all the colloquial Anglo-Indian expressions, words, phrases and "kindred terms," along with little essays and historical references. It was originally published in 1903 and has been updated periodically. It's a wonderfully absorbing 1,021-page book that you ought to consider for your library.

Anyway, under *pariah* it states that it is a Tamil word, which means it comes from Dravidian origins in the South and not the dominant Indo-Aryan or Arabic/Persian origins of northern India. It says that a *parai* is actually a large drum beaten at certain festivals, and the hereditary beaters of it are called *paraiyan* (singular) or *paraiyar* (plural) and that this lower caste made up 20 percent of the population of Madras at one time. (Not all of them were drum-beaters, or else a hell of a lot of us would be pariahs.)

I quote: "As with other castes low in caste-rank, they are also low in habits, frequently eating carrion and other objectionable food, and addicted to drink. From their coming into contact with and under observation of Europeans, more habitually than any similar caste, the name pariah has come to be regarded as applicable to the whole body of the lowest castes, or even to denote out-castes or people without any caste. *But this is hardly a correct use* (my emphasis). There are several castes in the Tamil country considered to be lower than the Pariahs, e.g., the caste of shoemakers, and the lowest caste of washermen. And the Pariah deals out the same disparaging treatment to these that he himself receives from higher castes."

I asked a friend of mine who is a Tamil Brahmin and a foreign ministry official (Brahmin is the highest, or priestly caste), and he said the proper pronunciation in Tamil is on the second syllable, pronounced pa-RAY-uh. As in anchors *aweigh.*

Steven R. Weisman
The New York Times Bureau
New Delhi, India

Semiotic Yoks

A comedian named Steve Wright has a routine that plays on the meanings of signs in a way that is causing much delighted chin-pulling among students of semiotics.

"Parked my car in a tow-away zone," he says. "Came out after the movies, and they had towed away the zone."

And: "I bought a pack of batteries, but they were not included."

And: "It said in the restaurant, 'Breakfast served at any time.' I ordered French toast during the Renaissance."

I, too, like the humor of Steven Wright. My favorite line from him is the query, "What's another word for 'thesaurus'?"

David A. Santogrossi
West Lafayette, Indiana

The Setting Agenda

Do you know what the 1986 elections were all about? They were about *setting an agenda.*

"The leadership of the Senate would set the agenda," crowed Senator Robert C. Byrd, Democrat of West Virginia, expecting to be the new majority leader. "The White House won't set the agenda."

"From the standpoint of setting the agenda," agreed Senator Robert Dole, Republican of Kansas, soon to be minority leader, "it's a very significant change." He added that he was happy not having "the burden of setting the agenda on a daily basis."

Hearing all this, Senator Joseph R. Biden, Jr., Democrat of Delaware, told the cameras, "We're going to have an opportunity to set the agenda," and Senator John Heinz, Republican of Pennsylvania, let it be known that "Democrats will now set the legislative agenda for the next two years."

Agenda-setting appears to be the hottest vogue item in the language of politics. Who started it?

President Jimmy Carter gave the phrase its currency in 1977, when he told a news conference that "we'll set an agenda for trying to resolve" problems with Mexico and Canada. He promptly repeated the phrase—"when I get there and see how we can, as I say, set an agenda for getting them resolved"—and the cliché became part of the journalistic firmament.

What does it mean? "Determine what is important" is one definition; "focus public attention on" is another; "prioritize" is what bureaucrats believe the phrase denotes. Political philosophers treat it as meaning "take the lead."

How long can a vogue phrase hang on? Jimmy Carter—whose "Moral Equivalent of War" (MEOW), taken from William James, has been forgotten and whose misuse of *reticent* for *taciturn* is receding into linguistic history—haunts us still with *set an agenda*. When the new legislative term starts, I intend to put the elimination of this phrase right at the top of my list of things to do.

Setup, Trumped-Up,
but not Framed-Up

A State Department spokesman said that the Soviet case against Nicholas S. Daniloff, an American newsman in Moscow, was based on charges that were "contrived," and many news stories promptly jettisoned that weak word for an informal but more widely understood usage: the newsman, it was reported, had been *framed*.

The New York Times, sensitive to the use of nonstandard English, reported that a White House official had "said 'a lot of people in this Administration are furious' about what he called the 'frame-up' of Mr. Daniloff."

The *Washington Post* made no effort to allude to the informality of the verb *frame* and headlined the news of an earlier such instance: "1984 KGB Attempt to Frame Daniloff Reported."

A week later, seeking to equate one of their diplomats accused of spying with the United States newsman who was, according to the Administration, taken hostage, the Soviets mimicked that American reaction of *frame-up*. The Soviet spy suspect, Gennadi F. Zakharov, held a news conference that generated this *New York Times* headline: "Zakharov Charges a 'Setup' by F.B.I." The *Washington Post* headline quoted the words spoken by Mr. Zakharov's Russian translator: "I Was Set Up."

I accept no moral equivalence between the case of the Russian spy suspect and that of the American reporter held hostage by doing my customary thing: examining the etymology of the words in the dispute, the nouns *frame-up* and *setup*, and the adjective *trumped-up*.

The noun *frame-up*, along with its short form *frame*, is defined by Eric Partridge in his Dictionary of the Underworld as "a criminal act in which an innocent person is made to appear to be a criminal." Venal prosecutors know that, in the verb form, only *frame* is used; you do not *frame up* someone in current slang. (An accused American native speaker would cry, "I'm being *framed*; it's a *frame-up!*"; if the accused insists, "I'm being *framed up*," he might be a Russian trying to use American slang, and the proactive Federal Bureau of Investigation would stop to frisk his vocabulary.)

In the sixteenth century, the Middle English noun *frame*, meaning "a construction," gained a more sinister meaning of "contrivance," something fashioned to gain an advantage or undue profit. "He openeth our eyes," wrote Bishop Thomas Watson in 1558, "to see the frames of our enemyes." In 1901, the Oxford English Dictionary labeled this sense "obsolete," but it turned out that this sense was not dead, only in hiding overseas, among sleazy characters far from its mother tongue's origins. In the first volume of the current O.E.D. supplement, published in 1972, that dictionary's readers were told to "delete *Obs.* and add later examples in *U.S. Slang*; especially = *Frame-Up.*"

Though *frame* as noun and verb is not always pejorative—we proudly hail the *framers* of the Constitution, and the business of *framing* pictures is getting more expensive all the time—we take the downside of the word from uses like Shakespeare's "frame of villainies." In 1900, "He could arrange a 'frame-up' " appeared in *The Powers That Prey,* a book about crime by "Josiah Flynt" and "Francis Walton" (pseudonyms of Josiah F. Willard and Alfred Hodder), and the *frame-up* became the standard cry of the accused.

The noun *setup,* in the sense of "entrapment," is much newer. In American slang, a *setup* was a billiards term for the opportune lie of the balls left for the next player, or the ice-and-soda fixings for a drink that needed only a shot of the patron's personal booze to turn into a highball. Since the 1920s, the notion of a *setup* being like the pins or ducks set up in a carnival booth to be knocked down has been used for boxers easily defeated. In the 1960s, it seems, the term was applied to people in general: the first use found so far is from the *Baltimore Sun* of October 13, 1968: "That's how the narcs [narcotics policemen] get most guys on possession of narcotics—through setups." (Please do not send in vivid recollections of having used that term in the 1940s after some memorable bust; only recorded citations count.)

The disillusioned young usagist will ask plaintively: How come the old term *frame-up* is hyphenated in most newspapers, and the much newer sense of *setup* is not? Answer: Virginia, your little stylebooks are wrong. Frequent use over time should determine the erosion of a hyphen; following that rule, I would write *frameup* and *set-up,* despite threats by legions of stylebook writers to clap me in grammarians' jail, accused falsely of misplaced hyphenation. (I also use *stylebook* as one word, on the analogy of *cookbook,* because it works well as an attributive noun, as in *stylebook critics.*)

Trumped-up should always be hyphenated to separate the past participle and the preposition. The compound is old, its etymology as uncertain as a trumpet that prepares nobody for battle.

The noun *trumpet* is imitative, from the Old High German *trumba,* and it is easy to see a connection with loud tooting in *trump up.* But Joseph Shipley in his Dictionary of Word Origins tells us that the *trump* in cards "is short for *triumph . . .* the card game was called *triomphe* in French," and from the French *trompe* "came *tromper,* to cheat, whence *tromperie,* cheating." From that might have come the English *to trump,* "to go one better," or *to trump up,* to deceive. Its first use in English to mean "forge" or "fabricate" was in 1695: "His Pouder being . . . disgraced, he was obliged to trump up another Medicine to supply its Defect."

There goes another bullet in the fusillade denouncing false accusations: *fabrication*. President Reagan, in a speech to the United Nations, married "fabricated accusations and trumped-up charges."

The Latin *fabrica* means "workshop" or "structure," similar to *frame*; a connection exists with the turning-from-truth sense of "to frame or invent." "The whole story was fabricated," wrote John Moore in a 1779 commentary on European society, sounding much like Ronald Reagan today; that is also the sense of *cut out of the whole cloth*, fabric that is defined by the O.E.D. as "a piece of cloth of the full size as manufactured, as distinguished from a piece that may be cut off or out of it for a garment."

The taking of an American newsman into custody churned up another question about Russian names. How come the difference in spelling and pronunciation of Andrei D. Sakharov, the valiant dissident, and Zakharov, whose arrest triggered the Soviet action? According to Ted Shabad, the *New York Times*'s revered source on the Russian language, SAKH-ar-ov is rooted in the Russian word for sugar, *sakhar*, accented on the first syllable; Za-KHAR-ov is rooted in the archaic first name for a male, *Zachar*, and follows the usual accent on the second syllable, as in Ro-MAN-ov.

The affair also apparently rattled the metaphoric stability of our usually unflappable Secretary of State, George P. Shultz. "There will be shoes dropped as we go along," he warned, "and people should keep their powder dry."

I can't understand how you could fail to adduce the Yiddish *trumbenik*. It came leaping at me over several decades of disuse as the term my parents used to designate a faker, con man, or phony.

Undoubtedly, my work as a psychoanalyst and the caseload this entails facilitated this association to your excellent piece.

Michael Green, M. D.
Springfield, Massachusetts

While you indicate that Zachar is an old name, you don't give a meaning or an etymology. It might be assumed that its origins are Russian, but I wonder. It seems much more likely to me that the name is derived from the Bible, and that in the first instance it is based upon the familiar name Zacharias in the New Testament: i.e., the priestly father of John the Baptist (Luke 1:5, etc.). This name, in turn, is derived from the common name Zechariah in the Old Testament; among the many examples, the prophet Zechariah stands out, and the righteous priest in II Chronicles 24:20–22, who is also mentioned in the New Testament. Altogether upwards of forty people in the Bible bear this name or ones related to it and derived from the same root:

z k r. The middle letter is pronounced *-kh-* (or *-ch-*) as I presume it is in Russian.

Another curiosity, which started me on this research and response, is that there is a biblical Hebrew word with the same root letters, *zākār* (pronounced *zākhār*) which means "male, man." It was the juxtaposition of the words "male" and *"Zac-har"* that brought to mind the Hebrew words, and while it may be pure coincidence, I thought it worth mentioning and investigating. There is a continuing discussion among Hebrew scholars as to whether there is any etymological connection between the terms *zākār* "male" and *zākār* "to remember, make mention of," with which the names are associated. I believe the prevailing view is that they are homonyms. In any case, I believe the Russian name "Zachar" is derived from the biblical source.

David N. Freedman
Professor of Biblical Studies
The University of Michigan
Ann Arbor, Michigan

"Stylebook" is ugly whereas "cookbook" is all right. The double "k" and the rhyming makes for a good word just as GOOD FOOD is the best sign I know of for a restaurant.

Tom Bates
Berkeley, California

You note that "the business of framing pictures is getting more *expensive* all the time." Recent visits to picture framing stores have convinced me that the business of framing must be getting more *lucrative.*

Marian Sofaer
Washington, D.C.

Simon Didn't Say

The Presidential Campaign Hotline is a computerized information service put out by the American Political Network. I was downloading its stuff when I came across a memory-jogging statement by Democratic presidential candidate Paul Simon of Illinois. (*Download* is computerese for "receive from a larger computer into a smaller unit," the opposite of *upload,* "send from a smaller to a larger computer"—both locutions out of *offload,* an 1850 South African expression meaning "unload," and the even earlier *overload,* a 1553 compound.)

Senator Simon had previously endeared himself to me by announcing early in the campaign, "I'm not a neo-anything," thereby putting down both neoconservatives and neoliberals (actually, Simon is a post-modern neoliberal, which means "old-fashioned New Dealer"). He told a San Antonio audience, "On fiscal policy, I am conservative."

That triggered a synapse in my head attached to "dynamic conservatism," a semi-oxymoron favored by President Eisenhower, who also fiddled around with "moderate progressivism." Adlai Stevenson of Illinois, preparing to run against the unbeatable Ike for the second time, had this to say:

"I am not sure what dynamic moderation or moderate dynamism means. I am not even sure what it means when one says that he is a conservative in fiscal affairs and a liberal in human affairs. I assume what it means is that you will strongly recommend the building of a great many schools to accommodate the needs of our children, but not provide the money."

A similar instance of unconscious harking back (not *hearkening* back—*hark* means "to turn" and *hearken* means "to listen," which the Gotcha! Gang once nailed me on) came out of the mouth of Nicaraguan strongman (or "Sandinist leader" or "Communist dictator") Daniel Ortega Saavedra.

Asked why he refused to conduct direct talks with the contra leader Adolfo Calero, President Ortega said, "We have nothing to talk about with Mr. Calero, because the owner of the circus is Mr. Reagan. We have to talk with the owner of the circus and not with the clowns."

The predecessor metaphor was in a line attributed to Winston Churchill. When the British Ambassador in Rome asked Prime Minister Churchill whether it would be wiser to raise a question with Mussolini or with Il Duce's Foreign Minister and son-in-law, Count Galeazzo Ciano, the British leader replied: "Never hold discussions with the monkey when the organ grinder is in the room."

If this keeps up, we will turn into a nation of paramnesiacs, all with a sense of déjà-voodoo economics. I harked myself back the other day in a piece on the collapse, drop or rolling readjustment of the stock market, suggesting some "had been taking credit for the rain and must now take the blame for the drought." That was an unconscious steal from Dwight W. Morrow, the banker who became President Coolidge's ambassador to Mexico.

You characterized Daniel Ortega Saavedra variously as "Nicaraguan strongman," "Sandinist leader," and "Communist dictator." Ortega's title is President of Nicaragua. He may also be the most powerful figure in the Sandinista Front and thus the government, but he rules in conjunction with others, and with the consent of many of the governed. "Strongman," "dictator," even "Sandinist leader" are allegations, not names. They are part of an argument about what

Ortega, and Nicaragua, are. And they are powerful weapons in that battle.

Ortega was elected President by approximately 60 percent of Nicaraguans who voted in an election that was widely viewed by independent monitors, including American congressmen, European observers, and the American press, as fair and open. There were no reports of murders or death threats or bombings of demonstrations committed by Sandinista activists against opposition parties, as there are in India, Jamaica, Mexico, and other "Western-style democracies" around the world where the winner gets to be called "president." The only contestants who did not participate did so of their own accord, under strong American pressure, and were unwilling to denounce the contra insurgency. Few other "democratic" countries would permit a party linked to an opposing guerrilla army to participate in elections, but the Sandinistas were willing to let them. They didn't want to.

Presidents elected elsewhere under much more controversial circumstances than in Nicaragua are honored with the title. "President" (strongman, or dictator) Napoleón Duarte was also elected by a mere majority in a country where political allies of the armed insurgency refused to participate, because they feared for their lives, they claimed. In El Salvador, the campaign process included such extra-parliamentary methods of persuasion as death threats, assassination and continued army intervention in contested areas. The total vote count exceeded the possible number of voters, and was widely regarded as rigged to inflate both the Christian Democratic majority and popular support for the election.

That President Duarte was elected under such circumstances doesn't disqualify him from being called "president," though perhaps it should. Daniel Ortega is at least as "presidential" as other strongmen and dictators worldwide, who nonetheless never seem to get that label in columns.

Mitchell Hartman
Brooklyn, New York

In Canada the government is currently formed by a political party that calls itself the Progressive Conservative Party. While I've never been able to figure out exactly what this means or what the party principles are, this name has been institutionalized as the party name since 1942. Even earlier in Canadian history, this same party was called the Liberal-Conservative Party.

Paul Gingrich
Regina, Saskatchewan

In describing computers' ability to transfer material to each other, you state that downloading involves receiving "from a larger computer into a smaller unit," and the opposite, upload, is sending "from a smaller to a larger computer." I submit size has nothing to do with it —rather, it's a matter of which computer is controlling, or initiating, the transfer.

For example, a larger computer is certainly able to "download" from a smaller unit—and this is often the manner by which much of the larger computer's material is obtained, just as a smaller computer can be set to receive files which are "uploaded" from a larger unit. These activities are expressed, not in terms of the relative *size* of the units, but in terms of who's doing what to whom.

Thomas P. Cobin
Flushing, New York

Smiles of a Summit Night

The world's ears were poised to pick up the awaited word. As Ronald Reagan and Mikhail Gorbachev stepped into the rain to say farewell after a newsless summit, the diplomatic words that would signal genuine progress in superpower relations would be *fruitful* and *productive*.

Instead, we heard the leaders characterize their dealings as *frank* and *businesslike* or call the meetings *a useful exchange of views*. In diplomatese, *frank* does not mean "candid, earnest, forthright," as it does in ordinary language; it means "we got nowhere, and he even hollered at me once or twice." Worse, an *exchange* is not a mere "chat, talk, interchange, colloquy"; among the striped-pants set, it connotes an exchange of salvos by ships of the line. As the Soviet translator was saying *exchange of views*, Dan Rather was secondarily translating for his CBS audience, "that means 'little or no progress.' "

International confabulations, with diplomats drawn up in what Winston Churchill called "vast cumbrous array" (and it was Churchill who first used "parley at the summit"), churn up exciting and sometimes stunning usages.

My first shock of the Washington summit came with the publication of the Intermediate Nuclear Forces Treaty, Article XV, Section 2: "Each Party shall, in exercising its national sovereignty, have the right to withdraw from this Treaty. . . ."

A misplaced modifier! *In exercising its national sovereignty* is a prepositional phrase (*in* is a preposition, followed by the gerund *exercising* and the rest of the phrase). As such, the phrase modifies, and therefore should be placed either immediately before or after, the subject *Each Party*. But this obviously flawed treaty (grammatically, perhaps not *fatally*, flawed) unnecessarily separates the auxiliary verb *shall* from the main verb *have*. You can get away with such a separation of a verb phrase to interrupt with a contradiction—as in *shall, however, have*—but no such contradiction is intended here. Somebody goofed.

As the Senate debates this, some roundheeled handmaidens for permissivism will claim that the prepositional phrase is being used adverbially, to modify the entire sentence, and not adjectivally, to modify the subject; these are the same apologists for détente who will swallow "designated facilities" as being adequate for "on-site testing." They are trying to avoid *killer amendments*.

"The important count is not how many votes there will be for [the treaty]," said Senator Alan Cranston, Democrat of California, "but how many votes there will be to withstand *killer amendments."* These amendments, explained Susan F. Rasky in *The New York Times,* "are those that would so substantially alter the treaty that it would have to be renegotiated with the Soviet Union."

In this noun phrase, the word *killer* becomes an attributive noun, performing the function of an adjective; its first appearance as such came in 1884 with *killer whale.* Then it leaped forward in 1931 with *killer instinct,* resurfaced two decades later with *killer bee* and, when Ronald Reagan once explained to angry environmentalists that trees sometimes absorb useful elements from the air, spawned the derisive *killer trees.*

On the subject of White House efforts to encourage Senate ratification, Senator James A. McClure, Republican of Idaho, said, "I'm not feeling pressure; I'm feeling *suasion."* A revealing distinction: *pressure,* from the Latin for "the application of force," has kept in its figurative extension the notion of force, as in *arm-twisting; suasion,* on the other hand, denotes the bringing of influence without compulsion, closer to *coaxing, inducing* than *forcing, coercing.*

What's the difference between *suasion* and *persuasion?* A matter of degree: the Latin prefix *per-* means "through" or "thoroughly," as in *perfect.* Thus, *suasion* is the act of urging or exhorting (moral *suasion),* while *persuasion* is the act of counseling to the point of inducing belief or action (hidden *persuasion).* Each is related to the Latin root of *suave,* which is why the summit persuaders, or "spin controllers," are usually smoothies.

The summit provided a few redundancies. The Squad Squad winced at Mr. Reagan's *fellow countrymen* solecism (it should be *my countrymen* or *my fellow citizens),* and we were offered an "old" proverb—"Trust but verify" —as if any proverb could not be old. (You can't have an *old adage,* either; you can say *old saying.)*

Mr. Reagan one-upped his Western ally, Margaret Thatcher, on the issue of parallel construction. As Mr. Gorbachev stopped off in Britain on his way to Washington, Prime Minister Thatcher put forward a proposal to finesse the thorny issue of Star Wars testing and announced, "I have the impression it is not only being considered, but has been talked about quite a bit." In that statement, *not only* should precede *is* for parallel construction with *but also* (not just *but*). Mr. Reagan used it properly in "On the table will be not only arms reduction, but also human-rights issues. . . ."

One locution chosen by Mr. Gorbachev was obscure but not incorrect: "History has charged the Governments of our countries . . . to undo the logic of the arms race. . . ." Here *logic* was used in its negative sense, as "something inevitable"; when this pejorative meaning is intended, as in *the logic of war,* the word means "a forced decision, independent of reason."

When Russians use Americanisms, the phrases are often slightly outdated. Georgi A. Arbatov, one of the "Americanologists" in the Soviet party, tried to explain how savvy his non-English-speaking boss was about things American: "If I use a phrase like 'Parkinson's Law' or the 'Peter Principle,' I don't have to explain." A younger American generation, however, might need an explanation of both: *Parkinson's Law,* attributed to the historian C. Northcote Parkinson, is "Work expands so as to fill the time available for its completion," and the *Peter Principle,* from the educator Laurence J. Peter, includes "In a hierarchy every employee tends to rise to his level of incompetence."

Mr. Gorbachev is also enamored of a Shakespearean phrase, which he used earlier this year and repeated in Washington: ". . . the winter of our discontent may one day come to an end." That was a phrase leading up to a pun, playing on *son/sun,* from *Richard III:* "Now is the winter of our discontent/Made glorious summer by this son of York." (The only other pun I heard during summittime was a punchy "*Glasnost* what your country can do for you . . .")

Mr. Reagan has been briefed to avoid the use of the word *Russian,* except in reference to the language, because the Soviet peoples (plural) include many others in addition to Russians. That was why, in his telecast with network anchormen, he told Tom Brokaw of NBC: ". . . this is the first Russian leader—or Soviet leader, I should say . . ."

Brokaw, incidentally, was the only newsman to have a line misattributed to him by the Soviet news agency Novosti. When it printed and distributed the text of the NBC Gorbachev interview, Novosti deleted the follow-up question about what the Soviet leader discussed with his wife Raisa; deleted was "Including Soviet affairs at the highest level?" as well as the response, "I think that I have answered your question in toto. We discuss everything." Novosti inserted the words "I accept your answer" into Mr. Brokaw's mouth, which he had not said, in lieu of the censored follow-up.

Coinages were few; *the D-word* was the chosen euphemism for unfashionable *détente,* and Jacques Barzun came up with *glasnostalgia.* However, Frank J. Gaffney, Jr., a Pentagon official bounced for his hard-line views, came up with *Gorbasm:* "The fleeting achievement, after frenetic activity and inflated expectations, of a momentary and unfounded atmosphere of good feeling."

You state that Tom Brokaw "was the only newsman to have a line *misattributed* to him by . . . Novosti." The construction not only is awkward, jumping from the page of otherwise elegant prose, but also incorrect.

First, by using *mis*attribute to describe the Novosti action, you seem to indicate that the statement attributed to Brokaw should properly have been attributed to someone else. This is clearly not the case as you demonstrate later in the paragraph. I would have said that Brokaw was the only journalist in whose name a statement was *fabricated*—in the sense described in Webster's New Collegiate Dictionary: "to make up for the purpose of deception."

Second, the prefix *mis* gives a meaning of something done badly or wrong—perhaps through inadvertence or oversight. However, what Novosti did was calculated to accomplish some end. The end is not important here, but the act is a chilling example of cynical manipulation of information by the Soviets in full view of the world press.

Patrick J. Brady
Vienna, Virginia

Not only is "in exercising its national sovereignty" a misplaced modifier, but (*also* is optional for parallelism) it is an egregious error in diction, the use of the preposition *in*. Prepositions probably represent the most flagrant examples of diction errors in several Proto-Indo-European languages, because idiom is based upon bias rather than rules. The correct preposition for the treaty sentence is *by*.

Richard J. Rome
Houston, Texas

Smoke and Mirrors

Arthur L. Liman, Counsel to the Senate in the Iran-contra hearings, wanted the witness to explain what sort of support was being given the Nicaraguan resistance during the period in which Congress had cut off aid.

"Basically it was *smoke and mirrors,*" laconically replied former National Security Adviser Robert C. McFarlane.

A few months before, the phrase surfaced in a speech by Ronald Reagan about the budget process: it's "wink and blink and smoke and mirrors," said the President, adding for emphasis, "and pulling rabbits out of hats."

The phrase, with a color added, was given currency in 1981 by Jack W. Germond and Jules Witcover as the title of the book *Blue Smoke and Mir-*

rors: How Reagan Won and Why Carter Lost the Election of 1980. Before that, it appeared in the *Washington Post* on November 13, 1979, in an article by Bill Peterson about a straw-poll win by George Bush, campaigning for the Republican nomination for President: "The victory was fleeting, meaningless except in the blue smoke and mirror world of politics."

Where does it come from? *Smoke* has long meant the stuff of confusion. In 1634, John Milton wrote of "the smoke and stir of this dim spot/ Which men call earth." Then the word took on the quality of deliberate concealment; the word is defined in George Washington Matsell's 1859 *Vocabulum; Or, The Rogue's Lexicon* as "humbug; any thing said to conceal the true sentiment of the talker." In Australian slang, *to go into smoke* is to go into hiding; in naval warfare, a *smokescreen* is the concealment device of a warship, and the metaphor has been applied in politics to mean a cover story intended to obfuscate an issue. (In Japanese politics, such evasion is more prettily described as *throwing up cherry blossoms.*)

But *blue smoke and mirrors* is a specific image; to politicians with a background in show business, such as President Reagan, the phrase conjures the world of stage magicians, where a rabbit is pulled out of a hat to the accompaniment of a puff of smoke and—on occasion—with the help of deceptive mirrors.

The phrase was coined in a 1975 book by Jimmy Breslin, *How the Good Guys Finally Won,* a salute to then Speaker of the House Thomas P. (Tip) O'Neill for engineering the removal of Richard M. Nixon. Breslin quoted Thomas Hobbes's "The reputation of power is power" and went on to opine that all political power is primarily an illusion.

"Mirrors and blue smoke," wrote Breslin, "beautiful blue smoke rolling over the surface of highly polished mirrors, first a thin veil of blue smoke, then a thick cloud that suddenly dissolves into wisps of blue smoke, the mirrors catching it all, bouncing it back and forth. If somebody tells you how to look, there can be seen in the smoke great, magnificent shapes, castles and kingdoms, and maybe they can be yours." The operator of the illusion comes to believe in it himself, "at the same time knowing that what he is believing in is mirrors and blue smoke."

Curiously, Breslin's phrase *mirrors and blue smoke* has been inverted in usage to *blue smoke and mirrors,* and the *blue* now shows signs of eroding. Even in its clipped and inverted form, however, the phrase evoked by Mr. McFarlane in the hearings most quickly calls up the picture that stands for the manipulations of illusion.

Somewhat Vulgar

When may a newspaper properly use the slang verb *to pee?*
John Irving, the novelist, called me to protest a decision made by *The New York Times* not to use that widely used euphemism in a book review he had written of *Seven Rivers West,* by Edward Hoagland.

One of the characters in the lusty tale, which Mr. Irving reviewed favorably, is a trader known for his prowess in long-distance urinating. The reviewer felt it important to refer to the character and his talent. Although authors of the stature of John Irving are cited in dictionaries to illustrate the development and acceptance of words, the following line was published in the *Book Review* section of the *Times:* "The wild journey that only Cecil and Margaret manage to finish ends outside the tent of a trader who's famous for winning bladder-voiding competitions."

"The word I wrote was *peeing,*" Mr. Irving affirms. "Totally inoffensive word—a euphemism, in fact, for *pissing,* a perfectly good English word. To me, *bladder-voiding* is repellent." Grumbling, he went along with the stylistic suggestion, because he wanted the sentence in the review, but wanted me to know that was not his style.

I have been noodling that over. *Pee* is certainly the gentlest of euphemisms, but it is a slang term, and once a publication admits the use of slang in describing bodily functions, it assaults the ramparts of taste. Newspapers that respect their readers' intelligence do not shy from such Standard English words as *urinate*—it was used in a *Times* front-page subhead recently in connection with drug testing—but draw the line against using slang words to denote the same function.

If the judgment were mine, I would ban *pee,* not because it is slang but because it is a baby-talk euphemism; instead, I would accept the word for which it substitutes as Standard English (that dread word will be avoided here as "vulgar"), but most people do not feel as strongly as I do about euphemisms.

It's a close call; I am reluctant to condemn editors as bowdlerists who argue that where standard words are available, slang or vulgarisms should be avoided. In Webster's New World Dictionary, however, *pee* is held to be only "somewhat vulgar" and the "somewhat" opens the door.

Then along came Mario M. Cuomo, Governor of New York, whose 1986 campaign for reelection included an episode that bears directly on this issue. Governor Cuomo, whose early refusal to debate his opponent drew some criticism, was appearing on a radio talk show that took telephone calls from the public. One of the callers was his opponent, Andrew

O'Rourke, who sought to engage him in impromptu debate, and the governor cut him off.

Asked to explain his refusal to continue the conversation, Mr. Cuomo was quoted in the *Daily News* as saying: "I'm on the radio, minding my business. A guy tries to hit me from behind; he calls up without telling us, and pees on my shoe."

Should that comment be reported? Yes. A way of reporting it without direct quotation, to avoid printing the slang term, would be this: "The Governor objected to his opponent's surprise call by comparing it to bladder-voiding on his shoe." But that would be silly. Governor Cuomo is a public person making a public statement on the record. He may one day be President of the United States; if he says "pees on my shoe," that comment deserves to be recorded as much as a picture of Nelson A. Rockefeller making a motion with his middle finger to a crowd of protesters (and that "single-digit salute" was printed everywhere).

What lesson can we draw from these two instances? That *pee* is now OK to use? No; that's too simple. Safire's Law (I write the "laws," but I don't edit the paper) is this: *Slang terms describing bodily functions that can understandably be denoted with standard words should be avoided when possible, but not when such avoidance becomes labored or ludicrous; also, when relatively inoffensive slang terms are used by a responsible and directly quotable news source, such terms may be used in context within quotation marks.*

John Irving and Mario Cuomo, like the Colonel's Lady and Rosie O'Grady,* have under their skins a common zest for the way people speak in real life. Their audiences are not shocked. Without abandoning our standards—indeed, while vigorously resisting most vulgarisms and barnyard epithets as falsely emphatic and in bad taste—I think we should make it possible for artists and political figures to express themselves colloquially.

Thanks for plugging my book. In my previous communication I drew your attention to the trappers' and hunters' term "touch-hole" for an animal's anus, a good example of what you say should be ineligible for newspaper use. But I've since figured out that its origin is probably the old cannoneer's term for the hind end of a cannon, where the flame touched the charge—a use of "touch-hole" that *would* be admissible, although slang.

In a piece of mine, "Dying Argots," I mentioned, among many slang circus-carnival-logging terms, "glomming geek," for a carnival geek who ate as well as simply bit the heads off chickens, snakes, etc., but confessed to not knowing where "glomming" came from. I've since heard that glomming meant, as recently as a couple of decades

* See "The Gotcha! Gang Strikes Again," pages ix–xi.

ago, eating too fast or greedily. At least, a friend of mine was shouted at by his father for "glomming" at meals.

Ted Hoagland
New York, New York

Regarding Rockefeller's one-finger salute, you wrote that it appeared everywhere. Not at first, it didn't. My recollection was that the editors of our paper deemed it unsuitable for publication, even though it was done by a public official in a public setting. For confirmation, it would require an examination of the newspapers of that week, but I recall that the *Times* barred the photo. But a week later, it appeared on page one of either *Newsweek* or *Time,* which then took a full-page ad on the back page of the *Times,* and then one could say that the picture appeared everywhere.

Irv [Molotsky]
The New York Times Bureau
Washington, D.C.

I was the primary organizer of the "mass pee-in" that was held at Cornell University. Members of the recently-formed group P.I.S.S.E.D. collected 139 urine samples in 4-oz. plastic cups, and sent some of the samples to the President to show our mock support for the Reagan administration's plans for the unconstitutional urine testing of Federal employees. The event was a great success, in that we got excellent (even responsible!) press coverage when 70 percent of Americans supported at least some mandatory urine tests.

My main reason for writing to you is to indicate how the media responded to the name of our group and to the event itself. Most of the local media, including the only TV station, either dodged the issue by leaving the event nameless or adopted our moniker, though whether with reservations or glee I am not sure. Ithaca is a very liberal town. The regional press started calling the event a "tinkle-in," which to me sounded too lighthearted—sure, we had a lot of fun, but urine testing is a serious issue too. If you can come up with a less disconcerting but equally catchy name for a pee-in, I'd appreciate it; it would be so nice to repeat the event with more refinement in the spring, when it's warm and sunny outside.

Jan Grygier
President, P.I.S.S.E.D.
Ithaca, New York

Pee is a childish word. Piss is a fine old Medieval French and Middle English word used by Chaucer's Wife of Bath and more recently by Clemenceau in reference to Lloyd George.

One mid-morning in Seville I was seized by a severe urgency and entered a café looking for a "gentleman's convenience." The place was crowded with men who showed no response to my various euphemisms. I suddenly became desperate and yelled, "Piss." Immediately every man stood up and with a smile escorted me to the proper place.

William S. Tinney, Jr.
Lancaster, Pennsylvania

As a footnote, consider "piddle," which my Webster's defines as a child's word meaning to "make water" or "urinate." That could serve as a definition of "pee," also, but "pee" doesn't make the dictionary. Ronald Blythe, in *Divine Landscapes,* says that there is a small town in Dorset which for centuries was called "Piddletown," but was renamed "Puddletown" in Victorian times. It lies on the river Piddle, which retains its original name. This village was the real locale of many of Thomas Hardy's novels—it is called "Weatherbury" in the novels, but not, I think, for reasons of delicacy.

V. T. Boatwright
Stonington, Connecticut

"Long-distance urinating"? That sounds like pissing by remote control. How about "long-range urinating" instead?

Patrick Kelley
Emporia, Kansas

Spaced-Out Precision

"Precision is closely related to accuracy," write Herbert E. Meyer and Jill Meyer in their new book, *How to Write,* "but it is not quite the same thing." (Why have husband-and-wife writing teams taken to repeating their last names? Why not "Herbert E. and Jill Meyer"? Save space.)

The authors of this superb beginner's book on writing, from Storm King Press, offer this sentence to show how you can be accurate but vague: "The first men to set foot on the moon landed there in the 1960s." To add precision, they suggest changing "in the 1960s" to "on July 20, 1969."

That reminds me of my most far-reaching grammatical error. A couple of months before the moonshot, a few of the speechwriters were sitting around the White House and noodling over what should go on the sign the astronauts would leave on the moon. "Here men from planet Earth first landed on the moon" had a nice ring of declarative precision, and "We come in peace for all mankind" was an upbeat message. (Pat Buchanan wanted to say "Two Americans," but I thought that was too parochial; in retrospect, he was right.)

But we had a problem: shouldn't there be some subtle plug for the Deity

—not a religious pitch, but at least some reference to show future generations these men from planet Earth believed in God?

The solution: put the date of the landing on the plaque, and use A.D.— the initials of the Latin words *anno Domini,* "in the year of our Lord." Brilliant. Low-key but definite. When NASA could not give us the exact date of the landing in time to cast a bronze plaque, I told the plaque-maker to go with "July 1969, A.D. "

That's what sits on the moon today, to be seen by space travelers eons from now, and the only trouble is that it is wrong. When the date is before the birth of Christ, you write B.C. (or B.C.E., "before Christian Era") after the numerals; when the date is after Christ's birth, the letters come before. As the Random House College Dictionary puts it: *"From 20 B.C. to A.D. 50 is 70 years."*

In a century or so, I hope some descendant of mine will take a sharp stylus on some weekend rocket to the moon and, while awaiting a transfer rocket to Mars, will draw a little circle around the A.D. and put an arrow placing it in front of the word *July.* This will show that human beings in the early days of space were grammatically fallible; that mankind (since changed to *humankind,* but you can leave it the old way on the plaque, Junior) is forever editing, and that a little precision is a dangerous thing.

Those of us who prefer B.C.E. and C.E. to B.C. and A.D. understand the C. to stand for "common" rather than "Christian." Of course, proper usage here is 1991 C.E.

> Michael Engber
> New York, New York

Please be advised that there is another pitfall in the A.D./B.C. nomenclature. When progressing from the B.C. to the A.D. era there is a discontinuity in the numbers because the year 1 B.C. is followed by A.D. 1. A zero year is lacking, and a correct Random House College Dictionary entry would be "From 20 B.C. to A.D. 50 is 69 years."

> Minze Stuiver
> Seattle, Washington

You point out the vagueness, improved by adding exact date, but make no comment on the repetition, i.e. "set foot on the moon . . . landed there."

It is necessary to land before one can set foot.

Personally, I prefer "man first set foot on the moon on July 20, 1969."

> Bill Alex
> San Francisco, California

Spellbound

It would be easier to get our allies to agree on overflight rights to a bombing raid on terrorists than to forge a consensus on a way to spell the name of the strongman of Libya.

Jack Gescheidt of New York City puts the problem succinctly, to the tune of the 1937 Gershwin song "Let's Call the Whole Thing Off":

> The News says, Khadafy
> The Times says, Qaddafi
> Time says, Gaddafi
> Newsweek, Kaddafi;
> MOO-a-mar
> Mo-AH-mar;
> LIB-ya
> Lib-ee-a;
> Let's blow the whole thing off.

There is no "correct" way to spell Qaddafi. When we use Western characters to signify sounds of the Arabic language, we are free to paint the page any way we like.

The first sound of the Libyan leader's last name, like the opening of the chief Iranian Ayatollah's last name, is referred to as *velar:* To make this kind of sound, the back of the tongue flutters against the soft palate, or *velum.* There is a difference in velar sounds depending on how far back in the throat each sound is produced. The "q" without a "u" in Qaddafi is produced, like a guttural "g," even farther back in the throat than the "k" with the "h" in Khomeini. Notice the different velar sounds in "cougar," for example.

Are Westerners the only ones being inconsistent? Not according to Pierre Cachia of Columbia University's department of Middle East languages and cultures: "Most Libyans would, in informal speech, pronounce his name as Gaddafi. . . . In its literary form, however, the first letter is indeed a velar 'k,' and nowadays this is transliterated as 'q' by most Arabists—but not by all."

This makes the West appear disorganized in the face of state terrorism. To remedy this, I am thinking about issuing a ukase (an uppercase ukase is a UKASE) on the spelling of our fricative friends. If my decision is not universally recognized, however, and my edict is ignored by go-it-alone editors, my authority would be undermined, and nobody would automatically accept the word on anything in this space as the Final Authority. For this pitiful, pusillanimous reason, I have held back, emitting instead these descriptive bleats on an uncertain trumpet. However, the next time either of those characters makes major news, I will put aside all restraint and retaliate with both a spelling specification and a pronunciation pronunciamento.

Libya, I am prepared to say now, should be three syllables. It is not analogous to *love-yuh*. "LIB-ee-uh" it is, with the final syllable a schwa, the most nebbish sound in the language.

In that regard, I received this telex message from Burt Weeks of Syracuse University: "Pls use yr consid influence to advise tv netwks that Tokyo has only two syllables instead of Tok-ee-o."

I remember that zippy language from the ads in the subway for a speed-writing institute (cn u read ths?) on my way up to the Bronx High School of Science. My reply: Tokyo is three syllables in *NBC Handbk of Prnunciashun* so stik consid influence in yr ear.

The "y" in both Libya and Tokyo is pronounced as "ee." Perhaps this is not exactly as the words are pronounced locally—and deference should always be paid to residents, because they have a right to their name—but the English-speaking world has adopted the three-syllable usage, and that's the way it is.

Dear Bill,

Your note on the syllabification of Tokyo reminded me of Ring Lardner's play *June Moon* about some Tin Pan Alley hacks. One of them writes a candidate for worst song ever. Its title: "Hello, Tokyo." It contains the great couplet:

> I would fly through fire and smoke-ee-oh
> Just to be with you in Toke-ee-oh . . .

I've only heard it rendered, haven't seen the script, but it's definitely three syllables.

Russ [Russell Baker]
The New York Times
New York, New York

Burt Weeks of Syracuse University is correct. Tokyo has a 2-syllable pronunciation. The NBC guidebook is, of course, incorrect.

Just as we are able to pronounce the word "cute" with its "y" sound after "c" and before "u" ("kyu"), so should we be able to pronounce "kyo" as one syllable! Newscasters, take note.

Ida I. Shimanouchi
New York, New York

It's obvious that your correspondent Burt Weeks of Syracuse University should lay off telexing advice to you. Your pronunciation guide regarding "Tokyo" in today's Sunday *Times Magazine* "On Language" column is certainly more correct than his. But he has a point, to a point. Maybe "Tokyo" is a two-and-a-half-syllable word.

There's no disputing that some Americans tend to hit the "kyo" too heavily on the KEY sound. The Japanese tend to swallow the "ky," making almost a grace-note elision of the "kyo" syllable. It sounds a good deal like our pronunciation of "kiosk."

During my numerous trips to Japan my native friends have kidded me about the way I used to say "ryokan," where I stressed the first syllable and came up with "REE-o-kahn." The proper pronunciation is more like "r'yo-kahn," with a definite "ee-O" sound but without a stressed syllable, since Japanese typically has no accentuated syllables.

Thus, "Tokyo" is obviously not a two-syllable word, even in the generally unstressed Japanese pronunciation. I wonder if Mr. Weeks would try to transform the ancient Japanese capital of Kyoto into a two-syllable word, too. If so, he might be hard-pressed to find a train ticket-seller who would recognize his intended destination.

Ted Benjamin
Elmsford, New York

I take exception to both Mr. Weeks of Syracuse University and to the *NBC Handbook of Pronunciation* in the matter of Tokyo. The Japanese word is actually 4 syllables: "To-o-kyo-o," since the Japanese count a lengthened vowel as a separate syllable and use it as a distinguishing feature. The classic example of this is "ko-mon" (adviser) versus "ko-o-mon" (anus). (See Jack Seward's book *Japanese in Action*, pp. 28–29.)

More to the point, the Japanese make a strict distinction between the sounds "ki-o," "kyo," and "ki-yo." Unlike the lengthened vowel, the differences in the sounds are relatively easy for non-Japanese to master. At a minimum, I would stress that all Japanese syllables must end in a vowel or "n," and so the syllabic division "Tok-ee-o" is not possible. You would undoubtedly do the cause of international relations a great service by advising the networks, etc., how to pronounce this word. No one may care if Qaddafi (sp?) gets his name spelled wrong (after all, what's one more insult?), but it is courteous (in the Japanese sense of courtesy) to get the names of our friends right.

Daniel Kohanski
New York, New York

The Spook Speaks

"They fluttered Mike the pill" was the word in the intelligence community recently. To the cogs in the cognoscenti, that meant that a Department of Defense official named Michael Pillsbury was banished from the Pentagon, supposedly after being *fluttered*—subjected to a test on a polygraph, miscalled a "lie detector," that sometimes sends the needle into wild oscillations, resulting in the suspicion that the person hooked up may be nervous. Real spies are trained in how to beat polygraphs.

Flutter is a verb in *spookspeak,* a word coined in the 1978 edition of my political dictionary on the analogy of George Orwell's *Newspeak.*

Comes now *The Dictionary of Espionage: Spookspeak Into English,* by "Henry S. A. Becket," a pseudonym combining Henry II with Thomas à Becket (chosen because the King gave a "deniable" order to kill Becket with the words, "Who will free me from this turbulent priest?"). In the spookspeak dictionary, *counterespionage* is defined as not merely defending against enemy intelligence operations, but specifically as " 'attempting to use the opposition's operation.' . . . The highest form of espionage chess."

I wonder. G. J. A. O'Toole of Mount Vernon, New York—that's his real name, as far as I know—wants to know if *counterintelligence* and *counterespionage* are synonymous. He is preparing an encyclopedia of intelligence, and has what is called in the trade a need to know. If any sheep-dipped Papakhas out of Mother K want to help this granny educate the schpicks, leak the poop to me at *The Times.*

State of Ploy

The hottest word in diplomatic parlance is *ploy.* When President Reagan and Speaker of the House Jim Wright issued their short-lived peace plan for Central America, doves in the United States promptly dubbed it a mere *ploy* to help speed aid to the contras when the Sandinistas turned it down. A reporter asked Secretary of State George P. Shultz, "Is it a *ploy*?" Replied Mr. Shultz, in a verbal snippet that made a nice sound bite on all the news shows, "It's not just a *ploy,* it's a serious effort." Soon afterward, when Central American presidents put their own plan forward, hawks here characterized Nicaraguan President Daniel Ortega Saavedra's quick rhetorical acceptance of that as a *ploy* of his own.

Obviously, students of diplomacy have a major accusatory word to contend with. What is the state of play on *ploy?*

Sir Charles James Napier (whose Latin-coded *Peccavi* informed his colleagues in London that "I have Sind" in India) used the word in 1842 to describe a military drill maneuver that formed a column out of a line, perhaps back-forming the word from *deploy:* "They acquire the art of ploying and deploying their troops."

Before that, *ploy* was being used as an informal short form of an archaic meaning of *employ:* "to use," as one would give full employ to a tool. The Scots used the word to mean "activity," and then "escapade"; that's where it picked up a roguish quality, as a pursuit that young rakes would adopt to amuse themselves, or to outwit or disconcert others.

In the United States, this useful old term—still, curiously, considered "informal" by many lexicographers—means "trick, sly action, mild deceit" in its pejorative sense, "maneuver, gambit" in a more admiring sense.

Be careful with the synonym *gambit,* which is in its figurative sense a *ploy;* a *ploy* is not always a *gambit.* That's because the essence of *gambit* is "opening, beginning." In chess, the term denotes the purposeful sacrifice of a pawn or other piece at the start of a game to gain an advantage; its meaning has been extended in the real world to "an opening move to gain an advantage," keeping the opening connotation while losing the sacrifice. An *opening gambit* is redundant; don't use it or the Squad Squad will get you.

Your note on *ploy* omitted one major source for the rejuvenation of the word particularly among those who may be of a generation close to Secretary Shultz. In the 1950s, the British humorist, critic, and linguist Stephen Potter used the word frequently in his volumes *Gamesmanship, Lifemanship,* and *One-Upmanship.* A ploy was a move by a gamesman or lifeman to put the opponent "one down," and thus make it easier to win. Unfortunately my copies are packed in boxes or I could give you a more exact reference, for I believe the term did not appear in the first volume, but in the second. Potter also used the term *plonking* to describe the tone of voice often used in a ploy; whether it was his coinage or not I am not sure.

The volumes are out of print, but they still contain a wealth of good advice.

Alan C. Purves
Melrose, New York

Here's a possibly pertinent limerick:

> When a male seeking lecherous joy,
> Finds the female he lusts for too coy,
>   And besots her with gin
>   In the hope she'll give in,
> Such a plying for play is a ploy.

J. F. O'Connor
Silver Spring, Maryland

Subliminal Score

In the debate among six Republican candidates for President on William F. Buckley, Jr.'s, "Firing Line," a spirited exchange took place between Vice President George Bush and former Secretary of State Alexander M. Haig, Jr.

In discussing the intermediate-range nuclear forces treaty, Bush said that Haig had previously supported such a treaty. Haig contradicted him and claimed to have vigorously opposed it.

When Bush in turn objected, Al Haig shot back: "And I never heard a wimp out of you. . . ."

Curious choice of a word. In context, the word obviously intended was *whimper*, in noun form meaning "peep, small cry, whine" or, in its slang sense, "mild objection." However, General Haig—who obviously crossed swords with Mr. Bush when both were on the National Security Council—did not choose to say, "I didn't hear a peep out of you." He used *wimp*. No such slang noun is current in the sense of "peep," although a 1925 usage has been found that shortens the echoic *whimper* to *whimp*.

The derogation *wimp*, rooted in *whimper*, means "timid, flaccid person," and "Fighting the 'Wimp Factor' " was the cruel headline of *Newsweek*'s cover story on the Vice President. The application of the clipped form of *whimper* to Mr. Bush by Mr. Haig was a brilliant rhetorical subliminal stroke, or a mean-spirited shot, depending on your point of view.

Was it a mistake, or was it on purpose? Candidate Haig, when serving in the Reagan Cabinet, was capable of using such adjectives as *nuancal*, meaning "nuanced, finely shaded." He would not be incapable of hearing a *wimp*. The Vice President has been caveatted.

Do you remember the funny radio character Wallace Wimple? Perhaps they spelled it Wimple, perhaps Wimpole. He was the Milquetoast on the Fibber McGee and Molly show.

He was referred to on radio as W i m p. He was constantly hen-pecked by his "big ol' wife, Sweetieface."

Sharon Brown
San Mateo, California

Supine Nonconcurrence

Three locutions from our nation's leaders exemplify the state of the language: "This senator," said a stern majority leader Robert Byrd, "is not going to stand supinely by in silence. . . ." *Supine*, describing a position of the body, means "flat on the back, face up." By metaphoric extension, it has come to mean "passive, inactive," which is often the way we are in that position; but when you put *supinely* in the middle of *stand by*, you are asking for a bodily contortion or mystic levitation difficult even for members of the Senate.

"I nonconcur in the recommendation to sell the aircraft," courageously objected Lieutenant General E. R. Heiberg III to the Army's Inspector General. Edward Lavitt of New York City, who sent in this citation of Pentagonese, writes, "I nonagree with his usage."

Concur, a verb from the Latin for "to run together," is a good way of saying, "I'll trot alongside of that." *Concurrence* is the noun, its opposite *nonconcurrence*; what is wrong with taking another step into a verb like *nonconcur*? Because the language does not need the verb. (And avoid sentence fragments.) *Nonconcur* made its first appearance in 1703 and flopped. We have *disagree with*, and the more principled *dissent from*; if the speaker wishes to use only the opposite of *concur*, he can say, "I do not concur." Zap *nonconcur* with a laser beam, General.

All is not supine nonconcurrence. Describing a modest advance in negotiations toward a strategic arms treaty, the negotiator Max Kampelman said, "We kicked the can down the road." What a superb use of metaphor. Who has not, as a kid, played kick-the-can, or in less organized fashion kicked a can or other nonbiodegradable container ahead?

Kick the Can, which effectively summarizes desultory but definite progress, is the title of a novel by Jim Lehrer; the opening words of the book are "I was too old to play kick-the-can anymore. . . ."

As long as we have negotiators creatively kicking the can, this department will do the same to errant senators and generals.

I concur in your attack at my use of "nonconcur." But I do note that the Army Inspector General, to whom I wrote my "nonconcurrence," understood precisely where I stand. I will, however, do my part to eradicate some of the ridiculous nonwords (and endless acronyms) that creep into our vocabulary.

Consider me zapped, Mr. Safire.

E. R. Heiberg III
Lieutenant General, U.S. Army
Chief of Engineers
Washington, D.C.

You don't like "nonconcur" and urge against its use. I think that there is need for such a word as "nonconcur." Unfortunately, that word does not sound right—and I think that this is why you don't like it. That is probably why it flopped back in 1703, and why it will flop again. But an obvious way around the rotten sound is to use "disconcur." It avoids all of the two-word synonyms which you do like and it runs along the same lines as disagree. "Nonagreement" is a word used frequently, but "nonagree" just doesn't sound right. So we use "disagree." "Disconcurrence" would not be needed as we have the "nonconcurrence" usage. As there are subtle differences in meaning between "concur" and "agree," so must there be a subtle difference in their opposites. I disconcur with your recommendation to use two words for the one that is necessary. But I don't disagree with your right to write it as you like.

James Hlavac
New York, New York

In my experience, desultory progress behind a resonantly protesting piece of metal, the activity to which Mr. Kampelman alludes, is entirely different from the game, which is a team contest akin to "capture the flag" or "ringolevio": the can is the objective of both sides' efforts and a team member's kicking the can is the climactic action signifying victory by one side or the other. The satisfying clank of contact between toe and can is the same, but the context is not. I am fairly sure, even without knowing the context of Mr. Kampelman's remarks, that this is not what he meant by his metaphor.

Sara Collins Medina
New York, New York

Surgeon General's Warning

C Everett Koop, Surgeon General of the United States Public Health
. Service, issued a report on AIDS that contained some straight talk
and used a word ordinarily avoided in polite conversation. For good reason, the word *condom* is no longer taboo.

In the section dealing with ways to protect yourself from infection, Dr.
Koop wrote to all those engaged in what he termed high-risk sexual activities: "If you jointly decide to have sex, you must protect your partner by
always using a rubber (condom). . . ." In a press conference, he added,
"The best protection against infection right now—barring abstinence—is
use of a condom."

New York City's Health Commissioner, Stephen C. Joseph, promptly
said, "The day of the condom has returned." A spokesman for the National Academy of Sciences was described in *The New York Times* as calling
for "a large-scale campaign in the news media, in education and by public
health groups to warn people, in explicit, understandable language, to
protect themselves against AIDS by using condoms."

In a conflict between public health and genteel language, health cannot
lose. Since readers must get used to the word in print and everyday parlance, this department will deal forthrightly with its etymology.

Francis Grose, editor of the 1785 *A Classical Dictionary of the Vulgar
Tongue*, attributed the invention of the prophylactic or contraceptive
sheath to a "Colonel Cundum" of the royal guards of Charles II, who
ruled England from 1660 to 1685. Subsequent dictionaries picked up Mr.
Grose's etymology, and Eric Partridge cited a 1667 work by the courtiers
Rochester, Roscommon and Dorset entitled "A Panegyric upon
Cundum." However, the Oxford English Dictionary Supplement disputes
this with a peremptory "Origin unknown," adding, "no 18th-century phy-
sician named Condom or Conton has been traced though a doctor so
named is often said to be the inventor of the sheath."

My guess is that the word is more frequently pronounced *cundum* and
more frequently spelled *condom*; as the spelling is seen in print more often,
the pronunciation will probably be affected. The synonym *rubber* is often
used—Surgeon General Koop used both words, seemingly interchangeably, in his statement—but not all condoms are made of latex-based rubber; the material for many is animal membrane, such as sheep's gut.

"Take your rubbers" is a phrase that can lead to some confusion, meaning "it looks like rain" or "you'll need erasers" or "don't forget your
condoms." Because the term *rubbers* more often denotes coverings for the

feet in rainy weather, the formerly taboo word may predominate as the name of the protective genital sheath. Other synonyms or euphemisms— *French letters* (called in return by the French *capotes anglaises,* "English cloaks"), *safes, circular protectors,* etc.—are likely to fade as *condom* gains acceptance.

Although "Colonel Cundum" remains a shadowy or even legendary figure in history, etymologists can be certain that *condom* is not a shortening of *condominium.* That word originally meant "joint rule" or "shared sovereignty," and is still used in that sense by geostrategists (Zbigniew Brzezinski's coinage) in describing overlapping spheres of influence. In the early 1960s, *condominium* came to mean "ownership of a single apartment rather than a share in the whole building," based on the sense in Roman law of joint ownership of the same property with individual rights of disposal; its clipped form is *condo,* to distinguish it from the other possible shortening.

On an unrelated matter, but attached to my file on this subject, is a cigarette ad with a little white box saying: "SURGEON GENERAL'S WARNING: Quitting Smoking Now Greatly Reduces Serious Risks to Your Health."

Get with it, Dr. Koop: that's no warning.

Here is background material from Volume 7 of Sir Richard Burton's translation of *The Arabian Nights,* 1885:
1. *Then he took a lamb and killing it, cut out the long intestine.*[2]

Footnote 2: Arab. "Al-Musrán" (plur. of "Masír") properly the intestines which contain the chyle. The bag made by Ali was, in fact, a "Cundum" (so called from the inventor, Colonel Cundum of the Guards in the days of Charles Second) or "French letter"; *une capote anglaise,* a "check upon child." Captain Grose says (Class. Dict. etc. s.v. Cundum) "The dried gut of a sheep worn by a man in the act of coition to prevent venereal infection. These machines were long prepared and sold by a matron of the name of Philips at the Green Canister in Half Moon Street in the Strand . . . Also a false scabbard over a sword and the oilskin case for the colours of a regiment." Another account is given in the *Guide Pratique des Maladies Secrètes,* Dr. G. Harris, Bruxelles, Librairie Populaire. He calls these *petits sachets de baudruche* "Candoms, from the doctor who invented them" (Littré ignores the word) and declares that the famous Ricord compared them with a bad umbrella which a storm can break or burst, while others term them cuirasses against pleasure and cobwebs against infection. They were much used in the last century.

John A. Myers
Redwood City, California

Numerous authors on the history of rubber credit one Charles de la Condamine, member of a party which crossed South America beginning in 1736, with the introduction to Europe of rubber as a useful material. Although I have found no indication that the word "condom" is derived from his name, the similarity is striking.

For more definitive information on the origin of "condom," I turned to Mrs. Ruth Murray and the staff of the Rubber Division (American Chemical Society) Library, located at the University of Akron. From a volume entitled *The First of Everything* by Dennis Sanders comes the first published use of the word, in an anonymous 1706 poem entitled "A Scot's Answer to a British Vision." The pertinent lines are:

> syringe and condum
> come both in request

Less poetic but perhaps more indicative of the source of the word is a reference in Taber's *Cyclopedic Medical Dictionary*, 14th edition, which cites the Latin *condus*, meaning receptacle, as the root of the word condom.

Incidentally, the word "rubber" derives from an early use of the material as an eraser, first popularized in England by Joseph Priestley.

Stephen Mariconti
Warwick, New York

There is a town in the South of France, west of Toulouse and near Auch, which is the center of the Armagnac district. Its name is Condom and while I have done no research on the subject, I seem to recall from visits to the area that the "condom" may have been originally produced or invented in its namesake town.

James E. McDonough
New York, New York

A Pack of Wolves, Please

Grammarians must be cooped up at the Surgeon General's office. The following sign appeared on millions of copies of cigarette ads: "SURGEON GENERAL'S WARNING: Quitting Smoking/Now Greatly Reduces Serious Risks to Your Health."

First, that can hardly be termed a warning; it's closer to the opposite, a promise of good times ahead.

Second, the meaning intended by C. Everett Koop, the nation's chief medical officer, was that health risks were reduced by "quitting smoking now." However, with the line broken in the wrong place—"Quitting Smoking/Now Greatly Reduces"—the meaning is warped; the *now* seems to be directed to the end of the sentence, as if only now does quitting smoking reduce health risks—as if it never used to be that way.

POP GRAMMARIAN'S WARNING: If you are going to issue warnings, Dr. Koop, stick to predictions of the direst of consequences, or you will be reduced to an object of snickering and contempt. If you want to point to green pastures and happy days, change your nonwarning to a *notice* or even a *pledge.*

And while I have the Surgeon General's attention: I noted in this space how his official use of *condom* had moved the word from relatively taboo usage out into the sunlight of parlor conversation, making the noun of obscure origin acceptable even to the bluest of noses.

Evidence of that crossover is supplied from this joke, marking the passing in the night of ships heading to and from the ports of condemnation: Man walks into a drugstore, says in a loud voice, "I'd like a package of condoms, please" and—whispering behind his hand—adds, *"and a package of cigarettes!"*

Tayee, Kemo Sabe

"Charles and Andrew have married two attractive and charming women," frowned an editorialist in *The Sunday Times* of London after stories appeared about high jinks among the younger members of the royal family. "But the Sloane Ranger aspect in them often overwhelms the more decorous behavior that royal rank should dictate, and the result is not always dignified."

In quoting that passage in a piece of my own, I defined Sloane Rangers as "swinging single women who frequent the area of London's Sloane Square." The location was right, but the limitation to women was wrong, and the slang adjective "swinging"—with its present connotation of "loose morals"—was an unfair slur on the residents of that area. (Can there be a "fair" slur, or are all slurs inherently unfair? I think some slurs, or aspersions, are fair reproaches. This was unfair because it was inaccurate.)

A Sloane Ranger (a rhyming play on the American radio hero, the Lone Ranger, whose sidekick, Tonto, referred to him as "kemo sabe") is a member of Britain's young moneyed elite. The term's originator, Peter York, often described as a pop anthropologist, first used the term in a 1975 *Harper's & Queen* article: "The Sloane Rangers . . . are the nicest British Girl. . . . The Sloane Rangers always *add tone*. They never put on prole accents. . . ."

Mr. York was quoted by *Newsweek* in a 1985 piece about the daring doings of the young royals: "Diana was pure, state-of-the-art Sloane. She was not overeducated, she didn't have 'views,' and she had a clear idea of her role as being maternal and decorative." This is, of course, a derogation, but not so severe as *Newsweek*'s description of Sloane Rangers as "the most decadent group of young people English society has seen since Regency days—heavily into drugs, homosexuality, cross-dressing and, in the memorable phrase of one of Winston Churchill's grandsons, getting 'hog-whimpering drunk' as often as possible."

That's not the way Mr. York and Ann Barr treated the phrase in their 1983 *The Official Sloane Ranger Handbook: How the British Upper Class Prepares Its Offspring for Life*. Their Ranger is similar to an American preppie (few of whom aspire to becoming DINKs—Double Income, No Kids) with many of the same gentrified affectations. In his book *British English, A to Zed*, Norman W. Schur sees Rangers as conservatively dressed women who "work as well-paid personal secretaries and spend weekends in the country hunting. . . . Not quite the old Mayfair, as the particular panache is lacking, but as close as one can get in these inflation-ridden times."

In speech, write Mr. York and Ms. Barr, understatement overrides: "One must be stiff-upper-lip. 'I've got this stupid arm' means broken in three places. Disaster and tragedy, wholesale mutilation are 'boring,' a motorway crash is 'a spot of bother on the way'. . . . It sometimes leaves outsiders thinking Sloanes are extraordinarily callous."

If we are to err, let it be on the side of kindness. "The term refers to young affluent Britons who 'range' around fashionable shops in Knightsbridge," writes Paul Schlesinger of Brooklyn. "It's shopping, not partying, that distinguishes a Sloane Ranger."

Jacques Azagury, one of London's leading couturiers, does not think of the term *Sloane Ranger* as necessarily snobbish, and certainly not decadent —he saw the term evoking an image of a fun-loving, youthful upper class. When I asked, "Not high fashion but never out of fashion?" the fashion authority responded, "Burberry raincoat, Hermès scarf tied under the chin."

As both an erstwhile Londoner and author of the *Newsweek* piece about the Princess of Wales that you cited, allow me to assure you that you were indeed correct in originally defining Sloane Rangers as exclusively female. The male counterpart of the Sloane is the notorious Hooray Henry, a kind of latter-day Bertie Wooster who typically combines the worst of British upper-class philistinism and American fraternity-boy rowdyism—the result being an astoundingly offensive creature as overbearing as he is inescapable.

Allan Mayer
New York, New York

How could you downgrade one of my idols—The Lone Ranger—by saying that his sidekick Tonto referred to him as "kemo sabe"?

These two friends were much subtler than you suppose, for "tonto" means "silly" or "fool" in Spanish. In return the Indian Tonto called the Lone Ranger "que no sabe," or "one who knows nothing," that is, a "nitwit." I always thought that this friendly exchange of insults was one of the best aspects of the series.

William N. Leonard
Tampa, Florida

The Telltale Adverb

A dverbs, often used to qualify or otherwise influence verbs, can get you in trouble. Consider *fully*.

"I was not fully informed," said President Reagan in dropping the bombshell of the diversion of Iranian arms profits to the contras, "on the nature of one of the activities undertaken in connection with this initiative."

At first, the reaction to the President's statement focused on his denial of having been aware of the apparently unlawful diversion. Then eyes turned to the adverb: why had Mr. Reagan, in a statement closely perused or perhaps prepared by the Attorney General, chosen to say he had not been *fully* informed? If he had not been told of the use of the arms-transfer profits, why did he not simply say, "I was not informed"?

The use of *not fully* implied *partially*, and in this case, to be partially informed was to be "a little bit pregnant." As Robert H. Bletchman wrote to the *Washington Post*, "his speech writers should have warned him what 'not fully informed' means. If President Reagan had no knowledge at all, that would have been easy to say straight out."

Reporters then hurled the question at him at the first opportunity; the President at first ducked it, then had his press spokesman say "flat out" that he had not been informed. Apparently, the President and his writer, in choosing the *fully* qualifier, had wanted to cover the possibility that he may have been informed in part, or wanted to avoid the appearance of a President admitting to being totally out of touch on a central point. Or perhaps they did not realize the significance of *not fully*.

Watch those adverbs. At the start of the controversy, it was said that Admiral John M. Poindexter was "not directly involved." The question that *-ly* adverb will trigger: "What do you mean by *not directly*?"

When President Reagan's script writer wrote that our Chief Executive was not "fully informed" about the Iran-Contra imbroglio, he was employing "weasel words" designed to leave his boss "wiggle room." Ditto for Don Regan when he claimed he wasn't "thoroughly briefed" on the same matter. All good bureaucrats quickly learn the importance of weasel words. We will never know if the stronger denials were linked to the sounds emitted by a document shredder being turned off in the Old Executive Office Building.

> *Luke Albee*
> *Colchester, Vermont*

". . . closely perused . . ." Sounds like a case for the Squad Squad.

> *Mike Spataro*
> *Brooklyn, New York*

Might one call your examples "little white lys"?
> *Paul Klein*
> *Judge, Housing Part*
> *Civil Court of the City of New York*
> *New York, New York*

That Secret Desire

We all read with different eyes to satisfy unique needs.

A KGB operative in Moscow reads American spy novels to pick up the latest tradecraft; a member of the Nitpickers' League reads my political harangues for the thrill of spotting a grammatical error that enables him to cry "Gotcha!"

Perhaps the best example of coming at a book from a specialized point of view is Ed Zern's 1959 column in *Field & Stream*, tongue-in-cheekily reviewing the reissue of D. H. Lawrence's *Lady Chatterley's Lover*: ". . . contains many passages on pheasant-raising, the apprehending of poachers, ways to control vermin, and other chores and duties of the professional gamekeeper. Unfortunately, one is obliged to wade through many pages of extraneous material in order to discover and savor these sidelights on the management of a Midlands shooting estate, and in this reviewer's opinion this book cannot take the place of J. R. Miller's *Practical Gamekeeping*."

I read racy novels. (And I prefer *racy* to the voguish *steamy* because it is less overworked, and I was influenced at an early age by the pulp magazine

Racy Detective Stories—or was it *Spicy Detective*?) Because I am embarrassed to admit to titillability (I buy *Penthouse* only to have a respectable cover into which to slip my copy of *National Review*), my excuse for haunting the upper reaches of the best-seller list is to search for current slang, especially in the important category of the language of secret lust.

Sally Quinn's novel *Regrets Only* has this sentence on page 34: "Edwina had known Lawrence in London and had always had a slight sneaker for him." What is a *sneaker*? The slang dictionaries suggest a motorboat or a tennis shoe, with a *Sneaky Pete* as a moonshine cocktail, but from the context of the sentence, these meanings seem to miss the point.

I reached the author and asked for a definition. "You never had a sneaker for anybody?" replied Ms. Quinn. When I became cagey, she said, "It's a *crush*, a sneaking admiration or desire for somebody. I've heard it used all my life." Informed that linguistic sleuths were mystified by her use of the term, she reached back into memory for its origin: "My college roommate's mother was Ellen McCloy, Mrs. John McCloy. It's the sort of word she used. Upper-class WASP." The author's husband, an author in his own right, suggested this term was a *goyishism*, a nice coinage along the lines of *Yiddishism*.

(Pressed for another goyishism, Ms. Quinn immediately came up with *to have a scunner on:* "When you say, 'I have a *scunner on* someone,' that means you're angry with him. You can have a *scunner against* something, too." This checks out: the Oxford English Dictionary tracks the verb *scunner* to 1375, defining it as "a. to shrink back with fear, to flinch; b. to be affected with violent disgust . . ." and the Supplement, which had its fourth and final volume published in 1986, gives the noun form a milder sense, "a grudge, repugnance, dislike.")

I think we have a winner in *sneaker*, because the language lacks a specific term for "secret desire." *Crush*, rooted in "the hart-breake crush of melancholies wheele" in 1599 and modified to mean "infatuation, fancy, puppy love," does not necessarily connote secrecy, and usually conveys a feeling of adolescence. Same with *smitten*, which is the past tense of a verb used to describe a state, and what we need is a noun.

What about *yen*? In such comments as "Gee, have I got a yen for her," or "I have a yen for a hot pastrami on seeded rye," the word means "craving." In matters of taste, *yen* is often replaced by *to have one's mouth fixed for*, as in "I have my mouth fixed for a combination pastrami, corned beef and smoked turkey with hot mustard and pickle relish, but I don't suppose you have that in a Chinese restaurant." In that restaurant, stick to *yen*, which is of Cantonese origin: the word comes from a Chinese opium-smoker's desire for his drug.

The hots, as in the infinitive phrase *to have the hots for*, is a 1940s term derived from *hot pants*, a state of near-permanent arousal. *Hot pants* saw the light of day in *The Barker*, a 1927 novel by John Kenyon Nicholson ("When you had him all hot pants you married him") and was immortalized in Mary McCarthy's *The Group* in 1963 ("I've still got hot pants for her, if you want to call that love").

The hots was first spotted by Wentworth and Flexner in their invaluable Dictionary of American Slang, citing 1947 as its first appearance: "I'd never get the deep undying hots for that rah rah collitch [boy]." However, no source suggests that *the hots* implies concealed desire; on my own authority, then, and with the blind certitude of the native speaker, I say that nothing about *the hots*—or *yen*, for that matter—suggests an urge that is essentially clandestine.

Thus, a place exists for *sneaker*, a secret desire for sexual contact, especially among upper-crust types with names like Edwina in Washington novels. In due course, as the term becomes more widespread, we can expect the metaphor to be extended, as *yen* was, far beyond its point of origin. Already I have a sneaker for that pastrami.

I've been subject to occasional "sneakers," as defined by Sally Quinn, all my life.

Before it grew into rock-and-roll, there used to be a category of music called rhythm-and-blues, a black-oriented combination of blues, jazz and heavier beat music. You'll find many uses of "sneakin' around" in the lyrics of this music.

Because some form of "sneaker" must have motivated the "sneakin' around" (as in "not to be true to"), I don't believe the term can be exclusively WASP.

> *Brooke S. Taylor*
> *Greenwich, Connecticut*

Your comment about "sneaker" when used as a "crush": Having discovered John O'Hara while an impressionable twelve-year-old, I eagerly devoured every word he wrote. I truly believe I learned more about American history and mores from his novels than I ever did in school. At any rate, "Elizabeth Appleton" notes that her husband, John, always had "a little sneaker" for Elizabeth's younger sister, Jean. Although at twelve I had never heard the expression before, I understood instantly what it meant, so forceful was O'Hara's ability to paint instant pictures in relationships.

> *Robin Rath Gaige*
> *Painted Post, New York*

In the slang of the Scottish Border country, where I come from, people get "scunnert" when they're absolutely sickened by some person or issue, as in "Ah'm fair scunnert by that laddy aye wiping his mucky nose on his sleeve."

> *Rodney Pinder*
> *Washington, D.C.*

You derive *the hots* from *hot pants.* But everyone who has ever served in any branch of the U.S. armed forces knows very well that it refers instead to *hot nuts*—servicemen's slang for orchitis.

I once saw a stripper come on stage carrying a tray with nuts which she threw into the audience while singing a song in the form of a street vendor's cry: "Hot nuts! Hot peanuts!" was the title of the song.

Incidentally, I admire your ingeniousness in concealing the disreputable political journal you wish to read under the respectable cover of *Penthouse.*

Alfred G. Meyer
Ann Arbor, Michigan

That was indeed *Spicy Detective.* In the middle of the book was a two-page comic strip featuring a female private eye called "Sally the Sleuth." Sally rarely made it past the third panel without having her clothes torn off.

Dick Cavalli
New Canaan, Connecticut

You describe "smitten" as "the past tense of a verb used to describe a state . . ." A very unsatisfactory construction, Mr. Safire. What was used to describe a state, the past tense or the verb? Also, when I was in school "smitten" wasn't the past tense of anything. It was the past participle of "smite." Way back then the past tense of "smite" was "smote."

Julian S. Herz
Indianapolis, Indiana

Third-Commandment Blues

After his televised altercation with Dan Rather, Vice President George Bush, according to the *Washington Post,* told some CBS staffers that he didn't like the "goddamn" network. After that came out in print, Mr. Bush said, "If I had known the microphone was on, I would not have taken the Lord's name in vain, and I apologize for that. I was not amused. . . ."

Except to the strictest of constructionists, who are probably supporting Pat Robertson anyway, no apology was necessary. Originally, *God-damn* was a profane oath, and can be found in print in 1431, spelled "Goddem," attributed to Joan of Arc "after the French *god-dam,*" according to the O.E.D. (The French often represented Englishmen as the sort who went around saying *goddam.*)

These days, especially in its adjectival use, the first syllable of *goddam* is not a reference to the Deity. Compare *God-fearing* with *godforsaken* and *godfather*; in *God-fearing*, the reference is clearly to the Supreme Being; the other words are children of a lesser god. Thus, in using *goddam* as currently understood—and I accentuate its nonprofane meaning by not capitalizing the word, and dropping the final *n*—the name of the Lord was not taken in vain. George Bush did not break the Third Commandment.

However, "I was not amused" is a reference to a remark made frequently by Queen Victoria—"We are not amused"—when she wanted to express her displeasure in the most regal fashion. It's not the sort of cultural identification sought by most American politicians.

> Mr. Bush is indeed off the hook, but not because he used the adjectival form of the expression, as you indicated. Mr. Bush is off the hook because he was never on it. The Third Commandment, many believe, has nothing to do with minor swearing; it refers, rather, to lying under oath—to perjury, not profanity. If this is so, then the commandment wasn't broken and Mr. Bush can rest easy.
>
> *Jay Stolar*
> *Marietta, Georgia*

> Your assertion that "goddam" doesn't count as swearing anymore, except among conservative Christians, convicts you of having spent too much time in the loose-lipped East. Out here in America's heartland, not even liberal Episcopalians talk like that. Merciful heavens, Safire, clean up your act!
>
> *Pamela Smith*
> *West Lafayette, Indiana*

Tongue-Speak

The Associated Press identified the televangelist James Bakker as "a charismatic," describing that type of preacher as one who "emphasizes such things as emotional expressiveness, speaking in tongues and laying on of hands."

Speaking in tongues is a modern adaptation of one of our language's great ancient phrases, first found in early Bible translations, such as this line from I Corinthians 12:30 in William Tyndale's 1526 version of the New Testament: "Do all speake with tonges?"

Many Pentecostals and charismatics (sometimes capitalized when used as a proper noun) do, and they are the people who make up the majority of the television ministry known as the PTL Club. The day of Pentecost (*pentekoste* means fiftieth, from the same Greek root as the "five" in Pentagon, a five-sided building) was the fiftieth day (seven Sundays) after Easter. On that day, according to the Acts of the Apostles 2:3–4 in the King James version, ". . . there appeared unto them cloven tongues like as of fire, and it sat upon each of them./And they were all filled with the Holy Ghost, and began to speak with other tongues, as the Spirit gave them utterance."

That was considered by some to be the miracle of *glossolalia,* a word coined a century ago to denote the practice by charismatics of speaking in a language that is not readily understandable to speakers of any of the known languages. The unintelligible sounds made in a state of religious frenzy are thought by believers to be manifestations of ecstatic spiritual emotion; believers see that ability as a gift of devotion, and those capable of being the vehicle for such expression are said to have "the gift of tongues." *Tongue* in that sense stands for "language," the same sort of metonym as the use of *crown* for "king," although many think that *tongue* is directly rooted in the Latin *lingua.*

Nonbelievers, as well as Christians who do not associate themselves with the activities of the most fervent sects, do not attribute the excitement—rolling on the floor and speaking in, or with, tongues—to be evidence of being seized by the Holy Spirit. (I'm not knocking *speaking in tongues;* I'm just being evenhanded.) The best way to remember the meaning of the phrase is to treat it as an ellipsis of "speaking in tongues unknown to Man."

On Pentecost: the "fiftieth" actually meant fifty days after Pesach (Passover), not after Easter. The Jewish Feast of Weeks was also named Pentecost, and was originally an agricultural holy day, but at least by the second century C.E. it was regarded as the day on which the Torah was given to the people at Mount Sinai. It was as Jesus' followers gathered on the Jewish holy day of the Apostles, as you noted in your column today, the Holy Spirit came to the gathered community. However, many New Testament scholars have pointed out that the "speaking in other tongues" mentioned in Acts 2:3ff was probably not the phenomenon of *glossolalia* at all, because Luke (the presumed author of Acts) says that "each one [present] heard them speaking *in their own language*" (Acts 2:6, emphasis mine; the same idea repeated in Acts 2:8: "How is it that we hear, each of us in his own native language?"; both as translated in the Revised Standard Version).

The Reverend Lois Ann Wolff
First Presbyterian Church
Bainbridge, New York

Pentagon literally means five-angled and not five-sided: πεντα (penta = five) and γωνια (*gonia* = angle).

Who knows? In non-Euclidean geometry, the number of angles a figure has might have nothing to do with the number of sides.

Elizabeth R. Cardman
Urbana, Illinois

Too Clever by Three Quarters

"Soviet Summitry: Too Clever by Half," editorialized *The New York Times*, irritated at the way Mikhail S. Gorbachev tried to use the Reagan desire for a summit meeting in Washington as a lever for preconditions. (Why *preconditions*, a term always used pejoratively? Why not just the neutral *conditions*? I cannot address that subject today, as I had not preplanned to.)

A year before, Francis X. Clines of the same newspaper, known to his colleagues as one of the classiest writers in journalism, limned Richard Darman, then a high Reagan administration official, as one who is "a very smart man, and does not hesitate to show it; a Senate leader accustomed to dealing with him even coined the term 'Darmanesque' to describe someone too clever by half at politics."

"In criticizing Mrs. Thatcher's use of the word *frit,*" wrote a reader from Nottinghamshire to *The Financial Times* in 1983, "John Hunt is too clever by half—or rather wholly ignorant of North Country slang. At school in the East Midlands, the future Prime Minister would have regularly heard and no doubt used the word as an abbreviation for *frightened.*"

Since there is the revival of a Russian play by Alexander N. Ostrovsky titled in English *Too Clever by Half* at London's Old Vic Theater this year, the time has come to examine the origins of, and the recent proliferation of, this fractional excess of adroitness.

The prepositional phrase *by half* must not be confused with its plural brother, *by halves,* which means "imperfectly, partially"—as Edmund Burke warned in 1790, "A king is not to be deposed by halves." (That's what happens when usurpers get frit.)

In singular, *by half* means much more: "considerably, by far, a great deal." It can be found before 1400 in *Morte Arthure, or The Death of Arthur;* in the past five centuries, it has been used in the description of a woman "fayrer by one halfe than shee was before" and in a comment in Richard Brinsley Sheridan's 1777 play *The School for Scandal* that could be applied today to one of our media scandalhounds: "Pshaw! he is too moral by half."

Too clever by half was coined in George J. Whyte-Melville's 1858 book, *The Interpreter*, and means "too smart for one's own good." It is a British-ism—like *early on, good show* and *have a go*—that has crossed the Atlantic but still retains its British flavor.

Clever, since we're at it, is a word with two sides. Probably from a Scandinavian root, the adjective *cliver* appeared in Middle English as a reference to quickness with claws. In one sense, the word has drawn on physical quickness and, by metaphoric extension, has come to mean mentally "nimble, adroit, skillful." (Clever boy!) In another sense, the nimbleness takes on a darker meaning, as "sharp, canny, cunning, tricky, opportunistic." (Clever pol!)

Never, until today, has the phrase changed the degree of its fraction; it is always *too clever by half.* Today's headline of this column seeks to pique attention by changing the half to three quarters, which many will consider arch, straining for effect, pushing it or too clever by the standard fraction.

To the Buck-Naked Eye

Norm, the accountant in "Cheers," a sitcom set in a Boston bar, was saying how his sexy sister-in-law was sitting in his house *"buck na- ked."* Cliff, the naïve mailman (all right, "postal worker"), reacted with a shocked *"Buck?"*

In the world of modifiers, *stark* is out and *buck* is in. "A phrase has caught my attention," writes Joan Irvine of Westport, Conn., "and al-though I understand it, I am curious about its origins. *Buck naked,* meaning 'stark naked' or 'in the nude'—does this come from the male deer, or from slang for a dollar, or is it a derivation of 'in the *buff*'?"

According to DARE, the invaluable Dictionary of American Regional English, the term is chiefly used in the South Atlantic and Gulf states. The first citation is from Julia Peterkin's 1928 Pulitzer Prize-winning novel *Scar-let Sister Mary*, set in South Carolina: "You ain' to stand up buck naked like dat. You's a grown 'oman now."

Buck has two related meanings: male and strong. The first, as Ms. Irvine suggests, points to the masculinity of an animal—originally a goat, or *bucca* in Old English—later to the male of a deer, antelope or rabbit. Another DARE entry, *buck nun,* is defined as "a celibate man." *Buck's* sense of strength dates to its Middle English meaning of "rigid"—like *stark's* root in the fixed-eyeball *stare*—and both senses were combined when the word was used as a racial slur.

Buck may be rooted in an alteration of *butt* from *buttocks,* as well as the "posterior" sense of *bum.* What about Ms. Irvine's speculation about *in the buff?* That phrase, meaning "naked," comes from the smooth, soft feel and skin-tone color of well-treated buffalo hide. Personally, I have never been turned on by a herd of buffalo, but that's a fairly certain etymology for the phrase *in the buff.* (The color *buff* is in vogue this year, used for contrast by taupe addicts.) To come full circle, *buff* is slightly lighter than most *buck-skin.*

The *buck* in *buck naked*—which is surely a whole lot older than the 1928 citation first given by DARE—is pretty clearly just a variant of the word given in both the O.E.D. and Webster's Second International as *bouk,* a Scots and dialect word meaning "body." If you are buck naked you are body-naked, not just naked to the waist or whatever.

No doubt from *buck naked* came the flavor of *buck* as meaning "bare, unadorned," and hence *buck private* and *buck sergeant.*

Thaddeus Holt
Carlisle, Pennsylvania

The words "Buck Fizz" headed the menu for a brunch served after a fashion show at Grosvenor House in London during the 1985 International Fiscal Association Congress. "Buck Fizz" turned out to be a pleasant mixture of champagne and orange juice. However, I was mystified by the name until I read recently that this is a favorite beverage of the inhabitants of Buckingham Palace.

Dorothy B. Diamond
Hartsdale, New York

Tough Medicine, Bitter Choices

"**M**r. Dole talks about making 'tough choices' and offering 'bitter medicine' to reduce Government spending," wrote David E. Rosenbaum in *The New York Times*, ". . . but he has not named particular budget items he would reduce or eliminate."

We are now into the lingo of unspecific sacrifice, a staple of presidential years. Generalized calls for *sacrifice* and *belt-tightening* are perceived as good, while any specific plan to carry out this ideal is seen as politically stupid. To be fair (as this column always is; the only sentence-opening phrase more fatuous is *to be sure*), Republican Bob Dole has specialized mainly in *bitter medicine* while Democratic Senator Paul Simon is the one who most often calls for *tough choices*. Mr. Dole laid claim to his metaphor by extending it: "People are willing to take the *bitter medicine*, but nobody wants to hold the spoon."

"Good medicine always has a bitter taste" was identified as a Japanese proverb by H. L. Mencken. That spirit undoubtedly builds their trade surplus but is not necessarily an Eastern concept: by Shakespeare's time, the sense of medicine's bitterness could be found in his comedy *Two Gentlemen of Verona*. Proteus and Valentine, the two gentlemen, discuss the woman that Valentine loves; Proteus refuses to overpraise her, saying, "When I was sick, you gave me bitter pills,/ and I must minister the like to you."

The medical trope has long been active in the budgetary domain. "The budget would have to contain *bitter medicine*," wrote *Newsweek* in 1975 about New York City's fiscal crisis. Last year, Albert M. Wojnilower, the economist most often called "Dr. Doom," was quoted as opining, "We may have some choice as to what recipe we concoct for the *bitter medicine*," offering at least a change of taste in the bitterness.

Lest we forget: this metaphor is based on the notion that if a medicine tastes bad, it must be good for you. That is a truism that is not necessarily true; sometimes we have to make the tender choices.

You claim that "to be sure" is the most fatuous sentence-opening phrase. I disagree.

The most fatuous of all sentence-opening phrases is "needless to say," which renders the remainder of the sentence, by the writer's own judgment, unnecessary.

Jeff Berman
Hoboken, New Jersey

True Believer

How do you spell the word: *Moslem* or *Muslim?* Lexicographers are having big headaches over this one. Publications are split, sometimes within a single issue. Nobody wants to offend.

The word is Arabic (for "true believer") and for that reason has no "correct" spelling in English; the spelling was transliterated into an English approximation of the sound in Arabic. Some heard the first syllable as "maaz" and spelled it *mos*; others heard "mus" and spelled it that way.

Most dictionaries have tended to prefer *Moslem* to *Muslim*. (No argument over capitalization: Like *Jew* and *Christian*, *Moslem/Muslim* is capitalized; *atheist* is not, which seems unfair.) But in the citation files, according to information compiled for Allan M. Siegal, assistant managing editor of *The New York Times, Muslim* is being used almost two to one.

Since adherents of Islam prefer that form, I say let's go with it. More than 554 million Muslims can't be wrong.

The Arabic word *Muslim* does not mean "true believer"; rather, it means "submitter," "one who submits or has submitted," explained by Muslim exegetes as "one who has submitted himself to the will of God." Grammatically, the word is the masculine active participle (feminine is *Muslimah*) of *aslama* ("he has submitted"). This is what Western grammarians call the fourth form, and Arab grammarians call the *af'ala* form, of the verb *salima* ("he is/has been safe, secure"). The verbal noun of the fourth or *af'ala* form of *salima* is the familiar word *islam*—"submission." The word has no connotation of belief, true belief, or truth.

Edward A. Jajko
Middle East Bibliographer/Curator
Hoover Institution
Stanford, California

The reason Muslim is the correct spelling is that technically Arabic contains only three vowels—"a", "i" and "u". The two that appear in the word Muslim, when written with vowels (Arabic, like Hebrew and other Semitic languages, is generally written without the vowels), are "u" and "i." Moreover, those who spell the word with an "o" in place of the "u" do so not because they hear "Maaz" but because they here "Moz" with the British pronunciation as in "hot" pronounced British-style. Muslim is the correct scholarly transliteration, and Muslims and Arabic speakers rightly insist upon it.

Judith Romney Wegner
Assistant Professor, Judaic Studies
Williams College
Williamstown, Massachusetts

Muslim/Moslem: There are two basic reasons why the variant occurs. Arabic writers often omit vowels when the intent is clear, and, as in many languages, there are regional variants in pronunciation. A good example is the Arabic word for mountain. Roman transliteration of the word would probably appear as *jbl*. The second vowel almost invariably comes out in speech as a schwa, but the first is spoken variously as jaybel, jahbel, jubbel, joobel, doubtless with subtle interpolations, making a standard transliteration of the language all but impossible. Furthermore, there are a few sounds in Arabic unknown to any European tongue known to me. There is, for example, a town in Libya transliterated on some maps as Ghat, on others, as

Rhat. On arrival, I asked about this. The answer: halfway between the two, a guttural from deep in the throat.

J. R. Coolidge
New York, New York

The Arabic word, pronounced "Moosslim" (not Moozlim) in crude phonetic representation, *does* have only one correct spelling in English! Arabic transliteration has long been standardized. You can consult the Library of Congress transliteration experts if you doubt me. The correct spelling is "Muslim." This Arabic word is pronounced differently by non-Arab Muslims, which creates confusion. For example, in the culturally very influential Persian language, the word is pronounced "Moslem." Second, "true believer" is a *Christian* concept. "Muslim" means "one who submits (to God)." Third, the population of Muslims is rapidly approaching *one billion* (you may have forgotten to count Indonesian and Indian Muslims).

Ann Mayer
Philadelphia, Pennsylvania

Could it be that "The Power of Positive Thinking" has triumphed again? Being a Christian, a Jew, or a Muslim is hardly an abstract matter. The absence of commitment pertaining to atheism quite clearly is.

Translated to the political realm, we have Republicans, Democrats, Monarchists, Communists, Fascists and a few others. So far as I have been able to discover, though, those who favor a cessation of any and all forms of government are labeled—lower case—anarchists.

Thomas G. Morgansen
Jackson Heights, New York

Useful Idiots of the West

Referring with derision to what he called "so-called notables who were convened as props for Gorbachev's speech," Zbigniew Brzezinski used a stinging phrase that has become a term of art among hard-line historians and former national security advisers: *useful idiots of the West.*

Certainly Zbig was not labeling "idiot" the likes of former Secretaries of State Cyrus R. Vance and Henry A. Kissinger, columnist Jeane J. Kirkpatrick and Bronx High School of Science alumnus Harold Brown—not in the sense of the Greek word for "peculiar," later applied to those with an I.Q. of less than 25, now loosely tossed about in rough equivalence to "jerk."

None of those foreign-affairs worthies took offense because they recognized the phrase as a derogation more historically resonant than *unwitting dupe* and less politically damaging than the outdated *fellow traveler.*

The phrase is in current use among the geostrategic cognoscenti. "Lenin had a name for these people," wrote Susan Spreen of Mission Viejo, Calif., to the editor of the *Los Angeles Times,* denouncing congressmen who were pro-Sandinista and anti-contra, *"useful idiots."*

"Maarten van Traa, the Dutch Socialists' international secretary," wrote John Vinocur in *The New York Times,* "insists that the party is not playing the role of the *useful idiots* for the Russians, a phrase used by Lenin to describe left-liberals and Social Democrats. . . ." Several months after this instruction within the story by correspondent Vinocur, a *Times* headline on another topic read: "Lenin's 'Useful Idiots' in Salvador." West German Chancellor Helmut Kohl was quoted in *Business Week* as rapping the "fellow travelers who support this [Soviet] propaganda effort in Western Europe. We call them *useful idiots.*"

This seems to be Lenin's phrase, once applied against liberals, that is being used by anti-Communists against the ideological grandchildren of those liberals, or against anybody insufficiently anti-Communist in the view of the phrase's user. But as one who has tied himself in knots looking for Lenin's supposed quote on another subject—"The capitalists will sell us the rope with which to hang them," or words to that effect—I wondered when and where Lenin said it.

"We get queries on *useful idiots of the West* all the time," said Grant Harris, senior reference librarian at the Library of Congress. "We have not been able to identify this phrase among his published works." A call to Tass, the Soviet news agency, gets a telephonic shrug and a referral to the Institute of Marxism and Leninism in Moscow; I tried them before, on the rope trick, and it's a waste of a stamp. I called Communist Party headquarters in New York City, thereby setting off tape recorders in a dozen FBI offices (it's only me again, fellas), but to no avail.

Librarian Harris got back to me, however, with a lead to the possible source of both the "rope" remark and the "useful idiot" attribution. Former Colgate professor Albert Parry writes in the *St. Petersburg Times*: "You will not find the rope prophecy in any of the voluminous Lenin works published in the Soviet Union." Right.

He suggests we look instead in the 1966 book *People and Portraits: A Tragic Cycle*, published in New York by Inter-Language Literary Associates, written by Yuri Annenkov, a painter and writer who had been commissioned in 1921 by the Communist Party to do a portrait of Lenin. After Lenin's death three years later, Mr. Annenkov said he was given access to the personal papers of the dead leader at the Lenin Institute in Moscow, as he was illustrating some books about him.

Here is what Mr. Annenkov claims he copied from notes in Lenin's handwriting, italics in the original: "To speak the truth is a *petit-bourgeois* habit. To lie, on the contrary, is often justified by the lie's aim. The whole world's capitalists and their governments, as they pant to win the Soviet market, *will close their eyes* to the above-mentioned reality and will thus transform themselves into men who are *deaf, dumb and blind.* They will give us credits . . . they will toil to prepare their own suicide."

Look, I know it's a little farfetched. I would be a lot happier with a photocopy of the original Lenin notes, but such proof is not readily available, and no explosion of glasnost in Moscow is going to allow Western scholars on-site inspection of all of Lenin's notes. However, this gives us one clue about the source of the "sell us the rope" attribution, and the "deaf, dumb and blind" phrase may be one of the phrases that helped start the "useful idiots," whether or not originally by Lenin. This investigation needs more work, and we can hope it will be put on the agenda of the next summit.

In the meantime, outspoken anti-Communists have permission to use *useful idiots of the West* as well as *the West will sell us the rope with which to hang them,* but must not precede either with "As Lenin said . . ." until more precincts are heard from. Instead, try "As Lenin was reported to have said . . ." or "In a phrase attributed to Lenin . . ."

Here is Lenin's famous line from *Left-Wing Communism:* "I want with my vote to support Henderson in the same way as the rope supports a hanged man . . ." Surely this is the Ur text for all subsequent "rope" quote variations.

Kevin Coogan
Bronxville, New York

Weather Report: Yucky

"**W**hat's it like out today?"
"*Yucky.*"

You reach for your raincoat and begin a search for your overshoes (which you used to call *rubbers* before that word became a euphemism for *condoms*), because you know that *yucky* means "inclement" (a word most often meaning "stormy," based on the opposite of the Latin *clemens,* "lenient, mild").

Yuck! is an interjection used in such sentences as "I have just stepped in the—*Yuck!*—mud," and is more expressive of disgust than *Eek!* which is now limited to the sound a cartoon elephant makes as he leaps on a small chair after spotting a mouse. Unlike most interjections (*Oops! Wow! Oh! Ugh!*), *yuck* spawned an adjective, *yucky,* a slang term that shows signs of serving a linguistic need and may, centuries from now, make it to Standard English.

According to the Reverend John Boag's 1852–53 *Imperial Lexicon* (which appeared on my expense account a few years ago and which I feel the need to justify), there was a local verb *yuck* that meant "to itch"; it was derived from the Scottish *yuke,* and since at least the 1700s, the adjective *yuky* has meant "itching with curiosity."

The slightly nauseated reader will recognize a link between the current *yuck* and *puke*; yes, each of these words is imitative, or onomatopoeic (which means it means what it sounds like). In this century, the verb *yuck* first appeared in this sense in Canada's Newfoundland dialect, and its retching, gagging sound and sense have since been euphemized by college students everywhere as *blow your cookies* or *drive the great white bus* or *embrace the porcelain altar.*

The comedian Fred Allen had much to do with the word's popularization as a noun. H. Allen Smith, in *Life in a Putty Knife Factory,* wrote: "*Yuck* is a word introduced into the language by Fred Allen. A *yuck* is a dope who makes a practice of going around appearing on quiz programs." This use may have been influenced by *yok* or *yock,* which has long been a theatrical slang term for "laugh," perhaps based on the English dialect *yocha* with that meaning. Saul Bellow, in his 1964 novel, *Herzog,* wrote of a character "boisterous, yucking it up."

Beginning in 1970, the word took the adjective form *yucky* and gained the sense of "nasty, sloppy, distasteful, to be avoided at all costs," closely allied to regurgitation. It seems to have triumphed over the similar *icky,* has resisted replacement by *gross* and its derivative *grody,* but is now being challenged by a variant form, the interjection *yecch* and its adjectival *yecchy.* I predict *yucky* will persevere, but let us watch the comic strips for developments.

Dear Bill,

In the column on *yuck* and *yucky* you missed a beat, which implies that you aren't raising a small child. If you had been, you would have had to mention "Mr. Yuk" [pictured on Poison Center labels in Madison, Wisconsin]. Stick one on every medicine bottle or pill box in your cabinet. The idea is that the little dears, not yet able to read, meeting this label, will recognize that the nasty-looking man has swallowed something yucky and will *yuk* right back. Mr. Yuk is the opposite of the happy-face. He does not smile invitingly; he makes you feel vomity. Yuck!

Frederic G. Cassidy
Chief Editor, DARE
Madison, Wisconsin

Just an additional bit of information relevant to the Scottish *yuke:* the everyday German verb (infinitive) for itch is *jucken.* The question is: who came first? Who borrowed from whom?

Ernest Gruen
New York, New York

Fliuch ("flyuch," with ch as in the German) is the Irish Gaelic for "wet." *Tá sé fliuch* ("tah shay flyuch") means "It's wet," often true of the Irish weather. "Very wet" would be *ró-fhliuch* (pronounced approximately "row lyuch": the fh is silent); and of course *"Tá sé ró-fhliuch"* is also often true in Ireland, where the weather can be downright *fhliuch*-y at any time of the year.

> Peter Kenny
> Glenn Dale, Maryland

I would like to give you a very old and still popular expression here in the Bahamas—"Don't yuck up my vexation as it dun already yuck up."

> Catharine Matheson
> Andros, Bahamas

You cite "grody" as a derivation from "gross." That may be. But I remember first hearing "grody" in the mid-'60s, at the time of the British pop music invasion, when it was widely believed to have derived from the mod London slang "grotty," a shortened form of "grotesque."

> Robert C. Cumbow
> Seattle, Washington

Native Minnesotans use the word (if you can call it a word) *ish* (i as in fish). Having grown up in a suburb of Buffalo, N.Y., I had never heard of ish since we used the words yuck, gross or ick to describe something disgusting. Minnesota is the only state in which I've heard *ish* used.

> Cora E. Musial
> Rochester, Minnesota

Weenies of the World, Unite!

"Y ou ever heard of the *pol-mil weenies?*" asked Susan F. Rasky, a colleague at *The New York Times.*

I replied that it sounded like a variant of the "Tolpuddle Martyrs," a band of heroic English unionists of the early nineteenth century; *pol-mil* might be a corruption of *pell-mell*, the Anglicization of the French reduplication *pêle-mêle*, "all mixed up," and not from Pall Mall, the street in London. (I speculate wildly that way to discourage further questions.)

She shook her head. "Hot new locution at the Puzzle Palace and the Fudge Factory: 'He's one of Carlucci's new *pol-mil weenies*.' Check it out."

Why would officials at the Pentagon and State Department refer to

Defense Secretary Frank Carlucci's aides that way? I have excellent sources at both departments; recently, after I described the Soviet radar facility at Krasnoyarsk as an illegal "phrased-array, battle-management radar," hordes of arms-control junkies wrote to tell me to drop the r in "phrased": the term is *phased array,* referring to communications technology in which an array of antenna elements can be used in phases to vary signal directions without moving the antenna.

Pol-mil was easy enough to trace: it stands for "political-military" (or "politico-military"), and in the State Department the pol-mil bureau is the place where a tiny collection of hawks is allowed to assemble. Pol-mil types, with their crassly undiplomatic solutions, are tolerated in the building to be trotted out when hawkish members of Congress come to visit.

But the trail to *weenie* was long and winding. We have here a slang term of suitably checkered provenance, now blossoming in the English language as it never had in its century-old existence.

Covering the Olympic skating championships in Canada, *Time* magazine reported a profound change in style with a change in trainers: ". . . it was goodbye Tech Weenie, hello Elegance Whiz. Out went the bouncy pop-rock medley. In came sobering, dramatic theme music."

Another recent usage, from a *Washington Post* story about gifts of computer software for children: "There's hope for the most timorous techno-weenie."

"It was inevitable, perhaps," wrote the *Los Angeles Times,* "that laser games would give rise to laser weenies."

In each of these instances, the noun *weenie* means "someone small." Since the 1780s, *weeny* or *weenie* has been used as a variant of the Scottish adjective *wee,* from the Old English *waege,* "weight," denoting something of little weight or size. The word has been influenced by, and has influenced, *tiny* and *teeny,* producing *teeny-weeny,* a reduplication used two generations ago to modify bikini swimsuits, which were then considered daringly small.

The first use in its meaning of "child" is credited by the Oxford English Dictionary Supplement to the nineteenth-century letters of Cecilia Ridley, who wrote in 1844: "Little weeny is growing visibly."

A second root, and source of more sinister senses, can be found. *Wiener-wurst,* meaning "sausage of Vienna," appeared in 1889; this cured cooked sausage, more slender than a frankfurter, became known in the United States in the early 1900s as a *wienie* or *weenie;* in 1920, Sinclair Lewis used it in his novel *Main Street.* In the mid-'20s, another sense surfaced: "the catch; the kicker; a surprise that may cause failure."

Wentworth and Flexner, in their Dictionary of American Slang, speculate that the origin may have been "in vaudeville or the movie industry, perhaps in reference to the large bladders used by comics to hit one another over the head in slapstick comedies. Such bladders are the descendants of the mock phallus wielded by ancient Greek comedians." It may also explain the word's frequent use in nursery talk as a euphemism for a child's penis.

College students know the noun in another sense, a slang term for "grind," "wonk" or "throat" (from *cutthroat*), meaning "serious student" or "obnoxious premed." This meaning now predominates; in 1929, the *Baltimore Sun* explained that "Girls are described as *weenies, janes, dames* and *broads."* By the 1960s, *American Speech* reported that the word had lost its sexist connotation and had become mixed in with the names of small animals to describe socially unacceptable persons: "*toad, squirrel* and *shrimp* all serve for the zoologically unsound but all-inclusive *weenie."*

Today, the word is used in a variety of its senses. Senator Pete Wilson, Republican of California, rose on the Senate floor last year to contend that an opponent of Star Wars wanted to disrupt practical work on the kinetic kill system and instead to explore more exotic technologies where results are decades away: "He is urging us today to drop the ham to pick up the weenie!" The senator, who is phasing away himself, was using the sausage-based metaphor.

"It's old news that [Margaret] Thatcher dislikes the royal family," wrote Alex Heard in the *Washington Post*, "and that it is stupid, weenie, expensive and unproductive except in terms of 'atmospherics.' " The writer uses *weenie* as an adjective synonymous with "small-minded," as does Washington sportscaster Glenn Brenner, who denounces unsportsmanslike conduct with his "Weenie of the Week" award.

Caution: Although a *weenie* has been known as a *hot dog* ever since the turn of the century, the new sense of *hot dog*—"one who performs ostentatiously"—is not applied to *weenie*. To avoid confusion with "show-off," some slanguists are using *tube steak* rather than *hot dog*. Pass that on to the hot-dog boss of the pol-mil weenies.

May I add three entries to your list of weenie words?

1. Ween dog. A super weenie; a student who studies excessively hard, even by weenie standards.
2. Weenoid. A techno-weenie; a science student; a pre-med.
3. Weenie wand. A yellow highlighting magic marker, used by weenies to underline their books.

All three words were current at Yale when I was an undergraduate (1978–82).

Alexander F. Cohen
New York, New York

A "weenie" in our vocabulary is usually prefixed by "road" as in "road weenie." These are the people who cut in front of your car in rush hour (also known as the weenie parade) only to slow down, who come to full stops at yield signs or who drive down the center line of the Taconic State Parkway.

Julie L. Henderson
Yorktown Heights, New York

Your most recent column ("Weenies of the World, Unite!") contains a reference to the term "tube steak" as a synonym for hot dog (as in frankfurter). While I was not familiar with that particular usage of the term, I had heard it used in a much less delicate manner. In *National Lampoon*'s list of euphemisms for the obscene, as well as in the popular song "Tube Steak Boogie," the aforementioned term is synonymous with, how shall I say this, a man's private parts.

This may or may not be news to you, as it would be a reasonable omission from your column. However, for the uninitiated your partial list of usages could lead to potentially embarrassing statements and/or requests.

Richard Lebowitz
New York, New York

Weigh to Go

"I was watching 'Wheel of Fortune,'" writes Dorothy Epstein of Brick Township, N.J., adding the defiant parenthesis: "(Yes, I watch word game shows.)" And in one show, she said, "they used the phrase *plans are under way.* Shouldn't it have been *weigh?*"

This is an etymological mistake that has celebrated its two hundredth anniversary. "We are all in high spirits," wrote the British dramatist Richard Cumberland in 1785, "getting under weigh." Richard Henry Dana, the American author of *Two Years Before the Mast,* picked up the common error and wrote in that classic in 1840: "She got under weigh with very little fuss. . . ."

With that kind of hoary provenance, a word or phrase usually gains "correctness," based on the First Principle of Descriptive Linguistics: "If it sticks around, it's right."

But it is incorrect, which means it is still viewed as a "variant" spelling by most lexicographers. The nautical term *under way,* spelled that way, meaning "having begun to move through the water," was first recorded in 1743 in England, and was used that way by Washington Irving in America four years before Dana botched it here.

The confusion is with *weigh anchor,* "to pull up an anchor before sailing," as in the song "Anchors Aweigh"; however, as Admiral William

Henry Smyth pointed out in his *Sailor's Word-Book* in 1867, "Some have written this *under weigh*, but improperly. A ship is under weigh when she has weighed her anchor. . . . As soon as she gathers way she is under way." Other salts hold that a ship is under way as soon as she is not at anchor, aground or made fast to a mooring, and does not have to be making way to be *under way*. I don't want to get into that scrap.

The sinking feeling experienced by Mrs. Epstein about spelling is widely shared, even by those who do not get defensive about watching game shows, but is dismissed as "folk etymology" by us folks in the language dodge. Our problem is the marriage of the two words in the phrase: the *Washington Post* spells it *underway*, *The New York Times* *under way*; you pays yer money and you takes yer choice. (And does anybody have the origin of that?)

(1) "Under weigh" refers to a ship that is strictly under anchor. It does not refer to a ship that is aground, or drifting in the water. In fact, there is no English word to refer to the condition of drifting in the water.

(2) "Underway" refers to the condition where a ship is in the actual condition of a controlled propulsion, be it sail, steam or nuclear power. The key to this term is hence in a state of controlled propulsion from either being tied up along the pier, after hoisting anchor, or in a state of drift. You are not either "underway" or "under weigh" if you are adrift in the water.

Arthur D. Steckel
Skokie, Illinois

Since you quote Dana using "under weigh," I thought you might be interested to know that Melville did likewise in *Moby Dick*. Near the beginning of Chapter XXII, "Merry Christmas," Melville explains Captain Ahab's absence from the decks of the *Pequod* as follows: "But then, the idea was, that his presence was by no means necessary in getting the ship under weigh, and steering her well out to sea."

Although I agree that "underway" is much more sensible, it is interesting to note that Webster's Ninth New Collegiate Dictionary dates "underway" to 1751 while "underweigh" is dated circa 1663.

Craig Curtis
Chapel Hill, North Carolina

You Pays Yer Money

"Y ou pays yer money and you takes yer choice," I wrote, using what I assumed to be an old Americanism meaning, as the oddsmakers say, "Pick 'em."

Mark Twain used the saying in 1884, at the end of chapter 28 of *Huckleberry Finn*, I am informed by Richard Bliss of New York City: ". . . here's your two sets o' heirs to old Peter Wilks—and you pays your money and you takes your choice!"

The origin, as dozens of other Lexicographic Irregulars stepped forward to say, is British, probably Cockney. The first time the saying saw print was in an 1846 *Punch*. A cartoon entitled "The Ministerial Crisis" has a showman telling a customer, "Which ever you please, my little dear. You pays your money, and you takes your choice."

The phrase still means "The right of choice is to the buyer," or a more sophisticated "Power belongs to those who have paid their dues," but a much different sense has emerged. "The phrase is used today," writes Edward C. Stephens, dean of Syracuse University's Newhouse School of Public Communications, "not so much as an invitation to choice as it is a rejoinder to complaint. It seems to be similar in intent to 'You made your bed, now lie in it.' Another variant is 'Look, if you don't like it, you can just lump it.' "

A third meaning is "Beats the hell out of me." In that regard, let us look at an even older cliché, *butter wouldn't melt in her mouth.*

This was a predecessor of today's *cool,* in its sense of "untouchable by emotion, admirably aloof and fashionably alienated." The saying, first cited in John Palsgrave's 1530 book on the French language, gained further currency in Jonathan Swift's writings: "She looks as if butter would not melt in her mouth, but I warrant cheese won't choak her."

In a 1781 comedy by Charles Macklin, the playwright used this expression in the sense it was used for centuries: "She looks demure and good: and is less good and demure than she looks."

The idea behind the phrase is that the person is so cold and proper that her mouth temperature would keep butter refrigerated and firm. In a warmhearted or hot-blooded person, the butter would melt, or at least turn all icky, but the phrase is never used in that form. You never hear someone say, "He's such a compassionate human being that butter would melt in his mouth." The phrase has always been used sarcastically.

In recent years, however, a new sense has developed, threatening to push the old meaning out. This current usage has not yet made the quotation books. The phrase now means "eager to please, oleaginous in an attempt to curry favor." It is now used to say, "She's all sweetness and light," as in "Ever since I won the lottery, butter wouldn't melt in her mouth." In this sense, the phrase has lost its etymological moorings, perhaps having sucked some meaning out of *buttery*, "oily, unctuous," or *to butter up*, "flatter."

In *The New York Times Magazine*, writer James Traub described Francis T. (Mickey) Featherstone, a former gang member, as looking like a cherub: " 'If you saw this guy, you'd swear that butter wouldn't melt in his mouth,' says an acquaintance of his. 'But you'd hear the most horrible stories.' "

Carl H. Snyder, a professor of chemistry at the University of Miami, who apparently knows the temperature at which solids turn to liquids, writes: "Assuming that butter doesn't melt in the mouths of cold-blooded reptiles but that it would flow sweetly in the mouth of a warm and cuddly cherub, it seems to me our first impression of the fellow ought to be that butter *would* melt in his mouth." The professor adds, "Not until after we had heard all the horrible stories would we expect the stuff to congeal."

He has a point, because the meaning has changed. When the unidentified source says, "If you saw this guy, you'd swear that butter wouldn't melt in his mouth," he does not mean "This person is cold-blooded." Rather, he means "This fellow's appearance is such that you would expect a mild and gentle soul"; the contrast is then made with "the most horrible stories."

So when you say, "Butter wouldn't melt in his mouth," you now confuse listeners. You can mean "He's uptight and frigid" in the old sense, or you can mean "He's all peaches and cream," which is the opposite.

You pays yer money and you takes yer choice. I'd let that particular cliché die until it sorts itself out.

> I am familiar with a variant form of "you pays yer money and you takes yer choice" from the writings of the innovative American composer Charles Ives (1874–1954). In his *Memos* (Norton, 1972), Ives recalls working on his orchestral tone poem *The Fourth of July* during a 1913 trip to visit his father-in-law at a sanatorium in Vermont. (According to Ives, a doctor looked at the score strangely and assumed Ives was a patient.) The composer gives a characteristically dualistic description of the piece: "This is pure program music—it is also pure abstract music—'You pays your money, and you takes your choice' " (*Memos*, p. 4).
>
> With customary thoroughness, the editor of the *Memos*, John Kirkpatrick, notes that Ives is quoting Mark Twain, from the end of Chapter 28 of *Huckleberry Finn*. A devotee of American literature, Ives certainly would have been well acquainted with the source of the quote. He also had other reasons for knowing his Twain: his father-in-law, whose illness seems at first to be peripherally related to Ives's

recollection of *The Fourth of July,* was Joseph Hopkins Twichell (1838–1918), the minister and close friend of Twain for many years. The indirect personal connection with Twain seems to creep into Ives's remembrance of his musical activities.

J. Philip Lambert
Assistant Professor of Music
Baruch College
New York, New York

You use the term "Pick 'em" to mean the same as "You pays yer money and you takes yer choice." Not so! Regardless of the odds/pointspread on a given game, you *always* pay your money and take your choice when placing your bet with a bookie. The term "Pick 'em" is used *only* if the teams are evenly rated. If Dallas were favored by 3 points over the N.Y. Giants the phrase would be, "Dallas, by 3." If the teams were evenly rated, it would be "Pick 'em."

Joel W. Grollman
Columbia, Maryland

What Happened to the Market?

On Black Monday, *crash* was the word most frequently used at first to describe the 508-point drop in the Dow Jones industrial average that occurred October 19, 1987, a day that many investors think will live in infirmity. Donald T. Regan, former Treasury Secretary, called C-Day "black and blue Monday," a nice play on the battered image of "black and blue" with the traditional bad-news sense of "black [whatever] day" and the don't-want-to-go-back-to-work sense of "blue Monday."

However, some considered *crash*—evocative of the "crash of '29"—to be alarmist. (As Kipling never said, "If you can keep your head when all about you are losing theirs, perhaps you don't understand the gravity of the situation.")

Among politicians, Senator Paul Simon called it a *plunge,* Jesse Jackson broadened it to a *crisis,* Governor Mike Dukakis preferred the milder *slide* and Congressman Jack Kemp used the mildest *drop.* White House aides used *panic,* stressing the unfounded and irrational nature of the cause of the sharp downward move of investor confidence, although President Reagan in his subsequent news conference preferred the upbeat *correction.*

In the news business, *The New York Times* used both *plunge* and *drop:* "Stocks Plunge 508 Points, A Drop of 22.6%"; later in the week, sensitive to the scariness of *plunge*, the *Times* gave readers a lesson in synonymy: "Stocks Fall, But Avert Plunge."

The Associated Press alternated between *plunge* and *decline*; at the *Washington Post*, *drop* was the key verb with *plunge* in the subhead, although its financial columnist, Hobart Rowen, chose the more vivid *collapse*.

In a column immediately after the event, I used the less formal *nosedive*. An editorial writer in the *Washington Post* preferred *nasty fall*, but the *Times*'s editorialist observed that "words like crash did not suffice; it was, people said, more like a meltdown."

Meltdown, offering the alliterative *market meltdown*, showed signs of becoming the noun of choice (Haynes Johnson, a *Washington Post* columnist, was even more alliterative with *the frantic, fearful falls of Black Monday*).

"Whether today was a financial meltdown or not," said John J. Phelan, Jr., unflappable chairman of the New York Stock Exchange, apparently responding to the use of the word in a question, "I wouldn't want to be around for one worse than this." *USA Today* headlined this as "Market 'Meltdown,' " grasping firmly at the aforementioned alliterative possibilities. (The most recent sense of the term is "ultimate nuclear-reactor accident," although the word *meltdown* originated in the ice-cream industry in the 1930s, according to the vanilla king Norman Beck of Beverly Hills.)

Let's hit the thesaurus key on the Xywrite word-processing program and see what is left to denote a sudden fall: *tumble* is still available, though that has a jocular quality, and *setback* and *downturn* are far too mild. *Slump* does not have the requisite suddenness in decline for this financial terminology, since it is often used as a synonym for "mild recession." Here's a good verb: *plummet*, from the Latin for the heavy metal we call lead, which sinks faster than most elements. This thesaurus does not have *shakeout*, a market term falling between the harsh *crash* and the more neutral *drop*.

Fall does not have the needed suddenness, or quality of the unexpected, implicit in *crash* or even *drop*, but do not underestimate this short verb; it recalls the fall of the rebellious angel, Lucifer, and post-mortems on the market are sure to be headlined "After the Fall."

Hence, loathed Melancholy: *rebound* has its family—*bounceback, snapback, comeback, recovery* . . .

> It is curious that when the market experiences a decline, members of the securities industry and the Administration refer to the phenomenon as a "correction." However, when the market goes up, the term "correction" is never applied. This linguistic disparity illogically implies that it is incorrect or unnatural for the market to be high, and correct for it to be low.
>
> It is intriguing to speculate (if you'll excuse the pun) on how such a verbal anomaly developed. Is it a reflection of the familiar gravitational adage that "whatever goes up must come down"? Do we suffer from a collective fear of flying? Do we feel guilty when we make too

much money in a bull market, and more virtuous when we suffer losses?

What we have here is an example of a particular brand of double-talk known as brokerese. Everyone knows that a bull market is wonderful (unless you've gone short). However, the securities industry feels it must sanitize a loss by describing it as a "buying opportunity," and a major decline as a "correction." President Reagan and Treasury Secretary James A. Baker III similarly invoke these terms to persuade the public that all is "correct" with the economy and the ship of state.

Ira J. Morrow
New York, New York

You did not mention "crumble" and "collapse"—two words which, in my opinion, are particularly apt.

Charles F. Gill
Mathews, Virginia

You missed one! We population ecologists use "irruption" to signify a precipitous decline in population size.

Can you imagine the headline? "STOCK MARKET IRRUPTS VIOLENTLY. BROKERS BURNED. INVESTORS INCINERATED."

Michael L. Rosenzweig
Tucson, Arizona

You write: "Here's a good verb: *plummet,* from the Latin for the heavy metal we call lead, which sinks faster than most elements."

This may be good morphology, but it's bad physics. The interpretation that you attach to *plummet* is based on a popular misconception—but one that physicists have repudiated since the days of Galileo and Newton. To be sure, Newtonian mechanics does not explain the motion of atoms and certain heavenly bodies. However, on an "ordinary" scale, disregarding viscosity effects, falling (or sinking) objects of various densities are observed to fall (or sink) at the same rate.

Rudolph L. Bertschi
Seattle, Washington

"When I Make a Mistake . . ."

"I'm not known to make many mistakes," said Senator Lloyd Bentsen modestly, in extricating himself from a fund-raising furor, "but when I do, it's a *doozie.*"

This is a botched use of a statement by New York Mayor Fiorello H. La Guardia. "When I make a mistake, it's a beaut." The Little Flower's confession became one of the great observations in political wisdom, comparable to Woodrow Wilson's suggestion that an opponent in difficulty should not be attacked, expressed as "Never murder a man who is committing suicide," and Navy Secretary Claude Swanson's paean to political loyalty in the New Deal era, "When the water reaches the upper deck, follow the rats."

Senator Bentsen would ordinarily be censured here for his half-remembered evocation of La Guardia's more succinct self-analysis, but the slang word he chose to substitute for "beaut" has merit.

Doozie is early 1930s slang, occasionally used by our senior statesmen, and has a nice Art Deco connotation; *dipsy doodle*, used by President Reagan jocularly to mean "deception," is from the same era. The definition of *doozie* is usually "something outstanding or excellent," but the slang word adds zest and enthusiastic emphasis; a second meaning has emerged of "a stunning event."

Its most common synonym is another slang term, *humdinger*, first listed in the 1905 *Dialect Notes* as a term of admiration in Nebraska dialect, the example being, "She's a *humdinger.*" A more recent slang term with a sense that overlaps *doozie* is *whopper*, though that word has, since the eighteenth century, been associated with size, and is often limited to a lie told in the national interest or the trade name for an extra-thick hamburger.

Doozie was spelled *doozy* in a *Washington Post* editorial applauding the senator's fund-raising retreat. This appears to be *Post* style: in a 1977 column by Nancy Collins, a Washington hostess was described as "just dead sure tonight's party for her friends . . . will be a guaranteed doozy because, as she's telling friends, 'I have 15 ambassadors and 20 senators.' " (Presumably, one was the senior senator from Texas, Mr. Bentsen.) Other spellings include *doosie* and *doosy*, but these do not express the *z* sound, which predominates.

I think the *-ie* ending suggests a noun, on the analogy of *floozie*; the *-y* ending, however, suggests an adjective or adverb, on the analogy of *woozy* and *woozily*. (A *boozer* is a noun synonym for "drinker," and the adjective is *boozy*; an early variant of *doozie* in the 1930s was *doozer*. Slang has a nice way of following patterns.) The earliest citation in Wentworth and Flexner's Dictionary of American Slang is this 1951 comment by bandleader Meredith Willson: "The first orchestra I ever had was really a doozie."

Unlike the roots of most slang terms, the roots of *doozie* are far from obscure: the expensive Duesenberg automobile captured the public imagination during the early 1930s, and a caption in a nostalgic issue of *Life* magazine in 1983 under a picture of the motorcar read: "*Doozies* like this boat-tailed '33 Speedster purred for Gable and Flynn at 100 m.p.h." (If this etymology turns out to be in error, will I have a riposte ready.)

I, too, thought of Fiorello when I read about Lloyd Bentsen, and another fine line of Hizzoner's (does anybody call a mayor "Hizzoner" anymore?) came to mind. Asked about the chances of both a Democratic and a Republican opponent one election year, La Guardia replied, "I could beat those bums running on a laundry ticket."

Question: Are we going to need a new word to describe idioms, or portions of them, for which the reference has totally vanished from society, such as "laundry ticket?" Do you think our kids—well, grandchildren—are going to understand the meaning of the words "clockwise" and "counter-clockwise"? (You see, kids, the old analog watches had hands—well, not really hands, more like pointers . . .")

Frank Mankiewicz
Washington, D.C.

When "No Plans" Means "Get Ready"

*P*revaricate is rooted in the Latin for "to walk crookedly" and is now a highfalutin synonym for the verb "to lie." A more subtle form of misleading can be called *postvarication*; this word has been freshly minted to denote the technique of setting forth an untruth in such a way that the listener will later find that the postvaricator had not actually been lying. Indeed, this verbal device, frequently used in Washington and other political capitals, includes a deliberate signal to the listener that less than the truth is being told.

No plans is a good example. If the postvaricator has every intention of making a trip but does not yet want to announce it, he or she seizes on this locution.

Assume that you, the postvaricator, have penciled the trip in on your calendar and have checked out the best restaurants at your destination. Because you have not yet bought the tickets, made the reservations or caused a flurry of cables to fly back and forth, you can truthfully say—with a straight face but a crooked smile playing on your lips—that you have "no plans."

"I have no plan to resign," said Secretary of State George P. Shultz, soon after the revelation of the secret Iran arms trading, which had been pursued against his better judgment. In fact, he had been giving active consideration to resigning, and was careful not to say, "I will not resign," or the more colloquially definitive "Resign? Not me!"

At that tense moment, just before the bombshell announcement of possible criminality in the White House basement, a tug-of-war was going on over control of our arms policy toward Iran. In a verbal straddle, President Reagan announced he had "absolutely *no plans*" to ship more arms to Iran; despite the *absolutely*, this *no-plans* escape hatch left him an opening to ship more arms at some future time. Accomplished postvaricators know that the one locution to avoid is a declarative sentence like "We will ship no more," if that's what you may do one day.

Not until the revelation of the diversion of Iranian arms funds to the contras did *no plans* disappear both from Secretary Shultz's statements on resigning and from the President's policy statements on arms shipments. President Reagan prevailed on Mr. Shultz to announce without equivocation his intent to stay. At that point, the Secretary of State abandoned the postvaricative *no plans* and put out the word that he would stay until the end of the Administration.

Meanwhile, however, Vice Admiral John M. Poindexter had been announcing from the basement of the White House, "I have no plans to resign." Soon after, in classic postvaricative fashion, he bailed out, as the embarrassed National Security Adviser must have suspected he was fated to do.

The Department of State has long been the foremost exponent of no-planning, which is in no way connected with planlessness; some of the most adept no-plans statements come from the Policy Planning Staff.

In an area only remotely related to the Iranian no-planning, Richard W. Murphy, Assistant Secretary of State for Near Eastern (formerly Middle Eastern) and South Asian Affairs, said about the Syrians: "We have *no plans* to consider further sanctions." That was a double postvarication: if sanctions move to the front diplomatic burner, the verb *to consider* offers a second buffer, as we adopt "plans to consider" sanctions—that is, we do not actively consider them.

Asked if he was soon going to the region, Mr. Murphy told a House Subcommittee on Europe and the Middle East (the House has no plans to consider changing "Middle East" to "Near East"), "I don't have any plans to go." Then, in a sudden surge of candor frowned on by his colleagues, the Assistant Secretary blurted, "But then I never seem to have plans."

Students of postvarication are always alert to a refinement in their lingo. When "I have *no plans* to go" changes to "I have *no present plans* to go," they rush home to pack their bags; and when the official takes the final step, "I have *no immediate plans* to go," experienced reporters hustle across the street to grab a toothbrush and a razor because the official's plane is warming up on the runway.

"Postvaricate" must be one of the worst-sounding neologisms of the year, or the generation.

Praevaricator was a betrayer, a lawyer who colluded with the other side. It comes from *varicus,* "to straddle." The definition "to walk crookedly" comes from a single use by Pliny (probably the Younger).

"Postvaricate" could mean "to straddle later," but my advice as an English-lover and friend is: forget it!

Arthur J. Morgan
New York, New York

Who Is an "American"?

Not long ago (a euphemism for "eleven months ago, but time flies"), a request was made of readers to submit substitutes for the word *American,* meaning "citizen of the United States." The reason was plain: other residents of the Americas were taking umbrage at this linguistic imperialism. Our persnickety good neighbors to the south are Americans, too; if we call them "South Americans," should we not refer to ourselves as "North Americans"? And if we do, would we thereby merge with Canada and Mexico by accident?

To open up the possibilities for a new moniker all our own, the Gringo Division of the Lexicographic Irregulars was formed. More than 280 submissions were received. That was nearly a year ago. As Dr. Lloyd I. S. Zbar of Glen Ridge, N.J., writes, "I have not read anymore in your column about the use of *American.* Have you reached a position?"

(One position is clear: *anymore,* in the sense of amount used by the noodging Dr. Zbar—meaning "anything additional"—should be written as two words. In the negative sense, meaning "any longer," the term is one word, *anymore.* Thus: I did not write any more, so Dr. Zbar won't be reading me anymore. A positive, dialectical use is on the rise, meaning "now, at present," which comes naturally to Midwesterners and sounds weird to coastal dwellers: I think I'll write about *Americans* anymore.)

The confusion began with Martin Waldseemüller, the German mapmaker, in 1507. Do not blame Amerigo Vespucci, the explorer from Florence, who sailed to this continent four times between 1497 and 1503 and named the place *Mundus Novus,* Latin for "New World." Good name. If good enough had been let alone, we would all be *Mundus Novusans* today. But Waldseemüller, who apparently did not think much of Christopher Columbus's 1492 trip, scorned Vespucci's coinage; in his *Cosmographiae Introductio,* the mapmaker dubbed the new land *America,* and in those days, cartographers had clout.

In a certain section of Mundusland beginning in 1578, *American* was used to refer to the dark-skinned natives; these natives were later miscalled "Indians," perpetuating a mistake by Mr. Columbus, who thought he was somewhere else. Clergyman Cotton Mather adopted the notion of calling the colonists from England *Americans* in 1697.

Almost a century later, the *United Colonies* sounded like a good name to many revolutionists, while others preferred the *United States of North America*. The pamphleteer Tom Paine, it is said, suggested the broader, and less colonially dependent, *United States of America*, which found its way into the Declaration of Independence. However, as Stuart Berg Flexner recounts in *I Hear America Talking*, the new government used the *United States of North America* as the official title until 1778, when the Continental Congress, thinking in multicontinental terms, passed an act dropping the *North.*

Now to the only extensive modern survey of suggested names for citizens of what has come to be known as the *U.S.A.*, or more jocularly and accurately, the *U.S. of A.* These letters are the initials of the name of the country and are not the trademark of a subsidiary of the Gannett Newspapers. (Since this bunch of letters was found in a deep drawer, it can be called an in-depth survey.)

Usans, pronounced YOU-senz, was the preference of many. Variants of this form include *Usanians* and *Usatians,* both popular, but the pacific *Usanians* might prompt the slogan "Usasia for the Usasiatics"; some entries went back to the acronym for United States of North America for *Usonians, Usonans, Usofans, Usofams* and *Usoans.*

Others like *USAmericans,* pronounced You-ess-Americans, and *USAers,* the ending to rhyme with naysayers. A jingoistic sense was added by Andrea Sharp of Berkeley, Calif.: "Better than *Usan* is *Ussin,*" or *Us'n* (pronounced USS-in). "All the citizens of the United States would be called *Ussins* and everybody else *Themins.* Headlines all over the world would read: '*Ussins* and *Themins* Meet Again in Geneva for Another Round of SALT Talks.'" (Another suggestion on these lines—*Ussies,* to rhyme with *hussies,* may be rejected as anti-feminist: *User,* coming from "one who uses," is subversive: and we can write off *Usurers,* sent in from some debtor nation.)

An original variation of the same beginning is from Tessa Blumberg of New York: *Usam,* preserving the mid-nineteenth-century image of Uncle Sam. Others trying to tie into the image wound up with *Uncles,* but the avuncular connotation of that was ruined by Mr. Reagan's hope that opponents would "say uncle." In the same way, *Samians* apes too closely the word *simians,* and *Samites* would invite anti-Samitism.

Turning to monikers taken from whole words, one entry is *Uniteds:* "If citizens of the Soviet Union are called *Soviets,* which means 'councils,'" writes David Halperin of Washington, "surely we should not mind being called *Uniteds."* On that line, David Kwartler of New York City turned in *Units,* on the analogy of *Brits* for the British, but that has an Orwellian connotation, like *United Statistics.*

More frequently suggested was *Statesider,* long a name applied to residents of the continental United States by expatriates or offshore residents. *United Staters* is simple and direct, analogous to *American,* and better than the pretentious and even sexist *United Statesman.*

Wild suggestions ranged from the acronym *Noncom* (NOrth Americans Not from Canada Or Mexico) to *Namericans,* slipping in the *n* for North, to the historic *Jonathan,* from the predecessor to Uncle Sam, "Brother Jonathan," who may have been Jonathan Trumbull, George Washington's friend.

Wait. "I feel compelled to inform you," writes David Draper from Moose Jaw, Saskatchewan, "that there are some 25,000,000 North Americans who do not refer to themselves as *Americans.* We, sir, are *Canadians."*

Same thing with *Mexicans;* that's what they call themselves. That means the only North Americans who call themselves *Americans* are us—or us'ns, if you will. That limits the problem to South and Central Americans. How about they call themselves whatever they like, and we continue to call ourselves *Americans,* with the limitation to the United States understood?

In that regard, we may use a linguistic device by which pronunciation changes spelling: centuries ago, *a napron* became *an apron,* and kids on Brooklyn playgrounds ask each other today "What is the fruit that begins with an *n? A norange!"* Intrahemispheric comity is in the ear of the beholder: when I travel in South America and I say, "I am an American," let the hearer hear "I am a Namerican." The understanding listener will know I am a North American and, since I have not claimed to be Canadian or Mexican, from the United States.

Although *Ussins* and *Themins* have their appeal, and *Yankee* and *Gringo* are useful synonyms, perhaps it is wiser to rely on the perceptiveness of our neighbors to the south and stick with *Americans* as the name for people from the United States, no colossusism intended. Our diplomats can point out it is short for *United States of Americans,* which is a mouthful.

That enables us all to lose our fear of jingoism and embrace the name that Waldseemüller coined, saving us from being called *Mundus Novitiates.* Remember that on the Glorious Fourth, and on I Am a Namerican Day.

I believe you are perpetuating a myth about the origin of the term "Indian." If there's one thing I've gleaned from reading your language and political columns, it's your admirable attention to detail.

If you check any map from Columbus's era of exploration, you will discover that India was nonexistent. The country we know by that name was referred to as Hindustan. Consequently, when Columbus came upon the natives he first encountered, he called them "Indio," from the Italian *in dio,* which means "in God." The rest is history, or at least a misinterpreted version of it.

Theo M. Carracino
Editorial Editor
El Paso Herald Post
El Paso, Texas

Your effort to find a substitute for "American" to designate a citizen of the United States of America is misconceived.

The full name of our country is The United States of America; the generic name (saying what kind of a country it is) is United States: the specific name is America. No other geographic entity is called America (without qualification). It is the most natural thing in the world for our country to be called America and its citizens Americans. It is highly unusual for a country to be referred to by its generic title, when other countries have the same generic specification. There are two countries officially called the United States in the continent of North America, namely, the United States of America and the United States of Mexico—or, if we are speaking Spanish, *Los Estados Unidos de América* and *Los Estados Unidos Mexicanos* (or *de México).* If anyone doubts that this name is still in current usage in Mexico, let him look at any piece of Mexican currency. There were also three United Stateses in South America at one time or another: the United States of Venezuela, the United States of Colombia (and before that, the United States of New Granada), and the United States of Brazil. Brazil's name lasted from 1891 to 1967, when it officially changed to the Federative Republic of Brazil.

I would think, then, that our Mexican neighbors would be more peeved about our arrogating to ourselves the name of United States, *tout court,* since we share this title with them, than at our being called after the name of our country, America.

H. A. Kelly
Department of English
University of California
Los Angeles, California

You may be interested to know that this question was settled in 1960, when that eminent archaeologist and author Robert Nathan unearthed the remains of a people known as "the Weans," whose country had a capital found to be named "Pound-Laundry."

"Sri. B'Han Bollek has called these people the Weans, because certain archaeological findings incline him to the belief that they called their land the WE, or the US. . . ."

"Pound-Laundry is in itself the richest of the diggings. It is believed that at one time this city (for recent excavations indicate the laundry, as we call it, to have been a city of considerable size) may even have been the capital of We itself, or at least to have had some political and historic importance. Obelgerst-Levy translates the first word of the name as washing; the second is obviously the sign for weight. It is not known what—if anything—was washed there."

I hope this settles the question.

> Yvonne R. Freund
> New York, New York

A museum here in Delaware houses remains of Delaware's oldest citizens.

"When did these Indians live?" I asked the curator.

"Madame," he replied with some acerbity, "the term 'Indian' is reserved for peoples living in America after Columbus, since that was his word for them. These are the remains of *prehistoric people.*"

Maybe after you get NAmericans settled, you'd like to take on that one.

> Bernadine Z. Paulshock, M.D.
> Wilmington, Delaware

As an expatriated New Yorker, I may perhaps be permitted two comments with regard to the Midwestern use of *anymore* in the sense of "now" or "at present."

First, the present signified by the Midwesterner's *anymore* is not simply the current instant; rather it is the present as contrasted to an unspecified (and seemingly better) past. This contrast is most often emphasized by an additional negative phrase: "Anymore, they don't grow white clover." The form "Anymore, they grow alfalfa," also may be heard.

Second—to my ear—the Midwesterner's use of *anymore* to mean "currently" requires the *anymore* to precede the rest of the statement: "You don't see windshield wipers on horses' asses anymore," rings true to someone from either coast. "Anymore, you don't see windshield wipers on horses' asses," is what you will hear in Columbus, Ohio.

> Joseph Cooper
> Worthington, Ohio

Was surprised that none of the contributors to your recent column came up with the appellation "Statist." According to the O.E.D., that is "a supernumerary actor on the stage who simply poses or stands by." Today we may call them "extras," but regardless, I can think of a lot of (mostly liberal) members of Congress who think of us that way anyhow.

> Laurence D. Skutch
> Westport, Connecticut

You refer to the use of the word Ussin, or Us'n. I am afraid you have the spelling all wrong. If the British pronunciation of the word "boatswain" is to be any example, obviously the term should be "Utswain."

Allon G. Percus
New York, New York

You quote David Halperin as saying that citizens of the Soviet Union are called *Soviets*. Yes, unfortunately, they are—by ill-informed Americans. It is, however, a misnomer. As Mr. Halperin correctly notes, the Russian word *soviet* means council; it has no secondary meaning to describe a person. I suspect that the misuse originated when American media misinterpreted the term *the Soviets* as applying to the Soviet people instead of the political bodies they designate.

What are Soviet citizens called in their country? Actually, they, too, could use a new term, because they have no single word. The common terms are *sovetsky chelovek* (literally, "Soviet person") and *sovetsky grazhdanin* ("Soviet citizen"). In English, I prefer *Soviet citizens* when referring to the population and, somewhat grudgingly and imprecisely, *the Russians* when referring to domestic- or foreign-policy issues, which Russians obviously dominate within the Soviet Union. But never *Soviets!*

Steven Shabad
New York, New York

Yankee came from the Dutch, who referred to the English in New Haven as *Jan Kees*, their version of John Cheese. This predates John Bull, which surfaced in 1712 in a pamphlet by John Arbuthnot called *Law, as a Bottomless Pit*. Too bad that Columbus did not run into the Hopi, which means people. We would all be Hopians.

Paul Maag
London, England

Who Shot John?

Nobody really cares who shot John. That's because *who shot John* is inherently dismissive, always used in the sense of a question that the speaker is not about to answer because it involves loathsome finger-pointing, unworthy of the fair-minded.

When Marlin Fitzwater, press spokesman for Vice President George Bush, was asked about Bush's support of the President's policy to ship arms to Iran, he said, according to the *Washington Post*, "that Bush does not want to discuss the process of 'who shot John' in making the Iran decisions." The reporter, David Hoffman, quoted the spokesman directly, adding, "This is a classic example of the kind of thing for six years that George Bush has never commented on, in good times or bad."

That derogation concerning blame-fixing has been steadily gaining currency. A 1977 recording by Nathan Page used those words as its title, and the expression must have been helped along by the "Who Shot J.R.?" promotion of the television drama "Dallas." "For the first three months of his campaign," wrote the *Washington Post*'s T. R. Reid about Senator Edward M. Kennedy's quest for the presidency in 1980, "Kennedy flailed around on a sprawling spectrum of issues ranging from who-shot-John-in-Teheran to the wiretap provisions of the criminal code bill."

Richard M. Nixon always liked the locution. In 1977, he told a reporter, Austin Scott, about the terrible personal pressures on former Attorney General John Mitchell, and concluded, "And so, that's the human side of the story, which . . . I know that you and the press, you can't be interested in that. You can only be interested in 'Who shot John.' Well, go ahead. . . ."

Stuart Berg Flexner finds in his file of old slang citations that "the earliest ones are British. Around 1860, there's a reference in the file to British Royal Military Academies where men sat around playing 'who shot John.' The Army phrase *play who shot John* might suggest its origin in a children's game, but there is simply not enough evidence."

John was a slang term for a student at the British military schools, which might account for the origin, but this mystery never received the attention given that of an unrelated crime, "Who killed Cock Robin?" (to which the sparrow confessed).

Those interested in the shooter of John are likely to run up against the stone wall of disdain at finger-pointing and contempt for the bandying-about of recriminations—as if those searching for the culprit were themselves blameworthy for being cruelly houndlike.

If we must deal with this expression slanted in favor of the concealer, let's adopt a style: I prefer hyphenating, *who-shot-John*, to putting quotation marks around the noun clause or trying to set it off with the capitalization of *Who*. Thus, instead of getting into a *"who shot John"* or descending to a *Who shot John*, I would rather not be drawn into a *who-shot-John*.

When I was growing up in Virginia, the expression was "who-struck-John." It was used in this situation: One party in a discussion would spin a tale as a diversionary tactic to obscure the real issue. To this, the other party might reply, "That's a lot of 'who-struck-John' " or, "Don't give me that 'who-struck-John'!"

As you can see, in this usage the identity or culpability of John's assailant is not at issue.

Jack H. Hopkins
Key Biscayne, Florida

"Who-struck-John" was an expression often used by my managing editor when I was a reporter in Trenton, New Jersey, in the early-mid 1950s. When he was giving me instructions on writing a story he would often say: "Leave out all the who-struck-John" or "Don't give me all the who-struck-John." For what it may be worth, my editor was from Philadelphia and was born around 1915.

David Hapgood
Hanover, New Hampshire

Who Steals My Per Se

In a televised debate, Democratic presidential candidate Richard A. Gephardt suggested that the government of South Africa be warned, just as the Soviet Union had been warned in Afghanistan, that "we're sending arms to the Afghan rebels." Asked if he meant that we should threaten to arm the African National Congress in South Africa, he replied, "Not *per se.*"

This Latin term, pronounced pur-SAY, means "by itself; in and of one-self, alone." First to use it in English was Archbishop John Whitgift in 1572: "For they belong unto God properly and *per se*, to man *per accidens.*" That used *per se* to mean "essentially, intrinsically, without reference to anything else"—if you prefer, "stand-alone"—and *per accidens* to mean "indirectly, by accident."

The meaning is broadening in political use. When the congressman replied, "Not *per se,*" he did not mean precisely "not in and of itself"; more likely, he meant "not exactly," or "that's not quite it," or "don't pin me down on that." As a get-out-of-trouble word, the Latinism has a scholarly ring, and with its meaning slipping old moorings, we can expect to hear it fuzz up debates for years to come.

Per accidens does not mean by accident (except very accidentally). It means rather something arising, not from the essence but from some nonessential attribute.

I fear that the ghosts of countless scholastics may rise to protest my oversimplification, but I feel I owe it to the Cause to try.

Francis D. Champion
Pittsford, New York

Will Grammar Survive?

W ho gives a hoot if a noun that modifies another noun is called *attributive?* Can't you get through life speaking clearly and writing in happy syntax without that information? Those are questions that percolate in the minds of those of us who are, late in life, studying grammar.

"Are you aware that teaching grammar is considered *outré* in the world of education?" writes Diane Ravitch, professor of history at Teachers College, Columbia University. "It is now dogma among teachers of writing that student papers should never, never be corrected for minor details like grammar, spelling, punctuation and syntax; to do so, goes the predominant wisdom, is to inhibit the student's ego and interest in self-expression."

Professor Ravitch is concerned that the advent of high-tech in schools will make matters worse, because the coming availability of spell-checkers and grammar-fixers in word-processing programs removes the need for a knowledge of the way letters and words come together. In other words, correctness of form is not important, say our strawmen-educators, and if and when it is, let the machine do it for you. Let's chew that over.

Divide all knowledge into knowledge for survival, knowledge for achievement, knowledge for pleasure. The first lets us move around in the jungle, the second gives us a sense of satisfaction, the third offers us intellectual and physical kicks.

Some of the knowledge for achievement—arithmetic, spreadsheeting, grammar—can be delegated to machines. One of my kids resisted learning the multiplication tables, now has a handy-dandy calculator that does it all and wants to know why I knocked myself out memorizing nine times seven. The philosophical question is a reprise of the spook's query: do we learn only what we have a need to know?

I think we have a need to know what we do not need to know. What we don't need to know for achievement, we need to know for our pleasure. Knowing how things work is the basis for appreciation, and is thus a source of civilized delight.

That's why I am not worried at the prospect of knowledge for achievement becoming available by easy purchase rather than by hard learning. The whole thing will move over into the next category of mental need. We'll break our heads over abstract art, and try to learn about the intricacies of music, and plow the fields of grammar not to show the damn machines we're smarter than they are, but to satisfy our human yearning for the pleasure of understanding.

Begin with "Teachers College." Should it have an apostrophe?

> I vote for Teachers' College, Doctors' Hospital, Veterans' Administration and Shoppers' Parking. I believe in both the subjunctive and objective genitive (or possessive): respectively, the crook's crime and the crook's sentencing.
>
> Arthur J. Morgan
> New York, New York

> The question isn't simply should Teachers College have an apostrophe, but where to put it? Notice that we here at St. John's University know the answer to both questions. Actually, as one who does correct student papers for grammar, spelling, punctuation, and syntax, I have found the use and location of the apostrophe (i.e., before or after the "s") to be one of the most common errors.
>
> Jeffrey W. Fagen
> Associate Professor of Psychology
> St. John's University
> Jamaica, New York

Winsome, Lose Some

When Indiana senator Richard G. Lugar was campaigning to be ranking Republican on the Senate Foreign Relations Committee, he circulated a letter to his colleagues recalling his record of constructive service as chairman when the Republicans were in control of the Senate. More to the point, he said the Reagan administration needed "skillful and winsome leadership in foreign policy issues."

Rick Hertzberg, former chief speechwriter for Jimmy Carter, sent that clip along with a little note: "I guess Lugar was out to fill the 'adorability gap' on the GOP leadership team."

Winsome does not mean "winning" any more than *noisome* means "noisy." (The *noy* in *noisome* is the *noy* in *annoy*, and means "malodorous, smelly, disgusting, causing nice people to hold their noses and say, 'Feh!' " *Noisy* is also rooted in the Latin *nausea* but affects only the ears.)

To be fair, *winsome* does mean "winning" in the sense of "to win one's affection," but not in the victorious sense, as in "to win an election." The old Anglo-Saxon *wynsum* meant "pleasurable, lifting the spirit, giving joy to the beholder," and that is still what the word means today. A ballpark synonym, as Mr. Hertzberg suggests, is *adorable*, though that word, like *lovable*, is rarely applied to a male.

Senator Lugar can claim that his smile is winsome, which it is, but his leadership cannot be described with that word. Nor, in this case, can he use *winning*; that's better applied to the victor in the jousting, Senator Jesse A. Helms. He will be the first to admit that nobody uses *winsome* to describe him.

With All Deliberate Vulgarity

If you are an impressionable minor, turn this page hurriedly without reading further; go watch the ax murder of a nude model by a lecherous alien on television instead. This is about vulgar speech in school and is too shocking for juvenile eyes.

Are schools allowed to discipline students for uttering dirty words out loud or, more specifically, for engaging in "indecent, lewd and offensive" speech?

You bet they are. Freedom of speech does not give a child the right to yell his favorite dirty word in a crowded assembly hall. Writing for the Supreme Court majority in *Bethel School District No. 403 v. Fraser*, Chief Justice Warren E. Burger held that "The First Amendment does not prevent the school officials from determining that to permit a vulgar and lewd speech . . . would undermine the school's basic educational mission."

The case was brought by an uppity, or gutsy, kid named Matthew N. Fraser who didn't like the way his teachers penalized him for waking up his high-school assembly. He made a campaign speech nominating a friend for student government by using an extended sexual metaphor; when faculty members—who had warned him beforehand not to try anything disruptive—slapped him down with a three-day suspension, he sued, and the Supreme Court flunked him on his test case with finality.

However, while going along with the majority on the issue of the discretion teachers have in teaching civil public discourse, Justice William J. Brennan, Jr., in a separate concurring opinion, raised a fascinating linguistic point: what is the meaning of *obscene, vulgar, lewd?* (The Court has not yet caught up with the hot vogue adjective for all this—*lubricious*, rooted in "slippery"—but give it time.)

Justice Brennan is a good egg with an interest in both free speech and precise language; he helped me recently in tracing the evolution of the phrase "with all deliberate speed"—from the second Brown decision, upset by Green, out of old English chancery law—for which I am grateful. Without blushing, the spry eighty-year-old jurist preceded his opinion by quoting the Fraser speech at the root of the controversy. (C'mon, kids, wouldn't you rather watch the scantily clad mud wrestlers shouting imprecations compatible with community standards on Channel 5? This strong stuff is not for the tender-aged.)

"I know a man who is firm," said the defiant young wiseguy, whose words are now enshrined in an opinion of our highest court, which is more than a lot of us can claim, "he's firm in his pants, he's firm in his shirt . . . a man who takes his point and pounds it in. . . . Jeff is a man who will go to the very end—even the climax, for each and every one of you."

Climax, let me interject (no, there is no double meaning to *interject*; what you kids watching the heavy breathing on "Dynasty" were thinking of is *ejaculate*, a Tom Swift verb based on the Latin for "javelin"), is rooted in the Greek for "ladder," and referred originally in rhetoric to an ascending series of propositions, before reaching its present meaning of only the highest step of such a series.

Climax gained a sexual meaning, as a euphemistic synonym for "orgasm" in 1918, when British birth-control advocate Marie Carmichael Stopes wrote: "In so many cases the man's climax comes so swiftly that the woman's reactions are not nearly ready." The euphemism has reversed itself: *climax* now has a more archly forbidden connotation than *orgasm*, now a clinical term so often discussed in popular magazines as to have become dull.

Justice Brennan read that kid's speech and did not register shock and horror. "Indeed, to my mind," he footnoted (the best stuff in the opinions these days is in the footnotes), "respondent's speech was no more 'obscene,' 'lewd' or 'sexually explicit' than the bulk of programs currently appearing on prime-time television or in the local cinema." He found the language not obscene (a judgmental word, from the Latin *obscaenus*, "illomened," originally a term of augury), but did find it intentionally disruptive, and held that school officials had the right to insure that a highschool assembly proceed in an orderly manner, without hoots and howls and all that snickering.

In dissent, Justice John Paul Stevens took a step further the Brennan footnote about the student's language being no worse than what kids see in the movies or on television. (OK, kids, get away from that screen, the mudfight's over and what they are showing now is unnatural.) He cited a 1926 opinion that "nuisance may be merely a right thing in the wrong place—like a pig in the parlor instead of the barnyard," adding that "vulgar language, like vulgar animals, may be acceptable in some contexts and intolerable in others." He would have upheld the student's freedom of expression, in part because in school corridors, "the metaphor in the speech might be regarded as rather routine comment."

Although I am a no-law-means-no-law First Amendment freak, I think Burger and Brennan were right to assert the school's right to rule that priapic pretension is out of order in an assembly; it's okay to shut up kids in formal settings when you are not trying to shut down their opinions. But I salute Justice Stevens for grasping the point of context in the meaning of *vulgarity.*

Vulgar once meant "the common people"; the Vulgate is the Latin version of the Bible from the Roman Catholic Church and comes from *vulgata editio,* "the edition in general circulation." A derogatory sense came in when some elitists thought of the common people as ignorant and inferior, and in the 1760s the word gained its present meaning as "not belonging in good society."

One sense of *vulgar* is undeniably "dirty, smutty," but another active sense is "out of place." Context determines vulgarity. A genteel cliché like *scantily clad* is as vulgar in a locker room as a four-letter shocker is in a garden club; each would be suitable and not vulgar in the opposite setting. To a dedicated radical, *liberal* is an obscenity; to a rootin'-tootin' reactionary, no more repellent vulgarism exists than *moderate.*

To the question, "Was that lewd?" must be added the questions, "Where was it said? To whom? On what sort of occasion?" Mr. Fraser, who was dealt with so firmly, could have delivered his speech with impunity—if it had been part of an assignment to analyze vulgarity or illustrate the belaboring of a metaphor. (In the preceding sentence, "firmly" may seem to be a vulgarism because of its smirking double meaning, but is not a vulgarism because it is being used to illustrate the point about context determining vulgarity. Become a language columnist and get away with murder.)

> Young Fraser delivered his "lewd" speech *not* in a classroom, but in a student assembly that was devoted to the delivery of *political* campaign speeches. Attendance was entirely voluntary. Thus, this was *political* speech for which Mr. Fraser was being punished.
>
> Secondly, it is simply not true that Mr. Fraser's speech in any way disrupted the political assembly. Indeed, this was probably one of the calmer political assemblies in American history! Yet the school regulation that purported to prohibit this kind of speech, purported to do so on the ground that it would be disruptive. The Supreme Court purported to buy the same line.
>
> I happen to believe that the *Fraser* case constitutes a very dangerous precedent for precisely these reasons. It is a green light for school authorities to impose a rather serious regimentation of political speech on the part of schoolchildren.
>
> *Harvey A. Silverglate*
> *Silverglate, Gertner, Baker, Fine,*
> *Good & Mizner*
> *Boston, Massachusetts*

The Word's the Thing

The first thing you learn in general semantics is "the word is not the thing"—that is, the referent is not the source, or, to put it understandably, *cow* is merely a word, a sign, a name, and is not the flesh-and-blood thing that has an udder and goes "moo."

Grasp that idea and the ghost of Alfred H. S. Korzybski, papa of this branch of the science of linguistics, smiles. Too many of us think of the word *cow* as the barnyard reality itself, and thereby lose the notion of particularity: the cow we call Bossy is not the cow we call Elsie, and the contented brown cow we call Elsie is not the same as the grumpy black cow of the same name. The word, the name of the kind of animal, is only a human sign for the bovine animal, and is more than once removed from the actual beast that comes up to the fence and gives our face a large lick.

Language is representative government, a step removed from direct democratic participation. Like paper money, it is worth only what we assign to it, and the words *a million dollars* are not worth a plugged nickel.

What's so hot about that insight? Why did *the-word-is-not-the-thing* sell so many copies of Stuart Chase's *The Tyranny of Words* and S. I. Hayakawa's *Language in Thought and Action?*

That blinding illumination reminds us to think of language not as reality, as so many passively regimented people do, but as a code to help us describe reality, made up differently by different people in different places. That, in turn, forces us away from accepting stereotypes, from thinking of all cows as the same, into asking the questions about the particular thing that separates every cow from the herd. We then investigate and evaluate the abstractions called words, and our evaluation brings us closer to reality, thereby humanizing our behavior. And this wonderful thing takes place when first we get it into our noggins that the word for the thing is not the thing itself.

Nowadays, this big idea in the meaning of meaning is shrugged off as obvious by students of semiotics, the academic indiscipline that puts semantics, syntactics and pragmatics into the same sign-language pot. But 'tis enough for today's essay; 'twill do for an introduction to the new use of the word *thing*.

Which brings us to the Deaver *thing*.

"Within the White House," goes a crisp Bernard Weinraub feature lead in *The New York Times*, "it is called, simply, 'the Deaver thing.' "

For five centuries, we have been modifying the noun *thing*: "the publique thinge," in 1436, meant the state or commonwealth, derived from the Latin *res publica,* source of the word *republic.* In Old Norse, *thing* meant "public assembly, cause, matter, affair," and still appears in our language with that meaning in the word *hustings.* Of the fifty most common words spoken in English—mostly articles, pronouns and prepositions—*thing* is the only noun that makes it. No name is as popular.

The new use of the grand old word harks back to that earliest sense of "public matter." Although the dictionaries do not yet show it, *thing* is frequently being used with an attributive noun, as in *this terrorism thing, the whole tax-reform thing* and *the Deaver thing.*

(Attributive nouns are nouns that modify—attribute meaning to — other nouns, as in *basketball star* and *Amityville horror*; we went into this last week, and if you were absent, the work cannot be made up. Readers of this space are not enrolled in a gut course. Next term, say you didn't mean to flunk semantics and sign up for semiotics.)

When a hip agnostic says, "I'm not into the God thing," he uses *thing* as a device to distance himself from the word that signifies the thing. "Now tell me about *this clogged-carburetor business,"* says the puzzled motorist, fearful of dealing directly with the clogged carburetor. "Tell Mr. Smoothie that Bubbles is on the phone to talk to him about *the pregnancy matter"* is another example of step-back speaking.

The use of *thing* in the step-back construction is usually a minimizer. The Deaver *thing* is to be discussed, avoided, brushed off; if it progresses to the Deaver *business,* it will have acquired a note of distaste; if we hear lawyers talking, it will be the Deaver *matter* or, more serious, the Deaver *case.* The word *problem* in this case is not pejorative—Lyndon Johnson had "the Bobby *problem"*—but *affair* is something to worry about: the Dreyfus *affair* rocked France almost a century ago, and the Lance *affair* troubled Jimmy Carter.

Escalate it further, or give it a criminal or sexual connotation, and you have a *scandal:* Crédit Mobilier and Teapot Dome were attributive nouns modifying *scandal* in the Grant and Harding administrations, and the Profumo *scandal* rocked the Macmillan government in Britain. A good indication of the degree of culpability placed on the Nixon administration is in the word used to characterize its agony: Mr. Nixon called it the Watergate *thing,* Europeans call it the Watergate *affair,* not such a big deal, but most Americans remember the Watergate *scandal.*

Worst of all, in political terms—just short of *massacre* or *atrocity*—is *mess:* Harry Truman's influence-peddling *mess* brought him a lower popularity rating than Nixon's.

"But do your thing, and I shall know you," wrote Ralph Waldo Emerson in 1841. We have been doing our *thing* thing today, and will keep an ear cocked for the moment when this mere *thing* moves up the ladder of synonymy into the Deaver *affair.*

Index

Vanauken, Sheldon, 55
Vance, Cyrus R., 349
Van Cleve, James, 26
Van der Velde, Marilyn V., 274
Van Horn, Mike, 282
Van Maarseveen, Alex, 288
Van Munching & Company, 66–67
Van Sciver, Alan E., 122
Vatican, the, 183–84, 185, 201
Veil (Woodward), 261
verbal irony, 103
verbal vs. *oral*, 89–90, 91, 102
verbification of nouns, 39, 273
Verity, William, 130
Vespucci, Amerigo, 367
Vest, John P. W., 158
Vicar of Wakefield, The (Goldsmith), 245
Vidal, Gore, 261–62
Viereck, Peter, 266
Village Voice, The, 273
Vinocur, John, 161, 349–50
violated, 50
Vogue magazine, 5
Von Maltitz, Frances Willard, 80
Voss, Laura A., 299
Vreeland, Diana, 292
vulgar (vulgarity), 377–78. *See also obscene;*
    scatology; specific terms

Waldheim, Kurt, 185
Waldseemüller, Martin, 367, 369
Wall Street Journal, The, 17, 42, 112, 270
Walpole, Horace, 132, 134, 242
Walter, Dan, 277
war, euphemisms and, 54–55
Ward, Michael, 14
warp one, 287
Warren, Earl, 66
"warts and all," 132–35
Washington, George, 286
*Washington Bedtime Stories: The Politics of
    Money and Jobs* (Stein), 101–2
Washington Post, 10, 11, 32, 33, 107, 115, 155,
    185, 187, 191, 214, 216, 263, 270, 273,
    284, 297, 306, 316, 336, 340, 355, 358,
    362, 364, 373
Wasserman, Arnold S., 3
Waste Land, The (Eliot), 258
Watergate, 220; *thing*, 381
Waterman, Rita, 194
Watson, Rita Esposito, 161
Watson, Thomas, 306
Watt, James, 284
Wattenberg, Ben J., 35
Webb, Thomasina, 126
Webb, Thompson, 255
Webber, Andrew Lloyd, 259, 260
Webster's New Collegiate Dictionary, 203
Webster's New World Dictionary, 288
Webster's Third, 80, 81
Weege, Reinhold, 191
Weeks, Burt, 323–24

weenies, 354–57
Wegner, Judith Romney, 347
Weidenbaum, Murray L., 131
weigh anchor, 357
Weinberg, Jerrold, ix
Weinraub, Bernard, 380
Weintraub, Stanley, 151
Weir, Benjamin F., 17
Weisman, Steven R., 303
Weiss, Gerald, 247
Wells, H. G., 106
went through the overhead, 15, 16
Wentworth, Harold, 103, 339, 364
wetbacks, 50
whatever, 3
Wheeler, Raymond David, 96
Whelton, Clark, 298
whence (whence comes), 35–36
which vs. *that*, 76, 77, 141–42
which vs. *who*, 98, 99
"While Zealots Sleep," 269
White, Theodore H., 5
white-collar, 61
Whitehead, Mary Beth, 200–4
white knight, 164
White Monkey, The (Galsworthy), 217
Whitgift, John, 374
Whitney, April, 204–5
Who Killed Society? (Amory), 292
whole nine yards, 42
who shot John, 372–74
who vs. *which*, 98, 99
who vs. *whom*, 100
Why England Slept (Kennedy), 269
Wick, Charles Z., 298
Wicker, Tom, 92
wiggler, 102
Wilcox, Michael F., 280
Wilde, Oscar, 265, 266–68, 272
Wiley, T. T., 155
Willebrands, John Cardinal, 183
Williams, Edward Bennett, 66
Williams, Thomas, 103
Willis, Jeannie, 113
Willson, Meredith, 364
Wilson, Harold, 35
Wilson, J. D., 239
Wilson, Pete, 356
Wilson, Richard Patrick, 19
Wilson, Woodrow, 37, 134, 364
wimp, 327–28
wines, names for, 61–63
winsome, 376–77
Winter, John E., 210
wiring diagram, 124, 125
Wirthlin, Richard, 105–6
Witcover, Jules, 315–16
Wodehouse, P. G., 12
Wojnilower, Albert M., 346
Wolff, Lois Ann, 342
womanizer, 214, 215–20, 273
Women's Travel Guide (Fine and Lasky), 5